LAW OF REMEDIES

LAW OF REMEDIES

A European Perspective

Edited by
Franz Hofmann
Franziska Kurz

intersentia
Cambridge – Antwerp – Chicago

Intersentia Ltd
8 Wellington Mews
Wellington Street | Cambridge
CB1 1HW | United Kingdom
Tel.: +44 1223 736 170
Email: mail@intersentia.co.uk
www.intersentia.com | www.intersentia.co.uk

Distribution for the UK and Ireland:
NBN International
Airport Business Centre, 10 Thornbury Road
Plymouth, PL6 7PP
United Kingdom
Tel.: +44 1752 202 301 | Fax: +44 1752 202 331
Email: orders@nbninternational.com

Distribution for Europe and all other countries:
Intersentia Publishing nv
Groenstraat 31
2640 Mortsel
Belgium
Tel.: +32 3 680 15 50 | Fax: +32 3 658 71 21
Email: mail@intersentia.be

Distribution for the USA and Canada:
Independent Publishers Group
Order Department
814 North Franklin Street
Chicago, IL 60610
USA
Tel.: +1 800 888 4741 (toll free) | Fax: +1 312 337 5985
Email: orders@ipgbook.com

Law of Remedies. A European Perspective

Artwork on cover: Clive Watts/Alamy Stock Photo

ISBN 978-1-78068-785-8
D/2019/7849/103
NUR 822

British Library Cataloguing in Publication Data. A catalogue record for this book is available from the British Library.

CONTENTS

PART III. FUNCTIONS OF REMEDIES

PART IV. UNDERLYING PRINCIPLES

LIST OF CASES

EUROPEAN UNION

GERMANY

UNITED KINGDOM AND THE COMMONWEALTH

UNITED STATES

OTHER

LIST OF AUTHORS

Paul S. Davies
Professor of Commercial Law, University College London, UK

Orit Fischman Afori
Professor of Law, Haim Striks School of Law, The College of Management, Israel

Jens-Uwe Franck
Professor of Private Law, Commercial and Competition Law, University of Mannheim, Germany

Andreas Funke
Professor of Public Law and Philosophy of Law, Friedrich-Alexander-University Erlangen-Nürnberg, Germany

Christian Heinze
Professor of Private Law and Intellectual Property Law, Leibniz University Hannover, Germany

Jan Felix Hoffmann
Professor of Civil Law and Civil Procedure, Director of the Institute for German and Comparative Civil Procedure, Department 1, University of Freiburg, Germany

Franz Hofmann
Professor of Private Law, Intellectual Property and Technology Law, Friedrich-Alexander-University Erlangen-Nürnberg, Germany

Martin Husovec
Assistant Professor, Tilburg Institute for Law, Technology and Society (TILT) and Tilburg Institute for Law and Economics (TILEC), Tilburg Law School, Tilburg University, The Netherlands

Franziska Kurz
Doctoral Candidate and Research Assistant at the Chair of Private Law, Intellectual Property and Technology Law, Friedrich-Alexander-University Erlangen-Nürnberg, Germany

Dorothea Magnus
Assistant Professor of Criminal Law, Free University Berlin, Germany

Jonathan Moss
Barrister, Hogarth Chambers, UK

Benjamin Raue
Professor of Private Law, Law of the Information Society and Intellectual Property Law, University of Trier, Germany

Klaus Ulrich Schmolke
Professor of Private Law, Commercial, Company and Business Law, Friedrich-Alexander-University Erlangen-Nürnberg, Germany

Luboš Tichý
Professor of Private and European Law and Chair of the Centre for Comparative law, Charles University Prague, Czech Republic

Christian Twigg-Flesner
Professor of International Commercial Law, University of Warwick, UK

PART I

THE ISSUE OF REMEDIES

INTRODUCTION TO THE 'LAW OF REMEDIES'

Franz HOFMANN and Franziska KURZ*

1. INTRODUCTION

Is there such a thing as a 'Law of Remedies'? The answer probably depends on your juridical provenance. Those who were educated in England, the United States or Australia will agree that quite a few scholars in these jurisdictions devote their writing, inter alia, to questions surrounding remedies. A. Burrows, for example, covers judicial remedies in his textbook, *Remedies for Torts and Breach of Contract*.[1] The focus is on principles governing the remedial law instead of substantive tort or contract law. Furthermore, the book is not restricted to remedies available, for example, for breach of contract, but 'treat(s) the area as a coherent whole'.[2] A. Burrows argues that this has the great advantage 'of enabling the many similarities, as well as the differences, between tortious and

* We are grateful to Fritz-Thyssen-Stiftung who funded a conference on the topic of Remedies.

1 A. BURROWS, *Remedies for Torts and Breach of Contract*, 4th edn., OUP, Oxford 2019.

2 A. BURROWS, above n. 1, p. xi (3rd edn., 2004).

contractual remedies and their governing principles to be fully appreciated'.[3] Similarly, S. Waddams points out that the 'Law of Remedies' 'is worthy of study because it enables illuminating parallels to be drawn that cross the boundaries between contract and tort, and between law and equity'.[4] Although there might be specific principles for the assessment of damages in intellectual property (IP) law or contract law,[5] there seems to be a value in looking at different types of remedies side by side.[6] In either case, textbooks in, for example, the UK, the US, Canada or Australia exclusively handle remedies, such as damages, account of profits, injunctions or specific performance.[7] Admittedly, this is a recent phenomenon.[8] The origins of a 'remedies scholarship' can be found in the 1970s.[9] It was only in 1972 that F.H. Lawson published the first scholarly work dedicated to remedies.[10] Since then, the 'Law of Remedies' appears to have become an increasingly 'stand-alone' research area. At the beginning of this century, R. Zakrzewski tried to classify remedies.[11] T.F. Cotter focuses on an economic and comparative analysis of remedies in patent law.[12] Recently, a conference at the University of Cambridge explored themes and controversies with respect to commercial remedies.[13] Previously, scholars reflected on how

---

3 Ibid.

4 S. Waddams, 'Remedies as a Legal Subject' (1983) 3 *Oxford Journal of Legal Studies* 113, 121.

5 Cf. Art. 13 Enforcement Directive (Directive of the European Parliament and of the Council 2004/48/EC of 29 April 2004 on the enforcement of intellectual property rights [2004] OJ L 195/16).

6 R. Zakrzewski, *Remedies Reclassified*, OUP, Oxford 2005, p. 23.

7 For example, J. Berryman, *The Law of Equitable Remedies*, 2nd edn., Irwin Law, Toronto 2013; D.B. Dobbs and C.L. Roberts, *Law of Remedies. Damages–Equity–Restitution*, 3rd edn., West Academic Publishing, St. Paul 2018; W. Covell, K. Lupton and J. Forder, *Principles of Remedies*, 6th edn., LexisNexis Butterworths, Chatswood 2015; D. Harris, D. Campbell and R. Halson, *Remedies in Contract & Tort*, 2nd edn., CUP, Cambridge 2005; J.M. Fischer, *Understanding Remedies*, 3rd edn., CAP, Durham 2014; R.L. Hasen, *Remedies*, 4th edn., Wolters Kluwer, New York 2017; R.L. Weaver, E.W. Shoben and M.B. Kelly, *Principles of Remedies Law*, 3rd edn., West Academic Publishing, St. Paul 2017; M.J. Tilbury, *Civil Remedies: Principles of Remedies*, vol. 1, 2nd edn., LexisNexis Butterworth, Sydney 2014 and *Civil Remedies: Remedies in Particular Contexts*, vol. 2, Butterworth, Sydney 1994; S.A. Smith, *Rights, Wrongs and Injustices: The Structure of Remedial Law*, OUP, Oxford forthcoming 2019.

8 W. Covell, K. Lupton and J. Forder, above n. 7, p. 3.

9 J. Berryman, 'The Law of Remedies: A Prospectus for Teaching and Scholarship' (2010) 10 *Oxford University Commonwealth Legal Journal* 123, 132.

10 F.H. Lawson, *Remedies of English Law*, Penguin Books, Harmondsworth 1972; see also K.H. York and J.A. Bauman, *Cases and Materials on Remedies*, West Publishing, St. Paul 1967; A. Ogus, *The Law of Damages*, Butterworth, London 1973; D.B. Dobbs, *Handbook of the Law of Remedies. Damages–Equity–Restitution*, West Publishing, St. Paul 1973.

11 R. Zakrzewski, above n. 6.

12 T.F. Cotter, *Comparative Patent Remedies. A Legal and Economic Analysis*, OUP, Oxford 2013.

13 G. Virgo and S. Worthington (eds.), *Commercial Remedies: Resolving Controversies*, CUP, Cambridge 2017.

to justify private law remedies.[14] More edited volumes can be located easily.[15] And finally, J. Berryman claimed that meanwhile '(t)he law of remedies has truly come of age'.[16]

On the contrary, there is a different approach to remedies in other European countries, for example Germany.[17] Each of the private law disciplines (i.e. contract, tort, property, commercial or IP law) considers remedies only as an addendum. Most civil law lawyers conceive remedies as a mere 'legal by-product'. If somebody has infringed a patent, for instance, the claimant could automatically claim an injunction. More precisely, the claimant would have a right against the defendant that he/she refrains from infringing the patent.[18] Particularly in contract law, rights and remedies seem to be inseparably connected ('monistic approach').[19] 'Specific performance' is not considered a remedy, but the 'backbone of the obligation'.[20] As such, specific performance is the obligation which is enforceable on its own terms. Unlike in common law countries, the question is not: which remedies are available to cure a wrong? Instead, German lawyers comprehend the legal system as a compilation of 'subjective rights'.[21]

In European private law, the picture is more diverse. The European notion of remedies can be perceived similarly to the common law approach. Especially in IP law, secondary European legislation has increasingly harmonised remedies.

---

14 C.E.F. Rickett (ed.), *Justifying Private Law Remedies*, Hart Publishing, Oxford and Portland 2008.

15 For example, A. Burrows and E. Peel (eds.), *Commercial Remedies. Current Issues and Problems*, OUP, Oxford 2003; J. Berryman and R. Bigwood (eds.), *The Law of Remedies. New Directions in the Common Law*, Irwin Law, Toronto 2010.

16 J. Berryman, 'The Law of Remedies: A Prospectus for Teaching and Scholarship' (2010) 10 *Oxford University Commonwealth Legal Journal* 123, 148.

17 Another example is given by the French debate on the use of the term 'remèdes', cf. S. Whittaker, 'The Law of Obligations' in J. Bell, S. Boyron and S. Whittaker (eds.), *Principles of French Law*, OUP, Oxford 2008, p. 349; D. Fairgrieve, *Comparative Contract Law in Practice – Contract Law in a Mid-Channel Jurisdiction*, Hart Publishing, Oxford 2016, pp. 144–146.

18 Cf. §139 (1) PatG (*German Patent Act*): 'Any person who uses a patented invention contrary to sections 9 to 13 may, in the event of the risk of recurrent infringement, be sued by the aggrieved party for cessation and desistance. This right may also be asserted in the event of the risk of a first-time infringement.' Translation provided by U. Reusch in cooperation with the Language Service of the German Patent and Trade Mark Office, https://www.gesetze-im-internet.de/englisch_patg/englisch_patg.html#p0755.

19 M.-P. Weller, *Die Vertragstreue: Vertragsbindung – Naturalerfüllungsgrundsatz – Leistungstreue*, Mohr Siebeck, Tübingen 2009, pp. 231 f., 372 with reference to B. Windscheid, *Die Actio des römischen Civilrechts vom Standpunkte des heutigen Rechts*, Düsseldorf 1856; cf. J. Berryman, *The Law of equitable remedies*, 2nd edn., Irwin Law, Toronto 2013, p. 14.

20 E. Rabel, *Das Recht des Warenkaufs. Eine rechtsvergleichende Darstellung*, 1st vol., Berlin and Leipzig 1936, p. 375.

21 H. Dedek, 'From Norms to Facts: The Realization of Rights in Common and Civil Private Law' (2010) 56 *McGill Law Journal* 77; cf. F. Hofmann, '"Anspruchsdenken" und "Remedydenken" im deutschen Privatrecht' (2018) 9 *Juristische Schulung* 833.

For instance, Art. 130 European Trade Mark Regulation[22] states that '(w)here an EU trade mark court finds that the defendant has infringed or threatened to infringe an EU trade mark, it shall, unless there are special reasons for not doing so, issue an order prohibiting the defendant from proceeding with the acts which infringed or would infringe the EU trade mark.' Whereas the claimant can apply for an injunction, it is for the court to decide whether to grant the injunction or not. Art. 130 European Trade Mark Regulation is a pure remedial provision distinct from substantive trade mark law, as well as – to provide another example – the remedial provision in Art. 8 para. 3 Information Society Directive.[23] The latter requires Member States to 'ensure that rightholders are in a position to apply for an injunction against intermediaries whose services are used by a third party to infringe a copyright or related right.' The Enforcement Directive[24] illustrates the structure of European private law even more clearly. This directive exclusively deals with remedies for the enforcement of intellectual property rights. The substantive IP law, by contrast, is harmonised in separate directives.[25] These directives explicitly differentiate between 'rights' on the one hand and 'remedies' on the other. Art. 3 Enforcement Directive even outlines some general principles. It states: '(R)emedies shall be fair and equitable and shall not be unnecessarily complicated or costly, or entail unreasonable time-limits or unwarranted delays.' Furthermore, damages and injunctions are designed as court orders. The same applies to the Trade Secret Directive, for example.[26] In contract law, in turn, the wording of remedial provisions is different. The directive on certain aspects concerning contracts for the supply of digital content,[27] for instance, provides that 'the consumer shall be entitled to' the remedies for lack of conformity in Art. 14. An identical wording is adopted in Art. 13 of the new directive on certain aspects concerning contracts for the sale of goods.[28]

---

22 Regulation of the European Parliament and of the Council (EU) 2017/1001 of 14 June 2017 on the European Union trade mark [2017] OJ L 154/1.

23 Directive of the European Parliament and of the Council 2001/29/EC of 22 May 2001 on the harmonisation of certain aspects of copyright and related rights in the information society [2001] OJ L 167/10.

24 Directive of the European Parliament and of the Council 2004/48/EC of 29 April 2004 on the enforcement of intellectual property rights [2004] OJ L 195/16.

25 E.g. the Information Society Directive, above n. 23.

26 Directive of the European Parliament and of the Council (EU) 2016/943 of 8 June 2016 on the protection of undisclosed know-how and business information (trade secrets) against their unlawful acquisition, use and disclosure [2016] OJ L 157/1.

27 Directive (EU) 2019/770 of the European Parliament and of the Council of 20 May 2019 on certain aspects concerning contracts for the supply of digital content and digital services [2019] OJ L 136/1.

28 Directive (EU) 2019/771 of the European Parliament and of the Council of 20 May 2019 on certain aspects concerning contracts for the sale of goods, amending Regulation (EU) 2017/2394 and Directive 2009/22/EC, and repealing Directive 1999/44/EC [2019] OJ L 136/28.

The entitlement to have the digital content or goods brought into conformity with the contract is not drafted as a court order but as a right within substantive law. Nonetheless, this 'remedy' can be analysed independently of the obligations outlined in Art. 5 and Art. 6 of the directive on digital content. Against this background, C. Twigg-Flesner will take a closer look on themes and controversies surrounding remedies in European contract law in his chapter. For sure, already these few examples illustrate the 'remedial structure' of European private law.

Although 'remedies' have not yet attracted special attention, particularly in German private law, the continent might have to become more sensitive: Remedies are an emerging issue as European private law is based on the distinction between substantive rights and corresponding remedies. Respective developments in European private law are a good reason for the establishment of a 'European Law of Remedies'.[29] Questions related to the enforcement of substantive rights, hence, deserve more attention. This book will explore remedies. For this purpose, it will focus on the issue of remedies in its own right. The following chapters of this book will introduce the issue of remedies from different angles, especially from the viewpoint of different jurisdictions, a law and economics perspective and an interdisciplinary point of view (Part I). The book will further set out mechanisms of enforcement (Part II), analyse the functions of remedies (Part III) and their underlying principles (Part IV). Moreover, special remedy-related controversies in contract law and IP law will be outlined (Part V). In doing so, the book aims to take on a genuine European perspective.

This first chapter shall introduce the 'Law of Remedies'. First, the respective terms are presented: What is a remedy – (2.) a court order, a claim, or rather a right? Subsequently, the task of defining the subject matter will be continued by narrowing down the term of enforcement. The enforcement of rights can be understood as an interdisciplinary task. Thus, (3.) the 'Law of Remedies' shall be presented within its relation to public enforcement and criminal law. This book is not about substantive law in its traditional, narrow sense concerning the rights and duties people might have. It is about the enforcement of those rights and duties. In other words, in a perfect world in which all rights and duties are accepted without reproach, a certain set of rules would be obsolete: those rules dealing with the enforcement of substantive rights and duties. From a theoretical point of view any legal provision written or unwritten can be assigned either to substantive law or to 'remedial law'. The term 'remedy' is not restricted to court orders only; more generally, the 'Law of Remedies' is about enforcement. Having carved out the scope of the 'Law of Remedies',

[29] For more reasons cf. F. Hofmann, *Der Unterlassungsanspruch als Rechtsbehelf*, Mohr Siebeck, Tübingen 2017, pp. 134–155.

(4.) characteristic features of this field of law shall be elaborated and underlying principles will be outlined. Finally, as these principles reflect a genuine European notion of remedial law, (5.) the European perspective shall be taken into account.

2. REMEDIES, COURT ORDERS, CLAIMS AND RIGHTS

Looking at a 'Law of Remedies' from an international perspective primarily triggers the question of what a remedy actually is. The answer seems to be quite straightforward. Arguably, in common law jurisdictions, a remedy is a court order.[30] The term is used to denote the relief that a person can seek from a court to counter an infringement.[31] Courts hereby obviously play an active role. Thus, scholars range remedial questions and remedial law as quite distinct from both substance and procedure.[32] At a second glance, the legal concept of remedies is more controversial, though. P. Birks identified five different meanings of remedies.[33] R. Zakrzewski recently suggested to use the term 'remedy' only in the sense of the rights arising from certain court orders or pronouncements.[34] According to him, rights which exist prior to the commencement of legal proceedings and the making of an order are not classified as remedies.[35] Still, his classification is based on the distinction between primary rights and secondary rights. The courts give effect to the latter by restating them in the court order ('replicative remedy').[36] Finally, yet importantly, equitable remedies are supposed to be 'discretionary remedies'. For instance, the court has a certain degree of discretion whether to grant an injunction or to order specific performance. On the one hand, this shall serve justice based on the facts of each case ('discretionary remedialism').[37] On the other hand, it is emphasised that the exercise of the discretion is 'rule-based'.[38] Both common law and equitable remedies are granted or refused in accordance with clearly established rules and

30 R. Zakrzewski, above n. 6, p. 44; S.A. Smith, 'Rights-Threats, Wrongs and Injustices: The Common Law's Causes of Action' (2017) 27 *New Zealand Universities Law Review* 1033, 1034 f.; *Attorney General v Blake* [2000] UKHL 45; [2001] AC 268, 284 (Lord Nicholls of Birkenhead: 'Remedies are the law's response to a wrong').

31 A. Burrows, above n. 1, pp. 3–4.

32 D.B. Dobbs, *Law of Remedies. Damages-Equity-Restitution*, 2nd edn., Irwin Law, St. Paul 1993, p. 2.

33 P. Birks, 'Rights, Wrongs and Remedies' (2000) 20 *Oxford Journal of Legal Studies* 1; for the various notions of 'remedies' in common law cf. P.S. Davies in this volume, pp. 27–43.

34 R. Zakrzewski, n. 6, p. 43.

35 Ibid., pp. 4, 50–61.

36 Ibid., p. 50.

37 S. Evans, 'Defending Discretionary Remedialism' (2001) 23 *Sydney Law Review* 463.

38 P. Birks, 'Rights, Wrongs and Remedies' (2000) 20 *Oxford Journal of Legal Studies* 1, 24.

principles.[39] The tense relation between the court's discretion and governing principles is illustrated in *Coventry v Lawrence*.[40] In that case the court had to decide whether to grant an injunction or damages in lieu of an injunction in a nuisance case. On the question how far the court's discretion to award damages in lieu is bound by relevant principles, Lord Neuberger said: 'Indeed, it is appropriate to give as much guidance as possible so as to ensure that, while the discretion is not fettered, its manner of exercise is as predictable as possible.'[41] Definitely, equitable remedies will not be granted automatically; those remedies will be denied if they cause injustice to the defendant.[42] Overall, three key features of 'remedies' can be identified. Firstly, substantive rights are something different from remedies. Secondly, the nature of remedies appears to be different from the nature of substantive rights. Thirdly, the active role of courts is evident – especially with regard to 'equitable remedies'. In his chapter, P.S. Davies will elaborate on the common law understanding of remedies and their distinctive character in more detail.

Unlike common law, German law appears to be less flexible when it comes to enforcement. As mentioned, the German legal system is supposed to be a collection of 'subjective rights'. Amongst others, a 'claim' is such a subjective right. Although the term 'remedy' is often used as equivalent to the term 'claim',[43] claims and remedies represent two different legal systems, at least 'different way(s) of thinking about law'.[44] These differences can be seen in three ways. First, in the civil law system, courts play only a passive role. The claimant does not apply for a certain remedy; he/she rather asks the court to 'confirm' his/her claim ('Anspruch').[45] 'Anspruch' is defined in §194 German Civil Code (BGB) as 'the right to demand that another person does or refrains from an act'. The claim itself is part of substantive law. Notwithstanding this, the distinction between primary rights and secondary rights can be established in German law as well (cf. also J.F. Hoffmann in this volume). Indeed, in property law, for example, there are provisions concerning the scope of the physical property right (§903 BGB: the owner's 'rights') and provisions on the available remedies (§1004 BGB: injunctive relief; §823 BGB: damages; §812 BGB: unjust

39 A. Burrows, above n. 1, p. 11.

40 *Coventry (t/a RDC Promotions) v Lawrence* [2014] UKSC 13; [2014] AC 822; [2014] 2 WLR 433.

41 Ibid., 121, 119–123.

42 *Jaggard v Sawyer and Another* [1994] EWCA Civ 1 para. 53; [1995] 1 WLR 269, 287.

43 Illustratory BGH 07.10.2004 – I ZR 91/02 = *GRUR Int.* 2005, 719 – *Lila-Schokolade.*

44 H. Dedek, 'From Norms to Facts: The Realization of Rights in Common and Civil Private Law' (2010) 56 *McGill Law Journal* 77, 77, 80.

45 M. Wolf and J. Neuner, *Allgemeiner Teil des Bürgerlichen Rechts*, 11th edn., C.H. Beck, München 2016, §21 para. 29.

enrichment; §§687 (2), 681, 667 and §816 BGB: disgorgement of profits). In a lawsuit, the claimant relies on this secondary right. A 'claim' equates with the secondary right. Even in contract law, some lawyers establish a distinction between the obligation and its enforcement ('specific enforcement').[46]

Secondly, claims clearly are within the realm of substantive law. Claims lack any procedural element.[47] Certainly, the wording of some of the provisions governing injunctive relief still reminds us of the ancient roots of those claims (cf. §12 BGB[48]). Originally, injunctions were indeed understood as court orders.[49] According to the modern view, injunctions are rights; solely the substantive law determines their scope.[50] Whether an injunction is granted or not is decided by substantive law, not by a court.

Thirdly, the relief available is rule-based. There is no discretion as to 'specific performance' or injunctive relief. A closer look, however, reveals that there are many parameters assuring that rights are enforced with a sense of proportion. Admittedly, private law does not address this in terms of remedies. A 'Law of Remedies' would foster transparency, though.

European law[51] tends to mirror features of the common law. As mentioned above, rights and remedies are indeed two distinct issues in the community law. The European notion of 'remedies' has substantive as well as procedural elements.[52] Yet, the European system is not a copy of the common law 'remedy-system'. Although some directives and regulations conceive remedies as court orders, others comprehend 'remedies' as rights.[53] Most importantly, European private law is aware of the fact that competing interests can be balanced via

---

46 M. Schmidt-Kessel and M. Kramme in H. Prütting, G. Wegen and G. Weinreich (eds.) *Bürgerliches Gesetzbuch. Kommentar*, 14th edn., Luchterhand Verlag, Köln 2019, §241 para. 22; cf. F. Hofmann, above n. 29, pp. 156–164 and 188–196.

47 B. Windscheid, above n.19, p. 1.

48 §12 BGB (*German Civil Code*) provides: 'If the right of a person to use a name is disputed by another person, or if the interest of the person entitled to the name is injured by the unauthorised use of the same name by another person, the person entitled may require the other to remove the infringement. If further infringements are to be feared, the person entitled may seek a prohibitory injunction.' Translation provided by the Langenscheidt Translation Service, https://www.gesetze-im-internet.de/englisch_bgb/englisch_bgb.html#p0048. However, this official translation misses that the second sentence says that the person entitled '*can take legal proceedings*'.

49 Cf. J. Fritzsche, *Unterlassungsanspruch und Unterlassungsklage*, Springer, Berlin, Heidelberg and New York 2000, pp. 114–120 and 535–537.

50 BGH 07.10.1982 – I ZR 120/80 = *GRUR* 1983, 127, 128 – *Vertragsstrafeversprechen*.

51 Cf. W. Van Gerven, 'Of Rights, Remedies and Procedures' (2000) 37 *Common Market Law Review* 501.

52 M. Ebers, *Rechte, Rechtsbehelfe und Sanktionen im Unionsprivatrecht*, Mohr Siebeck, Tübingen 2016, p. 79; C. Harlow, 'A Common European Law of Remedies?' in C. Kilpatrick, T. Novitz and P. Skidmore (eds.), *The Future of Remedies in Europe*, Hart Publishing, Oxford 2000, pp. 69, 73, yet, focusing on a procedural notion of remedies in Europe.

53 This chapter, 1; W. Van Gerven, 'Of Rights, Remedies and Procedures' (2000) 37 *Common Market Law Review* 501, 524–525.

the framework of remedies. Such equitable principles can be found in recent pieces of legislation. For example, the Trade Secret Directive[54] states in Art. 13: 'Member States shall ensure that, in considering an application for the adoption of the injunctions and corrective measures provided for in Article 12 and assessing their proportionality, the competent judicial authorities shall be required to take into account the specific circumstances of the case, including, where appropriate', inter alia, the conduct of the infringer (Art. 12 para. 1 lit. c), the public interest (Art. 12 para. 1 lit. g) or fundamental rights (Art. 12 para. 1 lit. h). Enforcement needs to be just and fair. Balancing is not only important for determining the scope of rights allocated and duties imposed, but also with respect to remedial provisions. In this regard, the Court of Justice of the European Union (CJEU) claims:

> (T)he Member States to provide for an appropriate system of sanctions with regard to professionals who employ unfair commercial practices, while ensuring that those sanctions comply, in particular, with the principle of proportionality. It is in this context that due account could be taken of factors such as the frequency of the practice complained of, whether or not it is intentional, and the degree of harm caused to the consumer.[55]

Thus, European private law's focus on proportionate enforcement is defined. Already, the principle of proportionality emerges as a fundamental principle of a European 'Law of Remedies' and will be outlined in more detail below.[56] Overall, it becomes apparent that it is time to independently analyse remedies, such as injunctions or damages, from a European point of view, thereby considering the issue of enforcement.

3. THE ISSUE OF ENFORCEMENT

Legal realists are primarily interested in the outcome. O.W. Holmes described the law as 'the prophecies of what the courts will do in fact, and nothing more pretentious, are what I mean by the law.'[57] He argued that it would be better 'to cease troubling ourselves about primary rights and sanctions altogether, than to describe, our prophecies concerning the liabilities commonly imposed

---

54 Above n. 26.

55 CJEU 16.4.2015, C-388/13, *Nemzeti Fogyasztóvédelmi Hatóság/UPC Magyarország Kft.*, ECLI:EU:C:2015:225 = *GRUR* 2015, 600 para. 58.

56 This chapter, 4.3; on 'proportionality as a mega-standard in European Private Law' cf. O. Fischman Afori in this volume, pp. 223–232; see also O. Fischman Afori, 'Proportionality – A New Mega Standard in European Copyright Law' (2014) 8 *International Review of Intellectual Property and Competition Law* 889.

57 O.W. Holmes, 'The Path of the Law' (1897) 10 *Harvard Law Review* 457, 461.

by the law in those inappropriate terms.'[58] Legal analysts demand, however, more accuracy. Indeed, the law can be described as the product of substantive rights and the means of enforcement. Figure 1 illustrates this. The 'law' as citizens at the end of the day experience it in their daily life – basically, this constitutes the legal realists' view – is represented by the area of the square.[59]

Figure 1. The 'law' as product of substantive rights and enforcement

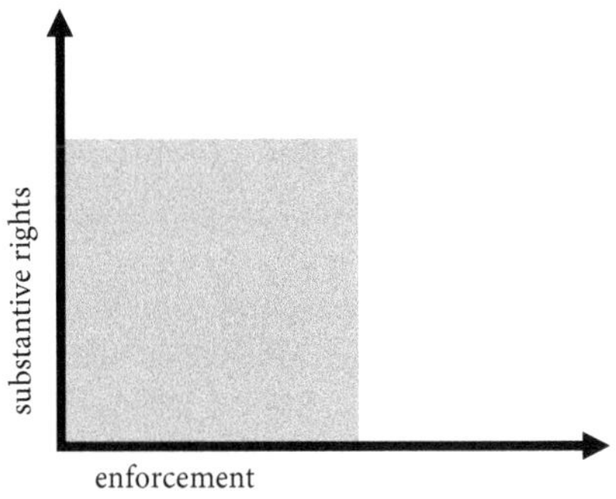

The stronger the enforcement regime, the broader the scope of substantive rights and vice versa. The value of a substantive right depends on the level of enforcement. Thus, questions of enforcement are crucial. Substantive rights eventually are shaped by their enforcement mechanisms. It is not only necessary to provide effective procedures to enforce rights, but also effective remedies. Irrespective of rules organising lawsuits etc. (procedural law), the question arises by which means rights are enforced. How, for example, can one vindicate his/her property or a copyright? By what means can a corporation enforce a contract? Which tools help consumers to defend their rights? In principle, at an institutional level there are three possible solutions (mechanisms of enforcement): (1.) Private enforcement, (2.) public enforcement and (3.) criminal enforcement.

Private rights are usually enforced by the means of civil proceedings. Within this original form of private enforcement, the right holders are in charge of the initiation and the course of the proceedings (i.e. by bringing evidence). In contrast, public authorities are generally competent to enforce public rights and values like public security. Nonetheless, private and public enforcement are converging. For instance, unfair competition law could be put into effect by administrative authorities, as well as by private lawsuits. Pursuant to Art. 11,

58 Ibid., 462–463.

59 Cf. F. Hofmann, 'Smart contracts und Overenforcement. Analytische Überlegungen zum Verhältnis von Rechtszuweisung und Rechtsdurchsetzung' in M. Fries and B.P. Paal (eds.), *Smart Contracts*, Tübingen 2019, pp. 125, 130–133.

the Unfair Commercial Practice Directive[60] leaves it to the Member States whether competitors combat unfair commercial practices or consumers can bring unfair commercial practices before an administrative authority, competent either to decide on complaints or to initiate appropriate legal proceedings. This dualism of enforcement raises the question as to what can be regarded as the most efficient means. On the one hand, authorities often lack both the resources and the relevant information to proceed effectively against, for example, misleading advertisements or aggressive commercial practises. On the other hand, they have discretion whether it is worth taking action or not. It might not be required to combat smaller infringements that are not significantly relevant to consumer behaviour, especially when the infringer ceases the unfair practice once he/she is informed that his/her conduct is unlawful. A sense of proportion can prevent overenforcement. Indeed, mechanisms of private enforcement can be considered highly effective. Yet, if there are no mechanisms which ensure proportionality, a 'purely' private enforcement might cause hardship. The infamous practice of 'cease-and-desist-letters', for instance in German unfair competition law, gives strong evidence of this finding. In turn, authorities can concentrate on those players who wilfully adopt unfair measures, who try to conceal their practices and attempt to infringe competition rules systematically. At the same time, this illustrates that enforcement rules which do not differentiate between different infringements are not just and equitable. Therefore, the effectiveness of public v. private enforcement has to be scrutinised. Against the background of CJEU case law, J.-U. Franck will look into that debate more deeply in his contribution to this volume. It can also be seen that private and public enforcement tools are interlocking. They are two sides of the same coin. The enforcement axis in Figure 1[61] relates to both private and public enforcement.

Criminal law is an enforcement tool, as well. In fact, criminal law intends to protect individual (private) rights, as well as rules established for the public interest.[62] The foundations of criminal enforcement will be presented in more detail by D. Magnus in her chapter. She points out that criminal enforcement is, however, at its heart public enforcement. It is even the strongest means of enforcement available. As such, it is the enforcement by criminal proceedings

---

60 Directive of the European Parliament and of the Council 2005/29/EC of 11 May 2005 concerning unfair business-to-consumer commercial practices in the internal market and amending Council Directive 84/450/EEC, Directives 97/7/EC, 98/27/EC and 2002/65/EC of the European Parliament and of the Council and Regulation (EC) No 2006/2004 of the European Parliament and of the Council [2005] OJ L 149/22.

61 This chapter, 3.

62 Cf. W. Hassemer and U. Neumann in U. Kindhäuser, U. Neumann and H.-U. Paeffgen (eds.), *Strafgesetzbuch NomosKommentar*, Band 1, 5th edn., Nomos, Baden-Baden 2017, Vorb. §1 para. 195.

that is said to distinctively characterise criminal law.[63] Criminal enforcement not only bears severe sanctions, like fines and imprisonment, but prosecutors can also rely on special procedures to discover further evidence (i.e. search warrants). Furthermore, criminal proceedings could cause 'collateral consequences'.[64] Thus, being treated as a 'criminal' can be a penalty in its own right. Therefore, interests in enforcing rights by means of the criminal law have to be balanced. Interestingly, this balance of interest concerns two different levels. On the one hand, the law must decide whether a wrongdoing shall be sanctioned by criminal law at all. D. Magnus argues in her chapter that a criminal sanction should only be imposed as last resort. The infringement of private rights as wrongdoing, however, could rather be enforced by means of private law, namely the law of tort.[65] On the other hand, interests need to be balanced concerning the specific sanction. The kind of sanction that is imposed by criminal law (i.e. fine or prison sentence) leaves space to weigh different factors, such as the state of mind of the wrongdoer, his/her intentions, the damage occurred, etc. Criminal courts have to ensure that there are different (appropriate) sanctions for different cases, even if the committed offence was identical. However, the line between criminal law and private law remedies is blurred concerning the preventive and potentially punitive function of certain remedies, especially in the law of torts.[66] Notably, L. Tichý will argue in favour of a genuine preventive function of private law remedies in his contribution to this volume. Whereas the functions of remedies will be dealt with in the following chapters,[67] this blur of private, public and criminal law reveals the relevance of addressing the questions of how to vindicate wrongs and how to enforce rights from a unified point of view. That is the perspective of enforcement.

4. PRINCIPLES OF THE LAW OF REMEDIES

So far, this introduction has focused on shaping the landscape of a 'Law of Remedies' within the field of enforcement. It has been pointed out that remedies can indeed be subject to distinct and genuinely European legal scholarship. Hence, (4.1) questions related to enforcement can be embraced by a distinctive area of law. Even the civil law can be analysed from a remedial perspective,[68]

63 G. Williams, 'The Definition of Crime' (1955) 8 *Current Legal Problems* 107, 123; R.A. Duff, *The Realm of Criminal Law*, OUP, Oxford 2018, p. 16.
64 R.A. Duff, above n. 63, p. 15 at n. 21 and p. 26.
65 For a 'rights based' approach to the common law, see R. Stevens, *Torts and Rights*, OUP, Oxford 2007.
66 R.A. Duff, above n. 63, p. 25.
67 Cf. this chapter, 4.2.
68 F. Hofmann, n. 29, pp. 122–249.

more than ever as the 'remedy-approaches' in European Private Law will influence national 'thinking'. Taking such a viewpoint reveals that certain legal problems can be gathered under the umbrella of enforcement issues. At the same time, underlying principles can be identified. They might deliver helpful 'guidelines' as C. Heinze will argue in his chapter with respect to damages. A few of underlying principles (4.2–4.6) shall be presented in the following.

4.1. DISTINCTIVE RESEARCH FIELD

The 'Law of Remedies' can be understood as an area of law 'shaped by its own set of distinctive principles and/or policies'.[69] Yet, its distinctiveness has to be scrutinised. In particular, the variety of remedies could draw a question mark on an inclusive approach. Even the common law perspective on a 'Law of Remedies' is not uncontroversial. P.S. Davies will pay particular attention to the English notion of remedies in his chapter, hereby considering the objections against and merits of a 'stand-alone' research field. Overall, he will demonstrate that an analysis of remedies comprising the different areas of law is, though, an important and genuine research task. As mentioned above, the traditional civil law is not used to a separate remedial view. Against this background, J.F. Hoffmann will, however, present an approach to analyse substantive private law as system of 'property rights' and 'remedial rights' in his contribution to this volume. Thus, a remedial analysis is possible.

The 'Law of Remedies' could go even further. Questions related to enforcement, in effect, have common features. Although the remedial nature is sometimes somewhat concealed, a certain set of rules serves the enforcement of 'rights antecedent'.[70] In contrast, the classic rules of substantive law aim to allocate rights and duties, as well as to describe their respective scope. In other words, there are two types of legal rules, rules of a categorical different nature – substantive rules and remedial rules. This can be illustrated by a simple test: could a certain provision be erased if the addressee of the rule obeys its order voluntarily? There would be no need for injunctions, for instance, if property rights were never violated. If the seller maintained his/her duty to perform, specific performance never would have to be ordered. It does not matter whether a norm is part of contract law or of the law of execution. The norm's function is decisive: agreed remedies might be discussed within contract law. However, these clauses primarily concern the question of enforcement, hence, the 'Law of Remedies'. For example, parties do not agree on a penalty

[69] J. Berryman, 'The Law of Remedies: A Prospectus for Teaching and Scholarship' (2010) 10 *Oxford University Commonwealth Legal Journal* 123, 134.

[70] Cf. T.E. Holland, *The Elements of Jurisprudence*, 12th edn., London 1916.

clause for its own sake, but to secure the performance interest of the creditor.[71] 'Cease-and-desist-letters' in German law can be analysed as contracts. A closer look, however, reveals their 'remedial nature'. The infringer promises to refrain from doing something. This promise substitutes legal proceedings, as a court would order the very same thing. Furthermore, a penalty clause substitutes the execution procedure due to a court order pursuant to §890 German Civil Procedure Act (ZPO).[72] The latest case law in European copyright law[73] can be analysed from such a remedial perspective, as well. As the CJEU has extended the concept of communication to the public, it is no longer restricted to primary infringements. For instance, Art. 3 Information Society Directive[74] has arguably adopted the German 'Störerhaftung' as a sort of secondary liability.[75] The development of remedies against intermediaries as innocent third parties will be further elaborated by M. Husovec in his chapter. From a law and economics point of view, K.U. Schmolke shows in his chapter that actions within corporate law (interestingly, despite their procedural nature) fall within the 'Law of Remedies', too. He also introduces the fundamental distinction between property rules and liability rules. This is a pure remedial question as entitlements might be protected in either way. Overall, it becomes apparent that questions surrounding remedies are indeed a distinctive field of research. Arguably, 'remedial law' covers rules telling courts what they shall order.[76] Yet, it deals with all types of questions related to enforcement. At the end of the day, it is about how substantive rights (in a narrow sense) are put into effect.

---

71 S. Rowan, 'For the Recognition of Remedial Terms Agreed Inter Partes' (2010) 126 *Law Quarterly Review* 448; S. Rowan, *Remedies for Breach of Contract*, OUP, Oxford 2012, pp. 207 ff.

72 §890 (1) ZPO (Code of Civil Procedure) provides: 'Should the debtor violate his obligation to cease and desist from actions, or to tolerate actions to be taken, the court of first instance hearing the case is to sentence him for each count of the violation, upon the creditor filing a corresponding petition, to a coercive fine and, for the case that such payment cannot be obtained, to coercive detention or coercive detention of up to six (6) months. The individual coercive fine may not be levied in an amount in excess of 250,000 euros, and the coercive detention may not be longer than a total of two (2) years.' Translation provided by Samson Übersetzungen GmbH, C. von Schöning, https://www.gesetze-im-internet.de/englisch_zpo/englisch_zpo.html#p3400.

73 CJEU 8.9.2016, C-160/15, *GS Media/Sanoma*, ECLI:EU:C:2016:644 = *GRUR* 2016, 1152; CJEU 26.4.2017, C-527/15, *Stichting Brein/Jack Frederik Wullems [Filmspeler]*, ECLI:EU:C:2017:300 = *GRUR* 2017, 610; CJEU 14.6.2017, C-610/15, *Stichting Brein/Ziggo [The Pirate Bay]*, ECLI:EU:C:2017:456 = *GRUR* 2017, 790.

74 Above n. 23.

75 A. Ohly, 'The broad concept of "communication to the public" in recent CJEU judgments and the liability of intermediaries: primary, secondary or unitary liability?' (2018) 6 *Gewerblicher Rechtsschutz und Urheberrecht Internationaler Teil* 517; J.B. Nordeman, 'EuGH-Urteile GS Media, Filmspeler und ThePirateBay: ein neues europäisches Haftungskonzept im Urheberrecht für die öffentliche Wiedergabe' (2018) 6 *Gewerblicher Rechtsschutz und Urheberrecht Internationaler Teil* 526; E. Rosati, 'Intermediaries and IP: 5 key principles of EU law' (2018) 16 *Praxis im Immaterialgüter- und Wettbewerbsrecht* 367, 369.

76 S.A. Smith, above n. 30, 1034 f.; cf. S.A. Smith, above n. 7; https://www.youtube.com/watch?v=-II0hSGU52I.

4.2. FUNCTIONAL APPROACH

Besides the generalised approach of a 'Law of Remedies', different remedies have different functions. The main ones are compensation, restitution, punishment, compelling performance, preventing a wrong and declaring rights.[77] Hence, depending on the facts of each case, the questions are: Which remedy is appropriate? Does the chosen remedy support the desired effect? Are there better remedial alternatives? Or as J. Moss asks in his chapter, is the effect of a certain remedy in accordance with the justification of the underlying intellectual property right? The economic analysis of law differentiates between 'property rules' and 'liability rules'.[78] Against this background, the law has, as mentioned, to decide whether to grant an injunction ('property rule') or damages as compensation instead ('liability rules'). In copyright law, for example, it is not possible to negotiate about copies for personal use. Therefore, injunctions cannot operate as a tool to foster market solutions, which could lead to a market failure due to high transaction cost. Just imagine, every student who wants to copy a few pages of a textbook would have to negotiate with the right holders. Unimaginable! Consequently, the Information Society Directive[79] allows Member States to provide for exceptions or limitations to the reproduction right (Art. 5 para. 2), albeit contingent on the condition that the right holders receive fair compensation. In other words, the copyright 'infringement' (although, according to the classic doctrine, there is no such infringement as the privileged use is legal)[80] triggers damages in lieu of an injunction. This example demonstrates that exceptions and limitations in copyright law can also be analysed in terms of remedies. K.U. Schmolke tells a similar story with respect to corporate law in his contribution to this volume. There is a special risk of hold-up situations, which can be cured by means of remedies.

Furthermore, not only the infringement of a right could cause a loss for the right holder, but an injunction could harm the infringer likewise. If he/she had to suspend production immediately, for instance, the incurring costs might be inappropriate. Additionally, avoiding another patent infringement might necessitate the infringer to adapt his/her production. Finally, the infringer has no chance to charge his/her expenses. Consequently, an injunction can have the same effect as punitive damages.[81] Is this intended by the remedy?

---

77 A. Burrows, above n. 1, p. vii (3rd edn., 2004); see also S.A. Smith, above n. 30 arguing for a 'modern' and broader understanding of 'causes of action' in remedial law.

78 G. Calabresi and D. Melamed, 'Property Rules, Liability Rules, and Inalienability: One View of the Cathedral' (1972) 85 *Harvard Law Review*, 1089.

79 Above n. 23.

80 More generally, cf. J.F. Hoffmann, in this volume, pp. 45–60.

81 P.J. Heald, 'Permanent Injunctions as Punitive Damages in Patent Infringement Cases', *Illinois Public Law Research Papers Series*, No. 10-38, available at: https://ssrn.com/abstract=1851681.

Within the 'Law of Remedies' the functions of each remedy can be analysed. As already mentioned, preventive elements in 'remedial law' will be investigated in detail by L. Tichý in his chapter. B. Raue will particularly consider punishing or deterrent effects of disgorging remedies in his chapter. He will argue that the degree of fault should be taken into account when assessing the extent of the monetary remedy. Whereas intended and reckless infringements of rights shall be sanctioned by a disgorging remedy, in other events (such as negligence or strict liability) the profit should not be allocated to the infringed right. Consequently, the infringer's efforts need to be considered and the remedy 'disgorgement of profits' would not be appropriate.

4.3. PROPORTIONALITY

Despite their respective functions, remedies in general need to be proportionate. A fundamental principle within the (European) 'Law of Remedies' is proportionality. Arguably, proportionality does not mean 'discretion', but rather some sort of flexibility.[82] As private law is generally faced with the task of adjusting numerous competing interests, remedies could provide an effective balancing tool. Of course, rights themselves have to be just and fair in the first place. For example, copyright protection for mere ideas, scientific theories etc., would hamper cultural or scientific life instead of promoting it.[83] Accordingly, inter alia, Art. 1 para. 2 Computer Programs Directive[84] provides that '(i)deas and principles which underlie any element of a computer program, including those which underlie its interfaces, are not protected by copyright under this Directive'. Arguably, tangible property does not allocate a right to exclusively take photos of the concerned property, in German law.[85] Finally, trade secrets do not prohibit reverse engineering.[86] Notwithstanding, balancing is not restricted to substantive rights in a narrower sense. In particular, European law suggests that competing interests can also be balanced via the framework of remedies (cf. the above-mentioned Art. 13 of the Trade Secret Directive[87]

---

82 At least in the German legal system 'discretion' is understood as a free decision by an authority; a working translation for 'discretion' could be *Interessenabwägung* (balancing of interests), cf. F. Hofmann '"Equity" im deutschen Lauterkeitsrecht? Der "Unterlassungsanspruch" nach der Geschäftsgeheimnis-RL' (2018) 1 *Wettbewerb in Recht und Praxis* 1, 6–7.

83 H. Schack, *Urheber- und Urhebervertragsrecht*, 7th edn., Mohr Siebeck Verlag, Tübingen 2015, §9 para. 194–196.

84 Directive of the European Parliament and of the Council 2009/24/EC of 23 April 2009 on the legal protection of computer programs [2009] OJ L 111/16.

85 Cf. BGH 17.12.2010 – V ZR 45/10 = *GRUR* 2011, 323 para. 15 – *Preußische Gärten und Parkanlagen*.

86 Art. 3 para. 1 lit. b Trade Secrets Directive above n. 26.

87 Cf. this chapter, 2.

and Art. 3 Enforcement Directive[88]). Art. 7 Trade Secrets Directive further provides that 'measures, procedures and remedies provided for in this Directive shall be applied in a manner that is proportionate'. In trade mark law, to mention a further example, remedies have to be proportionate, as well. Art. 130 Trade Mark Regulation[89] provides that when an EU trade mark has been infringed the court shall issue an order prohibiting the defendant from proceeding with the acts which infringed the EU trade mark 'unless there are special reasons for not doing so'. More generally, the CJEU reminds us that 'the Member States have to provide for an appropriate system of sanctions, while ensuring that those sanctions comply, in particular, with the principle of proportionality'.[90] Injunctions must be equitable and proportionate.[91] If the amount of damages is calculated on the basis of twice the amount of the hypothetical royalty and will exceed the loss actually suffered clearly and substantially, a claim to that effect could constitute an abuse of rights, which is prohibited by Art. 3 para. 2 of the Enforcement Directive.[92] Moreover, the CJEU stresses the importance of fundamental rights. The CJEU holds that in order to assess whether an injunction, for example, on the basis of Art. 8 para. 3 of the Information Society Directive,[93] is consistent with EU law, it is 'necessary to take account in particular of the requirements that stem from the protection of the applicable fundamental rights'.[94] Consequently, a fair balance has to be struck between the applicable fundamental rights protected by the European Union legal order.[95] Similarly, injunctions pursuant to the third sentence of Art. 11 of the Enforcement Directive 'may be pronounced only if it ensures a fair balance between the protection of intellectual property and the absence of obstacles to legitimate trade'.[96] As a consequence, academics endorse a proportionality test.[97] Notably, O. Fischman Afori argues in her chapter that the test of proportionality is the 'new mega standard', specifically

---

88 Above n. 24.

89 Above n. 22.

90 CJEU 16.4.2015, C-388/13, *Nemzeti Fogyasztóvédelmi Hatóság/UPC Magyarország Kft.*, ECLI:EU:C:2015:225 = *GRUR* 2015, 600 para. 57; cf. above this chapter, 2.

91 CJEU 7.7.2016, C-494/15, *Tommy Hilfiger*, ECLI:EU:C:2016:528 = *GRUR* 2016, 1062 para. 34.

92 CJEU 25.1.2017, C-367/15, *Oławska Telewizja Kablowa*, ECLI:EU:C:2017:36 = *GRUR* 2017, 264 para. 31.

93 Above n. 23.

94 CJEU 27.3.2014, C-314/12, *UPC Telekabel*, ECLI:EU:C:2014:192 = *GRUR* 2014, 468 para. 45.

95 CJEU 15.9.2016, C-484/14, *McFadden*, ECLI:EU:C:2016:689 = *GRUR* 2016, 1146 para. 83 and 89; CJEU 27.3.2014, C-314/12, *UPC Telekabel*, ECLI:EU:C:2014:192 = *GRUR* 2014, 468 para. 46–47; CJEU 29.1.2008, C-275/06, *Promusicae*, ECLI:EU:C:2008:54 = *GRUR* 2008, 241 para. 68 and 70.

96 CJEU 7.7.2016, C-494/15, *Tommy Hilfiger*, ECLI:EU:C:2016:528 = *GRUR* 2016, 1062 para. 35.

97 Cf. P. Teunissen, 'The Balance Puzzle: The ECJ's Method of Proportionality Review in EU Copyright Law' (2018) 40 *European Intellectual Property Review* 579.

in copyright law.[98] She suggests that the test should be introduced via the 'framework of remedies'.[99] Furthermore, she claims that 'remedies should not be viewed as simply a legal by-product of the determination that an infringement has taken place, but rather as a complimentary means of implementing policy'.[100] In her contribution to this volume she will further elaborate this thesis. Whereas O. Fischman Afori considers the proportionality test a strong policy vehicle, there are good reasons to rely on proportionality only as an instrument for 'fine-tuning'.[101]

4.4. SOPHISTICATED ENFORCEMENT

Remedial analysis sheds light on the significance of enforcement. De facto, the scope of the substantive law is influenced by the means of remedies. Strong remedies broaden the scope of substantive rights. For fear of awkward sanctions, actions legally allowed might be suspended. Namely, incalculable liability for damages enlarges the risk of emerging 'phantom rights'.[102] Such 'chilling effects' have been observed in the context of intermediary liability.[103] Figure 2 illustrates how enforcement can influence the scope of rights by enlarging or trimming them. The square representing the 'law' gets larger or smaller depending on the degree of enforcement. The question is whether the legislator intended the 'law' (represented by the extent of the square) to be so strong or weak.[104]

Figure 2. Different degrees of enforcement affecting the scope of the 'law'

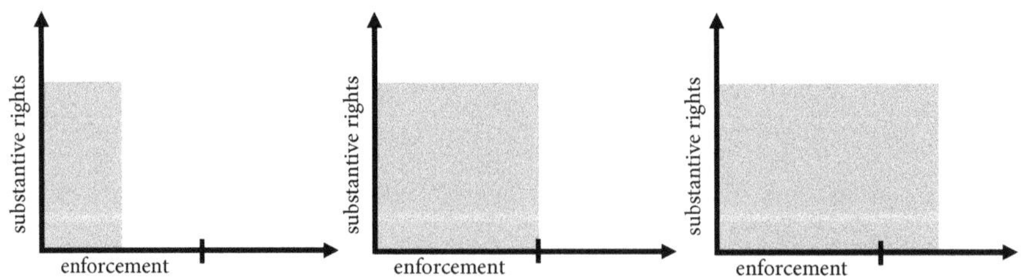

[98] O. Fischman Afori, 'Proportionality – A New Mega Standard in European Copyright Law' (2014) 8 *International Review of Intellectual Property and Competition Law* 889.

[99] Ibid., 890.

[100] Ibid., 892–893.

[101] J.F. Hoffmann in this volume argues, in turn, that proportionality is not a remedy-related question at all; the substantive law itself shall have to be just and equitable.

[102] B. Raue, 'Die doppelte Lizenzgebühr ist kein Strafschadensersatz' (2017) 4 *Zeitschrift für Urheber- und Medienrecht* 353, 354.

[103] Cf. ECHR 16.06.2015, 64569/09 para. 73, 92 – *DELFI AS / Estland II.*

[104] CF. F. Hofmann, n. 59, pp. 130–133 and pp. 137–140.

Some argue that if a right is not enforceable, it is not a proper right. Namely J.F. Hoffmann suggests in his chapter that balancing has to be undertaken as to the scope of the 'property right' itself, but not within remedial law. Who would care about any legal entitlement that is only found in textbooks, but not in courtrooms? Indeed, a substantive right is worthless if there are no effective means to enforce it. So, the more enforcement the better? The answer is no.[105] Rights need to be enforced appropriately, not maximally. The principle of proportionality already has been introduced. Furthermore, it has already been pointed out that injunctions are not always appropriate. Awarding damages might be sufficient. Thus, German unfair competition law developed 'grace periods' (*Aufbrauchfristen*).[106] This means that if an immediate injunction would cause hardship to the infringer, the injunction could be suspended temporarily. Damages, however, remain unaffected. This instrument is subject to the test of proportionality. The state of mind of the infringer, the consequences of the infringement, hardship to the infringer etc. have to be balanced. Thus, rights and duties are enforced sophisticatedly. Another example of this is the *McFadden* case. If Wi-Fi access is abused for copyright infringements the operator is not liable for damages (cf. Art. 13 E-Commerce Directive[107]), albeit the possibility of ordering an injunction.[108] Whether this policy fosters the disposability of Wi-Fi or not, European private law is sensitive that enforcement can be based on different remedies.

4.5. SUBSTANTIVE LAW

The 'Law of Remedies' is distinct from procedural law. More precisely, the rules governing civil procedure are complemented by the rules governing the remedies available to counter an infringement of a right. The question is whether this is a matter of procedural law as well/or a matter of substantive law. In England, P. Birks argued that remedies were rights.[109] Indeed, the 'discretion' of courts is said to be rule-based.[110] Certainly, European private law is flexible as to which conditions have to be met in order to, for example, grant an injunction. The latest evidence to that can be found in Art. 13 Trade Secret Directive.[111] Pursuant to subsection 3 of this provision, in specified

---

105 Cf. J. Basedow, 'Rechtsdurchsetzung und Streitbeilegung' (2018) 1 *Juristenzeitung* 1, 2–4.

106 BGH 10.05.2016 – X ZR 114/13 = *GRUR* 2016, 1031 para. 41 – *Wärmetauscher (patent law).*

107 Directive of the European Parliament and of the Council 2000/31/EC of 8 June 2000 on electronic commerce [2000] OJ L 178/1.

108 CJEU 15.9.2016, C-484/14, *McFadden*, ECLI:EU:C:2016:689 = *GRUR* 2016, 1146 para. 79.

109 P. Birks, 'Rights, Wrongs and Remedies' (2000) 20 *Oxford Journal of Legal Studies* 1.

110 Above n. 38.

111 Above n. 26.

constellations Member States shall provide that, if an injunction pursuant to Art. 12 could be granted 'at the request of the person liable to be subject to th(is) measure ..., the competent judicial authority may order pecuniary compensation to be paid to the injured party' rather than issuing the injunction. Provisions like that illustrate the linking, yet, distinctive nature of remedies, such as injunctions or pecuniary awards. The remedies point the way for the court's decision. Notwithstanding, the 'Law of Remedies' is part of substantive law – substantive law in a broader sense. The main reason is that substantive law itself has to decide how rights are enforced in detail and provide a framework for judicial review. Whereas common law courts rule on remedies with discretion, 'balancing' can be considered a functional equivalent.[112] Future case law shall give further guidelines in which cases which remedy is appropriate. Consequently, identical cases should be decided identically.[113] A. Funke supports this view from the perspective of German public law in his contribution to this volume. Instead of 'remedies', he talks about 'reactions of the law'.

4.6. NOTICE AND ACTION

Sometimes the boundary between substantive law in a narrower sense and remedial law can be difficult to find. As mentioned above, the CJEU, for example, fosters a broad understanding of the right to communication to the public.[114] Platforms, such as The Pirate Bay, users who set a hyperlink on the internet or sellers of devices which enable access to copyright protected material, can directly infringe copyright. None of them, though, commits the act of communication to the public on his/her own. They are sort of assistants. The CJEU, thus, recognises their specific role and considers them liable only if they had knowledge of the infringement. Therefore, subjective components are said to restrict the broad understanding of Art. 3 Information Society Directive.[115,116] Except for business models which are clearly based on copyright infringements (in which a liability can be established easily), the right holder has to notify the infringer before he/she can exercise his/her right. The CJEU holds that where it is established that a person 'knew or ought to have known that the hyperlink he or she posted provides access to a work illegally placed on the internet, ... it is necessary to consider that the provision

112 Above n. 82.

113 For a different view *Jaggard v Sawyer and Another* [1994] EWCA Civ 1 para. 56, [1995] 1 WLR 269, 288.

114 Cf. above n. 73.

115 Above n. 23.

116 B. Raue, 'Das subjektive Vervielfältigungsrecht – eine Lösung für den digitalen Werkgenuss?' (2017) 9 *Intellectual Property Journal* 514, 519–520; A. Ohly, above n. 75.

of that link constitutes a "communication to the public"'.[117] This is particularly the case when the person who posted the link 'was notified thereof by the copyright holders'.[118] The enforcement, therefore, depends on procedural requirements. The idea is clear: competing interests are balanced within the realm of enforcement. Particularly for intermediaries, it is difficult to positively realise that their platforms are abused for copyright or trade mark infringements. A general obligation to actively seek facts or circumstances indicating illegal activity is unreasonable.[119] The principal of proportionality opposes such an obligation.[120] Thus, liability depends on a 'notice-and-take-down-procedure' (cf. Art. 12 E-Commerce Directive). In contrast, if the intermediary had learned about an infringement, he/she may be forced to take measures which contribute to avoiding new infringements of the same nature by the same market-trader from taking place.[121] This can be described as 'procedural property rules'.[122] Injunctive relief (the remedy) depends on a notification. Without such a principle, there would be a risk of overenforcement. For that reason, the CJEU applied this principle to an organiser of a physical market as well.[123] Even in patent law the CJEU requires the proprietor of a standard essential patent (SEP), 'first, to alert the alleged infringer of the infringement complained about by designating that SEP and specifying the way in which it has been infringed'.[124] The CJEU argues that 'in view of the large number of SEPs composing a standard', it was 'not certain that the infringer of one of those SEPs would necessarily be aware that it is using the teaching of an SEP that is both valid and essential to a standard'.[125] Looking at these different cases through the lens of 'remedial law', once more supports the view that there is an analytical value to this perspective. Indeed, to manage complexity, remedies can depend on a prior notification.[126] Enforcement is modified.

---

117 CJEU 8.9.2016, C-160/15, *GS Media/Sanoma*, ECLI:EU:C:2016:644 = *GRUR* 2016, 1152 para. 49.

118 Ibid.

119 Cf. Art. 15 E-Commerce Directive, above n. 107; CJEU 12.7.2011, C-324/09, *L'Oréal/eBay*, ECLI:EU:C:2011:474 = *GRUR* 2011, 1025 para. 139.

120 CJEU 7.7.2016, C-494/15, *Tommy Hilfiger*, ECLI:EU:C:2016:528 = *GRUR* 2016, 1062 para. 34.

121 Ibid., CJEU 12.7.2011, C-324/09, *L'Oréal/eBay*, ECLI:EU:C:2011:474 = *GRUR* 2011, 1025 para. 141 and 144.

122 F. Hofmann, 'Kontrolle oder nachlaufender Rechtsschutz – wohin bewegt sich das Urheberrecht? Rechtsdurchsetzung in der EU zwischen Kompensation und Bestrafung' (2018) 1 *Gewerblicher Rechtsschutz und Urheberrecht* 21, 28 and 29.

123 CJEU 7.7.2016, C-494/15, *Tommy Hilfiger*, ECLI:EU:C:2016:528 = *GRUR* 2016, 1062 para. 34.

124 CJEU 15.7.2015, C-170/13, *Huawei Technologies/ZTE*, ECLI:EU:C:2015:477 = *GRUR* 2015, 764 para. 61.

125 Ibid., para. 62.

126 Cf. W. Van Gerven, 'Of Rights, Remedies and Procedures' (2000) 37 *Common Market Law Review* 501; F. Hofmann, 'Prozeduralisierung der Haftungsvoraussetzungen im Medienrecht – Vorbild für die Intermediärshaftung im Allgemeinen?' (2017) 2 *Zeitschrift für Urheber- und Medienrecht* 102, 105–109.

5. THE EUROPEAN PERSPECTIVE

As demonstrated above, remedies are increasingly important in European private law. The issue of enforcement, as well as underlying principles become more and more influenced by European legislation and the CJEU case law.[127] Thus, this book aims to provide a European view on remedies as an enforcement tool. This perspective shall foster the development of the previously outlined principles, thereby clarifying the crucial question about the available remedies. The answer to this question is, as illustrated in Figure 2,[128] an essential indicator for the level of enforcement. A 'Law of Remedies', hence, has to appreciate the distinct nature of remedies.[129] Therefore, it has to be freed from issues surrounding procedural enforcement in European law,[130] as well as debates solely concerning the scope of substantive rights.

To do so, this book will focus on remedies, such as damages, accounts of profits, injunctions or specific performance, in European private law. C. Heinze will address in his chapter the question whether it is possible to speak of a 'European Law of Damages' by analysing different sources of and underlying principles for damages in European private law. Further controversies in European contract law, inter alia, relate to remedies for non-conformity of digital data issued by the 'digital content' directive[131] or the Commission's plans to fully harmonise consumer sales of goods.[132] Even if the new Consumer Sales Directive explicitly addresses the issue of consumer's remedies in Art 13, damages are not included in its scope. In his chapter, C. Twigg-Flesner will present remedies in European contract law in more detail. Monetary awards, such as damages, are not only important in consumer law cases, but also play a decisive role for the adequate remedial response to an IP infringement. However, the rules on assessment of monetary remedies have to be scrutinised. J. Moss will consider this and further controversies on remedies in European IP law in his chapter.

A comprehensive approach to understanding remedies, thus, has to deal with various pieces of European legislation, as well as different national interpretations to get the whole picture. Finding and analysing this 'whole picture' is indeed the core task of a 'Law of Remedies'. The lack of a unifying legislative framework should not be an objection to but rather a justification for the demand for a distinctive field of research. Overall, it becomes apparent that a

---

127 This chapter, 1.

128 This chapter, 4.4.

129 See this chapter, 2.

130 On a procedural perspective on 'remedies' in European law cf. C. Kilpatrick, T. Novitz and P. Skidmore (eds.), *The Future of Remedies in Europe*, Hart Publishing, Oxford 2000.

131 Above n. 27.

132 Above n. 28.

'Law of Remedies' is not only a common law phenomenon. The enforcement of rights (not only with respect to procedural rules) is a unifying task. Besides addressing the various private law disciplines, as well as public and criminal law,[133] it applies to different jurisdictions likewise. Nonetheless, this book will not address the variety of European jurisdictions but rather focus on the English legal system as a common law perspective (P.S. Davies' contribution) and the German law as an example of a civil law jurisdiction. In general, the topic shall be presented within the overall structure of European private law.

6. CONCLUSION

The 'Law of Remedy' deserves attention. It is indeed a subject in its own right. Whereas in common law countries themes and controversies related to remedies in general are widely discussed, the continent lacks such a discussion. This should change for three reasons. First, taking a remedial view helps in analysing the structure of private law. It becomes much clearer that a certain set of rules aims to enforce rights instead of allocating rights. The boundaries in private law are set between substantive law and remedial law, not between IP, tort and contract law – at least with respect to enforcement. Secondly, European private law adopts this view. Clearly, a distinction between provisions governing the substantive law in a narrower sense and remedial provisions (substantive law in a broader sense) can be observed. Thirdly, via remedies competing interests can be balanced. Rights need to be proportionate; remedies secure the 'fine-tuning'. Hopefully, this book fosters the identification of controversies related to the enforcement of rights and explores principles concerning the issue of remedies. In order to stimulate this debate, within the following chapters international scholars provide several reasons for a 'European Law of Remedies'.

133 This chapter, 3.

REMEDIES IN ENGLISH PRIVATE LAW

A 'Stand-Alone' Research Area?

Paul S. Davies

1. INTRODUCTION

Are remedies in English private law considered to constitute a 'stand-alone' research area? There is no doubt that lawyers often talk about 'remedies' as a distinct area; books are written on remedies, and university courses on remedies seem to be increasingly common. Indeed, I have taught a course on 'Commercial Remedies' at graduate level for the past five years.[1] That partly reflects the fact that students are concerned to understand what courts do, and the potential relief available in the commercial context in which they hope to practise. But it does not necessarily mean that remedies should be considered to be a 'stand-alone' research area. There are obvious problems in divorcing remedies from substantive rights and causes of action. Conversely, there is clearly a strong link between rights and remedies.

This chapter begins by considering what it means for something to be a 'stand-alone' subject or research area. It will then briefly address the vexed

1 One of the editors of this collection, Franz Hofmann, attended some of these seminars in Oxford. Despite that, he kindly invited me to answer the question posed in the title of this chapter. I am grateful to him for that invitation, and thank all those who participated in the conference at which an earlier version of this chapter was presented for their questions and comments.

question of how the term 'remedy' should be understood. This is the cause of substantial disagreement amongst scholars. The final terminological clarification concerns the scope of 'private law' and its coherence as a subject. It will then be possible to discuss the idea of remedies as a stand-alone subject. The dangers of isolating remedies will first be outlined, before analysing the pragmatic approach that the common law has taken to remedies. Finally, it will be suggested that regardless of whether remedies is viewed as a 'stand-alone' research area, there is still much to be gained from courses and books on remedies.

2. WHAT MAKES A LEGAL SUBJECT?

It is surprisingly difficult to state how a 'legal subject' is defined.[2] In England and Wales there are currently seven foundational subjects that have to be studied at the academic stage in order to qualify as a solicitor or barrister: criminal law, contract law, tort law, constitutional and administrative law, land law, equity and trust law, and the law of the European Union.[3] These core subjects are well-defined: they each consist of a set of over-arching principles which are distinct from those of other areas, and each contains a large body of law which shows structural coherence. They are rightly regarded as the 'core' of English law, since they are the building blocks for a number of other subjects which would be hard to understand without these foundational subjects.

The core subjects are well-known and well-defined. But it is worth noting that even the integrity of these subjects has been sometimes doubted. For instance, Tony Weir once light-heartedly remarked that 'Tort is what is in the tort texts and the only thing holding it together is the binding'.[4] That was over-stating the position for comic effect,[5] but it is worth noting that setting clear boundaries of even the 'core' subjects may be difficult. Indeed, the utility of a taxonomy depends on its purpose,[6] and it is important that the law be presented in a clear and coherent way for a proper understanding to be developed.

---

2 I am grateful to Tamara Hervey for sharing her (as yet largely unpublished) thoughts with me for this section of the chapter, although she bears no responsibility for what follows.

3 This is likely to change in the imminent future with the introduction of the Solicitors' Qualifying Examination: https://www.sra.org.uk/sra/policy/sqe.page.

4 T. Weir, *An Introduction to Tort Law*, 2nd ed., OUP, Oxford, 2006, p. ix.

5 N. McBride and R. Bagshaw, *Tort Law*, 6th ed., Pearson, Harlow, 2018, pp. 13–15.

6 D. Sheehan and T.T. Arvind, 'Private law theory and taxonomy: reframing the debate' [2015] LS 480.

Beyond the 'core' subjects, it can be more difficult to establish what a subject is. For instance, Judge Frank H. Easterbook famously deprecated the notion that 'cyberlaw' was a true subject, arguing:[7]

> ... the best way to learn the law applicable to specialized endeavors is to study general rules. Lots of cases deal with sales of horses; others deal with people kicked by horses; still more deal with the licensing and racing of horses, or with the care veterinarians give to horses, or with prizes at horse shows. Any effort to collect these strands into a course on 'The Law of the Horse' is doomed to be shallow and to miss unifying principles.

This view has since been challenged as it applies to 'cyberlaw',[8] but even in that context remains influential. Many rules might concern a horse, but studying the law of the horse as a subject would not be very enlightening. Cyberlaw scholars continue to wrestle with this existential issue for their own subject.[9]

Some subjects have become established only more recently, and are subject to strong debates about what should be included within their scope. For instance, family law has evolved as a subject to do with families, and the scope of books on family law differ markedly.[10] Family law was previously largely broken up within the 'core' subjects, such as property, trusts, and tort law. What drove the subject forwards was the impetus provided by Bromley's seminal text,[11] which sparked greater interest and development. Similar processes may be discerned in other areas too, such as the law of unjust enrichment[12] and environmental law.[13] But in all these areas there remains debate about the nature of the subject and what should be included within its scope as particular to and definitive of that subject.

If remedies is a 'stand-alone' legal subject, that does not mean that one should expect its boundaries to be clear and uncontroversial. Its nature and

---

7 F. Easterbrook, 'Cyberspace and the Law of the Horse' (1996) *Uni Chicago Legal Forum* 207, 207.

8 See, most notably, L. Lessig, 'The Law of the Horse: What Cyberlaw Might Teach' (1997) 113 Harv. L. Rev. 501.

9 E.g. A. Murray, 'Looking Back at the Law of the Horse: Why Cyberlaw and the Rule of Law are Important', (2013) 10:3 *SCRIPTed* 310. http://script-ed.org/?p=1157.

10 For critical discussion, see e.g. A. Diduck, 'What is Family Law For?' [2011] CLP 287.

11 P. Bromley, *Family Law*, Butterworths, London 1957.

12 R. Goff and G. Jones, *The Law of Restitution*, Sweet & Maxwell, London 1966; the most recent edition of which is now titled *The Law of Unjust Enrichment*, 9th edn., Sweet & Maxwell, London 2016. See similarly P. Birks, *An Introduction to the Law of Restitution*, Clarendon, 1989 and *Unjust Enrichment*, Clarendon, 2003. For recent critical discussion, see R. Stevens, 'The Unjust Enrichment Disaster' (2018) 134 LQR 574.

13 See e.g. E. Fisher, B. Lange, E. Scotford and C. Carlarne, 'Maturity and Methodology: Starting a Debate about Environmental Law Scholarship', 21 *Journal of Environmental Law* (2009) 213.

content may evolve over time. Perhaps the greater attention paid to remedies by books and university courses will accelerate such developments. That will be considered once the scope of 'private law' and 'remedy' have been addressed.

3. THE SCOPE OF PRIVATE LAW

Private law is vast. It covers a huge area. The leading work, *English Private Law*,[14] covers not only contract, tort and equitable wrongs, but also families, companies, property, intellectual property, succession, agency, employment, and unjust enrichment. All these areas may be distinguished from public law, but it is difficult to draw common themes across such a range of subjects, and it is notable that *English Private Law* does not attempt such a feat. For instance, there are clearly significant differences between the law relating to families and banking contracts.

Considering remedies in English private law to be a 'stand-alone' area for research runs the risk of being so broad as not to be very helpful or illuminating. Remedies in the family law context include divorce decrees, decrees of nullity of marriage, separation orders and adoption orders. But these are clearly particular to the family context, and little is to be gained from considering them within a wider umbrella. Similar comments might be made regarding other areas, such as the appointment of an administrative receiver or liquidator and the winding up of a company, or the dissolution of a partnership.

It is suggested that if remedies is to be considered to be a 'stand-alone' area of research, the scope of the field should be narrowed to a more manageable ambit. Focusing on the core areas of contract, tort and equitable obligations may be sensible. However, even within these areas there are significant differences. For example, the law of personal injury in tort law has a large jurisprudence that is very different from more commercially-focused cases on economic loss. Similarly, within contract law, the 'standard' remedies for breach of contract have recently been displaced in the context of an action by a consumer against a trader by extensive provisions in the Consumer Rights Act 2015.[15]

For practical reasons, courses (such as the one I teach!) may choose to focus on commercial cases. Admittedly, there is no bright line between commercial and non-commercial cases, and the foundation of much of commercial law is to be found in generally-relevant cases concerning contract, tort, property and equitable obligations. Nevertheless, it is a crude way to avoid large and tricky topics such as personal injury and consumer remedies, and corresponds to the sort of areas in which many students hope to practise.

---

14 A. Burrows (ed.), *English Private Law*, 3rd edn., OUP, Oxford, 2013.

15 See generally S. Whittaker, 'Distinctive Features of the New Consumer Contract Law' (2017) 133 LQR 47, esp. Part IV.

4. WHAT IS A REMEDY?

Burrows has rightly observed that '[t]he concept of a remedy has rarely been subjected to rigorous analysis. Views may differ as to precisely what one is talking about'.[16] The language of remedies is often used loosely. In a typically powerful article, Birks ultimately concluded that the term 'remedy' could usefully be excised from our analytical vocabulary, and that the focus should instead be on events and responses.[17] Although Birks realised that this attack on the term 'remedy' was unlikely to prove completely successful, he hoped that it would at least focus attention on the need to be clear about what 'remedy' means, and to cut back its definition. Birks identified five different uses of the term 'remedy': (i) as an action or cause of action (such as 'conversion is your remedy'); (ii) as a right born of a wrong (such as a right to damages following the negligent infliction of personal injury); (iii) as a right born of a grievance or injustice (such as a right to restitution of a mistaken payment); (iv) as a right born of the order or judgment of a court (the remedy being the judgment which defined the claimant's enforceable entitlement); and (v) as a right born of a court's order issued on a discretionary basis (such as might flow from a 'remedial constructive trust'). Birks considered the language of rights to be sufficient.

Subsequent scholars have sought to establish a more stable core definition of remedy. For example, in his excellent book, *Remedies Reclassified*,[18] Zakrzewski has argued that the instability surrounding the term remedy is problematic, and in order to achieve a stable meaning it is important that remedies be restricted to the rights arising from certain court orders or pronouncements. Zakrzewski distinguishes between 'replicative' remedies which replicate the claimant's substantive rights, and 'transformative remedies' which confer rights different from the claimant's substantive rights. Significantly, one consequence of this is that damages do not fall within the subject of 'remedies': damages concern secondary rights which, together with primary rights, should not be considered part of the law of remedies but rather of substantive law.

Such a narrow approach to remedies seems unhelpful and diminishes the practical utility of the subject.[19] It is somewhat odd to consider the law of remedies to include the law on injunctions and specific performance, for example, but not the law on damages. Stephen Smith is currently engaged in an

---

16 A. Burrows, 'Judicial Remedies' in A. Burrows (ed.), *English Private Law* 3rd edn., OUP, London 2013, 21.01.

17 P. Birks, 'Rights, Wrongs and Remedies', (2000) 20 OJLS 1. See too P. Birks, 'Personal Property: Proprietary Rights and Remedies' [2000] KLJ 1.

18 R. Zakrzewksi, *Remedies Reclassified*, OUP, Oxford 2005.

19 See too A. Burrows, *Remedies for Torts and Breach of Contract*, 3rd edn., OUP, Oxford 2004, p. 2.

important project on explaining the law of remedies, and his forthcoming book could have a major impact on this area. Smith has already skilfully argued that there is no 'duty' to pay damages or make restitution, but rather defendants are under a 'liability' to be ordered by a court to do so.[20] This is controversial, and does not easily fit with aspects of the positive law, such as the fact that interest runs from the date of the wrong, rather than the date of the court order.[21] But Smith's approach encompasses both specific relief and damages, even if it moulds the law of remedies as based upon rules telling courts (rather than private actors) what they should do.

These theoretical differences are important. But for present purposes, the notion of a 'remedy' will be defined broadly. This matches the general use of the term by the courts and legislature. For example, in *Attorney-General v Blake*, Lord Nicholls cast the net widely in saying that '[r]emedies are the law's response to a wrong (or, more precisely, to a cause of action).'[22] The Civil Procedure Rules explicitly provide for 'interim remedies',[23] and the Oxford English Dictionary draws a comparison with 'medicine' and derives the noun 'remedy' from the prefix *re-* and the Latin root of *medior, mederi*, meaning 'to heal'. The courts speak of remedies in a broad sense, as Birks put it, as 'a cure for something nasty'.[24] Remedies may be personal or proprietary in nature, and may be obtained through court orders or self-help. On the basis of this broad conception of remedies, should remedies be considered a 'stand-alone' research area?

5. REMEDIES AS A 'STAND-ALONE' RESEARCH AREA

When approaching the issue of remedies, it is not uncommon to focus on the availability of certain remedies. But if that is the crucial question, it is difficult to justify remedies as a 'stand-alone' research area. The availability of a remedy is a question of substantive law, and dependent upon the cause of action at issue. There is little to be gained by considering the area of remedies to be distinct on this view.

In fact, the close link between the cause of action and remedies available means that it is perhaps doubtful whether remedies can ever truly 'stand-alone'. Rights and remedies are inextricably linked. This has long been

---

20 See e.g. S. Smith, 'Duties, Liabilities, and Damages' (2012) 125 *Harvard LR* 1727.

21 As pointed out by E. Shewin, 'Comments on Stephen Smith's Duties, Liabilities, and Damages' (2012) 125 *Harvard LR* 164, 165.

22 [2001] 1 AC 268, 284.

23 Civil Procedure Rules, Part 25.

24 P. Birks, 'Rights, Wrongs and Remedies' (2000) 20 OJLS 1, 9.

recognised. For example, in *Nocton v Lord Ashburton*, Lord Dunedin noted that:[25]

> in certain cases where common justice demanded a remedy, the common law had none forthcoming, and the common law (though there is no harder lesson for the stranger jurist to learn) began with the remedy and ended with the right.

More recently, Friedman has written that:[26]

> A discussion of the classification of legal rights and remedies may place the emphasis upon either. Much depends on the basic approach. Does one believe that the remedy is meant to protect the legal right (and the corresponding duty) and that this is, in fact, its sole purpose, or does one assume that it is the other way around? Rights and obligations were created in order to justify the granting of a remedy. In any event the idea that the choice of one leads to the abandonment of the study and analysis of the other seems to be misplaced.

In a similar vein, Golding J observed in Chase Manhattan Bank NA v Israel-British Bank (London) Ltd that:[27]

> Within the municipal confines of a single legal system, right and remedy are indissolubly connected and correlated, each contributing in historical dialogue to the development of the other, and, save in very special circumstances it is idle to ask whether the court vindicates the suitor's substantive right or gives the suitor a procedural remedy as to ask whether thought is a mental or cerebral process. In fact the court does both things by one and the same act.

Given the pragmatism of the common law, it is unsurprising to find that a piecemeal and practical approach towards remedies has been adopted. It also makes sense for remedies to be closely related to the primary rights and duties that have been breached. Stevens, for example, has strongly argued that damages are the 'next-best' thing to performance of the primary duty at issue.[28] Not only does this emphasise the link between the right and remedy, but imposes limits upon what the remedy can be. As Stevens has said:[29]

> (t)he reason that underlies the primary obligation places limits upon the form any obligation of next best compliance can take. This is just as true of obligations not to

---

25 [1914] AC 932, 964.

26 D. Friedmann, 'Rights and Remedies' (1997) LQR 424, 425.

27 [1981] Ch. 105, 124.

28 R. Stevens, *Torts and Rights*, OUP, 2007, Ch 4; R. Stevens, 'Damages and the Right to Performance: A Golden Victory or Not?' in J. Neyers, R. Bronaugh & S. Pitel (eds.), *Exploring Contract Law*, Hart Publishing, Oxford 2009.

29 R. Stevens, 'Rights Restricting Remedies' in A. Robertson and M. Tilbury (eds.), *Divergences in Private Law*, Hart Publishing, Oxford 2016, p. 161.

> punch someone on the nose as it is of promissory obligations to be at a particular place at a particular time. A caterpillar may be transformed into a butterfly, which appears to be a startlingly different thing, but it cannot be transformed into a water buffalo.

It is crucial to bear in mind the nature of the rights infringed and cause of action at issue when considering remedies. The two should not be divorced. This is true throughout private law. Contract law is a particularly good example. Contractual remedies are the essence of contract law. On one view, the whole point of entering into a contract is to access the expectation measure remedies that are available when a contract is breached. What governs the remedies awarded is the law of contract. There is no distinct area of law that determines what remedy will be awarded whenever a remedy is awarded.

Treating remedies as distinct is not without influential support. Some New Zealand cases suggest that there is simply a 'basket of remedies',[30] and Finn has welcomed 'the progressive divorce between remedy and doctrine' seen in Australia.[31] But as Birks has persuasively pointed out, this bestows great discretion on the judges and can undermine certainty and predictability (which are especially important in commercial law). Birks went so far as to call it 'a nightmare trying to be a noble dream'.[32] Whilst a weak form of discretion is present in the positive law – such as regarding whether to award specific relief – a strong form entitling a judge to pick whatever remedy appears best from an unlimited range of options is definitely not.

For example, the remedial constructive trust has been firmly rejected in England and Wales, unlike the antipodean jurisdictions home to Thomas and Finn.[33] In *Westdeutsche Landesbank Girozentrale v Islington LBC*, Lord Browne-Wilkinson said:[34]

> Under an institutional constructive trust the trust arises by operation of law as from the date of the circumstances which give rise to it: the function of the court is merely to declare that such trust has arisen in the past. The consequences that flow from such a trust having arisen (including the potentially unfair consequences to third parties who in the interim have received the trust property) are also determined by rules

30 For general analysis of this area, see the extra-judicial discussion of THOMAS J, 'An Endorsement of a More Flexible Law of Civil Remedies', (1999) 7 *Waikato Law Review* 23.

31 P. FINN, 'Equitable Doctrine and Discretion in Remedies' in W. CORNISH et al. (eds.), *Restitution, Past, Present and Future*, Hart Publishing, Oxford 1998, p. 260.

32 P. BIRKS, 'Rights, Wrongs and Remedies' (2000) 20 OJLS 1, 23.

33 *Re Polly Peck International (No. 2)* [1998] 3 All ER 812, 823 (Mummery LJ) and 830 (Nourse LJ). See also *Metall und Rohstoff AG v Donaldson, Lufkin and Jenrette Inc.* [1990] 1 QB 391, 478–80 (Slade LJ); *Halifax Building Society v Thomas* [1996] Ch 217, 229 (Peter Gibson LJ); *FHR European Ventures LLP v Cedar Capital Partners LLC* [2014] UKSC 45; [2015] AC 250.

34 [1996] AC 669, 714.

> of law, not under a discretion. A remedial constructive trust, as I understand it, is different. It is a judicial remedy giving rise to an enforceable obligation: the extent to which it operates retrospectively to the prejudice of third parties lies in the discretion of the court.

Lord Neuberger has recently deprecated attempts to introduce such a strong form of discretion into English law, wryly commenting that:[35]

> There is much to be said for the notion of a remedial constructive trust displays equity at its flexible flabby worst. I will seek to show, at least arguably, that it is unprincipled, incoherent and impractical, that it renders the law unpredictable, that it is an affront to the common law view of property rights and interests, that it involves the court usurping the role of the legislature, and, as if that were not enough, that the development of the remedial constructive trust is largely unnecessary. Apart from that, it's a pretty good concept.

In any event, if the remedial constructive trust is to be recognised in English law, it must be triggered by a cause of action. What might that cause of action be? It could be equitable wrongdoing but the constructive trust that is exceptionally recognised where there is a breach of fiduciary duty is institutional in form, arising by operation of law rather than judicial discretion.[36] Similarly, unconscionable retention of property triggers an institutional, rather than a remedial, constructive trust. The remedial constructive trust might be considered to be an appropriate response to the defendant's unjust enrichment but the fact that the defendant has been unjustly enriched at the claimant's expense is not a sufficient reason to recognise an equitable proprietary interest; the claimant should instead be confined to a personal claim against the defendant. A remedy without a cause of action is meaningless and for that reason, as well as the inherent uncertainty of this unbridled judicial discretion, the remedial constructive trust should not be recognised in English law.

This last point reflects the Latin maxim *ubi remedium ibi ius* – wherever there is a remedy, there is a right. This rule is almost invariably applied.[37] But caution should be exercised about the related maxim *ubi ius ibi remedium* – wherever there is a right, there is a remedy. This is not always true. For example,

---

35 Lord Neuberger, 'The remedial constructive trust – fact or fiction', delivered on 10 August 2014 to the Banking Services and Finance Law Association Conference, New Zealand: https://www.supremecourt.uk/docs/speech-140810.pdf.

36 See e.g. *FHR European Ventures LLP v Cedar Capital Partners LLC* [2014] UKSC 45; [2015] AC 250.

37 Cf *Cartier International AG v British Sky Broadcasting Ltd* [2018] UKSC 28; [2018] 1 W.L.R. 3259 where an injunction was granted even though not in support of substantive proceedings; see further P. Davies, 'Costs of Blocking Injunctions' [2017] IPQ 330.

a contract may be unenforceable, or a debt time-barred, but the claimant still has a right to be paid even if they cannot invoke the help of the court to assert it.

A further example of the dangers of focusing upon remedies as distinct from the underlying right may be found through analysing the recent decision of the Supreme Court in *Morris-Garner v One Step (Support) Ltd.*[38] In that case, the Supreme Court had to grapple with the remedies available for breach of contract and breach of confidence. Karen Morris-Garner set up and ran her own business, One Step At A Time, which provided support for young people leaving care. Her partner, Andrea Morris-Garner, later joined the business as its Operations and Area Manager. In 2002, the business was sold to One Step Support Ltd ('One Step'), which was owned 50% by Karen Morris-Garner and 50% by Charmaine Costelloe. The working relationship between the parties soon broke down, and in 2006 the Morris-Garners incorporated Positive Living Ltd, without anyone else at One Step being aware of this. Later that year, Mrs Costelloe purchased Karen Morris-Garner's shares in One Step for £3.15 million.

As part of the sale agreement, the Morris-Garners agreed, for a period of 36 months, not to engage in any business activity which would be in material competition with One Step, or to approach any clients of One Step. Karen Morris-Garner was also subject to provisions regarding the use of confidential information. However, in 2007 Positive Living began to offer similar services to One Step. Positive Living was very successful, and in 2010 the Morris-Garners sold their shares in the company for nearly £13 million. One Step, on the other hand, had experienced a significant downturn, and ultimately issued proceedings against the Morris-Garners. Both Phillips J at first instance[39] and the Court of Appeal[40] held that the restrictive covenants were not an unreasonable restraint of trade, and that Positive Living was in material competition with One Step. Moreover, the Morris-Garners were found to have breached the non-solicitation covenants, and Karen Morris-Garner to have breached her obligations of confidence. The sole issue for the Supreme Court was whether negotiating damages were available. Phillips J and the Court of Appeal had decided that they were. The Supreme Court disagreed.

The Supreme Court was clear that negotiating damages are compensatory. This settles the debate – as a matter of authority, at least – regarding the nature of such damages. Importantly for present purposes, the Supreme Court rejected

---

38 [2018] UKSC 20; [2018] 2 WLR 1353. For further discussion see P. Davies, 'One step backwards: restricting negotiating damages for breach of contract' [2018] LMCLQ 433; A. Burrows, 'One Step Forward?' (2018) 134 LQR 515.

39 [2014] EWHC 2213 (QB); [2015] IRLR 215.

40 [2016] EWCA Civ 180; [2017] QB 1.

that idea that such damages are restitutionary in nature.[41] Before *One Step* it was often suggested that there was a coherent subject of 'restitution for wrongs', and such damages could be awarded regardless of the nature of the wrong.[42] Admittedly that view looked increasingly suspect: only one appellate decision had awarded a distinctly gain-based remedy for breach of contract, and that was very much an outlier on extreme facts involving the breach of contract by a traitor,[43] whilst in tort law restitutionary damages have been limited to 'proprietary torts'.[44] *One Step* confirms that it is a mistake to start by thinking that restitution is a remedy that can be awarded as a response to wrongdoing; instead, it is crucial to start by considering the nature of the wrong.

In *One Step*, the key wrong was breach of contract.[45] The essence of contract law is to protect the parties' expectation interests, not to disgorge gain, and thus gain-based remedies were not awarded by the Supreme Court.

Commenting upon the decision in *One Step*, Day has perceptively remarked that:[46]

> Remedies should not be uniformly available across the law of obligations; their availability should reflect the nature of the cause of action. This is because a cause of action is the juridical recognition of an injustice.[47] Different causes of action are concerned with different injustices. As a remedy should undo the particular injustice recognised by the cause of action, it follows that different remedies should be available for different causes of action across private law. Put shortly, the premise should be one of coherence between causes of actions and their remedies, rather than of remedial uniformity across different causes of action.[48]

This is important, since it highlights that coherence may be found not across remedies, but between causes of action and remedies.

All the above might suggest that remedies should not be understood to be a stand-alone research area. Faced with such a stark proposition, Stephen Smith concluded that the law of remedies needs to be re-thought, and argues that

---

41 Cf *Marathon Asset Management LLP v Seddon* [2017] EWHC 300 (Comm) (Leggatt J).

42 See e.g. J. Edelman, *Gain-Based Damages*, Hart Publishing, Oxford 2002.

43 *Attorney-General v Blake* [2001] 1 AC 268.

44 *Devenish Nutrition Ltd v Sanofi-Aventis SA* [2008] EWCA Civ 1086; [2009] Ch 390; moreover, 'proprietary' has been narrowly defined: *Forsyth-Grant v Allen* [2008] EWCA Civ 505; [2008] 2 EGLR 16.

45 It is unclear why the equitable wrong of breach of confidence did not lead to negotiating damages: see further P. Davies, 'One step backwards: restricting negotiating damages for breach of contract' [2018] LMCLQ 433, 439–440.

46 W. Day, 'Restitution for wrongs: one step forward, two steps back?' [2018] RLR 60, 61.

47 Cf *Letang v Cooper* [1965] 1 QB 232, 242–243 (Diplock LJ).

48 For the avoidance of doubt, it is not denied that there is then a degree of uniformity of principle when it comes to the quantification of, for example, compensation in tort and contract or, for another example, restitution for wrongs and for unjust enrichment: see W. Day, 'An Application of *Wrotham Park* Damages' (2015) 131 LQR 218, 220–222.

remedies are exclusively about court rulings. This neatly explains why the law of remedies should be considered to be a distinct subject. But, as noted above, it is not clear how well this fits the positive law.[49]

In any event, it is suggested that it is not a waste of time to write books on remedies or to teach courses on the subject. Legal realists might argue that the only things worth studying are what the courts do in practice, and that remedies is therefore the principal topic of interest. Yet one does not have to be a legal realist to see the practical importance of remedies. When advising parties to a claim, their key interest is in the likely remedies, and scholars should be interested in this too.[50] So should students. There is, typically, insufficient time in undergraduate courses on contract, tort and trusts to deal with remedies in more than a relatively superficial manner; as a result, specialist options on remedies have developed.

Moreover, it is useful to consider aspects of remedies as they operate across private law. How loss is assessed, and how gains are quantified, should be similar regardless of the nature of the primary wrong. Looking at remedies as a stand-alone subject allows a greater range of cases to be introduced when considering how monetary remedies are quantified. For example, when considering the potential availability of an account of profits at common law or for breach of contract, it is useful to look across to the well-established jurisprudence on remedies for breach of fiduciary duty.

Treating remedies as a subject can be especially useful when considering concurrent liability.[51] The recent decision of the Court of Appeal in *Wellesley Partners LLP v Withers LLP* is instructive.[52] Wellesley Partners LLP ('Wellesley') claimed damages against its solicitors, Withers, for negligence in the drafting of a partnership agreement. Wellesley was a business specialising in head hunting in the area of investment banking. In order to expand, Wellesley entered into an agreement with a new investor, and consequently required a new partnership agreement to be drawn up. Unfortunately, Withers had negligently drafted the agreement so that an option for the investor to withdraw half its capital contribution could be exercised *within* the first 41 months of the agreement, rather than *after* 42 months, which is what had been intended. The courts found that this was a breach of Withers' duty of care. Wellesley sought to rely upon the more advantageous rules of remoteness in tort law.

---

49 See above.

50 Sir G. Leggatt has recently observed, extra-judicially, that 'the common law is a collaborative enterprise and we [judges] need all the help we can get': G. Leggatt, 'Negotiation in good faith: adapting to changing circumstances in contracts and English contract law' [2019] JBL 104, 121.

51 See generally P. Davies, 'Concurrent liability: a spluttering revolution' in S. Worthington, A. Robertson and G. Virgo (eds.), *Revolution and Evolution in Private Law*, Hart Publishing, Oxford 2018. See too A. Taylor, 'Concurrent Duties' (2019) 82 MLR 17.

52 [2015] EWCA Civ 1146; [2016] Ch 529.

A major reason why the tortious rules are generally preferred by claimants is that the type of loss only has to be foreseeable at the time of the tort,[53] rather than at the time at which the contract was concluded.[54] It appears to have been accepted that the 'reasonable contemplation' test in contract[55] is more restrictive than the 'reasonable foreseeability'[56] test in tort.[57] At first instance, Nugee J felt constrained by the weight of previous authority to apply the tortious rules, since the decision of the House of Lords in *Henderson v Merrett*[58] afforded the claimant freedom to choose how to frame its claim. However, the judge did say:[59]

> It seems odd, and to my mind distinctly unsatisfactory, that the law should give two different answers to the question "for what losses is a solicitor liable if he fails to take due care in carrying out a client's instructions?" depending on how the claim is framed. A rational system of law would only give one answer to that question.

The Court of Appeal unanimously agreed with the trial judge's concerns, and went on to hold that the contractual rules of remoteness should in fact apply. Their Lordships insisted that although *Henderson v Merrett* meant that the claim could be run in both contract and tort, that did not determine what rules of remoteness should apply to the tortious claim. As Floyd LJ said:[60]

> In a case such as the present (although not in all cases) the responsibility is assumed under a contract. It would be anomalous, to say the least, if the party pursuing the remedy in tort in these circumstances were able to assert that the other party has assumed a responsibility for a wider range of damage than he would be taken to have assumed under the contract.
>
> ...
>
> Nevertheless, I am persuaded that where, as in the present case, contractual and tortious duties to take care in carrying out instructions exist side by side, the test for recoverability of damage for economic loss should be the same, and should be the contractual one. The basis for the formulation of the remoteness test adopted in contract is that the parties have the opportunity to draw special circumstances to

---

53 *Overseas Tankship (UK) Ltd v Morts Dock & Engineering Co (The Wagon Mound)* [1961] AC 388.

54 *Hadley v Baxendale* (1854) 9 Exch 341.

55 Ibid.

56 *Overseas Tankship (UK) Ltd v Morts Dock & Engineering Co (The Wagon Mound)* [1961] AC 388.

57 E.g. [2015] EWCA Civ 1146, [2016] Ch 529 [74]. Ultimately, though, the Court of Appeal (disagreeing with the trial judge) concluded that the loss was not too remote in contract law anyway, so the point was moot.

58 [1995] 2 AC 145.

59 [2014] EWHC 556 (Ch); [2014] PNLR 22, [212].

60 [2015] EWCA Civ 1146; [2016] Ch 529, [68], [80]. See also, Roth J, [157].

> each other's attention at the time of formation of the contract. Whether or not one calls it an implied term of the contract, there exists the opportunity for consensus between the parties, as to the type of damage (both in terms of its likelihood and type) for which it will be able to hold the other responsible. The parties are assumed to be contracting on the basis that liability will be confined to damage of the kind which is in their reasonable contemplation. It makes no sense at all for the existence of the concurrent duty in tort to upset this consensus, particularly given that the tortious duty arises out of the same assumption of responsibility as exists under the contract.

Roth J explicitly agreed that 'the rationale for maintaining a broader principle of remoteness of damage for liability in tort than in contract … does not apply to a case of parallel liability, where the duty of care in tort rests on an assumption of responsibility arising from the contract'.[61] Longmore LJ emphasised that in these sort of cases '[i]t cannot, moreover, be right that a claimant can opt to recover a contractual measure of damages but then opt to apply the tortious rules of remoteness; measure of damage and remoteness of damage must be assessed by reference to one system or the other, not by a sort of "pick and mix"'.[62] Rules relating to the measure of damages and remoteness of damages should be consistent with one another.[63]

The decision in *Wellesley* is welcome. There is no reason to depart from the contractual rules when the parties are not strangers but able to make one another aware of special risks at the time of entering into their relationship. After all, even if the claim sounds in tort alone then a party might still add a disclaimer and thereby avoid liability for known risks.[64] The careful reasoning in *Wellesley* is convincing.

Wellesley highlights that focusing on the available remedies can be helpful, and can cast greater light on the nature of the primary rights at issue. This is important. However, whilst rules relating to the measure of damages should be consistent with one another, it is important to note that a term such as 'compensation' can be used in different ways. This has been highlighted in a string of cases concerning breach of trust in conveyancing transactions. When things go wrong in property transactions, solicitors tend to make obvious and attractive defendants. They are insured and can provide substantial monetary redress. Moreover, they may well have held deposits or mortgage monies on trust. This opens up the possibility of claims for breach of trust.

'The basic right of a beneficiary is to have the trust duly administered in accordance with the provisions of the trust instrument, if any, and the

61 Ibid. [151].
62 Ibid. [186].
63 Ibid. [187].
64 This was the case in *Hedley Byrne* itself: [1964] AC 465.

general law'.[65] The traditional means used to ensure the proper administration of the trust was for the beneficiary to take an account. Upon discovering a breach of trust, a beneficiary might falsify or surcharge the account. If the trustee had failed to exercise due care and skill leading to the fund's not being worth as much as would have been achieved by a reasonably prudent trustee, the account could be surcharged.[66] If the trustee misapplied trust monies in breach of trust, then the beneficiary was entitled to falsify that disbursement.[67] It is important that the two be distinguished, and to understand that the term 'breach of trust' takes in breaches of several different types of trustee duty, including the duty to comply with the terms of the trust instrument (breached when a trustee acts in an unauthorised way) and the duty of care (breached when a trust acts negligently). These are different duties from one another, and from the fiduciary duty that can be owed by trustees and other people. There is no reason to think that the same rules should necessarily govern the assessment of compensation payable for breaching them.

However, the courts appear to have failed to appreciate these differences. The most recent Supreme Court case on the matter is in *AIB Group (UK) Plc v Mark Redler & Co.*[68] Mark Redler & Co ('Redler') was a firm of solicitors which was retained to act for the Sondhi family and AIB, a Bank, on the re-mortgage of the Sondhis' family home. AIB advanced £3.3 million to Redler for this purpose. The mortgage monies were only to be released in exchange for a fully enforceable first legal charge over the property, but in breach of trust Redler advanced the monies without fully redeeming a first legal charge over the property already held by Barclays. Barclays therefore retained a first legal charge over the property of around £300,000. The Supreme Court refused to order that Redler reconstitute the trust fund to the tune of £3.3 million. AIB could only recover the loss it had suffered as a result of the breach of trust: £300,000.

The case has received a decidedly mixed reaction.[69] But it appears that the Supreme Court was focused on what it understood to be a universal remedy

---

65 *Target Holdings Ltd v Redferns* [1996] AC 421, 434; see too *AIB Group (UK) plc v Mark Redler & Co Solicitors* [2014] UKSC 58; [2015] AC 1503 [64] (Lord Toulson).

66 *Bristol & West Building Society v Mothew* [1998] Ch 1, 17; *Fry v Fry* (1859) 27 Beav 144; *Nestlé v National Westminster Bank plc* [1993] 1 WLR 1260; *Re Mulligan* [1998] 1 NZLR 481.

67 *Knott v Cottee* (1852) 16 Beav 77; *Re Massingberd's Settlement* (1890) 63 LT 296; *In re Dawson (dec'd)* [1966] NSWR 211.

68 *AIB Group (UK) plc v Mark Redler & Co Solicitors* [2014] UKSC 58; [2015] AC 1503 [57].

69 See e.g. P. Davies, 'Compensatory Remedies for Breach of Trust' (2016) 2 *Canadian Journal of Comparative and Contemporary Law* 65; N.A. Tiverios and C. McKay, 'Orthodoxy Lost: The (Ir)relevance of Causation in Quantifying Breach of Trust Claims' (2016) 90 *Australian Law Jounral* 233; D. Wright, 'Another Wrong Step: Equitable Compensation Following a Breach of Trust' (2015) 21 *T & T* 825; M. Conaglen, 'Equitable Compensation for Breach of Trust: Off *Target*' (2016) 40 *Melbourne University Law Review* 125; J. Edelman, 'An English Misturning with Equitable Compensation' in S. Degeling and J. Varuhas (eds.), *Equitable Compensation and Disgorgement of Profits*, Hart Publishing, Oxford 2017; L. Ho, 'Causation in the Restoration of a Misapplied Trust Fund: Fundamental Norm or Red Herring?'

of compensation, without clearly distinguishing between the strict duty not to misapply trust funds and the duty to take reasonable care. The two different duties have different remedies: hence the use of language such as 'falsification' as opposed to 'surcharge', or 'substitutive damages' as opposed to 'reparative compensation'. Surprisingly, Lord Toulson concluded that 'in a practical sense both are reparative compensation'.[70] This represents a marked shift in the law, and one which emphasises the primacy of (reparative) compensation above all else. Perhaps it should be limited to the commercial context where there is a concurrent cause of action in contract, which suggests that the contractual claims 'trump' the claim for breach of trust. But it is not clear why this should be so.

For instance, imagine that, in breach of trust, a trustee purchased a second-hand car rather than a brand new car. There was a clear logic behind equity's traditional recognition of the beneficiary's ability to choose to falsify the disbursement made and treat the car as having been purchased with the trustee's own money: on that approach, the unwanted second-hand car was the trustee's problem to deal with. The hassle of selling it to realise its value, for example, lay with the wrongdoing trustee rather than the innocent beneficiary. This is admittedly different from the approach at common law, but, as Lord Millett explained,[71] this might be justified by the higher standards demanded by equity. A trustee holds particular power over a beneficiary and a beneficiary's assets, and should be held up to a higher standard. It is important that a trustee complies with the terms of the trust instrument. This provided a sound justification for the traditional, strict approach in equity. The approach favoured by the Supreme Court in *AIB Group (UK) Plc v Mark Redler & Co* alters the important link between the duty breached and remedy awarded.

6. CONCLUSION

The law on remedies does not 'stand-alone' in the sense of being isolated from primary rights or causes of action. Rather, a clear analysis of remedies helps

in S. Degeling and J.N.E. Varuhas (eds.), *Equitable Compensation and Disgorgement of Profits*, Hart Publishing, Oxford, 2017; J. Penner, 'Falsifying the Trust Account and Compensatory Equitable Compensation' in S. Degeling and J. Varuhas (eds.), *Equitable Compensation and Disgorgement of Profits*, Hart Publishing, Oxford 2017; P.G. Turner, 'Want of Causation as a Defence to Liability for Misapplication of Trust Assets' in P. Davies, S. Douglas and J. Goudkamp (eds.), *Defences in Equity*, Hart Publishing, Oxford, 2018. See too *Main v Giambrone and Law (a firm)* [2017] EWCA Civ 1193, discussed in P. Davies, 'Equitable compensation and the SAAMCO principle' (2018) 134 LQR 165.

70 *AIB Group (UK) plc v Mark Redler & Co Solicitors* [2014] UKSC 58; [2015] AC 1503 [54].

71 P. Millett, 'Equity's Place in the Law of Commerce' (1998) 114 LQR 214.

to illuminate various matters concerning the primary rights at issue. This is useful in itself. But it is also helpful to analyse 'remedies' as a subject since doing so can highlight common principles underpinning the award of various remedies, most notably damages. This is an area of great practical importance and academic interest, and deserves to be a subject to which serious attention is given.

REMEDIES IN PRIVATE LAW FROM A GERMAN PERSPECTIVE

Jan Felix HOFFMANN*

1. DIVERGING INFLUENCES ON THE EVE OF THE CODIFICATION OF THE GERMAN CIVIL CODE

Put simply, the legal discussion prior to the codification of the German Civil Code was influenced by two schools of thought. On the one hand, there was the classical Roman approach of thinking in *actiones*. Private law

* This chapter aims at presenting questions of German law. It has no ambition to be comparative and does therefore not intend to highlight similarities or differences with other legal systems. The mere choice of certain terminology does not intend to suggest such similarities or differences.

was primarily perceived through the practical perspective of the remedies a *iudex* would grant. The *actiones* were at the centre of any effort of legal systematisation.[1] The *actio* combined aspects that today in German law are found to be subject to both procedural law as well as, partly, to substantive law.[2] Conceptually, one could say that the classical Roman approach of thinking in *actiones* granted by the *iudex* somewhat found a theoretical exaggeration in the theory of imperatives, even though no clear historical line can be drawn.[3] The theory of imperatives[4] not only focused in a practical way on what could be enforced judicially, but also denied the existence of legal norms in private law other than the enforceable imperatives altogether. The idea that imperatives serve to protect individual subjective rights was openly rejected.

On the other hand, on the eve of the codification of the German Civil Code, legal scholarship was also influenced by an already far-advanced idea of substantive subjective rights. As early as the Middle Ages some scholars are said to have differentiated between the judicially enforceable *actio* and the underlying substantive *ius*.[5] The idea of subjective rights was an important element of the doctrine of natural law.[6] Likewise, it played a central role in Kant's philosophy of law.[7]

Savigny combined the idea of subjective rights existing regardless of judicial enforcement with the Roman thinking in *actiones*. The connecting theoretical link was Savigny's idea of a 'metamorphosis'. Accordingly, every subjective right metamorphoses into a right of action as soon as it is infringed.[8] Following Savigny every *actio* is based on the existence and infringement of a subjective right. Savigny had the ambition to include both absolute as well as relative rights in his theory of a metamorphosis. An absolute right only yields an action once it is infringed. The proprietor's *rei vindicatio* is legitimised by the opponent's wrongful possession.[9] Hence, the same holds true for

---

1 Cf. e.g. H. Kaufmann, 'Zur Geschichte des aktionenrechtlichen Denkens' (1964) *JuristenZeitung* 482, 483.

2 H. Kaufmann, above n. 1, 482, 483.

3 See J.F. Hoffmann, *Zession und Rechtszuweisung*, Mohr Siebeck, Tübingen 2012, pp. 41–44.

4 Decidedly e.g. A. Thon, *Rechtsnorm und subjektives Recht*, 1878, passim.

5 In that sense H. Coing, 'Zur Geschichte des Begriffs "subjektives Recht"' in H. Coing, F.H. Lawson and K. Grönfors (eds.), *Das subjektive Recht und der Rechtsschutz der Persönlichkeit*, Alfred Metzner Verlag, Frankfurt am Main 1959, pp. 7, 13–14.

6 Cf. R. Dubischar, *Über die Grundlagen der schulsystematischen Zweiteilung der Rechte in sogenannte absolute und relative*, Tübingen 1961, pp. 60–65.

7 See J. Hruschka, 'Kants Rechtsphilosophie als Philosophie des subjektiven Rechts' (2004) *JuristenZeitung* 1085–1092.

8 F.C. von Savigny, *System des heutigen römischen Rechts, Band 5*, Moritz Veit, Berlin 1841, §204, 3 and F.C. von Savigny, *System des heutigen römischen Rechts, Band 1*, Moritz Veit, Berlin 1840, §59, 393.

9 F.C. von Savigny, above n. 8, §239, 281–284.

a relative right that only yields an *actio* in case of infringement. The claim for performance is legitimised by the debtor's wrongful non-performance.[10] Savigny's system shows striking parallels to Blackstone's model of rights, wrongs and remedies.[11]

The works of Windscheid had a great impact on the conceptualisation of the German Civil Code. An important element of Windscheid's ideas was the strict division between substantive and procedural law. Windscheid assumed that any procedural right of action had to correspond to a substantive right that he called *Anspruch*.[12] The notion of an *Anspruch* is as resistant to a precise English translation as the notion of a remedy is to a German translation. Windscheid's theory of an *Anspruch* today at its core is an undisputed element in German private law, serving as the foundation for the characteristic strict theoretical division between substantive and procedural law.[13] Judicial enforceability is conceivable only by means of a corresponding substantive right. Similar to Savigny, Windscheid declared that for rights with an absolute nature an *Anspruch* only emerges in the case of its infringement.[14] With regard to relative rights, Windscheid seems to have found a distinction between the subjective right and the enforceable substantive right (*Anspruch*) to be redundant and inconceivable.[15] Whereas Savigny was able to consistently combine the notion of subjective rights with the classical action-based approach, whilst not yet distinguishing between procedural and substantive law, Windscheid could not smoothly build upon both schools of thought: Absolute rights are supposed to yield the substantive basis for an *actio* only in case of an infringement of the right. Relative rights, however, are supposed to yield the substantive basis for an *actio* without an infringement.

2. THE CURRENTLY PREVAILING CONCEPT IN GERMAN PRIVATE LAW

These two different schools of thought are also manifested in the prevailing conceptualisation of German private law. Legal scholars and courts oscillate

10 F.C. von Savigny, above n. 8, §239, 285–289.

11 On Blackstone's concept see P. Birks, 'Rights, Wrongs and Remedies' (2000) 20 *Oxford Journal of Legal Studies* 1.

12 B. Windscheid, *Die Actio des römischen Civilrechts vom Standpunkte des heutigen Rechts*, Julius Buddeus, Düsseldorf 1856, passim.

13 See the comparison between civil law and common law in this respect presented by H. Dedek, 'From Norms to Facts: The Realization of Rights in Common and Civil Private Law' (2010) 56 *McGill Law Journal* 77.

14 B. Windscheid, above n. 12, §23, 222–223.

15 B. Windscheid, *Lehrbuch des Pandektenrechts, Band 1*, 6th edn., Rütten & Löning, Frankfurt am Main 1887, §122, 393–394.

between a concept based on subjective rights and a perspective that focuses on the judicially enforceable imperatives (*Anspruch*).[16] With regard to property, the dominant systematisation is based on subjective rights. Damages and restitution as remedies for the infringement of property are generally based on the perspective of the property right. Intellectual property law is also dominated by an approach that differentiates between the protected subjective right and the legal consequences of an infringement, i.e. the judicially enforceable imperatives that follow an infringement. However, there also supposedly exist judicially enforceable imperatives in the sense of an *Anspruch* that do not require the infringement of a substantive right. The prevailing doctrine does not classify certain constellations as the protection of subjective rights, but merely as legally recognised 'interests'[17] that result rather out of a reflex to the imperatives. When an aggrieved party can, for example, demand the compensation of a purely pecuniary loss that resulted from fraud, it is generally considered that the remedy of damages does not have a basis in a subjective right not to be defrauded.[18] With regard to claims, the protected subjective position also fades away beneath the judicial enforceability. By following the ideas of Windscheid, the prevailing doctrine does not differentiate between the claim and its (specific) performance.[19] The claim is primarily conceived to be identical to the remedy of specific performance.

One can justifiably say that presently German Private Law is torn between a concept of subjective rights and a concept of substantive imperatives. This has also led to a rather unclear terminological definition of the subjective right which encompasses both protected positions as well as judicially enforceable imperatives without any differentiation.[20]

---

16 F. Hofmann, '"Anspruchsdenken" und "Remedydenken" im deutschen Privatrecht' (2018) *Juristische Schulung* 833–838 seems to believe that German private law solely focuses on the category of an *Anspruch*. This might be an adequate description of the way that law students are generally instructed, but is in the author's view not representative for the perception of German private law by scholars and the courts.

17 Cf. e.g. A. Teichmann in *Jauernig, Kommentar zum BGB*, 17th edn., C.H. Beck, Munich 2018, §823 BGB, para. 41.

18 In that sense E. von Caemmerer, 'Wandlungen des Deliktsrechts' in E. von Caemmerer, E. Friesenhahn and R. Lange (eds.), *Hundert Jahre Deutsches Rechtsleben*, vol. 2, C.F. Müller, Karlsruhe 1960, p. 55; against this concept J.F. Hoffmann, above n. 3, p. 39; in-depth analysis by E. Picker, 'Das Verhältnis von §823 Abs. 2 zu Abs. 1 BGB im System von Rechtszuweisung und Rechtsschutz' in E. Becker-Eberhard, H.F. Gaul, L. Haertlein and C. Meller-Hannich (eds.), *Festschrift für Eberhard Schilken zum 70. Geburtstag*, C.H. Beck, Munich 2015, pp. 85–104; cf. recently also F. Hofmann, *Der Unterlassungsanspruch als Rechtsbehelf*, Mohr Siebeck, Tübingen 2017, p. 207; N. Jansen, 'Gesetzliche Schuldverhältnisse – Eine historische Strukturanalyse' (2016) 216 *Archiv für die civilistische Praxis* 112, 212.

19 Cf. e.g. M.-P. Weller, *Die Vertragstreue*, Mohr Siebeck, Tübingen 2009, pp. 231–232.

20 Critically against this terminology also F. Hofmann, above n. 18, pp. 175–181.

3. PRIVATE LAW AS A SYSTEM OF PROPERTY AND REMEDIAL RIGHTS

There is currently a growing number of German legal scholars who want to maintain the strict division between procedural and substantive law in Windscheid's tradition whilst at the same time, try to bridge the gap between an action-based thinking and the concept of subjective rights, in the spirit of Savigny. The works of Eduard Picker in particular stand out in this context.[21] This school of thinking differentiates between rights defining individual freedom and rights protecting this freedom. This dichotomy could terminologically be highlighted by separating primary from secondary rights. Another possible terminological differentiation could be the one between 'substantive rights' and 'remedies'. However, the already fixed term 'remedy' should be avoided because the protective rights in the presented classification are of a purely material nature and do not have any procedural implications.[22] For the same reason, the category 'substantive right' does not seem fitting for German law because it would imply that the protecting counterpart was not of substantive nature. The terms 'property rights' and 'remedial rights' seem to be neutral enough to accurately describe the presented model. They also run the least danger of being misunderstood.

3.1. PRIVATE LAW AS AN ORDER OF PROPERTY RIGHTS

This model views the system of private law in its entirety as an order coordinating and defining individual freedom.[23] Private law fulfils this task

21 See recently E. Picker, 'Das Deliktsrecht im Zivilrechtssystem' (2015) 4 *Zeitschrift für die gesamte Privatrechtswissenschaft* 385–434; E. Picker, 'Privatrechtsdogmatik und Eigentumsschutz' in M. Auer, H.C. Grigoleit, J. Hager et al. (eds.), *Festschrift für Claus-Wilhelm-Canaris zum 80. Geburtstag*, de Gruyter, Berlin 2017, pp. 579–615; see also F. Hartmann, *Der Anspruch auf das stellvertretende commodum*, Mohr Siebeck, Tübingen 2008, p. 22; J.F. Hoffmann, above n. 3, pp. 35–40; J.F. Hoffmann, 'Zum vermögensrechtlichen Schutz absoluter und relativer Rechtspositionen an der Schnittstelle zum Immaterialgüterrecht' (2014) *Juristische Ausbildung* 71–80; T. Lobinger, *Rechtsgeschäftliche Verpflichtung und autonome Bindung*, Mohr Siebeck, Tübingen 1999, pp. 89–106.

22 The procedural implications of a 'remedy' in common law are presented by S. Smith, 'Rights-Threats, Wrongs and Injustices: The Common Law's Causes of Action' (2017) 27 *New Zealand Universities Law Review* 1033, 1034–1035.

23 This concept has recently been radically attacked by T. Ackermann, 'Sektorielles EU-Recht und allgemeine Privatrechtssystematik' (2018) *Zeitschrift Europäisches Privatrecht* 741, 749–753 claiming that there is no room for a purely civil society in a democratic state. However, neither the national state nor the European Union theoretically have the power to fully dispose of the individual freedom that constitutes a civil society and that is the foundation of a private law system.

by recognising individual rights that are equipped with judicially enforceable material protective rights.[24] This liberal concept of private law is of course not of static nature but allows individuals to autonomously alter and redefine their spheres of individual freedom by concluding contracts. Accordingly, private law can be captured entirely with the theoretical constructs of contract and property – property being understood in a wider sense encompassing any domain that one individual may not breach without the consent of another, including, for example intellectual property rights, personality rights and physical integrity. One individual may demand an action or inaction by another individual only when it has been contractually promised to him/her or when his/her claim is legitimised by an infringement of a property right.

3.2. PRIVATE LAW AS AN ORDER OF REMEDIAL RIGHTS

In particular Picker highlighted the fact that property rights in private law are surrounded by a *triad* of remedial rights ensuring an all-round protection.[25] Private law has to grant the existence of remedial rights targeting the *realisation* of the property right, as well as *damages* and *restitution* of unjustified enrichment in order to ensure the implementation, the preservation and the value assignment indicated by the property right.[26] Already the drafters of the German Civil Code assumed the idea of a remedial triad with regards to tangible property.[27]

The remedial rights are activated when a property right is infringed. The notion of an infringement needs to be precisely defined: It neither requires fault nor an intentional act by the opponent. An infringement merely requires that one individual's sphere intendedly or unintendedly overlaps the legally defined sphere of freedom of another individual.

3.2.1. *Property*

Should the infringement be *completed* and the spherical overlap not be ongoing, the right holder will be granted remedial rights in form of restitution and damages. The right holder may demand *restitution* of the unjust enrichment

---

24 Cf. recently also N. Jansen, above n. 18, 112, 205 and with a few modifications F. Hofmann, above n. 18, pp. 122–249.

25 Whether disgorgement of profits should be included in the prototypical line-up of remedial rights shall not be discussed here; cf. in this volume B. Raue, pp. 153–167.

26 E. Picker, FS Canaris II, above n. 21, pp. 579, 608; there are some similarities to the model of common law's causes of action according to S. Smith, above n. 22, 1033.

27 See B. Mugdan (ed.), *Die gesammten Materialien zum Bürgerlichen Gesetzbuch, Band 3*, R. v. Decker, Berlin 1899, p. 218; similar concepts within the doctrine of natural law are highlighted by N. Jansen, above n. 18, 112, 206–207.

the opponent achieved by infringing upon the substantively protected freedom. Restitution is only granted as long as the enrichment is still positively detectable in the opponent's overall assets. As restitution is immanently limited to a continuing enrichment, no negligence is necessary.

In case the infringement has been caused by an opponent's at least negligent act, the right holder will be awarded *damages*. The remedial right to damages differs insofar categorically from the remedial right to restitution as restitution focuses on the opponent's assets whereas damages consider the assets of the right holder.

As far as the infringement is currently ongoing or probable in the future, the right holder will be awarded *realisational* remedial rights. The realisational remedial rights intend to protect the legal integrity of a property right. The opponent has to refrain from future infringements and injunctive relief is granted. Ongoing infringements in the sense that the opponent's factual sphere is overlapping the protected party's substantively assigned sphere have to be terminated. A prominent example for a realisational remedial right can be seen in the proprietor's right to recover possession from the wrongful possessor.[28] The realisational protection is decisively shaped by the property right itself. Its sundry manifestations are as manifold as the property rights in private law themselves. This can be demonstrated by the examples of a rectification of false allegations with regard to personality rights or the claim for destruction vis-à-vis goods that were produced contrary to intellectual property rights.[29] While restitution demands the opponent to reverse unjust enrichments that became part of his/her assets, realisational protection demands to stop the assumption of another individual's assets.

The remedial triad's specific elements of realisation, restitution and damages complement each other and grant the necessary protection in a liberal system of private law. In general, all three remedial systems are indicated to protect any property right. In particular, the *realisational* protection cannot be replaced discretionarily by damages against the right holder's will[30] because that would in effect dispose of the legal integrity of the position. However, it is

28 See J. Wilhelm, *Sachenrecht*, 5th edn., de Gruyter, Berlin 2016, para. 1175.

29 See J.F. Hoffmann, 'Der immaterialgüterrechtliche Vernichtungsanspruch' (2014) 3 *Intellectual Property Journal* 335–384.

30 The holder of the property right may choose between realisational and restitutional remedies under German law; if an opponent sells off another person's property, the proprietor may choose to activate restitutional remedies even if he/she has the right to recover possession from the new possessor; cf. BGH 06.05.1971, VII ZR 232/69 = *NJW* 1971, 1452. Against the prevailing opinion of legal scholars the right to choose between realisational protection and damages has also been granted by the BGH in the following case: The proprietor, instead of recovering possession, can also demand damages if the possessor does not recover the still existing good after the proprietor has fixed an additional period of time of reasonable length; BGH 18.03.2016, V ZR 89/15 = *BGHZ* 209, 270.

possible to attenuate the property right itself by imposing on the right holder to tolerate an infringement and be instead compensated for the value of his/her position. This is how German private law, for example, solves conflicts with regard to emissions that are locally customary yet significantly interfere with a real property right. In German law, this phenomenon is described illustratively as a claim in exchange for sacrifice (Aufopferungsanspruch). This constellation is systematically viewed as a modification not only of the remedial rights but of the property right itself,[31] which inevitably influences the realisational protection. The limitation of the property right itself in these situations can also be seen by the fact that not only realisational but also restitutional protection is ruled out. The phenomenon that the holder of a property right has to make his/her rights available against pecuniary compensation is widespread in German copyright law, even though the idea of a sacrifice is not as common. In copyright law these constellations are of great importance and are also predominantly viewed as a modification of the property right itself.[32]

3.2.2. Contract

The presented concept can also be used to systematise contract law and to free this field of private law from the predominantly action-based concept in Germany. The claims (*Forderung*) arising from the conclusion of a contract have to be seen as property rights protected by the remedial triad too. The most prominent aspect of a claim is the debtor's personal duty to perform. This is why the creditor is entitled to request performance from the debtor. Furthermore, the claim is a property right[33] that is protected against infringements by third parties and that constitutes a transferrable asset. The claim is on the one hand a static asset that enjoys absolute protection (erga omnes) while on the other hand at the same time being relatively

---

31 J. Wilhelm, above n. 28, para. 71, 754–757.

32 BVerfG 25.10.1978, 1 BvR 352/17 = *BVerfGE* 49, 382, 393 – *Kirchenmusik*; H. Schack, *Urheber- und Urhebervertragsrecht*, 8th edn., Mohr Siebeck, Tübingen 2017, §15, para. 512; M. Stieper, *Rechtfertigung, Rechtsnatur und Disponibilität der Schranken des Urheberrechts*, Mohr Siebeck, Tübingen 2009, pp. 141–142; against this view F. Hofmann, above n. 18, pp. 465–476.

33 Cf. e.g. C.-W. Canaris, 'Der Schutz obligatorischer Forderungen nach §823 Abs. 1 BGB' in E. Deutsch, E. Klingmüller and H.J. Kullmann (eds.), *Festschrift für Erich Steffen zum 65. Geburtstag*, de Gruyter, Berlin 1995, pp. 90, 96; H. Dörner, *Dynamische Relativität*, C.H. Beck, Munich 1985, p. 53; J.F. Hoffmann, above n. 3, pp. 104–106; E. Picker, 'Der deliktische Schutz der Forderung als Beispiel für das Zusammenspiel von Rechtszuweisung und Rechtsschutz' in A. Heldrich, J. Prölss, I. Koller et al. (eds.), *Festschrift für Claus-Wilhelm Canaris zum 70. Geburtstag, Band 1*, C.H. Beck, Munich 2007, pp. 1019; recently also N. Jansen, above n. 18, 112, 216–217.

(inter partes) focused on a dynamic transfer of assets by the debtor. This Janus-faced character of claims has posed great challenges for their systematisation.

3.2.2.1. A Claim's Relative Dimension

With regard to the relative dimension, a claim enjoys the described triple protection as a personal property right vis-à-vis the debtor.[34] The remedial rights protect the interest in contractual performance as promised by the debtor. In case the debtor does not perform by negligence, he/she will be liable for caused damages.[35] If the debtor generates unjust enrichments due to the non-performance, they will have to be restituted to the creditor.[36]

Next to remedial rights of restitution and damages a claim can also enjoy realisational protection, for example through entitlement to information. The most prominent realisational right concerning a claim is the right to require specific performance.[37] As a remedial right, specific performance is only relevant when the debtor's non-performance is a contractually wrongful act. This is the case when the debtor does not perform even though performance was due according to the contractual agreement. In German private law there are generally no further requirements for specific performance. Contrary to the currently predominant opinion in Germany, the claim and its specific performance should not be conceived as being identical but should be systematised according to the differentiation between property and remedial rights.

However, the basis for a termination of the contract in case of non-performance cannot be seen as remedial to the claim as a personal property right.[38] Even though it is common to speak of a 'remedy' in this context,[39] it is not the claim that is protected. Termination is possible in reaction to a debtor's breach of contract but it does not aim at enforcing the claim. Termination does serve as a remedial right to a property right but it is the creditor's private autonomy that is protected.[40] The creditor of a synallagmatic contract has

---

34 Recently also N. Jansen, above n. 18, 112, 222 n. 662.

35 Cf. §§280 ff. BGB (*German Civil Code*).

36 Cf. §285 BGB.

37 Differentiating between claim and specific performance also J. Schmidt, "'Actio". "Anspruch". "Forderung"' in M. Martinek, J. Schmidt and E. Wadle (eds.), *Festschrift für Günther Jahr zum siebzigsten Geburtstag*, Mohr Siebeck, Tübingen 1993, pp. 401, 415; J.F. Hoffmann, above n. 3, pp. 106–140; recently with a few modifications also F. Hofmann, above n. 18, p. 188.

38 J.F. Hoffmann, above n. 3, pp. 204–207.

39 Cf. Arts. 45 ff. CISG.

40 See T. Lobinger, *Die Grenzen rechtsgeschäftlicher Leistungspflichten*, Mohr Siebeck, Tübingen 2004, pp. 319–320.

not promised his/her performance in case of the debtor's non-performance and he/she may therefore declare the contract to be no longer binding upon him.

3.2.2.2. A Claim's Absolute Dimension

A claim in its absolute dimension enjoys the protection of the triad of remedial rights like any other property right. A claim is protected erga omnes by remedial rights targeting at realisation, damages and restitution. However, it is heavily debated in Germany whether claims can lead to damages in case of an infringement erga omnes.[41] Yet, it would not be coherent to grant remedial rights to realisation and to restitution[42] but not to damages in case of an erga omnes infringement of a claim.

Of course it is difficult to draw the line between the absolute and the relative substance of a claim. Without any doubt, only the debtor is obliged to perform and the extension of the protection erga omnes needs to be clarified. The creditor is protected from third parties assuming his/her position as holder of the claim as a static property right. Third parties may therefore not act as if they were the debtor's creditor. An obvious case of an infringement of a claim erga omnes would be for a third party to collect the performance of the claim with effects against the creditor; the effectiveness does of course depend on corresponding rules that allow the debtor to perform to a third party, which may in certain cases serve to protect the debtor's trust that the third party is his/her creditor.[43] Difficulties arise in cases where the third party manipulates the substance of the performance making it impossible for the debtor to perform.[44] Should a third party, for example injure an employee, this could lead to an impossibility to perform to the employer. In this case the third party negatively affects the claim as a property right because it may cease to exist during the period of time the employee is not capable of working. However, it is accurate not to protect the creditor against such effects on his/her claim caused by third parties because his/her position as the holder of the claim has not been infringed. A third party injuring an employee does not assume rights granted to the employer as the holder of the claim.

---

41 See on the one side e.g. C.-W. CANARIS, above n. 33, pp. 85–99 and E. PICKER, above n. 33, pp. 1020–1027 who favour such a protection, and against this idea e.g. D. MEDICUS, 'Die Forderung als "sonstiges Recht" nach §823 Abs. 1 BGB?' in E. DEUTSCH, E. KLINGMÜLLER and H.J. KULLMANN (eds.), *Festschrift für Erich Steffen zum 65. Geburtstag*, de Gruyter, Berlin 1995, pp. 333–345.

42 Cf. §816 (2) BGB.

43 Cf. §407 BGB.

44 Cf. §275 BGB.

4. THE MERITS AND LIMITS OF THINKING IN PROPERTY AND REMEDIAL RIGHTS

Legal doctrine is not an end in itself[45] and further development of the predominant status of systematisation has to be justified. Legal doctrine aims at reducing complexity by accentuating similarities of legal phenomena and therefore allows to prevent or to reverse inconsistent legal developments. However, developing abstract legal doctrine runs the risk of its potential being overestimated. The distilled legal categories can gain momentum and lead to concrete solutions being deduced from the abstract system without being intended by the original efforts of systematisation. Therefore, both the merits as well as the limits of thinking in property and remedial rights will be presented.

4.1. GENERAL THEORY OF REMEDIAL RIGHTS

On the one hand, this coherent model of private law in its entirety allows for a general theory of remedial rights. Stressing the commonality of all property rights, it opens the possibility to develop a general theory of restitution, of damages and of realisational protection that can be applied in any field of private law. This can also help to slow down the increasing drift between general private law and its more specific fields. It would, for example, allow property law and intellectual property law to use the same language and concepts.

Although the discussion of a general theory of *damages* is taking place in Germany – probably due to the fact that the German Civil Code has general rules for damages addressing property and contract law at the same time[46] – there are still communication barriers between general and specialised private law. For example, intellectual property law has developed concepts of damages that should be integrated into the general discussion of damages.[47]

The presented model here would allow for a general theory of *restitution* applicable in every field of private law. Restitutional remedies have only been recognised in German intellectual property law with delay[48] and the integration into general theory could still be intensified. Contract law in particular would

45 See R. Stürner, 'Das Zivilrecht der Moderne und die Bedeutung der Rechtsdogmatik' (2012) *JuristenZeitung* 10–24.

46 §§249 ff. BGB.

47 For an exemplary attempt at integrating the so called 'triple damages calculation' and the general theory of remedial rights see B. Raue, *Die dreifache Schadensberechnung*, Nomos, Baden-Baden 2017, passim; cf. also J.F. Hoffmann, 'Die Haftung in der Verletzerkette' (2017) 9 *Intellectual Property Journal* 72–97.

48 See R. Ellger, *Bereicherung durch Eingriff*, Mohr Siebeck, Tübingen 2002, pp. 591–619.

benefit from a general theory of restitution in order to identify and determine remedial rights available in the case of a breach of contract. Contract law could profit enormously from property law in this field.[49]

Realisational remedial rights are also far from being subjected to a general theory in the current discussion.[50] In particular, intellectual property law has developed special manifestations of realisational remedial rights like the claim for destruction or the duty to recall infringing goods from the channels of commerce that should be integrated into the discourse of general private law.[51]

On the other hand, the limits of the presented model have to be stressed in this context as well.[52] The remedial rights may be comparable across all different property rights. However, they are determined by the protected property rights. A remedial right can only protect the freedom that the property right confers upon the right holder. That in itself can be seen as progress for the current German discussion because it highlights the idea that a judicially enforceable right in the sense of a remedial right can only be granted if a protected individual position can be recognised in the first place.[53] Above all, it has to be stressed that the comparability this system allows for does not deny the heterogeneity of property rights. The restitutional protection of tangible property, intellectual property and a claim may be comparable in essence. However, the protected property rights that determine the range of the restitutional protection are very disparate in their features. Especially when dealing with contractual claims, one obviously has to bear in mind that there is no such thing as a prototypical claim because the contractual agreement defines the (relative) property right. Realising that contractual claims are equipped with a restitutional protection, just as property is, does of course not absolve the courts from precisely interpreting the contract in order to define the features of the (relative) property right and ultimately its restitutional protection.

4.2. GENERAL OBSERVATIONS ON THE RELATION BETWEEN PROPERTY AND REMEDIAL RIGHTS

The differentiation between property and remedial rights also allows for general findings regarding their relation to each other. In this context the remedial triad can be split into a dichotomy of remedial rights.[54] On one hand,

49 See F. Hartmann, above n. 21, passim.
50 F. Hofmann, above n. 18, passim, has recently presented a general theory of injunctive relief.
51 See J.F. Hoffmann, above n. 29, pp. 335–384.
52 See again below 4.3.
53 E. Picker, 'Das Deliktsrecht im Zivilrechtssystem' (2015), above n. 21, 385–434.
54 J.F. Hoffmann, above n. 3, pp. 56–74.

realisational rights protect the legal integrity of a position, whereas on the other hand damages and restitution are a projection of the already infringed right and demand a transfer of assets by the opponent. This dichotomy shows, on the one hand, why realisational protection is not subject to the distributional scheme of bankruptcy in the form of the *pari passu* principle. When claiming realisational protection of an absolute property right, the right holder is not trying to gain access to the estate but merely defends his/her absolute right by extricating his/her asset from the estate.[55]

On the other hand, this dichotomy captures that realisational remedial rights can, according to the prevailing German doctrine,[56] not be assigned in isolation without the property right, whereas claims for restitution and damages can be assigned regularly. The realisational remedial rights are shaped significantly by the absolute nature of the property right and are an integrating part of the property right, whereas the remedial rights of restitution and damages give rise to regularly assignable claims which, in turn, can be classified as property rights.

4.3. FLEXIBILITY

Since the differentiation between property and remedial rights recognises the particularities of each property right, it can be adapted to any position of private law. This flexibility is an advantage of the presented model especially in times when new property rights, for example with regard to data, are being discussed.[57] The presented system is also able to absorb the aforementioned constellations of a compensation for the legally demanded sacrifice of a position.[58] The property right itself is limited in these cases and restricted to a claim for compensation. In German private law there is no need for more flexibility by introducing the idea of discretionary remedial rights.

However, this flexibility also limits the extent to which general rules can be stated – a fact that cannot be stressed enough.[59] The characteristic and principal challenge of many specialised fields of private law is to accurately define the features of the respective property rights. This problem is evident when dealing with intangible goods. A contractual claim has to be assessed through an interpretation of the contract. In particular, intellectual property

---

[55] J.F. Hoffmann, *Prioritätsgrundsatz und Gläubigergleichbehandlung*, Mohr Siebeck, Tübingen 2016, pp. 233–252.

[56] Cf. e.g. G.H. Roth and E.-M. Kieninger in *Münchener Kommentar zum BGB*, 8th edn., C.H. Beck, Munich 2019, §399 BGB para. 21.

[57] Cf. e.g. the articles in *Intellectual Property Journal* (2017) 9, Vol. 3.

[58] See above 3.2.1.

[59] See already above 4.1.

law is a field that primarily deals with the just definition of the scope of the granted rights. The differentiation between property and remedial rights cannot contribute to the solution of these problems.[60] The precise determination of the features of the property right can also be problematic when dealing with tangible goods, even though this is often not seen in the current discussion. When dealing with tangible property the extent of the property right is problematic, for example when the proprietor of a machine cannot use his/her machine because a third party negligently damaged a public power cable and the machine cannot be supplied with the necessary energy.[61] A similar problem arises when it is discussed whether a proprietor also has exclusive rights to photographs taken on or of his/her property.[62] This problem of assessing the protected individual spheres of freedom becomes even clearer when dealing with purely pecuniary damages. The conceivable possible conceptualisations of a law of torts can only be addressed by the presented model with the postulate that the assets as a whole could be considered to be a property right and the extent of this right is difficult to discern in the light of the opponent's freedom of action.

4.4. PRIVATE LAW SYSTEMATOLOGY

Furthermore, it should be stressed that the presented model deals with the recognition and protection of individual freedom. The propagated concept builds upon the traditional continental European approach that allows for private law as a whole to be broken down to contract and property and to be clearly separated from public law. It systematises a legal system in which private law solely addresses the issue of coordinating individual freedom and which only interferes when disparities in contractual negotiations need to be balanced. The incentives, deterrence, sanctions or even the enforcement of

---

60 Dissenting F. Hofmann, 'Die Systematisierung des Interessenausgleichs im Urheberrecht am Beispiel des Rechts der öffentlichen Wiedergabe' (2018) *Zeitschrift für Urheber- und Medienrecht* 641, 645–649.

61 See BGH 04.02.1964, IV ZR 25/63 = *BGHZ* 41, 123; T. Bernhard, 'Das rechtsverletzende Handeln als Grundlage der deliktischen Haftung in §823 Abs. 1 BGB' in T. Lobinger, R. Richardi and J. Wilhelm (eds.), *Festschrift für Eduard Picker zum 70. Geburtstag*, Mohr Siebeck, Tübingen 2010, pp. 83–112.

62 BGH 19.12.2014, V ZR 324/13 = *GRUR* 2015, 578 – *Preußische Kunstwerke*; BGH 01.03.2013, V ZR 14/12 = *GRUR* 2013, 623 – *Preußische Gärten und Parkanlagen II*; BGH 17.12.2010, V ZR 45/10 = *GRUR* 2011, 323 – *Preußische Gärten und Parkanlagen I*; BGH 20.09.1974, I ZR 99/73 = *GRUR* 1975, 500 – *Schloss Tegel*; H. Schack, (2011) *JuristenZeitung* 375–376; H. Schack, (2013) *JuristenZeitung* 743–744; D. Yang, 'Bilder von Bildern: Urheberrechtliche und eigentumsrechtliche Fragen der Kunstfotografie' (2017) *Zeitschrift für Urheber- und Medienrecht* 951–955.

public welfare that the remedial rights can effectively provide for are a mere reflex and not the primary objective of remedial rights.

The proposed system, therefore, does not provide further insight when private law is not used to coordinate individual freedom but to (primarily) promote public welfare. It is doubtful whether private law should be used to this end when the concerned legal system provides for an efficient and not purposefully understaffed administrative body.[63] From the viewpoint of a legal culture that does not generally mistrust public authority,[64] private enforcement is at most a 'second-best' solution. However, this is not a question the presented concept directly answers or even addresses. Phenomena have to be considered where private law is being instrumentalised in the sense of private enforcement or in order to simply (punitively) sanction certain behaviour. Whether private enforcement should be implemented through damages, restitution or realisational protection (e.g. injunctions) has to be decided by public law and this decision is not restricted or pre-shaped by structures of individual freedom. It would not be coherent to apply the idea of a remedial triad in a context of private enforcement or private sanctioning.

However, the propagated model is able to clearly identify purely sanctioning instruments that cannot be solely legitimised by civil law. This can facilitate a transparent discussion on the reasonableness of such instruments. Cases of private enforcement can also be more clearly distinguished from the traditional parts of private law protecting individual freedom. This could allow for a separate systematisation of instruments of private enforcement and prevent a hybridisation of private law system that would, in the long run, be detrimental to both individual freedom as well as public welfare.

From the point of view of a liberal system of private law it should be dealt carefully with a general use of the principle of proportionality.[65] The principle of proportionality might have its merits in public law and could possibly be transferred to the private enforcement of public interests. It would, however, need thorough adaption in a context where solely individual freedom needs to be recognised. Even though individual freedom also needs to be coordinated, the idea of proportionality can be problematic in this context because the purpose of classic private law as a whole is to recognise individual freedom neutrally.

---

63 Cf. M. Reimann, 'Präventiv-Administrative Regulierung oder Private Law Enforcement?' (2009) *Bitburger Gespräche, Jahrbuch 2008/I* 105–146 and the chapter of J.-U. Franck in this volume, pp. 107–131.

64 In this context the vision of G. Wagner, 'Prävention und Verhaltenssteuerung durch Privatrecht – Anmaßung oder legitime Aufgabe?' (2006) 206 *Archiv für die civilistische Praxis* 352, 447 of a civil society that is not monitored by governmental institutions but by each and every individual seems rather alarming and leaves in fact no room for a 'civil' society.

65 As e.g. propagated by O. Fischman Afori in this volume, pp. 223–232.

5. CONCLUSION

The two divergent conceptualisations of private law either as a system of subjective rights or as a system of *actiones* can be combined harmoniously within the differentiation between property and remedial rights. This concept can also take into account the strict theoretical division between substantive and procedural law that is characteristic to German private law (but could also easily be modified to a more procedural understanding of the remedial rights as 'remedies'). This not only allows for a seamless systematisation of all fields of private law but also for a general theory of remedial rights. As a synthesis of the two historically prominent schools of thinking about private law, this system provides for a language that could be adapted by legal systems of both traditions, bearing in mind the different approaches to separating substantive from procedural law.

RIGHTS AND REMEDIES IN PUBLIC LAW

Andreas Funke

1. INTRODUCTION

It is fair to say that the concept of remedies does not play a significant role in contemporary public law doctrine. Certainly the English expression 'remedies' is used frequently in English publications on public law. This applies to works from common law authors as well as to works from continental scholars writing in English. But 'remedies' then does not have an autonomous specific meaning. It is rather a generic term used to assemble the various ways of redress against public authorities. Normally, two basic elements are identified as such remedies in public law: judicial review and state liability. For instance, in a major treatise on EU administrative law, Paul Craig states that in EU law, as well as in every domestic legal system, there are two main remedies available 'for holding public bodies to account': annulment and compensation.[1] This proposition is representative for the common view.

In this chapter this view will be referred to as the 'standard picture' of a public law of remedies and it will be presented and described in more detail. The author is of the opinion that it represents an approach that is not convincing. The standard picture is flawed. An alternative, basically a scheme of basic legal

[1] P. Craig, *EU Administrative Law*, OUP, Oxford 2006, p. 749.

positions arising from public law norms will be introduced, and it will be shown how these positions are linked to particular claims. Some of these claims form a branch of law that many scholars are not aware of. In German, it is sometimes called *Reaktionsrecht* which can be translated literally as 'law of reactions' or 'law of responses'. The law of reactions could be seen as a regime of remedies, yet then remedies are not understood in the generic sense just introduced, but rather in a new, narrow sense.

Eventually, the 'law of reactions' will not be linked with the idea of remedies. For the law of reactions is purely substantive law. It gives the grounds for action, whereas the term 'remedies' often refers to lawsuits or actions themselves (and sometimes even to their outcomes).[2] Or, to put it differently, according to a common view 'the law of remedies falls somewhere between substance and procedure'.[3] But there is a long path to follow in this chapter before these conclusions on the law of reactions can be reached. (2.) will start with a reflection upon the issue of a 'public law of remedies' as such. It will be clarified why it can be helpful to apply a remedies perspective to public law, and how this can work. In (3.) the standard picture of public redress – remedies in the broad sense – will be introduced in detail and it will be argued that it needs clarification and refinement. This thesis is elaborated in two steps. First, proceeding critically, some arguments against the standard approach will be discussed. Two revisions of the standard picture will be considered: in (4.) an 'internal' one, arguing from inside a remedy perspective, and in (5.) an 'external' one, looking from the outside at the law of remedies. Subsequently, (6.) will proceed constructively by sketching a new picture.

2. WHY AND HOW 'REMEDIES IN PUBLIC LAW'

What can be gained by applying a remedies perspective to public law? As already mentioned, when public law lawyers use the term 'remedies', it is probably without systematic meaning. In a comparative context, the term 'remedies' allows one to comprehend several instruments of legal protection – namely actions and claims – under a common frame.[4] In legal texts, the term 'remedies'

2 On the various meanings of 'remedies' see the useful synthesis in P. Birks, 'Rights, Wrongs, and Remedies' (2000) 20 *Oxford Journal of Legal Studies* 1, 9–17.

3 A quote cited in H. Dedek, 'From Norms to Facts: The Realization of Rights in Common and Civil Private Law' (2010) *McGill Law Journal* 56, 77, 83.

4 Some authors seem to prefer a narrow understanding of remedies in public law; they restrict it (without further elaboration) to judicial review, see for instance J.N.E. Varuhas, 'Taxonomy and Public Law' in M. Elliott, J.N.E. Varuhas and S.W. Stark (eds.), *The Unity of Public Law? Doctrinal, Theoretical, and Comparative Perspectives*, Hart Publishing, Oxford 2018, pp. 39–78, 66, or A. von Bogdandy, P.M. Huber and S. Cassese (eds.), *The Max Planck*

often refers to actions.[5] The author's intention is not to implant a certain civil law remedial structure into public law but rather to think about what could count as a law of remedies in public law. The discussion about remedies can be utilised as a resource for arguments. The author is not a comparative lawyer, but will make some comparisons. With an eye to the composition of the contributors in this volume, the scope of the comparison is restricted to English, German and European administrative law. The author's own doctrinal research interest lies in German public law.[6] Some of the arguments applied in this chapter are grounded there.

Some preliminary notes on the approach to the topic are necessary. First, it is an assumption that the question of remedies – now, in a generic sense – arises under certain circumstances of social life. Actually, the very issue is which circumstances these are. In a very rough first account, it may be said that in public law an individual feels impaired by an authority. He/she brings this allegation to a court. There is dispute between the authority and the individual and the court has to decide which party is right. The law is in a state of disorder somehow.[7] That is why the investigation of remedies is heading for judicial actions. The aim is to understand them properly. The remedies perspective could render a productive tool to give the best possible account of judicial actions. In a way, the author tries to reconstruct the procedural judicial actions as substantive claims. Some may call this approach 'action-based',

Handbooks in European Public Law, Vol. 1: The Administrative State, OUP, Oxford 2017, issued by two German scholars and an Italian scholar, where the term remedies is included in the register (p. 682), but the entries refer only to issues of judicial review. The idea of 'remedies' is not explained in the volume. The field of compensation is covered in this volume by the references collected as 'state liability'. It refers to some domestic rules on public liability for torts. Others subsume public liability under the idea of remedies, see for instance J. Chan, 'Vindicatory Damages for Violation of Constitutional Rights: A Comparative Approach' in M. Elliott, J.N.E. Varuhas and S.W. Stark, above, pp. 327–350, 327.

5 An example taken from EU law: Pursuant to Article 19 para. 1 TEU the EU Member States 'shall provide remedies sufficient to ensure effective legal protection in the fields covered by Union law'. In this provision, the expression 'remedies' is also used in an unspecific way. The German version of this article translates 'remedies' as 'Rechtsbehelfe', which is usually understood as a generic term for actions, viz. in a procedural way. The French version goes along these lines: 'voies de recours'. The provision is complemented by Article 47 EUCFR, which provides for the right to an effective remedy. A systematic account can be found in T. Eilmansberger, 'The Relationship between Rights and Remedies in EC Law: In Search of the Missing Link' (2004) *Common Market Law Review* 41, 1199.

6 With respect to earlier considerations, see A. Funke, 'Perspektiven subjektiv-rechtlicher Analyse des öffentlichen Rechts' (2015) *Juristenzeitung* 369.

7 Compare D. Medicus, 'Anspruch und Einrede als Rückgrat einer zivilistischen Lehrmethode' (1974) *Archiv der civilistischen Praxis* 174, 313, 322. But there is still an element of order in the system of legal positions set forth in the following. The two statuses (see section 4.3), and probably also the additional positions of the legal power to enforce these positions, are basically important as elements of the law seen as an order of behaviour. The disorder begins with the law of reactions, or vice versa the reaction begins with the violation (of the order).

aktionenrechtlich. However, this term is ambiguous. The approach is 'action-based' only insofar as the legal material shall be structured and presented by way of an adjustment to particular judicial procedures. The legal material is to be arranged in accordance with and in dependence on the trials.[8] Besides this, 'action-based' can also mean to derive substantive claims directly from procedural positions. With the exception of one minor point (discussed in the last section of this chapter), this is not the method applied in this text. Finally, the term 'action-based' can be used to label an approach that does not suppose that there are claims existing independently of actions. Such an understanding does not neglect rights in general. But the action at hand would define and shape the concrete scope of the rights.[9] Such a view is directly opposed to the approach presented and defended here; however, it is indeed held in contemporary German administrative law doctrine.

This point already leads to a second methodological remark. The debate on rights and remedies is carried by a fundamental belief: It is not *l'art pour l'art*, but serves doctrinal purposes. A comprehensive, sophisticated scheme of 'rights and remedies' enables us to advance a coherent reconstruction of legal norms and legal positions. The more coherent the law can be apprehended, the more is it fair and just.[10] The English discussion on remedies, propelled by the force of Peter Birks' works on private law, focuses on what Birks called a taxonomy of rights and remedies.[11] In Germany, systematisation is the keyword,[12] embracing classification and concept formation based on principles. In common private law, a taxonomy of the events causing a right to a remedy is at stake. In public law, the issue of 'rights and remedies' similarly refers to a taxonomy of public behaviour having an impact on the rights of the people.

But, thirdly, a reconstruction of actions must also take a distinctive feature of administrative adjudication into account: it has two functions.

---

8 For instance, the German private law professor Dieter Medicus, who popularised the method of thinking private law by means of claims and exceptions, also pursued such a project (see ibid.); more radical E. Bucher, 'Für mehr Aktionendenken' (1986) *Archiv für die civilistische Praxis* 186, 18; and a fresh account in F. Hofmann, *Der Unterlassungsanspruch als Rechtsbehelf*, Mohr Siebeck, Tübingen 2017.

9 J. Buchheim, *Actio, Anspruch, subjektives Recht: Eine aktionenrechtliche Rekonstruktion des Verwaltungsrechts*, Mohr Siebeck, Tübingen 2017, pp. 24–25.

10 H. Kantorowicz, *The Definition of Law*, CUP, Cambridge 2014, p. 32.

11 See P. Birks, above n. 2, pp. 3–4; picked up for instance in J.N.E. Varuhas, above n. 4, p. 48. On Birks taxonomy project and its massive impact see M. Flohr, *Rechtsdogmatik in England*, Mohr Siebeck, Tübingen 2017, pp. 203–238.

12 See W. Höfling, '§51 Vom überkommenen Staatshaftungsrecht zum Recht der staatlichen Einstandspflichten' in W. Hoffmann-Riem, E. Schmidt-Aßmann and A. Voßkuhle (eds.), *Grundlagen des Verwaltungsrechts, Vol. 3: Personal, Finanzen, Kontrolle, Sanktionen, staatliche Einstandspflichten*, Beck, München 2013, pp. 1051–1115, 1054; M. Morlok, '§52 Allgemeine Elemente der Einstandspflichten für rechtswidriges Staatshandeln', ibid., pp. 1117–1170, 1118.

Administrative courts do not only have to protect individual rights, but they also have to control the administration. Ordinary courts do not have this function. They are not supposed to 'control' the parties' behaviour. This may be relevant for the remedies perspective in public law. Yet, the control function of administrative courts does not allow for a one-and-only solution but has to be taken into consideration at different points and with contextual solutions.

The last methodological consideration is a caveat. A truly comprehensive account to public law remedies *in general* would have to do justice to important differentiations. A comparison of civil (continental) and common public law is a complex enterprise: there are many important differences between the two. The common law does not represent a monolithic block of administrative law; in fact it embraces various systems. English administrative law, which is chosen here, has always been fragmented.[13] Moreover, there are important differences between human rights litigation and administrative law litigation. The competences of constitutional courts and of the regular courts deserve separate attention. The starting point here is administrative law, more precisely the administrative courts, yet, a certain human rights dimension is involved. In neglecting necessary differentiations to a great extent, it is supposed that at an abstract level the civil law system of public law and the common law system of public law share basic features. Certainly, future research, paying attention to these differentiations, would allow for much more depth of focus.

3. THE STANDARD PICTURE

Following the standard picture, remedies in public law rest on two pillars: judicial review and public state liability. The liability-part of the picture is basically tort law.[14] For instance, the German civil code, in its chapter on torts, contains a special provision for official liability (*Amtshaftung*).[15] Thus, the reader

---

13 Emphasised in G. Kleve and B. Schirmer, 'England und Wales' in J.-P. Schneider (ed.), *Verwaltungsrecht in Europa, Vol. 1: England und Wales, Spanien, Niederlande*, V & R Unipress Univ.-Verl. Osnabrück, Göttingen 2007, pp. 35–180, 36.

14 A useful comparison in O. Dörr (ed.), *Staatshaftung in Europa: Nationales und Unionsrecht*, de Gruyter, Berlin 2014.

15 Section 839 German Civil Code (Liability in case of breach of official duty):

> "(1) If an official intentionally or negligently breaches the official duty incumbent upon him in relation to a third party, then he must compensate the third party for damage arising from this. If the official is only responsible because of negligence, then he may only be held liable if the injured person is not able to obtain compensation in another way.
>
> (2) If an official breaches his official duties in a judgment in a legal matter, then he is only responsible for any damage arising from this if the breach of duty consists in a

might expect an elaboration on remedies in public tort law but this approach would tend to narrow the remedy concept too much. Rather it will be considered whether and how the two pillars are connected, so that a clear sight of the picture arises before revisions can be placed (below, 4.).

To begin with public liability law, whether or not it is seen as a part of tort law, a public liability claim basically requires a violation of an official duty.[16] Such a violation at any rate is given if an official violates a right of an individual, an individual right (in German: *subjektives Recht*).[17] If all requirements of the liability claim are fulfilled, the legal effect is that the state is obliged to give a compensation for the damages.[18] The compensation can be owed as a restitution in kind (*Naturalrestitution* = '*specific performance*') or as a certain amount of money, which is compensation in a strong sense. The EU provision on state liability, Article 340 para. 2 TFEU, allows for restitution in kind and for financial compensation as well. In Germany, only financial compensation can be obtained.

In EU law, the Court of Justice of the European Union is competent for judicial review as well as for liability claims. In the German legal order, the two pillars reach into the realm of the court system. The recourse to the courts is split. Judicial review is administered by special administrative courts, whereas state liability falls into the ordinary jurisdiction (*ordentliche Gerichtsbarkeit*). The reasons for this divide are mainly historical.[19] For instance, when the idea of a public law tort claim against the state was accepted – roughly in the eighteenth century – there plainly were no administrative courts, but only ordinary courts.[20] An administrative judicial branch slowly emerged parallel to this in the

---

criminal offence. This provision is not applicable to refusal or delay that is in breach of duty in exercising a public function.

(3) Liability for damage does not arise if the injured person has intentionally or negligently failed to avert the damage by having recourse to appeal."

16 Whereas the element of guiltiness does not seem to have taxonomic value insofar.

17 See O. Dörr, '§5 Deutschland' in O. Dörr, above n. 14, pp. 121–156, 137. Notably it is possible to extend the scope of public tort law beyond violations of rights, see B. Grzeszick, 'Notwendigkeit und Grundzüge eines Staatshaftungsgesetzes' (2015) *Zeitschrift für Rechtspolitik* 162, 164.

18 Article 34 German Constitution: "Where any person, in the exercise of a public office entrusted to him, violates his official obligations to a third party, liability rests in principle on the state or the public body which employs him. In the event of wilful intent or gross negligence, the right of recourse against the holder of a public office is reserved. In respect of the claim for compensation or the right of recourse, the jurisdiction of the ordinary courts may not be excluded."
For Section 839 German Civil Code see n. 15 above.

19 P. Dagtoglou, 'Comment on Article 34' (Second treatment 1970) in W. Kahl, C. Waldhoff and C. Walter (eds.), *Bonner Kommentar zum Grundgesetz*, C. F. Müller, Heidelberg 2018, margin nr. 365.

20 See the detailed treatment in K.-P. Sommermann and B. Schaffarzik (eds.), *Handbuch der Geschichte der Verwaltungsgerichtsbarkeit in Deutschland und Europa*, Springer, Berlin 2019.

nineteenth century. The founders of the German constitution in 1949 decided to continue this tradition. Nowadays most commentators argue in favour of a monistic system where the administrative courts would also be responsible for public torts.

Judicial review, as opposed to state liability, is usually aligned with a particular act of a public authority. Basically, the review consists in the annulment of that act, given that the act renders as illegal. This is most notably the case if the act violates an individual right. Every legal order provides for special lawsuits to initiate that review.[21] An example is the action on the grounds of Article 263 TFEU. In Germany, it is the action for annulment, *Anfechtungsklage*,[22] that serves this purpose. If an administrative act is illegal and violates a claimant's right, then the administrative court quashes the act.[23] The act, which had been valid up to that point, is void, as an effect of the decision of the court. In many cases, this is enough to save the claimant's interests. Nothing else is necessary. For instance, if the authority orders that person A shall take down a building because it was not erected in accordance with the law, and if the court concludes otherwise, namely, that the building in fact has been erected in accordance with the law, then in many cases it is sufficient to declare the authority's order void. Consequently, A's building can persist.

Besides the 'annulment function', judicial review may also include declarations about the illegality of an act. In Germany, the declaratory action applies (*Feststellungsklage*). A further example is offered by the European Convention of Human Rights. The European Court of Human Rights does not have the power to declare a domestic act that violates the convention void. It can only declare that a violation of the convention has occurred.[24]

---

21 According to Timothy Endicott, judicial review is not as such a remedy but a procedure for asking a court to give a remedy (T. Endicott, *Administrative Law*, OUP, Oxford 2009, p. 347 (n. 4)). This statement may reflect the English view. Note that the point of 'judicial review' is that it is not 'merit review'. The latter is the task of tribunals who are allowed to substitute its own decision 'on the merits' for that of the administration, whereas the former applies to courts. The courts are restricted to legal errors and cannot decide as if they were an administrative body (P. Cane, 'Judicial Review and Merits Review: Comparing Administrative Adjudication by Courts and Tribunals' in S. Rose-Ackerman and P.L. Lindseth (eds.), *Comparative Administrative Law: Research Handbooks in Comparative Law*, Edward Elgar Publishing, Cheltenham, UK, Northampton, MA, USA 2017, pp. 426–448; G. Kleve and B. Schirmer, above n. 13, pp. 128–129).

22 The translation is not easy. Likewise the translation in A. von Arnauld, 'Damages for the Infringement of Human Rights' in M. Schmidt-Kessel (ed.), *German National Reports on the 19th International Congress of Comparative Law*, Mohr Siebeck, Tübingen 2014, pp. 545–580, 545; alternatives: revocatory action, action for rescission, act to set aside (the latter in G. Robbers, *An Introduction to German Law*, Nomos, Baden-Baden 2017, p. 108), suit for invalidity (M. P. Singh, *German Administrative Law*, Springer, Berlin 1985, p. 118).

23 In English administrative law, the quashing order is one of the prerogative remedies, aside of the prohibition and the mandatory order (G. Kleve and B. Schirmer, above n. 13, p. 133).

24 Compare section 41 and section 46 ECHR.

The two pillars – judicial review and state liability – represent the core idea of the rule of law. There are good reasons to claim that a state governed by the rule of law shall, on the one side, provide for judicial review along the lines considered above. Manifesting this spirit, Article 19 para. 4 German Constitution (*Grundgesetz*) provides: 'Should any person's rights be violated by public authority, recourse to the court is open to him.' This provision was praised as 'inserting the apex in the arch of the *Rechtsstaat*' by a contemporary commentator.[25] Besides the judicial review, the rule of law surely requires the state to provide for a minimum compensation, in case the state harms basic interests of its citizen. But still, the idea of the rule of law is indeterminate. It needs to be interpreted, and it allows for different systems of public redress. Viewed in this light, thinking about remedies in public law is an attempt to interpret the rule of law.

4. INTERNAL REVISION: FROM RIGHTS TO ACTIONS

4.1. THE COMMON GROUND OF THE TWO PILLARS

The standard presentation of remedies in public law obviously creates an asymmetrical arrangement. It assembles procedural instruments on the one hand (actions in judicial review) and substantive claims (torts, liability) on the other. The two pillars are not of the same kind. This already indicates that a further step is necessary to reach a balanced, symmetrical arrangement.

Of course, the torts-pillar also has a procedural side. There are certain actions available to realise a tort claim. Again, in Germany these claims fall into the ordinary jurisdiction. In EU law, the court of justice is responsible for claims invoking a claim on the grounds of Article 340 TFEU. These actions normally do not attract special attention when it comes to the issue of redress against public authorities. Only the judicial-review-pillar is represented in combination with procedure. This reflects the widespread assumption that in public law the procedural side is much more important for the operating of the law, and, hence, for the understanding of its provisions, than in private law.[26]

Though, judicial review is a complicated issue. It stands beside other forms of control of public administration. There are commissions, ombudsman, auditors and so on. Judicial review as such is also diverse. There are important

---

25 See R. Thoma, 'Über die Grundrechte im Grundgesetz für die Bundesrepublik Deutschland (1951)' in R. Thoma, *Rechtsstaat – Demokratie – Grundrechte: Ausgewählte Abhandlungen aus fünf Jahrzehnten*, ed. by H. Dreier, Mohr Siebeck, Tübingen 2008, pp. 468–482, 468.

26 A short discussion of this point in T. Endicott, above n. 21, p. XI.

differences between the legal systems. Comparing the legal systems of Germany, England and the EU, different types of judicial review can be identified, depending on their relation to rights and how the issues of standing and merits are treated.

Standing can be rights-based or non-rights-based. The *actio popularis* (group or collective action), which is provided for particularly in environmental law, is of a non-rights-based nature. An important example is the EU Public Participation Directive[27] which requires that, inter alia, certain non-governmental organisations shall have access to judicial review procedures in environmental matters.[28] Standing solely depends on the formal recognition of an organisation as such an authorised organisation. Besides this, standing can be grounded on mere interest. This is the overall approach in England. A rights-based standing is given only if the claimant can substantiate the possibility of a violation of a right. This is the traditional German model, yet it has always been accompanied by forms of non-rights-based forms of review.

The merits are structured and shaped in accordance to the requirement of standing. For example, the court must scrutinise the illegality of the act or it must examine whether a claimant's right was violated. With regard to standing as well as to the merits, a further distinction applies. Some legal orders give the courts discretion when assessing the criteria. So a table of judicial review types can be created (see Table 1 below).

A discretionary model of the merits can be found in English administrative law. The courts have discretion whether to grant a remedy and if the remedy is a declaratory order, a quashing order or something else.[29] The claimant does not have to invoke and does not have to have a right to the remedy.[30] This arrangement certainly represents the dominance of the public function of judicial review.[31] The public function prevails over the idea of individual legal protection. Actually, a system of such a judicial review cannot be interpreted as protecting rights.[32]

---

27 Directive 2003/35/EC of the European Parliament and of the Council of 26 May 2003 providing for public participation in respect of the drawing up of certain plans and programmes relating to the environment and amending with regard to public participation and access to justice Council Directives 85/337/EEC and 96/61/EC, Official Journal of the European Union, L 156/17.

28 The directive relates to the 'UNECE Convention on Access to Information, Public Participation in Decision-making and Access to Justice in Environmental Matters' (Aarhus Convention) from 1998. The domestic law of the EU Member States implementing the directive ensures compliance with the convention.

29 J.N.E. Varuhas, above n. 4, p. 66 (with some modifications especially for human rights litigations owed to the influence of the Human Rights Act).

30 T. Endicott, above n. 21, pp. 395, 608, 615.

31 See for instance J.N.E. Varuhas, above n. 4, p. 67.

32 See the bitter comments in P. Birks, above n. 2, p. 36, with regard to common private law: 'Discretionary remedialism is a view of the law in which the people subject to the law have

Table 1. **Judicial review types compared**

	Rights-based	**Non-rights-based**		
Standing measure	possibility of a violation of the right	no substantive requirements (*actio popularis*)	interest	
assessment	non-discretionary		discretionary	non-discretionary
Merits measure	violation of the right	illegality of the act	illegality of the act	illegality of the act
assessment	non-discretionary	non-discretionary	discretionary	non-discretionary
Examples	action for annulment (Germany)	domestic actions, as implementation of Directive 2003/35/EC (in England guaranteed by an extensive construction of interest-based standing[33])	quashing order (England)	procedure under Article 263 para. 4 TFEU

In Germany, a rights-based access to the courts as well as a non-rights-based-access are available.[34] Within the rights-based access, rights are necessary for standing (a right being possibly violated) as well as for the merits (a right being definitely violated).

At least within a right-based model of judicial review, it could be said that a symmetry between the two pillars of public redress exists. The substantive claims of state liability would be complemented by the rights being administered in judicial review. But at this point a look closer at the concept of a right is necessary. A right does not necessarily include all the positions that come into being if the right is violated. This is actually one of the basic assumptions of the law of remedies in common law. A right is not the same as the legal positions

no defined rights.' This goes hand in hand with a profound criticism of the remedy-as-discretionary-measures-view, see ibid., p. 23: 'a nightmare trying to be a noble dream … destruction of the fragile intellectual structure of the law'.

33 See Milieu (ed.), 'Measures on access to justice in environmental matters (Article 9(3)). Country report for United Kingdom', 2007 (http://ec.europa.eu/environment/aarhus/pdf/conference_summary.pdf, accessed 12.11.2018), p. 11.

34 In Germany, there is much dispute on the question if the rise of non-rights-based-review, initiated by EU law, is alien or contrary to the German system (see for instance K.-P. Sommermann, '§55 Entwicklungsperspektiven der Verwaltungsgerichtsbarkeit' in K.-P. Sommermann and B. Schaffarzik, above n. 20, pp. 1991–2014, 1992). The debate can be deflated, recognising that there are just two systems, working side by side. However, this discussion does not affect the dispute mentioned in the text, concerning the correct understanding of the merits within a rights-based model that is introduced in the following pages.

needed to enforce the right. A distinction must be drawn between the right and the remedies that are created by the violation of the right. This applies to public law as well, which leads to the next point.

4.2. JUDICIAL REVIEW BASED ON SUBSTANTIVE CLAIMS

If judicial review rests on a violation of a right, what does 'violation of a right' mean?

To tackle this problem, the action-based approach outlined above will be followed (2.). Legal positions have to be developed by way of an adjustment to actions. The venture starts with the action for annulment, from then on leaving the comparative task behind and focusing on German administrative law. As shown, the action for annulment is well founded if the invoked right is really violated. The relevant provision of the Administrative Courts Act (section 113 para. 1 *Verwaltungsgerichtsordnung*) necessitates that the act renders illegal and violates a claimant's right. The remedy of annulment (*Aufhebung*) does not lie in the court's discretion. Yet, caution is needed here to appreciate the exact role of rights. The question is: Can the right that is violated be identified with the right that feeds the annulment? Or to put in terms of remedies: is the right violated the right to the remedy?

In the author's view, and also in the view of other scholars, there is need for an additional legal position. This is a substantive claim/entitlement to annulment (*Aufhebungsanspruch*). Judicial review is thus based on a substantive claim.[35] But this thesis is challenged in German administrative law doctrine. Some authors argue in favour of an understanding that does not rely on such an entitlement. The violated right as such would be sufficient. A comprehensive discussion of the issue is beyond the scope of this chapter; only the crucial point shall be identified and illustrated by way of presenting some essential arguments (and the reader may excuse the one-sidedness of the considerations).

First, what is the thesis about? When an act is illegal and violates a person's right, this person is entitled to claim the annulment of that act. Notably, this claim is not directed to the court. It is directed towards the administrative body that has enacted the act. Yet, one may ask why it is necessary to shift the

---

35 The key reference is H.H. RUPP, *Grundfragen der heutigen Verwaltungsrechtslehre: Verwaltungsnorm und Verwaltungsrechtsverhältnis*, Mohr Siebeck, Tübingen 1991, pp. 249–261; a recent position for instance C. ENDERS, '§53 Abwehr und Beseitigung rechtswidriger hoheitlicher Beeinträchtigungen' in W. HOFFMANN-RIEM, E. SCHMIDT-AßMANN and A. VOßKUHLE, above n. 12, pp. 1171–1241, 1177. The opposite standpoint is forcefully developed in J. BUCHHEIM, above n. 9.

focus from the court to the administration. In the author's view, an account of administrative law is needed that depicts it as an order of behaviour. If the annulment of an administrative act is conceived as being owed purely by the court, the fact that administrative law primarily is directed to public authorities would not be taken into account. It regulates their competences vis-à-vis the citizens. Administrative law regulates legal relations between authorities and citizens. Purely procedural remedies would not fit into a system of such relations. Ultimately, one is thrown back to the idea of the *Rechtsstaat* (rule of law) at this point, and how it should be construed. Of course, it is a major achievement if judicial review against every act of the public power is available and if the constitution guarantees such a protection. But this represents only a fallback position. Primarily, the right holder is in a certain position towards the administrative body.[36] Rights must be respected. If rights are violated at all, it would be better if the rights-holder could rectify the situation without the help of the courts, in direct confrontation with the authority itself. And if it had to be the court that declares the act void instead of the administrative authority, then the court's decision expresses an accusation toward the authority: in principle, the authority should have done the annulment itself, in fulfilling the individual's claim.

Yet, judicial review embraces more than the annulment of a legal act. There are cases in which the violation of an individual right cannot be repaired by an annulment. The administrative body is then obliged to do something else. If the public authority violates a right by a non-legal act, the rights-holder cannot be protected by an annulment, since a real or physical act cannot be annulled. Annulment is an activity proceeding in the realm of 'ought'. It cannot happen within the realm of facts. A classic example: If the state instructs homeless people to a building, and if the instruction violates the owner's right, the mere annulment of the instruction order does not remove the people from the house. They may not voluntarily leave the house. In such a case the owner is entitled to demand from the administrative body that it removes the people. Or if an authority publishes an offending declaration, the offended person can claim that the authority removes the declaration, if possible, and that the authority apologises for the offense. In these examples, in German law, the claim for removal of consequences applies, *Folgenbeseitigungsanspruch*. If the interference had factual consequences which cannot be repaired just by revoking the legal act, the individual can demand the action which is necessary to do away with these consequences.

---

36 This proposition is contested by S. Haack, *Theorie des öffentlichen Rechts*, Mohr Siebeck, Tübingen 2017, pp. 18–20, but without rejecting the claims-oriented view of judicial review (ibid., p. 66).

If the authority does not fulfil obligations of that kind, it will be condemned by the court to do so. The claim supports the action for performance, the *Leistungsklage*.[37] By this action the court can oblige a public authority to grant something to the individual. In the German legal system, the action for performance explicitly rests on a substantive claim that bears the performance. Thus, the court has to examine if the conditions of the basis of the claim are fulfilled.

4.3. FROM RIGHTS TO ACTION

Thus, all actions rest on substantive claims. Yet, there are many analytical steps to take before understanding how a claim arises from a norm. To refine the revision of the standard picture, these steps must be elucidated. The considerations are somewhat abstract and they are presented in very condensed way, although they provide evidence for the conception argued here. They serve as the analytic frame for everything else.[38]

Every norm creates a duty, but it does not necessarily create a right. Some norms, however, may grant something to an individual. Such a granting can take two different forms that can be grasped by the way they operate from the view of the beneficiary. If the norm promises not to interfere with the interest shaped by the duty, it grants the individual a negative status. An example are liberty rights in their 'classic' understanding, seen as creating a defence position against the state. Yet, ordinary statutes may also grant such a position, for instance, if a provision of construction law prescribes a minimum distance between neighbouring buildings. The buildings' owners are granted with a right, embracing the maintenance of the distance. The classic view of human rights – understanding them as defensive rights – conceives of such rights as creating free spaces for the individual. If the state interferes with this sphere, it violates the liberty of the individual. Such a liberty, as a legal phenomenon, is basically a *status* of that person, defined by the entitlement produced by the human rights norm. The status is transformed into a right only at a second stage, as the law endows the status-holder with a right to omission of

37 Translated as 'general suit for affirmative relief' in SINGH (above n. 22), p. 118.

38 There are many resources for the following analysis to be found in the German public law literature. Beside of analytical legal theory, the author refers to the seminal investigations done by Georg Jellinek, see G. JELLINEK, *System der subjektiven öffentlichen Rechte*, 2nd edn., Mohr Siebeck, Tübingen 1905, p. 105; an elaborated account is H.H. RUPP, above n. 35. Further references are given in A. FUNKE, above n. 6. In contrast, Wesley Newcomb Hohfeld's famous studies on legal relations, which English readers may expect as a major reference insofar, rather resemble a parallel development in analytical legal thinking.

interferences. The entitlement for omission is rather the legal power to enforce the basic status. Actually, the individual has this right always and everywhere, but it often comes into sight only if an interference is imminent. Yet there is a third stage: if the status is violated, that is to say if the states interferes with the liberty unlawfully, a new entitlement is triggered: the citizen has a right to removal. A right to removal in turn can take different forms. If the interference consists in an obligation created by an administrative act, the citizen has a claim to revoke the act. Notably, this claim is directed to the administrative body that issued the act. If the authority does not fulfil the claim, it can be brought to court.

Other norms do not create a negative status, but a positive status. They grant a benefit. The benefit can stem directly from a statute or from a contract.[39] Such a positive status is actually again a bundle of positions. First, there is the sheer granting of a benefit arising from the norm; second, this position is typically combined with the ascription of the legal power to enforce the granting. This entitlement is the claim for performance (of the benefit). Performance means that the individual has a right vis-à-vis the authority to perform an action. This substantive claim is, if not fulfilled, brought to court.

With regard to the actions realising these claims, things are certainly complicated. It is most important to see that the scheme of actions is not simply congruent with the two statuses. The action for performance covers all the claims, except those claims that can be fulfilled by the court itself. These claims are assigned to the action for annulment. Thus, two chains of entitlements – regarding the negative and the positive status – can be constructed, as is summarised in table 2.

Table 2. From rights to action – the chains of entitlements

Negative status
Norm → duty → granting of a non-interference → legal power to enforce the granting (right) → claim for removal of an act that violates the right → action for annulment
Positive status
Norm → duty → granting of a benefit → legal power to enforce the granting (right) → claim for the benefit → action for performance

Thereby closing the 'internal' revision of the two-pillars-model, can be summarised: The pillar of judicial review, just as the pillar of state liability, is grounded on claims. In judicial review, these claims are basically about the omission and the removal of acts violating rights.

39 A benefit is even related with the negative status, insofar the claim triggered by a violation of negative right ('third stage' in the paragraph before) is concerned.

5. EXTERNAL REVISION: BEYOND VIOLATIONS OF RIGHTS

An external revision of the standard picture constitutes the next step. The operation starts with the observation that remedies are not exhaustive to cover judicial actions against the state.[40] Administrative bodies do not always act wrongly, however, they are confronted with legitimate claims. There are at least two areas where the courts judge upon individual rights *without* having to assume that a right was violated. The courts truly give redress, and in a way, they review the behaviour of an authority, but the claims they decide upon do not arise out of violation of rights. To put it differentially: there are substantive claims against the state that cannot be conceived as stemming from a violation of a right.

Two groups can be identified in this respect. The first one, again, is linked to the action for performance (*Leistungsklage*). This action not only operates as a reaction to a violation of a right. A statutory provision may grant the position to get a building permission under fixed conditions or to get a certain amount of social welfare. Or a public authority may enter a contract with an individual providing for a government aid. In all these cases, the beneficiary gets a certain entitlement. Such an entitlement is a simple (or direct) claim for a performance (*Leistungsanspruch*) created by a beneficial norm, be it a statute or a contract. In other words, the norm creates a positive status.

So, what happens with the entitlement if the authority does not fulfil the claim for a performance? Similar to the claim for annulment, one may think that a new, further claim is triggered in such a case. But this would be a needless duplication. The claim remains the same. If the state does not award the building permission, if it does not grant the social welfare, if it does not grant the government aid – it would make no sense to count this behaviour as a wrong that causes a legal reaction. Of course, the behaviour is wrong, but it does not change the beneficiary's primary legal position. This position persists. If an action is brought to court, the court does decide upon this original legal position. Thus, one can conclude that – unlike in English private law, where specific performance is conceived as a remedy – the idea of remedy does not apply. The core idea of judicial review, consisting in an annulment of a particular act, is left.

However, there is another group of claims for performance. These claims are a little bit closer to violations of rights, but still the courts grant redress without having to assume that a right was violated. A classic example is expropriation.

---

40 This is similar in common law, where the remedies perspective neither is sufficient. '(T)he language of wrongs and remedies cannot properly be applied to every case the claimants bring into court', P. Birks, above n. 2, p. 6.

It is widely accepted that under certain conditions the state is allowed to expropriate the owner of a property. The state only has to pay a compensation for the expropriation. There is indeed an interference with the property right, but this interference is justified. So, there is definitely no violation of that right, but still, the state is obliged to give financial compensation for the loss. Some legal orders also provide for compensatory claims in similar situations. For instance, in Germany, the ordinary courts are responsible for compensations resulting from 'sacrifice' (*Aufopferung*), a specific claim for someone who bears a special load for public interests.[41] For example, if a policeman fires at an aggressive attacker, and one bullet hits an innocent passer-by, this person has a right to compensation for his/her losses. The group of claims for compensation resulting from expropriation or sacrifice somehow stands between the two pillars of judicial review and public tort. A right may be restricted, or an interference may happen, but on a legal basis. Again, the standard picture of public redress – judicial review and state liability side by side – gets blurred.[42]

6. A NEW PICTURE: PUBLIC REDRESS, STRICTLY BASED ON CLAIMS

It is time to transform the rather critical observations into a positive account. How can one conceive of public redress in German administrative law?

When asking this question, one should not forget that courts have jurisdiction over administrative law issues without having any rights involved. This is the area of group actions and of interest-based actions (see above, 3.). From the outset, no scheme of rights can grasp this area. Yet, even some of these actions may be open to a right-based reconstruction. With regard to rights, the main result of the foregoing considerations is, as simple as it is: There are more than two pillars in public redress, but they are of the same kind and can be called claims. This result, which is represented in table 3 below, does not change the law, but it is supposed to change our assessment of the law.

If a claims follows from the positive status established by a norm, no further ordering is necessary. If a claim is related to the negative status, things are getting very complex. The individual negative right and the claims resulting from a violation require precise structuring, subject to the practical aims the claimant pursues, to the 'translation' of these aims into doctrinal purposes and to the legal bases of the claims.

41 Labelled 'Sacrificial encroachment' in A. von Arnauld, above n. 22, p. 554.

42 And again, the author's corrections correspond to the criticism by Peter Birks, who points out that the courts are not only concerned with wrongs (P. Birks, above n. 2, p. 25).

Table 3. German public redress revised[43]

	Negative status			Positive status
Practical aim of the rights-holder	Negation: realisation[44] of a right	Reparation: settlement of the consequences of a violation of the right	Compensation: settlement of the consequences of certain burdening public conduct	Realisation of a right
Purpose in terms of doctrine	(1) Prevention of a violation of a right (2) Establishment of the state that would exist if a violation of the right would not exist anymore	Establishment of the state that would exist if a violation of the right would never have happened	Removal of a loss of property that has been caused by a lawful public conduct	Performance of a claim
Claim	(1) Claim for omission of an act violating a right (2) Claim for removal of an act violating a right (including removal of the consequences of the act)	Official liability (restitution in finance)	Compensation for an expropriation compensation for a sacrifice (different forms)	Claim in dependence of its legal basis (e.g. statute)

Law of reactions (*Reaktionsrecht*) =
law of remedies in a narrow sense

There arises a new branch of law which can be called 'law of reactions' (*Reaktionsrecht*).[45] The law of reactions – as a law of remedies in a narrow sense –

[43] The table cannot be discussed in every detail. To keep it accessible, not all relevant claims are depicted. The systematisation builds on recent accounts to the topic (but includes some refinements), see W. Höfling, above n. 12, pp. 1055, 1100; M. Morlok, above n. 12, p. 1119; C. Enders, above n. 35, pp. 1176–1177. The traditional, conventional model, which presumably is the predominant one, is represented by the classic monograph F. Ossenbühl and M. Cornils, *Staatshaftungsrecht*, 6th edn., Beck, München 2013.

[44] The term is adopted from J.F. Hoffmann, in this volume, pp. 45–60.

[45] This terminology is occasionally used in German public law doctrine, see for instance J.F. Lindner, *Theorie der Grundrechtsdogmatik*, Mohr Siebeck, Tübingen 2005, p. 509; B. Grzeszick, *Rechte und Ansprüche: Eine Rekonstruktion des Staatshaftungsrechts aus den subjektiven öffentlichen Rechten*, Mohr Siebeck, Tübingen 2002, p. 140; H. Sauer, *Folgen hoheitlicher Rechtsverletzungen: Theorie und Dogmatik des öffentlichen Reaktionsrechts*, Düsseldorf 2014 (unpublished manuscript); W. Höfling, above n. 12, p. 1089; C. Enders, above n. 35, p. 1175.

is just a part of a comprehensive corpus of rights and claims. The 'reactions' can be conceived of as remedies, but not as if they would be different from rights. The reactions themselves are rights, in the form of substantive claims. Which of these positions is seen as primary depends on the point of view. From the point of view of adjudication, the legal reactions are the essence. From a behavioural point of view, which must not be neglected, the rights basically protect the individual's negative status. Moreover, the term 'remedies' blurs the line between claims and actions, hence, between substance and procedure, whereas the importance of this line has been most strongly emphasised in the foregoing considerations.

A view that identifies a law of reactions this way has important consequences. Only a few of them can be highlighted here. The scheme directly serves doctrinal purposes. Statutory provisions can be seen in a new light. For instance, the rules on administrative procedure also have an effect on these claims (especially the claim to abolish an administrative act). The German Administrative Procedure Code provides for a time limit that the addressees of an administrative act have to meet if they want to revoke the act. Such a provision also shapes the claim for an annulment. It does not touch upon the right not to be interferred with public action, but it limits the claim for annulment of such an action temporally.

The perspective of a law of reactions can help us to determine where new statutory rules are necessary, and how they should be shaped. Within the standard picture, much of the consequences of a violation of a right are processed within the single concept of a right. Once rights and claims are distinguished, it may be observed that there is no logical connection between a right and certain reactions. Legal regulations are needed. The rights as such may keep untouched, but the reactions can be shaped by the legislator. A claim for removal of a violation may expire under some circumstances, but this does not affect the right that was violated. At the moment much of the law of reactions operates on a slippery base. The statutes regulate this regime only partially. The rest is governed by general principles of administrative or public law which oscillate between customary law and legal doctrine. One should consider that these principles are often constructed by case-law, which does not always evolve coherently (not to say it is arbitrary from time to time).

The formation of a law of reactions is particularly important for the doctrine of human rights. In the foregoing only a small section of this has been observed. There is room for legislative design of such a law regime.[46] Since such a design, although necessary as a definition of legal reactions, must preserve the sense of

46 Although there is much literature on state liability, there is only a small number of enquiries about this point. Positive exceptions are J.F. Lindner, above n. 45, pp. 509–533; B. Grzeszick, above n. 45, pp. 153–154; M. Morlok, above n. 12, p. 1162.

the rights, the legislative task arising is highly complicated. If legal provisions are assessed as being relevant for the law of reactions, they can be evaluated more precisely with regard to their constitutionality. For instance, insofar the law of reactions restricts claims for removal of interferences with human rights, a constitutional matter arises.

With regard to the relation between the individual on the one hand, and the administrative body on the other, it can be seen that there is an administrative procedure necessary to assert the claims. In German administrative procedure law, opposition proceedings (*Widerspruchsverfahren*) may be initiated in such a case. Such proceedings have to be conducted by the administrative authority which has issued the act. The authority must prove the legality and the practicality of the act. The claimant must first run through the opposition proceedings before his/her action before the court is admissible. Yet, in the last years the scope of this proceedings has been restricted by the legislation. This means that in many cases the claimants have to go directly to the court to get redress. Further consideration must be given to the question of whether it is constitutionally necessary – by means of the rule of law – that such ordinary proceedings are available for the claimant.

Last but not least: legal education. Judicial review and state liability are traditionally taught in separate courses, and they are treated in separate textbooks. Once it is understood that both are based on claims, they converge. In a way, judicial review is a part of the doctrine of state liability, understood as the regime of the claims against the state.[47] Barely an author has so far deeply reflected this point and its consequences for legal training.

7. CONCLUSION

'At the bottom of a problem always a German is sitting.' Voltaire is supposed to have said this. He could have had the author in his mind, whose opinion is that the standard picture of public redress, presenting judicial review and state liability as two distinct pillars, is flawed. A central argument in favour of this thesis is that judicial review has to be interpreted in a 'claims-kind' way. Judicial review is not a procedure that can be initiated if a right was possibly violated, but serves the enforcement of a substantive claim that arises from the violation of the right. Public redress, if concerned with rights (which is not the case with group actions), then can be coherently constructed and set on one ground: claims.

Of course, there are many open questions that were not raised in this chapter.

First and foremost, they concern the public control function of the administrative courts. This control function, for instance, bears group actions

[47] Compare M. Morlok, above n. 12, p. 1119, and C. Enders, above n. 35, p. 1216.

(see above, 4.1), and, thus, the coexistence of subjective and objective modes must be managed by the courts as well as by legal doctrine.[48] The manifold reductions of judicial competences, pertinent if administrative norms create margins for the administration, provide another implication of the control function. The most important example is discretion. Pursuant to the traditional account of this problem, the courts' competences must be reconciled with the administration's competences.[49] Judicial and executive functions have to be separated. If the administrative body has discretion, the court must respect it; deference to the authority's decision is necessary. This is relevant for the claimant's individual rights: there is only a right to an error-free exercise of the discretion. In contrast, in the perspective of a law of reactions the question arises if this reduced competence can be explained as a function of the claimant's substantive legal position. Thereby the focus shifts, and new doctrinal questions arise. Instead of asking if deference shapes the individual's right, one would rather have to explain deference as a function of substantive claims. However, in doing so one would run the risk of eliminating the control function of the administrative courts. This function still needs to be maintained.

---

48 See above, n. 34.

49 W. Brohm, 'Zum Funktionswandel der Verwaltungsgerichtsbarkeit' (1984) *Neue Juristische Wochenschrift*, 8; E. Schmidt-Aßmann, *Kohärenz und Konsistenz des Verwaltungsrechtsschutzes: Herausforderungen angesichts vernetzter Verwaltungen und Rechtsordnungen*, Mohr Siebeck, Tübingen 2015.

ECONOMICS OF REMEDIES

The Perspective of Corporate Law

Klaus Ulrich SCHMOLKE

1. INTRODUCTION

The notion of remedies as a distinct field of research comes easily to a law-and-economics scholar. This is due to the fact, that law and economics employs a functional approach to law. And since the function of law, i.e. the promotion of welfare,[1] is perceived to be the same across the different fields of substantive law, it is only to be expected that this common function results in common features of remedies which are not specific to a certain field of substantive law.[2] Acknowledging the common function and, as a consequence, the common features of remedies it makes perfect sense to consider the law (and economics) of remedies as a discrete and cross-cutting field of research which helps to avoid 'duplicated work and missed insights.'[3]

However, it has only recently been lamented that the substantial interaction which would be expected between scholars in the fields of 'law and economics' and 'remedies' is not taking place.[4] The author of this lamentation attributes the sorry state of affairs largely to the effect that law-and-economics scholars tend to ignore the black-letter law and the doctrinal background remedies scholars have to take into account.[5] This critique, however, assumes a service function of law and economics for doctrinal research that is not self-evident. It appears to be rather the task of remedies scholars to translate the concepts and insights of law and economics to the law of their respective jurisdictions.[6] This can be done in order to interpret the law as it stands in a way that serves efficiency,[7] or to evaluate such law and to compare it to alternative legal arrangements.

This chapter endeavours to accomplish the latter task in respect to the remedial issues of corporate law and, therefore, proceeds as follows: After (2.) a brief introduction to some core concepts of the economics of remedies, (3.) these concepts will be applied to some of the remedial issues of current corporate law. This will be done by referring to some highly contested issues of the German stock corporation law (*Aktienrecht*), namely the appropriate design of the shareholder rescission suit, the idea of expanding the appraisal remedy and the desirability of shareholder derivative suits.

---

1 See further below sec. 2.1.

2 A. Porat, 'Economics of Remedies', in F. Parisi (ed.), The Oxford Handbook of Law and Economics, OUP, Oxford 2017, pp. 308, 308–309.

3 Cf. S.L. Bray, 'Remedies, Meet Economics; Economics, Meet Remedies' (2018) 38 *Oxford Journal of Legal Studies* 71, 82. For a famous example of such a 'unified perspective' see G. Calabresi and A.D. Melamed, 'Property Rules, Liability Rules, and Inalienability: One View of the Cathedral' (1972) 85 *Harvard Law Review* 1089. However, while it is a promising endeavour to identify common features and issues of remedies across the different fields of substantive law, legal scholars have to remain sensitive with regard to the idiosyncrasies and divergences in the different fields of law, cf. A. Porat, 'Introduction' in A. Porat (ed.), *The Economics of Remedies*, Edward Elgar, Cheltenham and Northampton 2012, p. ix.

4 S.L. Bray, above n. 3.

5 S.L. Bray, above n. 3, p. 80.

6 Cf. H. Fleischer 'Europäische Methodenlehre: Stand und Perspektiven' (2011) 75 *The Rabel Journal of Comparative and International Private Law* 700, 725–726 (German), according to whom legal scholars assume the role of 'interface actors'.

7 As to the notion of welfare maximisation and efficiency in the legal context, see below sec. 2.1.

This is, of course, not to introduce the reader to the delicate and complex idiosyncrasies of German company law, but to give illustrative examples for cross-jurisdictional issues and problems in the field of corporate law.

2. FOUNDATION: ECONOMICS OF REMEDIES

2.1. THE GOAL: MAXIMISING SOCIAL WELFARE

From the economist's view the primary goal of remedies is to enhance social welfare by minimising social costs.[8] Thus, remedies should be designed in order to achieve efficiency. Like legal rules in general, remedies promote efficiency by setting incentives for the persons concerned to act in an efficient way.[9] Thus, tort liability, for example, is not perceived as a means that is primarily aimed at compensating the victim of the tortious activity for his/her losses. In the economist's view, tort liability has the same purpose as tort law in general, namely reducing the cost and frequency of accidents.[10] Or to put it in the famous words of Guido Calabresi: '[T]he function of accident law is to reduce the sum of the costs of accidents and the costs of avoiding accidents.'[11] Therefore, tort liability should be designed to provide the incentives for the potential injurer as well as the potential victim of a tort to act accordingly.

Essentially the same holds true for contractual remedies. In the realm of contracts the welfare maximisation goal is generally translated into the maximisation of the 'contractual surplus' of the parties to the contract.[12] These parties are also the addressees of the incentives to act efficiently provided by (remedial) contract law.[13]

The idea of incentivising human actors by the design of a remedy or otherwise rests on the assumption of humans being rationally self-interested

---

8 See, e.g., R.D. Cooter and A. Porat, *Getting Incentives Right*, Princeton University Press, Princeton and Oxford 2014, passim; A. Porat, above n. 2, pp. 308–309; from an external point of view and contrasting it with the goal of achieving the plaintiff's rightful position S.L. Bray, above n. 3, p. 80.

9 Cf. the programmatic title of R.D. Cooter and A. Porat, *Getting Incentives Right*, Princeton University Press, Princeton and Oxford 2014.

10 R.D. Cooter and A. Porat, above n. 8, p. 1 et passim.

11 G. Calabresi, The Costs of Accidents, Yale University Press, New Haven and London 1970, p. 26.

12 Cf. e.g. B.E. Hermalin, A.W. Katz and R. Craswell, 'Contract Law' in A.M. Polinsky and S. Shavell (eds.), *Handbook of Law and Economics*, vol. 1, Elsevier, Amsterdam 2007, ch. 1, p. 13; A. Porat, above n. 2, p. 309; third-party effects are typically no issue in contract law and are therefore generally ignored.

13 See, again, A. Porat, above n. 2, p. 309, stressing the common features of (remedial) tort and contract law.

beings (*homo economicus*).[14] Thus, human actors maximise their individual welfare (utility) of their own accord. What they neglect is the impact of their behaviour on the utility of others. In order to align the self-interest of human actors to the interest in maximising social welfare external costs and benefits have to be internalised. In other words: legal remedies can be perceived as a means of internalising external effects.[15]

A straightforward example for this economic function of remedies is the victim's right to damages in a case where he/she incurred losses due to a tortious act. The tortfeasor's duty to make the victim whole by paying damages ex post is the necessary consequence of showing the (potential) tortfeasor ex ante that the tortious behaviour comes with a price to be paid. If, however, the advantages of the tortious behaviour for the potential tortfeasor outweigh the disadvantages incurred by the potential victim(s) the tortious act will result in an overall welfare gain. It would therefore be efficient for the potential tortfeasor, as well as for the society as a whole, if he/she acted accordingly. Deontologically minded legal scholars will find this latter consequence hard to accept where they perceive the tortious behaviour as inherently evil or wrong. Nevertheless, at least in Continental Europe, where punitive damages are a very rare exception to the rule, the tortfeasor's victim is generally entitled only to compensatory damages. However, where a tortious act has been committed intentionally criminal sanctions are often added to the damages claim of the victim.

The aforementioned reference to a (compensatory) damages claim shows that the efficiency goal may go along with putting the claimant in his/her rightful position vis-à-vis the respondent. However, since efficiency is about *social* costs and benefits economists also take into account the effects remedies have on third parties or society as a whole.[16] Thus, *private* costs incurred by the claimant are per se of no concern to the economist as long as they are offset by benefits accruing to someone else (positive externalities), thereby reducing social costs to zero. This divergence of private and social costs leads Cooter and Porat to advocate applying the *net* harm principle in tort law.[17] Accordingly, the tortfeasor should only be liable for the harm done to victims *minus* the external

---

14 For an overview of the model of *homo economicus* and the underlying assumptions of this model, cf., e.g., S. Hargreaves-Heap and C.G. Clark 'Economic Man' in Macmillan Publishers Ltd (eds.), *The New Palgrave Dictionary of Economics*, 3rd edn., Palgrave Macmillan, London 2018, with further references.

15 Cf. also with regard to corporate law remedies A. van Aaken, 'Shareholder Suits as a Technique of Internalization and Control of Management' (2004) 68 *Rabel Journal of Comparative and International Private Law* 288, 299–300.

16 See S.L. Bray, above n. 3, p. 80.

17 This is actually an application of the Kaldor-Hicks-Criterion which asks for the net welfare gain of a certain state where all effects – positive as well as negative – are considered.

benefits of the activity.[18] In short, the internalisation of externalities via (tort) liability should also cover positive externalities. Cooter and Porat illustrate their point by the following example:

> '[A] man who owns a small company flirts with a female employee. He mistakes her politeness for encouragement and, consequently, acts improperly. In law his improper act is the tort of sexual harassment, but not a crime. As news of the event spreads, the owner suffers a loss of reputation that he values at $25. The owner's loss of reputation enables potential victims of his future misbehavior to avoid other uncompensated harms worth $40. The employee sues and the court finds that damages of $100 will perfectly compensate the victim. [... E]fficient deterrence requires the court to set damages equal to the victim's harm ($100) minus the benefit to others ($40). By setting damages equal to $60, the court will cause the wrongdoer to internalize the external cost of his wrongdoing.'[19]

2.2. CONCEPTUAL DERIVATIONS FOR THE ECONOMICS OF REMEDIES

What has been illustrated so far is that the idea of maximising social welfare and minimising social costs serves economists as the normative background for developing their concepts of an efficient remedial design. The discussion can now proceed to some of the most influential and famous economic concepts and ideas in the field of remedies.[20] The following presentation, however, has to confine itself to some rough sketches thereby omitting the finer points of the concepts.

2.2.1. *Protecting Entitlements by Property Rules or Liability Rules*

One of the most important contributions to the economics of legal remedies is authored by Guido Calabresi and A. Douglas Melamed.[21] In their seminal article on the protection of legal entitlements Calabresi and Melamed distinguish

---

18 R.D. Cooter and A. Porat, above n. 8, pp. 11–12 and pp. 165 et seq.; others argue for a negligence rule instead of strict liability when the respective activity involves positive externalities, cf. J.-Y. Kim, 'Strict liability versus negligence when the injurer's activity involves positive externalities' (2006) 22 *European Journal of Law and Economics* 95. The difference between this idea of Cooter and Porat and the traditional views of remedies scholars has been pointed out by S.L. Bray, above n. 3, p. 80.

19 R.D. Cooter and A. Porat, above n. 8, p. 192.

20 Cf. also the publications referred to by S.L. Bray, above n. 3, p. 74–75; and A. Porat, above n. 2, p. 309 et seqq.; furthermore the texts collected in A. Porat (ed.), *The Economics of Remedies*, Edward Elgar, Cheltenham and Northampton 2012.

21 G. Calabresi and A.D. Melamed, above n. 3.

'property rules' and 'liability rules'. A property rule protects an entitlement to the extent 'that someone who wishes to remove the entitlement from its holder must buy it from him in a voluntary transaction in which the value of the entitlement is agreed upon by the seller'. To put it differently and in legal terms: under a property rule the holder of the entitlement may claim injunctive relief in order to defend his/her rights. He/she has a veto power effectively hindering others from infringing his/her entitlement. A liability rule, in contrast, allows the destruction or transfer of an entitlement 'on the basis of a value determined by some organ of the state rather than by the parties themselves'. The obvious manifestation of a liability rule is a claim for damages. The liability rule does not come with a veto power of the holder of the entitlement. Why does law not always employ a property rule thereby leaving the valuation of the entitlement to the parties involved, i.e. to the market?[22] According to Calabresi and Melamed the answer is to be found in market failures where market valuation of the entitlement is unavailable or too expensive compared to a collective valuation, i.e. employing a liability rule. Such situations occur where one or more parties have an incentive to hide their true valuation of the entitlement, for example in a hold-out or free-rider scenario.[23] But the organisation of a market for the entitlement may be simply too costly to establish. To illustrate this latter point the authors refer to pre-accident negotiations where all who engage in activities which might injure individuals would have to buy the right to 'knock off an arm or a leg' in advance. On the other hand, liability rules come with costs of their own. First, there are the costs the court or public authority has to spend in order to calculate the price for the entitlement in question. Secondly, the court may fail to assess the value of the entitlement correctly, be it that it does not come up with the correct 'objective' value or that the valuation of the holder of the entitlement differs from what the entitlement is worth 'objectively'. Where these costs are higher than the costs of a market solution, the property rule is the more efficient means of protecting the entitlement.[24]

The ideas of Calabresi and Melamed have sparked a lively debate on the comparative desirability of property and liability rules. The discussion has led to certain refinements of the concept.[25] However, the distinction between property

22 As to the following see G. Calabresi and A.D. Melamed, above n. 3, pp. 1106–1110.

23 Cf., for a detailed explanation of these terms, L. Cohen 'Holdouts and Free Riders' (1991) 20 *Journal of Legal Studies* 351.

24 G. Calabresi and A.D. Melamed, above n. 3, p. 1110 also point to the fact that liability rules allow for a combination of efficiency and distributive effects.

25 See, e.g., L.A. Bebchuk, 'Property Rights and Liability Rules: The Ex Ante View of the Cathedral' (2001) 100 *Michigan Law Review* 601, with further references in n. 3; furthermore, the selective list of publications compiled by A. Porat, above n. 2, pp. 312–313; A. Porat (ed.), above n. 20, Part I (pp. 3 et seq.).

and liability rules and the different features associated with the two categories are still highly valued tools in the toolbox of every law-and-economics scholar dealing with remedies.[26]

2.2.2. *Allowing for the Efficient Breach of Contract and Law*

Probably the most famous, but definitely the most notorious remedial concept deriving from the application of the efficiency rationale is the idea of efficient breach.[27] The concept of efficient breach is typically associated with the realm of contract law where the theory is used to decide whether the breach of contract should be primarily remedied by specific performance or by damages. This remedial dichotomy can be understood as an application of the property/liability rule framework[28] with specific performance being a property rule and damages being a liability rule.[29] Stephen Shavell was one of the first to elaborate on the concept of efficient breach in contract law.[30] He first points out that in a *complete contingent contract* defined as an agreement that specifies the obligations of the contracting parties and the payments to be made under each conceivable circumstance the parties would reach a deal that meets their mutual interests best (*Pareto efficiency*). Under these assumptions the parties would want the contract to be honoured without exception. In the real world, however, contracts are usually incomplete. This incompleteness is, according to Shavell, the reason why they are enforced by means of damages, expectation damages in particular. He illustrates his point by the following example:

> 'Suppose that a buyer contracts with and pays a seller at the outset to produce and deliver a machine, that the value of having the machine to the buyer would be $200, and that the relevant contingencies concern production cost, which will become apparent to the seller before he actually begins the production process. Assume first

26 Cf. by A. Porat, above n. 2, p. 313: 'very useful in many contexts'; see also below sec. 3 where this concept is applied to remedial issues of German stock corporation law.

27 S.L. Bray, above n. 3, p. 83: 'Where economic analysis has been introduced in remedies scholarship, it tends to resemble as stock character – often a villain, usually a grizzled one, like that old gangster Efficient Breach.' For a harsh rejection of the theory, see, e.g., R.R. Anderson, 'The Compensatory Disgorgement Alternative to Restatement Third's New Remedy for Breach of Contract' (2015) 68 *SMU Law Review* 953, 958–959 with further references.

28 See above sec. 2.2.1.

29 See for this perception, e.g., A.T. Kronman, 'Specific Performance' (1978) 45 *The University of Chicago Law Review* 351; A. Porat, above n. 2, p. 313; D. Markovits and A. Schwartz, '(In)Efficient Breach in Contract' in F. Parisi (ed.), The Oxford Handbook of Law and Economics, OUP, Oxford 2017, p. 20.

30 See also for the following, S. Shavell, 'Damage Measures for Breach of Contract' (1980) 11 *The Bell Journal of Economics* 466. Arguably the first statement of the concept of efficient breach was made in 1970 by R.L. Birmingham in his article on 'Breach of Contract, Damage Measures, and Economic Efficiency' (1970) 24 *Rutgers Law Review* 273, 284 et seqq.

> that contract is Pareto efficient and depends on production costs. Such a contract would *specify* that the seller should proceed with production if the cost is less than $200 value of the machine to the buyer, and that the seller should not proceed with production if the cost exceeds $200. Now assume that the contract does not depend on production cost. [...] Clearly, under this contract, the seller would be *induced* to behave just as he was *explicitly obligated* to behave under the terms of the complete contingent contract: if the production cost is less than $200, it would be cheaper for the seller to perform than to default and pay damages; and if the cost is greater than $200, it would be cheaper for the seller to default and pay damages than to perform. (And, equally clearly, it would not be in the mutual interests of the buyer and seller to set damages for breach so high that the seller would always satisfy his contractual obligation.)'[31]

The bottom line, thus, is: damage measures for breach of contract can serve as a kind of substitute for complete contracts.[32] More deontologically minded scholars have their difficulties in accepting the idea of efficient breach.[33] But these reservations are unfounded. Elsewhere Shavell rightly points out that efficient breach does not amount to breaking a promise in a moral sense if one accepts that the completely specified contract represents the promise which ought to be kept and not the incomplete contract.[34] Tying the concept of efficient breach to the incompleteness of the contract also shows (some of) its limitations. Where the parties or statutory default rules provide for an excuse if, as in this example, production costs exceed the price agreed upon, the remedy of specific performance will also lead to efficient results.[35] Apart from that it may be more efficient to provide for specific performance, i.e. a property rule, where the courts have difficulty in estimating the value of performance.[36]

---

31 S. Shavell, above n. 30, pp. 467–468. Cf. also S. Shavell, *Foundations of Economic Analysis of Law*, Belknap Press of Harvard University Press, Cambridge and London 2004, Chapter 15 on production contracts (pp. 338 et seq.).

32 As to the reasons why there is a need for such substitutes see only S. Shavell, above n. 30, pp. 468–469.

33 For a summary and analysis of this critique of the theory on moral grounds, see, e.g., G. Klass, 'The Rules of the Game and the Morality of Efficient Breach' (2017) 29 *Yale Journal of Law and the Humanities* 71, with further references; cf. also S.L. Bray, above n. 3, p. 83.

34 S. Shavell, above n. 31, pp. 309–310. That is why D. Markovits and A. Schwartz, above n. 29, want to do away with the theory of efficient breach. They want to focus on the interpretation of the contract at hand instead. Guided by efficiency considerations they would come up with the complete contract in terms of Shavell's concept. As a consequence, efficient breach would not be a breach at all; cf. D. Markovits and A. Schwartz, above n. 29, p. 21: 'Efficient breach theory should vanish because no breach is efficient. To see why, assume that contracting agents can contract in their self-interest and that it is in the agents' self-interest to choose efficient contract terms: [...] It follows that the analyst's or court's first order question is interpretative: what does the contract at issue require, permit or forbid?'.

35 See also S. Shavell, above n. 31, pp. 312–313 with regard to the desirability of specific performance.

36 S. Shavell, above n. 31, p. 313.

Furthermore, looking at sales contracts or, more generally, at contracts for the transfer of possession instead of production contracts, the comparative evaluation of specific performance versus (expectation) damages may change again. Taking account of outside bids for the item sold, specific performance is *ceteris paribus* more desirable where the buyer has equal or better access to outside bids than the seller. The case for specific performance becomes even stronger where the likelihood of underestimating the true value of the item to the buyer is considerable. It is this rationale by which Shavell tries to explain that specific performance is the standard remedy for breach of contracts in French and German law.[37]

The general idea of efficient breach can also be applied outside the realm of contracts, namely to the infringement of the law in general. Polinsky illustrates this point in his textbook by referring to the example of double parking:

> The practice of double parking disrupts the flow of traffic and thereby imposes costs, in the form of annoyance and lost time on other drivers. By assumption the total cost imposed on other drivers is \$10 for each incident of double parking. The benefits from double parking vary depending on the circumstances. They might be below \$10 if, for example, double parking allows someone to save a couple of minutes while running into a store to buy a bar of chocolate. Or these benefits might be above \$10 if, e.g., double parking saves several minutes to obtain urgently needed (life-saving) help.[38]

An efficient legal design dissuades people from double parking where the costs are below the benefits (\$10), while it does allow double parking where the benefits exceed the costs. As a consequence, the fine for double parking should be set so that the double parker internalises the social cost (\$10) of his/her behaviour, but should not be mandated to pay more.[39] According to Gary S. Becker this concept of criminal punishment would significantly change the traditional approach to criminal law, since part of traditional criminal law would become a branch of tort law, i.e. 'social torts', in which the public would collectively sue for 'public' harm.[40]

This concept is, however, subject to qualifications. Probably, the most important qualification is that there are certain crimes 'so heinous that no amount of money could compensate for the harm inflicted', like murder or rape.[41]

---

37 S. Shavell, above n. 31, pp. 378 et seq.; for further refinements of the efficient breach concept cf. the summary given by A. Porat, above n. 2, pp. 315–316.

38 A.M. Polinsky, *An Introduction to Law and Economics*, 4th edn., Wolters Kluwer Law & Business, New York 2011, pp. 79–80.

39 Ibid. For a generalisation of this notion, see the pioneering work of G.S. Becker, 'Crime and Punishment: An Economic Approach' (1968) 76 *Journal of Political Economy* 169, 192, 193 et seqq., 198.

40 G.S. Becker, above n. 39, p. 198.

41 G.S. Becker, above n. 39, p. 196.

In such cases there is no breach of the prohibition to kill or to rape that is efficient. Therefore, one wants – from an efficiency perspective – to prevent each and every single incident of such a crime.[42] On the other hand, the law sometimes exempts efficient behaviour from the general prohibition of certain activities by way of justification or excuse without demanding any compensation in terms of fines.[43]

2.2.3. Negotiated Compensation: Liquidated Damages and Valuation Clauses

In the last decades the law-and-economics debate on remedies dealt extensively with questions of the scope of liability and the measure of damages.[44] Part of this major debate focuses on the efficiency implications of liquidated damages and the extent to which judicial review of contract clauses providing for such damages is justified.[45] With regard to the Calabresi/Melamed framework introduced earlier[46] such remedial solutions appear – at least at first glance – especially appealing. The underlying reasoning is as follows: compensatory remedies like damages are liability rules in nature. These rules are typically characterised by the employment of the courts (or public authorities) for pricing the entitlement at issue. As has been illustrated, this delegation of the pricing decision to the courts comes at a cost.[47] However, in the case of liquidated damages or – to take an example from company law – valuation clauses that provide for the measurement of the compensation to be paid to an exiting shareholder for the loss of his/her interest in the company,[48] the price (or the method of its calculation) has already been negotiated by the parties involved. Thus, by liquidated damages clauses and similar contractual provisions, the parties can avoid (or at least mitigate) the costs of external

42 Over-deterrence is, as such, no issue in these subset of crimes, see A.M. Polinsky, above n. 38, pp. 88–89.

43 With regard to the concept of efficient breach of contract some traditional contract scholars would also point to the doctrine of excuse to defend the general notion that promises have to be honoured and/or specific performance as the default remedy in case of breach. Cf. J.L. Harrison, 'A Nihilistic View of the Efficient Breach' (2013) *Michigan State Law Review* 167, 202.

44 Cf., the compilation of texts provided by A. Porat (ed.), *The Economics of Remedies*, Edward Elgar, Cheltenham and Northampton 2012, pp. 301–601; see furthermore the summary given by A. Porat, above n. 2, pp. 317 et seqq.

45 For a recent summary of the debate on liquidated damages, cf., again, A. Porat, above n. 2, pp. 325–327.

46 See above sec. 2.2.1.

47 See above sec. 2.2.1. with n. 24.

48 Cf., for a discussion of the German case law on the validity and enforceability of such clauses in a partnership agreement or the articles of association of a close corporation (*GmbH*), K.U. Schmolke 'Expulsion and Valuation Clauses – Freedom of Contract vs. Legal Paternalism in German Partnership and Close Corporation Law' (2012) *European Company and Financial Law Review* 380–419.

valuation which are the main drawback of liability rules.[49] Furthermore, the parties enjoy certainty regarding the amount to be paid in case the trigger event becomes reality in the future. There is, of course, still a cost-benefit trade-off involved when considering such clauses: the party agreeing to pay the negotiated compensation ex ante takes the risk of paying too much ex post, while the counterparty takes the risk of being paid too little. The second scenario leads to under-compensation and, therefore, creates incentives for the compensating party to trigger the compensation event, even when this would be inefficient (ex-post opportunism). The first scenario, on the other hand, leads to over-compensation which keeps the (potentially) compensating party from triggering the compensation event, even where this would be efficient.[50] In addition, the over-insured party may be inclined to provoke the event that entitles her to compensation on her own account (problem of moral hazard).[51] The parties, thus, have to take these risks into account and trade off the ex ante advantages of the compensation clause against the ex post risks.

Courts, however, who tend to focus on the ex post perspective for obvious reasons are prone to 'correct' such negotiated compensation clauses where the amount agreed upon deviates considerably from the value of the interest to be compensated, i.e. the actual loss incurred. This judicial review may vary in its intensity.[52] It appears to be justified to the extent that judges control for systematic decision-making errors of the contracting parties, leading to unrealistic expectations and assumptions about the future.[53] Be that as it may, the stricter the judicial scrutiny with regard to such clauses, the less the comparative advantages of negotiated compensation.

2.3. BEYOND THE LAW: LEGAL REMEDIES AND SOCIAL SANCTIONS

In recent times the law-and-economics literature emphasises the fact that one has to look beyond legal remedies to get the whole picture of what drives

49 See above sec. 2.2.1.

50 Cf., as to the concept of efficient breach, above sec. 2.2.2.

51 For a description of moral hazard, cf., e.g., K.J. Arrow 'Uncertainty and the Welfare Economics of Medical Care' (1963) 53 *The American Economic Review* 941, 961–962; for a very brief explanation of the term, K.U. Schmolke 'Contract theory and the economics of contract law' in E.V. Towfigh et al., *Economic Methods for Lawyers*, Edward Elgar, Cheltenham 2015, pp. 96, 110–111.

52 Cf., with regard to (the enforceability of) liquidated damages clauses and penalty clauses the contributions compiled in issue 3 of 2015 and issue 1 of 2017 of the *European Review of Private Law*. As to the enforceability of valuation clauses under German partnership and close corporation law, see again, K.U. Schmolke, above n. 48.

53 Cf. K.U. Schmolke, above n. 48, pp. 406–413.

human behaviour. Therefore, law-and-economics scholars start to investigate the interaction between legal and social or reputational sanctions.[54]

Given the efficiency goal of legal remedies, the acknowledgment of extra-legal sanctions may lead to a change in the legal design.[55] This may be the case where the sum of legal and extra-legal sanctions would lead to over-deterrence, but also where the extra-legal sanction conveys a benefit to others. The latter effect is illustrated by the sexual harassment example of Cooter and Porat presented earlier where the reputational loss of the tortfeasor conveys a benefit to others thereby reducing the overall social cost of the wrongdoing.[56]

However, courts do not necessarily need to take into account reputational sanctions for the sake of efficiency where the reputational loss solely affects the wrongdoer. To illustrate this latter case, one has only to modify the aforementioned sexual harassment example:[57]

> '[The] man who owns a small company flirts with a female employee. He mistakes her politeness for encouragement and, consequently, acts improperly. His improper act is the tort of sexual harassment, but not a crime. As news of the event spreads, the owner suffers a loss of reputation that he values at $25. The owner's loss of reputation does not benefit anyone. The employee sues and the court finds that damages of $100 will perfectly compensate the victim. Should the court award damages of $100 or $75?'[58]

Cooter and Porat argue for awarding $100: to minimise social costs the wrongdoer should generally have to internalise all the harm caused by his behaviour. In the example, the owner caused $100 of harm to the employee and $25 of harm to himself. To efficiently deter him from committing the wrong he, therefore, has to bear the whole $125 including $100 of compensatory damages awarded to the employee.[59]

Legal and reputational sanctions merge into one where the legislator provides for public denunciation of the wrongdoer. This sanction of 'naming and shaming' has been used rather frequently in new legislation. For example, Article 34 of the European Market Abuse Regulation[60] provides that 'competent

[54] Cf., e.g., E.M. Iacobucci, 'On the Interaction between Legal and Reputational Sanctions' (2014) 43 *Journal of Legal Studies* 189, providing further references; S. Baker and A.H. Choi, 'Reputation and Litigation: Why Costly Legal Sanctions Can Work Better than Reputational Sanctions' (2018) 47 *Journal of Legal Studies* 45; also R.D. Cooter and A. Porat, above n. 8, pp. 187 et seqq.

[55] Cf., in this context, also E.M. Iacobucci, above n. 54, who points to the fact that changing legal sanctions may, in turn, change the reputational effects of the sanctioned misconduct.

[56] See above sec. 2.1 with n. 19.

[57] See above sec. 2.1.

[58] This example is – again – taken from R.D. Cooter and A. Porat, above n. 8, p. 189.

[59] R.D. Cooter and A. Porat, above n. 8, p. 189.

[60] Regulation (EU) No 596/2014, OJ L 173, 12.6.2014, p. 1.

authorities shall publish any decision imposing an administrative sanction or other administrative measure in relation to an infringement of this Regulation on their website immediately after the person subject to that decision has been informed of that decision.' Thus, the overall legal (!) sanction is composed of a conventional administrative sanction, like a fine, plus public denunciation intended to result in (additional) reputational losses.

Finally, negative reputational effects – as probably the most important kind of extra-legal/social sanction – may affect the calculus of the prospective claimant whether to enforce a remedy or not. This is the case where reputational effects of a wrongdoing turn against the wronged party (and not only against the wrongdoer). Such a peculiar scenario can occur in the corporate law context where the infringement of the law or other wrongdoings are not only attributed to the human agent who acted on behalf of the company, but also to the company itself. Due to this mechanism the directors of a company may tend to abstain from enforcing a liability claim against a fellow director or executive lest the compliance breach at issue is brought to the attention of the public.[61]

3. APPLICATION: REMEDIES IN CORPORATE LAW FROM A LAW-AND-ECONOMICS PERSPECTIVE

Having laid the conceptual groundwork, this discussion may now enter the realm of corporate law in order to apply the concepts and principles of law and economics in general and the property rule/liability rule framework developed by Calabresi and Melamed in particular to the specific remedies of this field. Before doing so (3.3.), however, some clarifying words on the function of corporate law (3.1.) and the contribution of corporate law remedies to this function are in order (3.2.).

3.1. THE ECONOMICS OF CORPORATE LAW: A PRIMER

One main function of corporate law is the management of conflicts of interest among corporate constituencies, i.e. the shareholders, the managers and other stakeholders like creditors or employees.[62] These conflicts take the shape of what economists call an 'agency problem': one party, the 'principal', relies on the other

---

61 This issue is discussed in the famous German corporate law case *ARAG/Garmenbeck*, see BGH 21.4.1997, *NJW* 1997, 1926.

62 J. Armour, H. Hansmann, and R. Kraakman, 'Agency Problems and Legal Strategies' in R. Kraakman et al., *The Anatomy of Corporate Law*, 3rd edn., OUP, Oxford 2017, pp. 29, 29–31.

party, the 'agent', to act on his/her behalf. Thus, the agent's behaviour affects the welfare of the principal. The agent, however, tends to act in his/her own interest which may deviate from the interest of the principal. Thus, incentive problems arise under the condition of uncertainty, that is, uncertainty of the principal about the actions of the agent. These incentive problems result in 'agency costs' that are caused by the agent acting opportunistically to the detriment of the principal and/or the principal spending (monitoring) costs to prevent the agent from acting this way.[63]

There are three main agency problems which affect the corporation. The first involves the conflict between the shareholders as the owners of the firm and the management (board) as their agents. The second involves the conflict between majority and minority shareholders, where the former can be perceived as the agents of the latter. The law's task here is to take care of the minority's interests by preventing the majority from expropriating the minority. The third and last agency problem involves the conflict between the company and its shareholders on the one hand and the other parties with whom the company enters into contractual relationships, i.e. creditors, employees or customers, on the other.[64] With the exception of creditor protection, this third agency problem is typically not addressed by corporate law but by other fields of law, most notably labour and contract law. In German company law, however, the interests of employees are also taken care of by means of codetermination rules affecting the organisational design of the company, namely the composition of the supervisory board (*Aufsichtsrat*).

3.2. THE ROLE OF REMEDIES

Company law, thus, addresses the above-mentioned agency problems by reducing the associated costs.[65] But how so? First, company law tries to achieve this goal through organisational rules establishing a framework of checks and balances. Taking the German stock corporation law as an example, this organisational framework can be sketched out as follows: the shareholders of the corporation elect the members of the supervisory board (*Aufsichtsrat*) who, in turn, appoint the members of the managing board (*Vorstand*) for a maximum term of five years. The managing board has to manage the business of the corporation independently while owing a duty of care and loyalty to the corporation, viz. the shareholders in their entirety (*shareholder value approach*). Prior to the end of their term, members of the managing board can, as a general

63 J. Armour, H. Hansmann, and R. Kraakman, above n. 62, p. 29; see also K.U. Schmolke, above n. 51, pp. 111–113.

64 J. Armour, H. Hansmann, and R. Kraakman, above n. 62, pp. 29–30.

65 See above sec. 3.1.

matter, only be removed from office for cause. Members of the supervisory board which monitors the managing board on behalf of the shareholders can be removed anytime without cause by a supermajority vote of the general meeting. While the managing board runs the business of the corporation independently, without being bound by instructions of the supervisory board or the shareholders, the general meeting has to vote on certain critical issues like fundamental changes of the corporation, i.e. charter amendments, the issuance of new shares or mergers and divisions,[66] or the distribution of the annual profits.[67] When voting in the general meeting shareholders face fiduciary duties vis-à-vis the corporation as well as vis-à-vis their fellow shareholders obliging them to take the interests of the corporation and their fellow shareholders into account. Furthermore, stock corporation law provides for certain minority rights protecting the minority shareholders vis-à-vis the majority shareholders (and the board which for obvious reasons is inclined to do the majority's bidding).

This organisational framework is supported and buttressed by specific company law remedies. Such remedies protect the legally acknowledged interests of the respective principal (or their 'entitlements' in terms of the property/liability rule framework) against opportunistic behaviour of the agent. They do so by bestowing veto powers on the principal so that the agent cannot proceed without the consent of the principal (property rule). Alternatively, they provide for monetary compensation (liability rule).[68] The latter may take the form of a claim for damages or of appraisal rights[69] which in cases of fundamental change (e.g. merger, forming of a contractual group by control agreement) allow the shareholders to leave the company while retrieving the fair value of their investment.[70]

An example of a property rule under German corporate law is the right of each individual shareholder to demand the rescission of unlawful resolutions of the shareholders' meeting by bringing a claim before the court (*Anfechtungsklage*).[71] In contrast, the company's claim for damages in cases where its directors breach

---

66 Cf. for an overview of how corporate law deals with such fundamental changes E. Rock et al., 'Fundamental Changes' in R. Kraakman et al., *The Anatomy of Corporate Law*, 3rd edn., OUP, Oxford 2017, pp. 171 et seq.

67 Most of these rules originate in EU law, see, e.g., with regard to the issuance of new shares, mergers and divisions Art. 68(1), Art. 93, 109 and Art. 139, 156 of the Directive (EU) 2017/1132 relating to certain aspects of company law, OJ L 169, 30.6.2017, p. 46.

68 See above sec. 2.2.1. for a rough sketch of the property/liability rule framework.

69 As to the latter, see below sec. 3.3.2.

70 For a definition, cf. also J. Armour, H. Hansmann, and R. Kraakman, 'Agency Problems and Legal Strategies' in R. Kraakman et al., *The Anatomy of Corporate Law*, 3rd edn., OUP, Oxford 2017, 29, 34: '[A]ppraisal permits shareholders who object to a significant transaction to claim the value that their shares had prior to the disputed transaction – thus, avoiding a prospective loss if, in their view, the firm has made a value-reducing decision.'

71 See below sec. 3.3.1, for further details.

their duties (*Organinnenhaftung*) is a prominent example for a liability rule in corporate law.[72] Both remedies, however, may generate costs of their own which have to be borne by the company, i.e. the shareholders in their entirety. In view of these costs, the risk of nuisance suits being brought by individual shareholders who only sue to get paid for abandoning their claim has to be taken care of. The desirable design of both the rescission suit as well as the derivate shareholder suit for damages on behalf of the company have not only been the subject of considerable debate among scholars, but have also repeatedly induced the German legislator to amend the German Stock Corporation Act (*Aktiengesetz*). While having taken place against the background of the German stock corporation law, these debates touch on issues which are relevant for corporate law remedies across jurisdictions. Thus, it appears worthwhile to take a closer look.

3.3. ISSUES IN CORPORATE LAW REMEDIES: THE GERMAN CASE

The remainder of this chapter, therefore, endeavours to illustrate issues in corporate law remedies along the lines of the liability rule/property rule framework by drawing on current debates in German stock corporation law. As already indicated, the probably most prominent of these debates deal with the appropriate design of the shareholder rescission suit (3.3.1) and the German equivalent of a shareholder's derivative suit (3.3.3). Some remarks on the German version of the appraisal right[73] (3.3.2) complete the picture.

3.3.1. Rescission of Corporate Resolutions: Shareholders' Veto Power and its Drawbacks

Under German stock corporation law, a resolution of the general meeting that goes against the law or the articles of association is void only in exceptional cases. Generally such resolutions are merely voidable.[74] After a certain period of time (one month) the resolution becomes incontestable, unless a specific suit is brought against the company by which the claimant demands the rescission of the unlawful resolution (*Anfechtungsklage*).[75] If the claimant is successful

72 Cf. A. van Aaken, above n. 15, esp. p. 300 with n. 35.

73 For some general remarks on the appraisal right, see above sec. 3.2.

74 Cf. ss. 241, 243 German Stock Corporation Act (*Aktiengesetz*).

75 Cf. s. 246 German Stock Corporation Act. For a comparative description and analysis of the German shareholder rescission suit, see M. Gelter 'Mapping types of shareholder lawsuits across jurisdictions' in S. Griffith, J. Erickson, D.H. Webber, and V. Winship (eds.), *Research Handbook on Representative Shareholder Litigation*, Edward Elgar, Cheltenham 2018, pp. 459–481, esp. pp. 475–478.

the court will declare the resolution void.[76] According to the German stock corporation law, each single shareholder has the right to bring such a suit even if his/her individual rights are not affected by the unlawful resolution (so-called 'policing function' of the rescission suit).[77] This arrangement puts the single shareholder in a strong position, which has led to frequent abuses in the form of nuisance suits. That is because the suing shareholder can halt the execution of the respective resolution for a considerable time and – in the worst case – thwart the underlying transaction. This is especially true where the statutory law forbids the registrar to enter the resolution in the commercial register while a rescission suit is pending, thereby preventing the underlying transaction from becoming effective (e.g. s. 16 para. 2 of the Act on Corporate Reorganisation [*Umwandlungsgesetz*] with regard to mergers). Thus, a pending rescission suit comes with a nuisance value. As a result, some professional claimants (*Berufskläger*) entered the stage and exploited this feature of the rescission suit and turned it into a business model.[78] This undesirable development led to legislative countermeasures: First and foremost, the German lawmaker introduced a fast-track clearance procedure (*Freigabeverfahren*)[79] which later on was successively expanded. As a result, the corporation can, under current stock corporation law, seek clearance for the registration of certain fundamental changes (like mergers, increase of the legal capital or the conclusion of a group agreement [*Unternehmensvertrag*]), regardless of a pending rescission suit. This clearance is granted by the court where (1) the claimant's investment in the corporation falls below a certain de-minimis threshold, (2) the claim for rescinding the resolution is obviously without merit, or (3) the delay of the resolution's effectiveness creates costs for the corporation that outweigh the harm inflicted on the claimant by granting clearance and the alleged infringement of the law is not exceptionally severe. Apart from this clearance procedure the legislator introduced a rule that bars shareholders from bringing a rescission suit where the alleged infringement of the law refers to the correct information about the calculation, amount or adequacy of certain compensatory payments and the law provides for a specific appraisal procedure (*Spruchverfahren*) to remedy the inadequacy of such payments.[80]

---

76 The court decision takes effect towards all shareholders and board members regardless of whether they have been party to the suit or not; cf. s. 248 para. 1 sent. 1 German Stock Corporation Act.

77 Cf. s. 245 no. 1–3 German Stock Corporation Act.

78 For brief summary of these developments, cf. M. Gelter, above n. 75, pp. 475–477.

79 Cf. s. 246a German Stock Corporation Act, introduced by *Gesetz zur Unternehmensintegrität und Modernisierung des Anfechtungsrechts (UMAG)*, September 22, 2005, Federal Law Gazette (*Bundesgesetzblatt*) I 2802; furthermore s. 16 para. 3 Corporate Reorganisation Act.

80 For an overview of the legislative measures that have been taken to thwart the 'nuisance suit industry' cf., e.g., W. Bayer and T. Fiebelkorn, 'Vorschläge für eine Reform des

These countermeasures were successful insofar as the number of nuisance suits declined substantially.[81] However, German corporate law scholars see the need for further reform. Especially with regard to small shareholders they are not convinced by the disparity between the substantive right to claim the rescission of an unlawful resolution and the procedural means to effectively enforce this right. A considerable number of influential scholars nowadays suggest the adoption of a more nuanced approach when it comes to the legal consequences of a shareholder suit claiming the illegality of a shareholders' resolution. They want the court to rescind the resolution only in cases of exceptionally severe infringements of the law whereas the courts should have the power to choose among a number of different remedies ranging from awarding damages, imposing a pecuniary penalty on the company or measures of 'naming and shaming' to voiding the resolution, but only with effect for the future. The court's choice of remedy should be in proportion to the severity of the infringement of the law. To support their view some authors point to section 996 of the English Companies Act 2006 according to which the Court may '[i]f it is satisfied that a petition under this Part [of the Act] is well founded, [...] make such order as it thinks fit for giving relief in respect of the matters complained of.'[82] Some scholars like to add a further differentiation according to which only shareholders who hold a sufficiently large amount of shares (*quorum*) have the power to claim the rescission of the resolution while owners of smaller shareholdings are relegated to less far-reaching remedial relief.[83]

Thus, the case of the rescission suit under German stock corporation law illustrates very well that complex remedial scenarios may call for a delicate and nuanced combination of property and liability rules in order to efficiently balance the different and partly diverging welfare implications.

3.3.2. *Appraisal Rights as a Specific Corporate Law Remedy*

The appraisal right mentioned earlier[84] is a specific corporate law remedy[85] that allows (minority) shareholders who are entitled to a compensation for leaving

---

Beschlussmängelrechts der Aktiengesellschaft' (2012) *Zeitschrift für Wirtschaftsrecht* 2181, 2182–2183 (German).

81 S. 243 para. 4 sent. 2 German Stock Corporation Act, introduced by *Gesetz zur Unternehmensintegrität und Modernisierung des Anfechtungsrechts (UMAG)*, September 22, 2005, Federal Law Gazette (*Bundesgesetzblatt*) I 2802.

82 J. Koch 'Empfiehlt sich eine Reform des Beschlussmängelrechts im Gesellschaftsrecht?' in Ständige Deputation des Deutschen Juristentages (ed.), *Verhandlungen des 72. Deutschen Juristentages*, vol. 1, C.H. Beck, München 2018, pp. F 38–39 (German) with further references.

83 Cf. W. Bayer and S. Möller, 'Beschlussmängelklagen de lege lata und de lege ferenda' (2018) *Neue Zeitschrift für Gesellschaftsrecht* 801, 804 (German) with further references.

84 See above sec. 3.2.

85 This appraisal right has a long tradition in corporate law, cf., e.g., R.B. Thompson 'Exit, Liquidity, and Majority Rule: Appraisal's Role in Corporate Law' (1995) 84 *The Georgetown*

the company (*Abfindung*) to seek a judicial assessment of the 'fair value' of their shares (*Spruchverfahren*). In Germany, this court procedure is available where (dissenting) shareholders leave the stock corporation in the course of a successful transaction constituting a fundamental change (e.g. a merger or the formation of a contractual group by control agreement) or of a coercive buy-out (*Squeeze-out*)[86].[87] This appraisal remedy represents a liability rule in terms of the conceptual framework developed by Calabresi and Melamed.[88] In accordance with this framework the origins of the appraisal remedy are tied to the emergence of large corporations and the increasingly dispersed ownership of publicly traded corporations which, in turn, led to holdout problems.[89] The recent extensions of the appraisal remedy by the German legislator at the expense of the right to claim the rescission of a shareholders' resolution referred to earlier[90] are based on a very similar logic: while the (potential[91]) veto power coming along with the right to claim the rescission of a shareholders' resolution (= property rule) creates a significant nuisance value that promotes frivolous suits, the appraisal remedy lacks such veto power.[92] It is therefore only to be expected that German corporate law scholars support the idea that shareholders are generally relegated to the appraisal remedy and, as a consequence, barred from bringing a rescission suit where the calculation, amount or adequacy of compensatory payments or of the price of newly issued shares are at issue.[93]

However, the benefits of switching from a property rule (i.e. rescission claim) to a liability rule (i.e. appraisal remedy) come at a price: the courts'

Law Journal 1, 11 et seqq. (for the U.S.); and D. Kubis in W. Goette, M. Habersack, and S. Kalss (eds.), *Münchener Kommentar zum Aktiengesetz*, 4th edn., C.H. Beck, München 2015, Vor §1 SpruchG, marg. no. 1–3 (for Germany).

86 Cf., ss. 327a et seqq. German Stock Corporation Act. In Germany, this coercive buy-out procedure is typically referred to as 'Squeeze-out'. However, in the U.S. such procedures are typically called 'freeze-outs'.

87 For a precise description of its scope of application, see s. 1 No. 1–6 German Appraisal Act (*Spruchverfahrensgesetz*). In contrast, s. 262 of the Delaware General Corporation Law (DGCL) provides for an appraisal remedy only in merger transactions, cf. C.R. Korsmo and M. Myers 'Recent developments in stockholder appraisal' in S. Griffith, J. Erickson, D.H. Webber, and V. Winship (eds.), *Research Handbook on Representative Shareholder Litigation*, Edward Elgar, Cheltenham 2018, p. 243, 244.

88 For an overview of this concept, see above sec. 2.2.1.

89 Cf., with regard to the legal developments in the U.S., W.J. Carney 'Fundamental Corporate Changes, Minority Shareholders, and Business Purposes' (1980) 5 American Bar Foundation Research Journal 69; for a brief summary C.R. Korsmo and M. Myers, above n. 87, p. 244.

90 Cf. above sec. 3.3.1; furthermore, e.g., J. Koch, above n. 82, pp. F 65–66; W. Bayer and S. Möller, above n. 83, p. 806.

91 As to the clearance procedure (*Freigabeverfahren*) by which the veto power of the suing shareholder can be overcome, see above sec. 3.3.1 with n. 80.

92 As to the (remaining) nuisance value of pursuing appraisal litigation, cf. J. Koch in U. Hüffer and J. Koch (eds.), Aktiengesetz, 13th edn., C.H. Beck, München 2018, §3 SpruchG marg. no. 8–9 (German).

93 Cf., e.g., J. Koch, above n. 82, p. F 65.

determination of the 'fair value' of the shares is costly and fraught with uncertainty.[94] In the absence of a real market transaction, the courts have to estimate what the 'fair' value of the shares at issue is. In order to accomplish this estimation task the judges have to rely on the assessment of experts, i.e. public accountants, and/or the price paid in a proxy transaction.[95] With regard to the German appraisal procedure in particular, one of its main drawbacks and the subject of constant critique is its overlong duration.[96] Due to legal amendments which were introduced when the legislator extended the procedure's scope of application[97] the (estimated) average duration of an appraisal procedure has been reduced to less than three years.[98] Concededly, this leaves still room for improvement.

The appraisal procedure, thus, comes with certain costs of its own. With regard to the legal situation in Germany, however, these costs appear to be considerably lower than the costs associated with a shareholders' rescission suit.[99] As a consequence, the case for switching from the shareholders' rescission suit to the appraisal remedy under German law, where the calculation or amount of a compensation payment or the share price is concerned, remains convincing. Having said that, the legislator should seize the opportunity to further reduce the costs of the appraisal procedure when broadening its scope of application.[100]

3.3.3. *Derivative Suits for Damages: Incentivising Shareholders to Act in the Interest of the Company*

An overview of the remedial issues of corporate law would be incomplete without some remarks on the shareholder derivative suit. By means of such

94 Cf. above sec. 2.2.1.

95 As to the question under which circumstances a transaction is deemed to be a suitable 'anchor' for determining the 'fair value' of the shares at issue, cf. R. Ronnen 'Appraisal rights in complete tender offers in Israel: a look into Israeli case law' in S. Griffith, J. Erickson, D.H. Webber, and V. Winship (eds.), *Research Handbook on Representative Shareholder Litigation*, Edward Elgar, Cheltenham 2018, pp. 229–241.

96 Cf. D. Kubis, above n. 85, marg. no. 2–3, 7, with further references; also J. Koch, above n. 82, pp. F 65–66.

97 As to the latter, cf. above sec. 3.3.1.

98 K. Henselmann, M.J. Munkert, N. Winkler and C. Schrenker, '20 Jahre Spruchverfahren – Empirische Ergebnisse zum gerichtlichen Verfahrensgang und zum Ausgang von Spruchverfahren' (2013) *Die Wirtschaftsprüfung* 1152, 1156–1158 (German); However, since there are no official statistics on the duration of the German appraisal procedure, this estimation is not undisputed. Cf. also The Company Law Committee of the Federal Bar (*Bundesrechtsanwaltskammer*), Evaluierung des Spruchverfahrensgesetzes, Opinion No. 33/2013, July 2014, sub II.1.1 with further references, online <https://www.brak.de/zur-rechtspolitik/stellungnahmen-pdf/stellungnahmen-deutschland/2014/juli/stellungnahme-der-brak-2014-33.pdf> (German). Cf. also the lists provided by VzfK e.V., online: <http://www.vzfk.de/>.

99 See above sec. 3.3.1.

100 Cf., e.g., J. Koch, above n. 82, pp. F 65–66.

a derivative suit a shareholder may claim damages on behalf of the company for a director's breach of duty.[101] Directors of the corporation are bound in their actions (and omissions) on behalf of the company by a duty of care as well as a duty of loyalty. A director who negligently breaches his/her duty to the corporation can be held liable for damages. The organisational design of the German stock corporation bestows the competence to enforce the company's claim for damages against a member of the managerial board (*Vorstand*) on the supervisory board (*Aufsichtsrat*) and vice versa. According to a famous court decision the members of the supervisory board are, in principle, obliged to enforce such liability claims against negligent members of the managing board (and vice versa). It is, thus, not within the board's free discretion whether to claim damages from the negligent director. Rather, the board may only abstain from enforcing the damages claim of the corporation where substantial interests of the corporation suggest doing so.[102] However, until very recently there were very few liability suits brought before the court. This did not come as a surprise since the members of the managing and the supervisory board develop bonds of collegiality. Furthermore, a liability suit against a managing director may raise questions about the diligent exercise of the supervisory board's duty to monitor the managerial board.

To address this (potential) enforcement problem the German Stock Corporation Act provides for a shareholder derivative suit. However, the shareholder is only entitled to claim damages on behalf of the company after he/she has passed an onerous clearance procedure before the court (*Klagezulassungsverfahren*, s. 148 German Stock Corporation Act). This clearance procedure was introduced to prevent nuisance suits which the lawmakers were afraid of due to their experience with the shareholder rescission suit.[103] The nuisance value of a liability suit – so the argument goes – derives from its negative reputational impact on the company and the absorption of the directors' resources.[104] Even so, when the current regime was introduced some authors feared that the legislator had opened the proverbial Pandora's box. However, it turned out that these fears were unfounded. To date the shareholder derivative suit is practically non-existent. Why is that? The obvious reason is that the lawmakers forgot to provide sufficient incentives for the shareholder to

---

101 For an overview of contemporary issues and questions regarding the shareholder derivative suit under U.S. law, cf. the contributions of J. Erickson, R.A. Booth, and C.R. Korsmo in S. Griffith, J. Erickson, D.H. Webber, and V. Winship (eds.), *Research Handbook on Representative Shareholder Litigation*, Edward Elgar, Cheltenham 2018, pp. 58 et seqq.

102 BGH 21.4.1997, *BGHZ* 135, 244 = *NJW* 1997, 1926 – *ARAG/Garmenbeck*; cf. also BGH 8.7.2014, *NJW* 2014, 1058; BGH 18.9.2018, *NZG* 2018, 1301.

103 As to the shareholder rescission suit under German Stock Corporation Law, see above sec. 3.3.1.

104 Cf. K.U. Schmolke, 'Die Aktionärsklage nach §148 AktG' (2011) 40 *Zeitschrift für Unternehmens- und Gesellschaftsrecht* 398, 419 (German), with further references.

initiate a derivative suit for such a suit has certain features of a public good:[105] If the shareholder succeeds the damages will be paid to the corporation of which the individual shareholder only owns a (small) fraction. The effort and costs of the suit, however, are borne by the shareholder. Therefore, rational shareholders will tend to free-ride, i.e. wait for another shareholder to bring the suit and profit from his/her success by way of their share in the company. The law tries to alleviate this problem by obliging the company to recompense the shareholder who lost the lawsuit (if the claimant were successful, the defendant, i.e. the director, would have to recompense the claimant/shareholder). This is, however, not enough. By this rule the shareholder only gets back what he/she spent beforehand. Furthermore, the risk remains that the shareholder has to bear the costs of the clearance procedure. And finally, the current legal regime does not take care of the free-rider problem.

Therefore, some scholars suggest that the law should provide for the payment of a premium to the successful shareholder.[106] However, this proposal has met harsh resistance. The opponents fear that such a premium would lead to too many actions with a rather low probability of success.[107] For the time being the incentive structure of the current regime prevents small shareholders from bringing suit.

4. CONCLUSION

From a law-and-economics perspective the primary goal of (legal) remedies is to enhance social welfare by minimising social costs. Remedies, like legal rules in general, promote this goal by setting incentives for the persons concerned to act in a way that takes account of the social costs of their actions. Because human actors are by assumption self-interested, they take account of social costs only insofar as they have to bear these costs. External costs, therefore, have to be internalised by the actor. Remedies help to achieve this cost internalisation since they provide means by which third parties who are negatively affected

---

105 Cf., also with regard to the following analysis K.U. Schmolke, above n. 104, 404–410 (German).

106 See, e.g., K.U. Schmolke, above n. 104, pp. 434–437; furthermore G. Wagner, 'Organhaftung im Interesse der Verhaltenssteuerung – Skizze eines Haftungsregimes' (2014) 178 *Zeitschrift für das gesamte Handels- und Wirtschaftsrecht* 228, 270–272; cf. also M. Adams, 'Reform des Kostenersatzrechts bei Aktionärsklagen mit Drittwirkung' (2000) *Die Aktiengesellschaft* 396, 406–410 (German).

107 Cf., e.g., M. Habersack 'Staatliche und halbstaatliche Eingriffe in die Unternehmensführung' in Ständige Deputation des Deutschen Juristentages (ed.), *Verhandlungen des 69. Deutschen Juristentages*, vol. 1, C.H. Beck, München 2012, pp. E 95–96 (German) with further references; T. Bezzenberger, 'Die derivative Haftungsklage der Aktionäre – Deutsches und US-amerikanisches Recht' (2018) *Zeitschrift für Unternehmens- und Gesellschaftsrecht* 584, 621–625 (German).

by the respective action are entitled to veto the action (property rule) or to claim compensation for their losses (liability rule). While property rules aim at inducing voluntary market transactions in which the right holder discloses the price for waiving his/her veto power, liability rules delegate the valuation of the entitlement to the courts. Both types of rules are employed in the company law context to protect the interests of shareholders. Examples from German stock corporation law illustrate the respective strengths and weaknesses of both types of rules. The right of each single shareholder to claim the rescission of an (allegedly) unlawful shareholders' resolution by which the shareholder can effectively stall the execution of the underlying transaction (property rule) can lead to very expensive holdout problems. Liability rules like the shareholder's appraisal remedy, on the other hand, may suffer from valuation problems. Additional incentive issues occur where the law employs the shareholder to protect the interests of the company, i.e. the interests of the shareholders in their entirety.

PART II

MECHANISMS OF ENFORCEMENT

PRIVATE ENFORCEMENT VERSUS PUBLIC ENFORCEMENT

Jens-Uwe FRANCK

1. INTRODUCTION

There is a shared vision of public enforcement: a government agency investigates suspicious activities. It requests information, interviews persons, inspects firms. If the agency finds a breach of the law, it brings a case before a court or it may directly require that the infringement be ceased or even impose a fine on the infringer. In contrast, private enforcement appears to be less clearly defined. The gist of the concept is that a private individual can bring an action against an infringer[1] to force them to end an illegal activity or to compensate a loss caused by an infringement. Thus, plaintiffs not only protect their own interests but also serve en passant the general interest in effective and efficient enforcement of the law. Consequently, where private individuals are in a position to file suit against a public authority to force it to take enforcement measures, this can be conceived as a hybrid that involves both private initiative and public capacity to enforce the law.

To see clearly that there can be a regulatory choice between private and public enforcement, it is useful to take the type of rule as a point of departure that might be described as 'incomplete' since it only imposes obligations on a certain individual, but – if considered in isolation – does not foresee legal consequences in case of breach. Examples may include rules such as:

- 'A business must not engage in misleading commercial practices.'[2]
- 'An undertaking must not form a cartel.'[3]
- 'An issuer that offers a security to the public must previously publish a prospectus.'[4]
- 'Manufacturers of cars must not use defeat devices that reduce the effectiveness of emission control systems.'[5]

---

1 Certainly, in a few cases an action can also be brought against an innocent third party, typically an intermediary, who is in a position to end an infringement. See M. Husovec's contribution to this volume, pp. 233–248.

2 See Article 5 of Directive 2005/29/EC of the European Parliament and of the Council of 11.05. 2005 concerning unfair business-to-consumer commercial practices in the internal market and amending Council Directive 84/450/EEC, Directives 97/7/EC, 98/27/EC and 2002/65/EC of the European Parliament and of the Council and Regulation (EC) No 2006/2004 of the European Parliament and of the Council [2005] OJ L 149/22.

3 See Article 101 TFEU.

4 See Article 3(1) in conjunction with Article 6(1) of Directive 2003/71/EC of the European Parliament and of the Council of 4 November 2003 on the prospectus to be published when securities are offered to the public or admitted to trading and amending Directive 2001/34/EC [2003] OJ L 345/64.

5 See Article 5(2) of Regulation (EC) No 715/2007 of the European Parliament and of the Council of 20 June 2007 on type approval of motor vehicles with respect to emissions from light passenger and commercial vehicles (Euro 5 and Euro 6) and on access to vehicle repair and maintenance information [2007] OJ L 171/1 ('The use of defeat devices that reduce the effectiveness of emission control systems shall be prohibited.').

Such obligations can either be supplemented by a set of rules that establish a competent authority and define its investigating and sanctioning powers, or they may be complemented by rights and remedies which are allocated to individuals, typically (but not necessarily[6]) to those individuals who are (potentially) negatively affected by an infringement. Considering the aforementioned examples, such private rights of action can be conferred upon competitors, suppliers, consumers, or investors. Certainly, any kind of mixture or combination of the two enforcement strategies is conceivable as well.

In contrast, where an area of the law has developed around rights that are attributed to certain persons, as in the case of intellectual property law, the legislator's choice in regard to potential enforcement strategies is restricted from the outset since the option of purely public enforcement is not available. Similarly, it is the very essence of a contract that the breach of an obligation the parties agreed upon triggers a remedy which is available to the aggrieved party. Thus, while it is certainly possible that contractual obligations are *also* enforced by a public authority,[7] a purely public enforcement of duties agreed upon by contract would run against the essence of contract law. As it lies in the nature of a contract that it confers private rights and imposes private obligations, to speak of 'private enforcement of contractual promises' may indeed seem tautological or irritating.

The picture changes, however, if the issue is viewed from a different angle and the option of private enforcement *through* contract law is considered. If, for instance, a defeat device that reduces the effectiveness of emission control systems and which is prohibited pursuant to the aforementioned rule, has been installed in a car, and if this means that the car is not in conformity with the contract,[8] then any contractual remedy available to the purchaser of the car will contribute to an effective enforcement of the prohibition of defeat devices. It seems clear then that contract law can be conceptualised as an instrument of private enforcement.

---

6 Rights of action can be granted, as a matter of principle, not only to parties aggrieved by a breach of the law but to everybody who wants to enforce the law in the general interest ('actio popularis'). See, e.g., P. Bucy, 'Private Justice' (2002) 76 *Southern California Law Review* 1, 13 ('common good private justice actions').

7 See, e.g., Article 7 (Right to Compensation), Article 8 (Right to reimbursement or re-routing), and Article 9 (Right to care) in conjunction with Article 16(1) ('Each Member State shall designate a body responsible for the enforcement of this Regulation as regards flights from airports situated on its territory and flights from a third country to such airports. Where appropriate, this body shall take the measures necessary to ensure that the rights of passengers are respected.') of Regulation (EC) No 261/2004 of the European Parliament and of the Council of 11 February 2004 establishing common rules on compensation and assistance to passengers in the event of denied boarding and of cancellation or long delay of flights, and repealing Regulation (EEC) No 295/91 [2004] OJ L 46/1.

8 See Article 2 of Directive 1999/44/EC of the European Parliament and of the Council of 25 May 1999 on certain aspects of the sale of consumer goods and associated guarantees [1999] OJ L 171/12.

In the following, some light shall be shed on the 'private-vs.-public enforcement' debate. In the first part, using EU internal market law as an example, it will be illustrated that the ('relative) effectiveness of private and public instruments of enforcement can be significant not only from a policy point of view but indeed in regard to questions of a legal nature in a strict sense. In the second part, taking a functional perspective, an overview of some essential considerations in the 'private-vs.-public-enforcement' debate will be provided. Finally, possible conclusions that can be drawn from these insights will be touched on briefly.

2. EU INTERNAL MARKET LAW AND THE DEBATE ON 'PRIVATE vs PUBLIC ENFORCEMENT'

In the context of EU internal market law, the question as to the appropriate roles of private enforcement and public enforcement arises not only as part of a general policy debate but regularly comes up as a legal issue. This is because to achieve the goal of a common market[9] and to remove barriers to trade due to diverging national standards, the EU legislature has traditionally focused on the harmonisation of substantive law.[10] While this focus has gradually changed over the last two decades, enforcement of EU internal market law was for a long time, by and large, left not only to the institutions of the Member States but also to domestic law. This explains why EU internal market law still contains many rules that can be characterised as 'incomplete,' as described in the introduction. As a matter of fact, the examples mentioned are all taken from EU law. But that is not the end of the story: in the ECJ's adjudication, three strands can be identified which are partly intertwined and which all became important in regard to an effective enforcement of EU internal market law.

First of all, an *effet utile*-interpretation of rules that are drafted as if they contained only a duty imposed on a private individual may indeed unveil implicit rights. For instance, Article 101 TFEU provides for the prohibition of cartels but not – at least not explicitly – for remedies or sanctions in case of an infringement.[11] Therefore, at first glance it may look as if the choice of the appropriate enforcement mechanism had been left completely to the EU legislature[12] or – in the absence of EU secondary legislation – to the Member States' legislatures who had to decide then, inter alia, whether or not to foresee

---

9 See Article 26 TFEU.

10 The effective protection of Community rights examines e.g. W. Van Gerven, 'Of Rights, Remedies and Procedures' (2000) 37 *Common Market Law Review* 501.

11 But see Article 101(2) TFEU.

12 See Article 103 TFEU.

instruments of (active) private enforcement such as competition damages claims. However, the ECJ clarified in *Courage v Crehan* that Article 101 TFEU not only contains the obligation for undertakings not to engage in coordinated activities that have as their object or effect the restriction of competition, but that it also confers a right to claim damages on those individuals who are negatively affected by an infringement of this obligation:

> The full effectiveness of Article 85 of the Treaty [now art.101 TFEU] and, in particular, the practical effect of the prohibition laid down in Article 85(1) would be put at risk if it were not open to any individual to claim damages for loss caused to him by a contract or by conduct liable to restrict or distort competition.[13]

The Court made it clear that by ascertaining a right to claim damages it intended to create a deterrent effect and thus, to strengthen the enforcement of competition law:

> Indeed, the existence of such a right discourages agreements or practices, which are frequently covert, which are liable to restrict or distort competition.[14]

Secondly, there is a longstanding adjudication based on the principle of loyal cooperation between the EU and the Member States according to which it is the latter's obligation to ensure that national rules are not

> framed in such a way as to make it in practice impossible or excessively difficult to exercise the rights conferred by European Union law (principle of effectiveness).[15]

Positively rephrased, this yardstick amounts to a test of 'practical possibility.'[16]

Thirdly, alongside the principle of effectiveness, another line of case law coexists, which is also based on the principle of loyal cooperation pursuant to Article 4(3) TEU and which specifically addresses the minimum standard

---

13 Case C-453/99, *Courage Ltd v Crehan and Crehan v Courage Ltd*, ECLI:EU:C:2001:465, para. 26.

14 Ibid., para. 27.

15 See, e.g., Case C-505/14, *Klausner Holz Niedersachsen GmbH v Land Nordrhein-Westfalen*, ECLI:EU:C:2015:742, para. 40. This requirement of effectiveness goes back to Case C-33/76, *Rewe-Zentralfinanz eG and Rewe-Zentral AG v Landwirtschaftskammer für das Saarland*, ECLI:EU:C:1976:188, para. 5 ('In the absence of such measures of harmonization the right conferred by Community law must be exercised before the national courts in accordance with the conditions laid down by national rules. The position would be different only if the conditions and time-limits made it impossible in practice to exercise the rights which the national courts are obliged to protect.'). In its subsequent case law, the Court amended the wording and introduced the phrase 'virtually impossible or excessively difficult ...'. See Case C-199/82, *Amministrazione delle finanze dello Stato v San Giorgio*, ECLI:EU:C:1983:318, para. 14.

16 P. Craig and G. de Búrca, *EU Law*, 6th edn., OUP, Oxford 2015, p. 228.

the Member States have to guarantee when they sanction infringements of EU secondary law. In the leading decision, the so-called *Greek Maize* case, the ECJ held:

> [W]hilst the choice of penalties remains within [the Member States'] discretion, they must ensure in particular that infringements of Community law are penalized under conditions, both procedural and substantive, which, in any event, make the penalty effective, proportionate and dissuasive.[17]

Subsequently, the EU legislature has taken up this triad of attributes ('effective, proportionate and dissuasive') and inserted it in a large number of EU legislative acts which, thus, contain a general provision on 'sanctions' such as, for instance, Article 17 of the Directive on Takeover Bids:[18]

> Member States shall determine the sanctions to be imposed for infringement of the national measures adopted pursuant to this Directive and shall take all necessary steps to ensure that they are put into effect. The sanctions thus provided for shall be effective, proportionate and dissuasive.

This finding is of particular interest in regard to the 'public-vs.-private-enforcement' debate because such a legal framework raises questions on the relative effectiveness of instruments of private and public enforcement. The Member States which have to guarantee an effective enforcement of EU internal market law in a certain field such as environmental law, securities regulation, consumer protection law, etc. find themselves typically not in the position to design enforcement mechanisms from scratch. Typically, since the national legislatures do not see any good reason to deviate from their established enforcement mechanisms, they make use of the instruments as they are already established to enforce domestic environmental law, securities regulation, consumer protection law, etc. This means, of course, that the same rule of substantive law – as it is part of EU law or transposed EU law – will be complemented in some Member States by elements of private enforcement, in other Member States through instruments of public enforcement, and in yet other Member States by a mixture or a combination of the two.

For instance, in the ECJ's seminal judgment in *Dassonville*, as the importers of whisky infringed the rules on the protection of designations of origin in Belgium, the Public Prosecutor instituted proceedings against them.[19]

---

17 Case C-68/88, *Commission of the European Communities v Hellenic Republic*, ECLI:EU:C:1989:339, para. 24.

18 Directive 2004/25/EC of the European Parliament and of the Council of 21 April 2004 on Takeover Bids [2004] OJ L 142/12.

19 Case C-8/74, *Procureur du Roi v Benoît and Gustave Dassonville*, ECLI:EU:C:1974:82.

In contrast, under German law such rules are traditionally enforced solely by means of private enforcement which – as will be illustrated in turn – has provoked infringement proceedings by the EU Commission. Indeed, against the background of the aforementioned general EU law requirements concerning effective enforcement, the diversity and path-dependency of (national) enforcement mechanisms therefore made it necessary from time to time for the ECJ to adopt a position – though often only implicitly – on the relative effectiveness of private and public enforcement in different institutional contexts. From a general point of view, this adjudication addresses in particular two issues which are essential in view of this topic.

- Does effective enforcement require that the Member States provide for mechanisms of public enforcement even if (well-functioning) instruments of private enforcement are available to aggrieved parties?
- Does the principle of effectiveness require the availability of private rights of action as enforcement instruments even if there are (well-functioning) mechanisms of public enforcement in place?

In the following, a brief overview will be given of how the ECJ has dealt with these two questions.

2.1. DOES EFFECTIVE ENFORCEMENT REQUIRE ELEMENTS OF PUBLIC ENFORCEMENT?

The question of whether or under which circumstances public enforcement is dispensable was addressed by the ECJ in the *Parmesan Cheese* case. The Commission had brought infringement proceedings against Germany on the grounds that, inter alia, Germany had not established an administrative practice to pursue infringements of the rules that protect designations of origin under Regulation No 2081/92.[20] The Commission maintained that an effective enforcement of the regulation concerning the protection of designations of origin should include 'administrative and penal measures.'[21]

---

20 Council Regulation (EEC) 2081/92 of 14 July 1992 on the protection of geographical indications and designations of origin for agricultural products and foodstuffs [1992] O.J. 1992, L 2081/1. See on enforcement in particular Article 10 of the Regulation which, however, according to the Court, does not require that public authorities take administrative action on their own initiative against infringements. Case C-132/05, *Commission of the European Communities v Federal Republic of Germany*, ECLI:EU:2008:117, paras 72 et seq.

21 Ibid., para. 58.

It argued that, in particular, the intended protection of the consumers would be compromised 'if the enforcement of the prohibitions laid down by the regulation were completely dependent on the taking of legal action by private economic operators.'[22]

The Court disagreed. It stressed that under German law rights to take action were not only available for the holders and legitimate users of a protected designation of origin but also to competitors of the infringer, business associations and consumer organisations. The Court found that:

> [i]n those circumstances, such legislation is capable of guaranteeing the protection of interests other than those of the producers of the goods protected ... in particular the interests of consumers.[23]

Thus, the Court answered the first initial question in the negative. Instruments of private enforcement alone may be regarded as sufficient to guarantee effective enforcement. This holds true even if it is not only the protection of certain individual rights that is at stake but also if the legislation in question pursues public policy objectives such as, for example, the protection of consumers. Yet in the latter case effective enforcement might require that a larger class of persons including, for example, the infringers' competitors and/or consumer protection associations are entitled to bring an action.

2.2. DOES EFFECTIVE ENFORCEMENT REQUIRE ELEMENTS OF PRIVATE ENFORCEMENT?

In regard to the question concerning the indispensability of private enforcement, two diverging strands may be observed in the Court's case law.

2.2.1. *Private Enforcement is Indispensable: The Judgments in* Courage v Crehan *and* Muñoz

2.2.1.1. Enforcing Competition Law: *Courage v Crehan*

As already mentioned in the introduction, the ECJ found in *Courage v Crehan* that Article 101 TFEU contains an implicit right to claim damages for parties who have been affected by an infringement of this prohibition of anticompetitive agreements and facilitative practices.[24] The Court followed in this decision a

22 Ibid., para. 60.
23 Ibid., para. 70.
24 See above n. 13 and accompanying text.

line of its case law that goes back to *Francovich*[25] and *Van Gend en Loos*[26] as it derived individual rights from the Treaty to supervise the implementation and effective enforcement of EU law. Moreover, the Court explicitly stressed that the envisaged actions for competition damages should serve as a mechanism of (private) enforcement of the competition law rules.[27] Thus, the Court did not leave it to the Member States or the EU legislature to decide if EU competition law rules should be enforced via actions for damages. Remarkably, in taking this decision, the ECJ has not taken into consideration – at least not in any way recognisable to the reader of the judgment – whether or not the existing mechanisms of public enforcement which were in place both on the EU law level and on the level of the national laws,[28] could have guaranteed an effective enforcement of the EU competition law rules.

The judgment in *Courage v Crehan* must be understood against the background of the far-reaching decentralisation of the public enforcement of EU competition law which was already proposed by the Commission and the implementation of which was predictable at the time the ECJ rendered its decision. Administrative enforcement should no longer be monopolised in the hands of the EU Commission. However, as the envisaged decentralised enforcement by Member State authorities was met with a fair amount of distrust, *Courage v Crehan* came at a convenient time for the EU legislature.[29] The judgment highlighted that damages actions could have a part in complementing public enforcement and, in particular, could function as a safety net in the event of public enforcement failing.

2.2.1.2. Enforcing Rules on the Labelling of Grapes: *Muñoz*

A strong commitment to private enforcement can be identified in the ECJ's judgment in *Muñoz*. The Court of Appeal of England and Wales referred the question to the Court whether a trader must be capable of instituting civil proceedings against a competitor who breached the rules established by two (successive) EU regulations[30] on the labelling of certain types of grapes.

---

25 Case C-6/90, *Francovich and Bonifaci v Italian Republic*, ECLI:EU:C:1991:428, para. 31.

26 Case C-26/62, *Van Gend en Loos*, ECLI:EU:C:1963:1 at 12.

27 See above n. 14 and accompanying text.

28 See Articles 4 and 5 of Council Regulation (EC) No 1/2003 of 16 December 2002 on the implementation of the rules on competition laid down in Articles 81 and 82 of the Treaty Regulation 1/2003 [2003] OJ L 1/1.

29 See A.P. Komninos, 'New Prospects for Private Enforcement of EC Competition Law: Courage v. Crehan and the Community Right to Damages' (2002) 39 CML Rev. 447, 485 ('The importance of this ruling for the modernization plans of DG COMP is evident.').

30 Regulation (EEC) No 1035/72 of the Council of 18 May 1972 on the common organization of the market in fruit and vegetables [1972] OJ L 118/1, and Council Regulation (EC) No 2200/96 of 28 October 1996 on the common organization of the market in fruit and vegetables [1996] OJ 1996 L 297/1.

The necessity of private enforcement was particularly doubtful because the regulations in question explicitly stipulated that the Member States must establish mechanisms of public enforcement.[31] Nevertheless, the Court answered in the affirmative:

> [T]he full effectiveness of the rules on quality standards and, in particular, the practical effect of the obligation laid down by Article 3(1) of both Regulation No 1035/72 and Regulation No 2200/96 imply that it must be possible to enforce that obligation by means of civil proceedings instituted by a trader against a competitor.[32]
>
> The possibility of bringing such proceedings strengthens the practical working of the Community rules on quality standards. As a supplement to the action of the authorities designated by the Member States to make the checks required by those rules it helps to discourage practices, often difficult to detect, which distort competition. In that context actions brought before the national courts by competing operators are particularly suited to contributing substantially to ensuring fair trading and transparency of markets in the Community.[33]

It is very telling how the ECJ argued to reach this quite remarkable conclusion.

First, the Court reasoned the availability of private enforcement without (rhetorically) establishing an implicit right, i.e. the Court did not argue – or at least not explicitly – that the obligation imposed on traders to comply with certain labelling rules contained a corresponding implicit right by competitors, the effective protection of which required that the Member States had to provide an effective remedy, i.e. the possibility to institute civil proceedings. Instead, the Court argued straightforwardly that there must be private rights of action available as otherwise an effective enforcement of the rules could not be guaranteed. Therefore, the remedy established by the Court in *Muñoz* cannot reasonably be integrated in a classical concept of private law.[34] At most, a certain reconciliation could be reached if one understood the judgment as conferring on each market actor a right to require from their respective competitors that they comply with the labelling laws in question. But to posit such an implicit right would seem to amount to a mere fiction.

Secondly, even though the High Court of Justice in England and Wales – which had dismissed the action brought by *Muñoz* – had found that the mechanism of public enforcement foreseen had failed in the case at hand,[35]

---

31 See Article 8 of Regulation (EEC) No 1035/72 and Article 7 of Regulation (EC) No 2200/96, respectively.

32 Case C-253/00, *Antonio Muñoz y Cia SA and Superior Fruiticola SA v Frumar Ltd and Redbridge Produce Marketing Ltd.*, ECLI:EU:C:2002:497, para. 30.

33 Ibid., para. 31.

34 For an outline of the features of such a classical concept of private law see J.F. Hoffmann's contribution to this volume, pp. 45–60.

35 *Antonio Muñoz y Cia SA v Frumar Ltd* [1999] 3 CMLR 684, 708 (1999) ('Through its lawyers [Muñoz] has complained to HMI about the mis-marking of the defendants' products. HMI

and even though this aspect was recognised in the ECJ's summary of the factual background of the case,[36] the Court did not indicate in any way that the requirement that private enforcement must be available would depend on the failure or at least on a specific, i.e. not merely abstract, risk of failure of the established mechanisms of public enforcement. More in particular, the Court did not address the question whether perhaps the availability of a remedy against the competent authority, i.e. the possibility to force the authority to take measures against infringers, could make a right of direct action against infringers dispensable.

Thirdly, the ECJ gave one reason why the (parallel) availability of private enforcement might effectively strengthen the effectiveness of enforcement as it implied that through actions brought by competitors before national courts private knowledge about infringements can be put to good use. This consideration – which is indeed essential in the discussion about potential advantages of private enforcement[37] – contrasts with the arguments put forward by the High Court to explain why private enforcement should be regarded as inadequate in the context of *Muñoz*:

> The primary line of enforcement here is placed in the hands of a body which has already developed, or will develop, the necessary technical expertise, i.e. HMI. No doubt there are equivalent bodies in other Member States. They not only know what they are doing but, importantly, they should be neutral. Their remit is not to advance one trader's interests at the expense of another's. These Regulations create types of consumer protection measures which are eminently suited to being policed by experienced but neutral enforcement agencies. They are quite unsuitable to be the subject of private litigation brought by customers or trade rivals.[38]

Thus, the High Court had advocated for a monopolisation of enforcement in the hands of the competent public authorities. It had argued that, first, expert know-how could thereby be (more) efficiently acquired and put to use. Secondly, the Court had suggested that it should rather be a 'neutral' entity – by which the Court apparently meant an entity which in contrast to a competitor has no specific self-interest in pursuing infringers – that decides if and how enforcement

---

has done nothing. So far as I am aware it has not even explained its failure to act. Based on the information before me, it should have instructed Frumar to stop using the names White Seedless, Sult and Coryn and to use Superior Seedless instead. Muñoz acted correctly when it complained to HMI and asked it to intervene.').

36 Case C-253/00, *Antonio Muñoz y Cia SA and Superior Fruiticola SA v Frumar Ltd and Redbridge Produce Marketing Ltd.*, ECLI:EU:C:2002:497, para. 19 ('Muñoz and Fruitola complained on several occasions to the [Horticultural Marketing Inspectorate] ... the HMI took no action in response to those complaints.').

37 See below sec. 3.1.

38 *Antonio Muñoz y Cia SA v Frumar Ltd* [1999] 3 CMLR 684, 708 (1999).

measures should be implemented in the case of an infringement of rules that have been enacted in the general interest (as in this case to protect the consumers).

2.2.2. *Enforcement May Be 'Effective' without Private Rights of Action:* Bankinter *and* Schmitt

In the aftermath of *Courage v Crehan* and *Muñoz*, both judgments were regularly invoked in the literature to substantiate that certain rules of EU internal market law embodied implicit rights and remedies to the benefits of those parties who suffer damage in the case of an infringement, or, to put it in other words, that the EU law principle of effectiveness required the availability of private enforcement. This has been argued, for instance, in regard to the obligation to assess the creditworthiness of the consumer pursuant to Article 8 of the Consumer Credit Directive.[39]

However, since then the ECJ has rendered at least two judgments – *Bankinter* and *Schmitt* – by which it disappointed those who had wished *Courage v Crehan* and *Muñoz* to be a beacon for all-embracing private enforcement of EU internal market law. In both cases, the Court left it to the Member States whether or not non-compliance with a provision of EU internal market law should trigger private rights of action. Thus, it was the implicit assumption in both cases that the Member States could guarantee an effective enforcement of the rules in question solely by means of public enforcement.

2.2.2.1. Enforcing Investment Firms' Conduct of Business Obligations: *Bankinter*

In *Bankinter*, the ECJ had to address whether EU law required that an infringement of the assessment requirements laid down in Article 19(4) and (5) of the Directive on Markets in Financial Instruments (MiFID)[40] as part of the conduct of business obligations imposed on firms that provide investment services must result in contractual consequences under national law. The Court responded as follows:

> It should be noted that, although Article 51 of Directive 2004/39 provides for the imposition of administrative measures or sanctions against the parties responsible

[39] See, e.g., P. ROTT, E. TERRYN and C. TWIGG-FLESNER, 'Kreditwürdigkeitsprüfung: Verbraucherschutzverhinderung durch Zuweisung zum Öffentlichen Recht?' [2011] *Verbraucher und Recht* 163, 167–168. See for a critical appraisal of this proposition J.-U. FRANCK, *Marktordnung durch Haftung*, Mohr Siebeck, Tübingen 2016, pp. 281–286.

[40] Directive 2004/39/EC of the European Parliament and of the Council of 21 April 2004 on markets in financial instruments amending Council Directives 85/611/EEC and 93/6/EEC and Directive 2000/12/EC of the European Parliament and of the Council and repealing Council Directive 93/22/EEC [2004] 145/1.

> for non-compliance with the provisions adopted pursuant to that directive, it does not state either that the Member States must provide for contractual consequences in the event of contracts being concluded which do not comply with the obligations under national legal provisions transposing Article 19(4) and (5) of Directive 2004/39, or what those consequences might be. In the absence of EU legislation on the point, it is for the internal legal order of each Member State to determine the contractual consequences of non-compliance with those obligations, subject to observance of the principles of equivalence and effectiveness.[41]

Thus, the Member States may decide whether or not they want to foresee – in addition to the measures of public enforcement required by the Directive – contractual remedies which would then serve as an instrument of private enforcement of the conduct of business obligations the Directive imposes on investment firms.[42]

2.2.2.2. Enforcing Duties of Care on Part of Notified Bodies under the Medical Devices Directive: *Schmitt*

The ECJ's judgment in *Schmitt* reveals some reluctance on the part of the Court to recognise a need for civil liability based on general principles of EU law. When asked about the obligations of notified bodies under the Medical Devices Directive[43] and the sanctions in case of an infringement, the Court established that the Directive imposes on notified bodies such as the *TÜV Rheinland* in the case at hand a 'general obligation to act with all due diligence when engaged in a procedure relating to the EC declaration of conformity.'[44] The body is under a 'duty to be alert' which means that it must react if evidence indicates that a medical device may not comply with the requirement laid down in the Directive.[45] Moreover, the Court found that the notified body acts, inter alia, to protect the health of end users of medical devices: 'with regard to the involvement of the notified body in the procedure relating to the EC declaration of conformity, it is apparent from the wording and overall scheme of Directive 93/42 that the purpose of that procedure is to ensure protection for the health and safety of persons.'[46]

---

41 Case C-604/11, *Genil 48 and Comercial Hostelera de Grandes Vinos v Bankinter and Banco Bilbao Vizcaya Argentaria*, ECLI:EU:C:2013:344, para. 57.

42 J.-U. Franck, above n. 39, p. 375, n. 345. But cf. S. Grundmann, 'The Bankinter on MIFI Regulation and Contract Law' [2013] *European Review of Contract Law* 267, 278.

43 Council Directive 93/42/EEC of 14 June 1993 concerning medical devices [1993] L 169/43.

44 Case C-219/15, *Elisabeth Schmitt v TÜV Rheinland LGA Products*, ECLI:EU:C:2017:128, para. 46.

45 Ibid., para. 47.

46 Ibid., para. 53.

Nevertheless, in regard to a potential liability of a notifying body under tort law or contract law, the Court stressed that:

> it does not necessarily follow from the fact that a directive imposes surveillance obligations on certain bodies or the fact that one of the objectives of the directive is to protect injured parties that the directive seeks to confer rights on such parties in the event that those bodies fail to fulfil their obligations, and that is the case especially if the directive does not contain any express rule granting such rights.[47]

Thus, the Member States remain free to foresee or not to foresee contractual or non-contractual liability on the part of a notified body vis-à-vis the end users of medical devices in the case that the former breaches its obligations under the Directive. This clear statement seems to be particularly telling as it was not necessarily warranted by the preliminary reference, and thus, as one observer remarked, appears 'to convey an averseness to private enforcement.'[48] In the same spirit as in *Bankinter*, the Court assumed that an effective enforcement of those obligations imposed on the notifying bodies is conceivable without making private rights of action available to those who suffer injury as a result of a culpable failure on the part of notified bodies.

2.3. PRELIMINARY CONCLUSIONS

The ECJ's jurisprudence on the question whether public and/or private enforcement is required under general principles of EU law to effectively sanction certain provisions of internal market law is a telling illustration of how the debate on private-vs.-public-enforcement may be relevant in regard to a legal question in the strict sense. What can be inferred is that there is no general obligation on the part of the Member States to provide in each context for mechanisms of both private *and* public enforcement to guarantee a sufficient level of compliance. More in particular, private enforcement alone may be sufficient even if not only the protection of certain right holders but also of general interests such as the protection of consumers is at stake *(Parmesan Cheese* case*)*. Also, public enforcement alone may be sufficient even if compliance with provisions that protect individual interests, such as personal health, is at stake *(Schmitt)*.

The ECJ gave hardly any guidance on the question why it considered private rights of action indispensable in *Courage v Crehan* and *Muñoz*. The Court does at least indicate that such rights facilitate the harnessing of private information

---

47 Ibid., para. 55.

48 A. Wallermann, 'Pie in the sky when you die? Civil liability to notified bodies under the Medical Devices Directive: *Schmitt*' (2018) 55 Common Market Law Review 265, 276.

on infringements of the law and may therefore contribute to increasing the detection rate.

As the author has argued in detail elsewhere,[49] one piece of the puzzle to distinguish *Courage v Crehan* and *Muñoz* from *Bankinter* and *Schmitt* may lie in the fact that while the latter cases involved the enforcement of obligations laid down in a directive, the former concerned the enforcement of Article 101 TFEU and of a labelling obligation enshrined in a regulation and thus, EU law obligations which are directly applicable between individual market players. Therefore, where an obligation is imposed on private parties by way of a Directive, the general duty to provide for effective enforcement should not be read as requiring that the Member States have to foresee private enforcement in every case.

While the ECJ's adjudication seems to be influenced by (only) implicit assumptions on the effectiveness of instruments of private and public enforcement, some of the insights presented in the following part can assist in critically evaluating how the Court uses general principles such as 'effectiveness' to require from the Member States the adoption of (additional) instruments of public and/or private enforcement.

3. THE COMPARATIVE ADVANTAGES OF PRIVATE AND PUBLIC ENFORCEMENT

The debate on whether private or public enforcement or a combination of the two should be preferred encompasses various dimensions. Whilst the following discussion will focus on functional considerations, it must not be neglected that the discussion also touches upon, first, questions of democratic legitimacy and accountability and, secondly, the legitimacy and intensity of the interference in the individual freedom which comes along with any enforcement measure. Suffice it to recall here[50] that there is no reason to describe private rights of action as a superior mode of enforcement in these regards.

The quest for an enforcement strategy that is optimal from a functional perspective raises a number of theoretical and empirical issues. Universally valid answers are sparse and typically rather abstract. One may hardly emphasise too strongly the eminent importance of the specific institutional framework. What appears to be promising – though of course cumbersome and costly – is to take into consideration empirical analyses that focus on the effectiveness, strengths and weaknesses of certain enforcement instruments in a specific legal and institutional context. Such empirical studies may concern quite diverse

49 J.-U. Franck, above n. 39, pp. 265–269.

50 For a more detailed elaboration of these aspects see J.-U. Franck, above n. 39, pp. 29–39.

topics ranging from the failure of criminal prosecution of insider trading in Germany[51] to the preventive effects of tort law liability in road traffic in Quebec.[52] The following discussion will be restricted to providing an overview of aspects which reveal (relative) advantages and disadvantages of instruments of private and public enforcement.[53]

3.1. DETECTION OF INFRINGEMENTS

There is a wide perception that private individuals have a systematic informational advantage over a public enforcement body as they 'naturally' possess information about an infringement and the identity of the respective violator.[54] Therefore, in a system with purely public enforcement, the detection of infringements is relatively costly. An agency can use its (scarce) resources to monitor for violations. In addition, it can trust that private individuals and in particular victims, report infringements as they want the authority to stop them and as they may obtain retributive satisfaction from reporting infringers and the expectation that these will be punished. Ultimately, an agency can also try to incentivise individuals to provide information, for instance by way of whistle-blower rewards programs.[55]

Yet the availability of private rights of action creates an additional way which allows use to be made of private information about legal infringements.

---

51 A. Hienzsch, Das deutsche Insiderhandelsverbot in der Rechtswirklichkeit, Nomos, Baden-Baden 2006.

52 R.A. Devlin, 'Some Welfare Implications of No-Fault Automobile Insurance' (1990) 10 *International Review of Law and Economics* 193–205; R.A. Devlin, 'Liability Versus No-Fault Automobile Insurance Regimes: An Analysis of the Experience in Quebec' in G. Dionne (ed.), *Contributions to Insurance Economics*, Kluwer Academic Publishers, Boston, Dordrecht, London 1992, pp. 499–520; M. Gaudry, 'Measuring the Effects of the No-Fault 1978 Quebec Automobile Insurance Act with the Drag Model' in G. Dionne (ed.), *Contributions to Insurance Economics*, Kluwer Academic Publishers, Boston, Dordrecht, London 1992, pp. 471–498.

53 For a good survey of the literature see L. Klöhn, 'Private versus Public Enforcement of Laws – a Law & Economics Perspective' in R. Schulze (ed.), *Compensation of Private Losses*, Sellier, München 2011, pp. 179–98.

54 See, e.g., S. Shavell, *Foundations of Economic Analysis of Law*, Harvard University Press, Cambridge, Mass. and London 2004, pp. 578–9; K. Roach and M.J. Trebilcock, 'Private Enforcement of Competition Laws' (1996) 34 *Osgoode Hall Law Journal* 461, 472, 480; B.H. Thompson, 'The Continuing Innovation of Citizen Enforcement' (2000) *University of Illinois Law Review*, 185, 191–2; M.C. Stephensson, 'Public Regulation of Private Enforcement: The Case for Expanding the Role of Administrative Agencies' (2005) 91 *Virginia Law Review* 93, 108–9.

55 Such programs are used for example in the United Kingdom, South Korea, and Hungary to detect antitrust infringements, see K.R. Sullivan, K. Ball and S. Klebolt, 'The Potential Impact of Adding a Whistleblower Rewards Provision to ACPERA', *The Antitrust Source*, October 2011, pp. 1–6.

Aggrieved parties can bring an injunction to stop an illegal activity which could cause them (further) damage. The availability of damages actions may not only incentivise direct actions against the infringer but may also create an incentive to inform the public authority, trusting that it will pursue the infringement, which in turn may make it easier to subsequently sue for compensation by way of a so-called follow-on action.

3.2. INCENTIVE STRUCTURE

One of the main concerns with public enforcement has always been that the agents that act for an authority are under-incentivised to pursue infringements. They cannot pocket the fines which they impose on violators nor do they usually have any other (direct) monetary incentive to enforce the law effectively. This creates threats of corruption, i.e. of collusion between infringers and public enforcement agents, which results in a socially suboptimal level of law enforcement.[56] Moreover, a public authority might be captured by an interest group, for instance if the government decides that a representative of the food industry should chair the food safety agency and the like.

However, one should not be too quick with a critical evaluation of the civil servants' incentive structure. For one thing, whilst civil servants indeed typically receive a fixed salary, in a well-organised public bureaucracy they might rightly expect that doing a good job will pay off through a rise in the hierarchy which will in turn lead to more power and a higher salary. For another thing, civil servants might be sufficiently eager to enforce the law based on non-monetary incentives. They act in the awareness that their work serves the general interest and the public good. Those who enforce environmental law, antitrust law, consumer protection law, etc. will often draw their motivation from the conviction that they belong to the 'good guys.'

Yet, private 'plaintiffs' may as well be driven by similar non-monetary incentives based on moral, ethical or political convictions. More in particular, aggrieved parties usually have a non-monetary incentive to see the infringer identified by a court as a lawbreaker. If, in addition to this, they can expect a monetary gain from their enforcement actions on top, at least a certain plausibility that private enforcement entails, in the aggregate, stronger enforcement incentives than public enforcement can be established. This, however, also includes the possibility that private individuals are over-incentivised to bring suit.

First, depending on the institutional framework, it might be a rational profit-maximising strategy to bring a case (almost) without merit, in the hope that

---

56 G.S. Becker and G.J. Stigler, 'Law Enforcement, Malfeasance, and Compensation of Enforcers' (1974) 3 *Journal of Legal Studies* 1, 3–4.

a defendant might be pushed into a private settlement as this will save legal costs and excludes the (even if only marginal) risk of losing the case, or that a court might award damages on a whim. Certainly, to prevent the waste of social resources that comes along with such unmeritorious actions, it is not necessary to forego private enforcement altogether. Rather, strike suits should be discouraged by appropriate rules of procedure and fee allocation.

Secondly, it is the aggrieved persons or, to be more precise, the persons who consider themselves as being aggrieved by a breach of the law, of whom one would think that they have the greatest incentive to bring suit. Insights of behavioral science indicate that these parties might even be inclined to over-invest in litigation. This is related to the phenomenon of loss aversion: 'losses loom larger than gains,'[57] i.e. a loss hurts more than a gain in the same amount delights.[58] Consequently, individuals tend to prefer avoiding losses to acquiring gains, and seem to be willing to take higher risks to avoid losses than to achieve gains.[59] What is more, experimental research indicates that the aggrieved individuals' reference point – which is crucial for their valuation of any compensation they might obtain via a lawsuit – is *before* the harmful event.[60] This suggests that they conceive the prospect of a successful action for damages as a chance to avoid a loss rather than to acquire a gain. Such a negative framing is expected to induce greater risk-seeking and to make it more difficult to reach a settlement with the opposing party as this is conceived as a bargain about the distribution of a loss.[61] These findings suggest a risk that victims of infringements might be tempted to file suit even if the expected value is negative.

Finally, it is worth mentioning that 'corruption' in the sense of a collaboration between an infringer and a potential plaintiff or even a judge is also possible in the case of private enforcement. It has been demonstrated, for example, that through rationing inputs at low prices, an upstream cartel may shield itself from private damages actions by forwarding a share of the cartel profits to its direct purchasers.[62] Such a risk of collaboration can be reduced

---

57 D. Kahnemann and A. Tversky, 'Advances in Prospect Theory: Cumulative Representation of Uncertainty' (1992) 5 *Journal of Risk and Uncertainty* 297, 298.

58 D. Kahnemann and A. Tversky, 'Advances in Prospect Theory: Cumulative Representation of Uncertainty' (1992) 5 *Journal of Risk and Uncertainty* 311 (estimating that losses are 2.25 times more powerful, psychologically, as gains).

59 D. Kahnemann and A. Tversky, 'Prospect Theory: An Analysis of Decision under Risk' (1979) 47 *Econometrica* 263, 268–9.

60 R.B. Korobkin and C. Guthrie, 'Psychology, Economics, and Settlement: A New Look at the Role of the Lawyer' (1997) 76 *Texas Law Review* 77, 99.

61 D. Kahnemann, 'Reference Points, Anchors, Norms, and Mixed Feelings' (1992) 51 *Organizational Behavior and Human Decision Processes* 296, 297–8.

62 M.P. Schinkel, J. Tuinstra and J. Rüggeberg, 'Illinois Walls: How Barring Indirect Purchasers Suits Facilitates Collusion' (2008) 39 *RAND Journal of Economics* 683–698.

significantly if a broad class of aggrieved parties enjoys standing rights, for example in the case of a cartel also indirect purchasers and suppliers.

3.3. ECONOMIES OF SCALE

To reduce the costs of law enforcement, the actors who enforce the law should preferably be in a position to achieve economies of scale and scope. Expertise should be accumulated to create synergies, be it in the form of persons that are specialised in enforcing a specific branch of the law or be it in form of technical devices, such as databases, which allow for an efficient processing of information, etc.

This consideration is typically viewed as an argument in favour of 'monopolistic' enforcement, and consequently, in favour of public enforcement.[63] This is because only in such a context does a system seem practically conceivable where only one party has the capacity to enforce the law. In contrast, private enforcement seems (almost) by definition to be to a greater or lesser extent 'competitive.'[64]

However, it is not clear why competing 'private enforcers' should not be in a position to exploit economies of scale. If such effects indeed play an important role in an efficient enforcement, it seems plausible to assume that this will affect the structure of the market for law enforcement. Consequently, one should expect to observe a market with a few specialised firms that have accumulated a certain expertise, and which are therefore in a position to handle a certain type of action on a large scale.

Legislators can facilitate the exploitation of economies of scale by providing, for instance, the option for class-action lawsuits or other legal mechanisms by which claims can be bundled such as the assignment to a special purpose vehicle.

3.4. EFFICIENT USE OF RESOURCES

Competition among private entities that provide the 'enforcement services' has led to the expectation that 'enforcement was provided at cost.'[65] In contrast, public enforcement is often associated with an inefficient use of resources as the enforcement agents spend not their own but taxpayers' money. What is more,

---

63 See, e.g., A.M. Polinsky, 'Private versus Public Enforcement of Fines' (1980) 9 *Journal of Legal Studies* 105, 107.

64 L. Klöhn, above n. 53, p. 188.

65 G.S. Becker and G.J. Stigler, 'Law Enforcement, Malfeasance, and Compensation of Enforcers' (1974) 3 *Journal of Legal Studies* 1, 14.

public servants may have an interest not to optimise the level of enforcement in the general interest but to maximise their own benefit. This might explain a tendency to raise in particular those cases that promise public attention or to focus on cases the successful handling of which promises the acknowledgement by their superiors.

Similar principal-agent problems may certainly also occur in the context of private enforcement. Lawyers, for example, have of course a strong interest in maximising their fees, and their services may to a great extent be characterised as a credence good:[66] clients can hardly observe or evaluate its quality.

Hence, the assumption that 'production efficiency' is higher in the case of private enforcement rests upon the premise that principle-agent problems are dealt with more effectively in a competitive framework. Whilst this does not look implausible, it implicitly presumes certain institutional safeguards, such as for instance strict fiduciary duties imposed on lawyers that are carried out conscientiously, as infringements are promptly and effectively sanctioned.

3.5. 'HIGH SANCTION/LOW PROBABILITY' STRATEGY

Monopolistic enforcement – which in practical terms means (purely) public enforcement – makes it possible to implement a 'high sanction/low probability' strategy. If it is assumed that the deterrent effect of a sanction is a function of, first, the severity of the penalties threatened and, secondly, the likelihood that an infringement will be detected and that the penalty will be imposed on the infringer, a public enforcer can choose the combination which minimises costs. This includes the option to accept a relatively low detection rate (to minimise enforcement costs) but to combine it with relatively severe sanctions.[67] Such a strategy faces in any event certain limits, not least fundamental rights restrictions. Yet, if private enforcement is available alongside public enforcement, the objective of such a strategy, namely to minimise the social costs of enforcement, could not be secured as there is no mechanism available to control and restrict the (private) resources invested in detecting and pursuing an infringement.[68]

3.6. INNOVATION

Competition is generally seen as a driver of innovation and it has therefore been argued in regard to law enforcement that private enforcement is desirable

---

66 The term has been established by M.R. Darby and E. Karni, 'Free Competition and the Optimal Amount of Fraud' (1973) 16 *Journal of Law & Economics* 67, 68–69.

67 G.S. Becker, 'Crime and Punishment: An Economic Approach' (1968) 76 *Journal of Political Economy* 183–4.

68 L. Klöhn, above n. 53, p. 186.

as private actors, if competing with each other, have stronger incentives to pursue new (innovative) strategies.[69] This may include the development of new means or techniques of evidence, such as, for example, the introduction into forensic practice of econometric techniques to estimate damage, but also the advancement of new legal arguments, for example in an attempt to reach a change of established case law.

3.7. POSITIVE EXTERNALITIES

Litigation enables courts to clarify legal standards and thus, to create a public good,[70] as others may anticipate more clearly where to draw the line between legal and illegal activities and adjust their conduct accordingly. Administrative guidelines can substitute for this only to some extent as they may have a certain binding effect on the issuing agencies but they will typically not bind the courts. Whilst public enforcement may also result in litigation and the setting of precedents, it seems plausible to assume that at least a well-functioning system of private litigation will be characterised by higher rates and will therefore give the courts more opportunity to flesh out legal standards.[71]

3.8. LONG-TERM STRATEGIES

In order to safeguard an optimal level of compliance in the long run, it might be preferable that those who are in a position to enforce – be it private actors, be it a public agency – enjoy the leeway *not* to pursue or *not* to file suit in the case of every infringement observed.

Private parties who have suffered damage due to a violation of the law by their contractual partners (customers, suppliers or investors) may have, for one thing, a rational interest in maintaining a sustainable long-term relationship. Thus, they may find it reasonable to forego the option to take active enforcement measures, such as in particular by way of actions for damages, but nevertheless to signal that a particular unlawful conduct will not be acceptable from now on. What is more, mechanisms of private enforcement may provide leeway so that those whose conduct is subject to a certain law

---

69 B.H. Thompson, 'The Continuing Innovation of Citizen Enforcement' [2000] *University of Illinois Law Review* 185, 188, 206–7; M. Stephenson, 'Public Regulation of Private Enforcement: The Case for Expanding the Role of Administrative Agencies' (2009) 91 *Virginia Law Review* 93, 112–13.

70 G.L. Priest and B. Klein, 'The Selection of Disputes for Litigation' (1984) 13 *Journal of Legal Studies* 1.

71 K. Roach and M.J. Trebilcock, 'Private Enforcement of Competition Laws' (1996) 34 *Osgoode Hall Law Journal* 461, 472, 481.

and those who are potentially affected by a breach of this law may (explicitly or implicitly) agree on a somewhat adjusted standard. Such an act of self-regulation which effectively softens the adverse effects of a top-down approach may be in the public interest if it means that a rule is, for instance, tailored to the conditions in a certain market sector, and if it ensures a higher level of compliance at the same time.[72] This must not be read as a plea for purely private enforcement, but public enforcers should be aware of the beneficial effects of such mechanisms and should consider them when exercising their discretion in their enforcement activities.

Following a similar logic, it can be essential for an agency to develop a cooperative relationship with the firms and individuals who have to comply with certain laws the agency has to enforce. Thus, in order to ensure a high level of long-term compliance, it may be preferable not to pursue a particular infringement or to leave it at a cease-and-desist order without imposing a fine. Yet, private enforcement actions may thwart such a public enforcement policy and thus, prevent the strategy which would have served compliance best in the long run.[73]

4. CONCLUSION

The previous section has revealed a plethora of aspects that may play a role in the private-vs.-public-enforcement debate. An essential finding of those functional considerations is that neither a model of purely private enforcement nor a model of purely public consideration can be constructed as a 'first-best-enforcement solution.' This is mainly because, on the one hand, private enforcement is characterised by inherent advantages in regard to the harnessing of private information about infringements and therefore the efficient detection of breaches of the law, as well as in regard to the incentive structure of those who are in the position to take enforcement measures. On the other hand, public enforcement entails certain advantages concerning the possibility to manage the allocation of enforcement resources, particularly as it allows for the pursuit of a 'high sanction/low probability'-strategy.

Therefore, if there is one lesson that can be learnt from these theoretical insights, it is that the most one can hope for is a robust second-best enforcement strategy. This will often require a mix of elements of private and public

72 See H. Collins, *Regulating Contracts*, OUP, Oxford, 1999/reprinted 2005, p. 65.

73 K. Roach and M.J. Trebilcock, 'Private Enforcement of Competition Laws' (1996) 34 Osgoode Hall Law Journal 461, 485–487 and 503; M. Stephenson, 'Public Regulation of Private Enforcement: The case for Expanding the Role of Administrative Agencies' (2009) 91 *Virginia Law Review* 93, 117–119.

enforcement – but not necessarily so: there are circumstances conceivable where purely private or purely public enforcement appears to be the best available enforcement strategy. However, in most cases, such a 'pure' system will be virtually impossible to implement due to institutional path-dependencies.[74]

How much weight should be lent to the aforementioned arguments which tend to speak in favour of public enforcement or of private enforcement, depends very much on the institutional framework in question or, to put it in other words, on the question of what is actually at stake: the enforcement of environmental law in Alaska, or of the laws on species protection in Brazil, or of employment protection provisions in Sweden? On the one hand, there may well be varying assessments of how trustworthy public enforcers are in respect of their professional or technical qualification, their proneness to corruption or their democratic legitimacy and accountability. On the other hand, equally depending on the country and the particular legal field, one may more or less trust that private attorneys and judges are better qualified and less corrupt than civil servants and thus, private litigation may function well as a (superior) substitute or at least as a useful complement to enforcement by public agencies.

Certainly, as indicated a few times in the previous section, to a significant extent the legislature has it in its hands to prevent potential flaws which may undermine the effectiveness and efficiency of instruments of private or of public enforcement. But at the end of the day, one must not overlook the simple truth that 'the working of institutions, as of fortresses, depends ultimately upon the persons who man them.'[75] Certain preconceptions and convictions may result in a self-fulfilling prophecy. In a society where it is a generally accepted belief that public agencies work effectively and efficiently in the interest of the common good, such a reputation may indeed make it a lot easier to hire well-qualified and highly-motivated civil servants. In contrast, in a society where every ambitious and self-respecting graduate from a law school would at all costs rather become a lawyer than work for a public authority, this may be viewed as an indication that it is not only the reputation but also the effectiveness and efficiency of the agencies which leave much to be desired.

Turning to the enforcement of EU internal market law, this should be a reminder that it may be a good idea to leave the Member States some leeway to do justice to their diverse legal traditions and institutional differences.

---

74 Cf. H. Hovenkamp, *The Antitrust Enterprise*, Harvard University Press, Cambridge/Mass. and London 2005, p. 59 ('If we were writing on a clean slate we might wish to create a system of purely public antitrust enforcement in which the role of private parties is limited to the filing of complaints with the government agencies, who then investigate and decide whether to sue and what kind of relief to request.').

75 K.R. Popper, *Conjectures and Refutations*, Harper and Row, New York 1963, p. 133.

Therefore, the question whether the European Union should make use of its power to harmonise not only the substantive law in a certain field but also the respective enforcement mechanisms should be cautiously answered by the EU legislature or by the ECJ in its application of the principle of effectiveness and other general principles.

What is more, if one considers those aspects in respect of which private enforcement tends to have a comparative advantage over public enforcement – namely the incentive structure of the persons responsible for taking enforcement action and the harnessing of private information about infringements – it seems plausible to assume that these aspects are typically more significant in the internal market context, in particular in view of a cross-border enforcement of the law, compared to purely domestic contexts.[76] Hence, to have private enforcement available as a safety net in case of a failure of public enforcement or to correct a (potential) under-enforcement by public enforcers appears to be more necessary in an internal market context than in a domestic context. This may be one reason to legitimise the important role which in particular the ECJ has assigned to private enforcement.

Finally, it should be stressed that the choice between private or public enforcement as such does not take centre stage in the policy debates about the enforcement of EU internal market law. Issues that are high on the EU agenda[77] are in particular the interplay between public and private enforcement and the cooperation between national enforcement authorities, but also detailed improvements of existing enforcement mechanisms as illustrated by the recent legislative initiatives that aim at fostering the enforcement of consumer protection law.[78] Nevertheless, it is important to see that the aforementioned insights into the comparative advantages of private and public enforcement, respectively, remain significant even after the fundamental choices for enforcement design in a particular

---

76 J.-U. Franck, above n. 39, p. 182.

77 For a perspective from political science see T.A. Börzel and E.G. Heidbreder, 'Enforcement and compliance' in C. Harlow, P. Leino and G. della Cananea (eds.), *Research Handbook on EU Administrative Law*, Edward Elgar, Cheltenham, UK and Northampton, MA, 2017, pp. 241–262.

78 European Commission, 11.4.2018, COM (2018) 184 final, Proposal for a Directive of the European Parliament and of the Council on representative actions for the protection of the collective interests of consumers, and repealing Directive 2009/22/EC. European Commission, 11.4.2018, COM (2018) 185 final, Proposal for a Directive of the European Parliament and of the Council amending Council Directive 93/13/EEC of 5 April 1993, Directive 98/6/EC of the European Parliament and of the Council, Directive 2005/29/EC of the European Parliament and of the Council and Directive 2011/83/EU of the European Parliament and of the Council as regards better enforcement and modernisation of EU consumer protection rules.

field of the law have been made. As, for example, the ECJ established in *Courage v Crehan* that a breach of Article 101 TFEU must trigger private rights of action, these actions for competition damages should be designed in such a way that the comparative advantages of private enforcement can indeed be fully reaped. Therefore, standing rights,[79] for instance, should be given primarily to those who have the highest likelihood of being informed about infringements because this will encourage market players to act upon their private information on infringements.

[79] The term 'standing right' is used here in a non-technical sense, embracing a plurality of rules which may effectively delimit the class of potential plaintiffs such as 'remoteness of damage', 'causation in law' and the like.

CRIMINAL ENFORCEMENT

Dorothea MAGNUS

1. INTRODUCTION

This chapter presents thoughts on criminal enforcement. Since there is only very limited material at the European level on this subject, the chapter will concentrate on the national perspective of criminal law, focusing on the question how far criminal provisions are enforced in the German legal system and what role criminal procedural law and private persons play in this context. Wherever possible and adequate, the difference between civil and public enforcement will be emphasised. There are different questions that arise from the topic. There are three main questions that are raised by criminal enforcement:

1. *The first question is:* How is substantive criminal law enforced?
2. *The second question is directly linked:* How are criminal sanctions enforced?
3. *And last, but not least, the third question is:* How can private persons influence the enforcement of criminal sanctions? This question especially concerns the relation of private versus public enforcement.

2. HOW IS SUBSTANTIVE CRIMINAL LAW ENFORCED?

The government has an arsenal of enforcement tools to compel compliance with criminal law.[1] The regulations vary from penalisation to dispensing with prosecution. Criminal investigations and criminal prosecutions do not have to lead inescapably to a conviction of the perpetrator. There are factual and legal reasons for non-enforcement.

2.1. FACTUAL REASONS FOR NON-ENFORCEMENT

Factual reasons for non-enforcement are most of all lack of evidence or lack of the offender (unknown or escaped). Obviously, a criminal sanction cannot be enforced if the police or public prosecutor cannot get hold of the alleged perpetrator, or if the evidence is not strong enough to prove his/her guilt.[2]

---

1 See F. Streng, *Strafrechtliche Sanktionen*, 3rd edn., Kohlhammer, Stuttgart 2012; B. Meier, *Strafrechtliche Sanktionen*, 4th edn., Springer, Berlin, Heidelberg and New York 2014; B. Bannenberg and D. Rössner, *Strafrechtliches Sanktionenrecht*, C.H. Beck, München 2018; G. Kett-Straub and H. Kudlich, *Sanktionenrecht*, C.H. Beck, München 2017; B. Meier and S. Noetzel, *Fallsammlung zum Sanktionenrecht*, Springer, Berlin, Heidelberg and New York 2009.

2 Federal Statistical Office (Statistisches Bundesamt), *Statistisches Jahrbuch 2017*, p 309 <https://www.destatis.de/DE/Publikationen/StatistischesJahrbuch/StatistischesJahrbuch2017.pdf>.

About 67 per cent of all registered crimes cannot be prosecuted because there are not sufficient grounds for suspicion or the guilt is negligible.[3] Even if a crime is committed, i.e. a person being robbed, a house set on fire, a person being drowning or murdered, the alleged person must be set free for lack of proof. A criminal sanction cannot be enforced.

2.2. LEGAL REASONS FOR NON-ENFORCEMENT

Besides the factual reasons, there are legal reasons for non-enforcement. In these cases, there is clear evidence that the alleged person has committed a crime, yet, there must be an acquittal. The discharge may be based on substantive or procedural criminal law.

2.2.1. Substantive Law Reasons for Non-Enforcement

Substantive law reasons are, for example, lack of culpability (Sec. 20 Criminal Code)[4] or intent (see Sec. 15 Criminal Code),[5] or justifications such as self-defence (Sec. 32 Criminal Code), or justified emergency (Sec. 34 Criminal Code), or the informed consent of the victim, or errors in fact (Sec. 16 Criminal Code) or in law (Sec. 17 Criminal Code), as well as (procedural) impediments such as limitation on prosecution (Sec. 78 Criminal Code), or no request to prosecute (Sec. 77 Criminal Code). All these reasons lead to a judgment of 'not guilty'.[6] The criminal penalty will not be enforced. If, on the contrary, substantive law is met, meaning there is an action that at least satisfies the requirements of the criminal norm, has been done voluntarily, was intentional or negligent, unlawful and culpable, and moreover all evidence proves the perpetrators' guilt, there can however still be an acquittal.

2.2.2. Procedural Law Reasons for Non-Enforcement

This is when there are procedural law reasons for non-enforcements. The following will not concentrate on inadmissibility of evidence or procedural

---

3 Nearly half of all registered crimes remain unsolved, see FEDERAL STATISTICAL OFFICE, *Statistisches Jahrbuch 2017*, p 315.

4 In the following Criminal Code is used for Strafgesetzbuch (German Criminal Code). For Sec. 20 Criminal Code see F. STRENG, in W. JOECKS and K. MIEBACH (eds.), *Münchener Kommentar zum Strafgesetzbuch*, 3rd edn., C.H. Beck, München 2017, §20 para. 1 et seq.; B. WEIßER and W. PERRON, in A. ESER (ed.), *Schönke/Schröder Strafgesetzbuch*, 29th edn., C.H. Beck, München 2014, §20 para. 1 et seq.

5 I. PUPPE in U. KINDHÄUSER, U. NEUMANN and H. PAEFFGEN (eds.), *NomosKommentar Strafgesetzbuch*, 5th edn., Nomos, Baden-Baden 2017, §15.

6 W. BEULKE, *Strafprozessrecht*, 12th edn., C.F. Müller, Heidelberg 2012, p 212.

impediments,[7] or other ways that impede a criminal procedure[8] and, therefore, have effect on criminal enforcement but rather will focus on the main cases of non-prosecution where there is no need for punishment. These cases are of highly practical relevance and show how procedural law influences criminal enforcement.[9]

2.2.2.1. First Example

The main example is the non-prosecution of minor offences (Sec. 153 Code of Criminal Procedure).[10] It states that 'if a misdemeanour is the subject of the proceedings, the public prosecution office may dispense with prosecution with the approval of the court competent to open the main proceedings if the perpetrator's guilt is considered to be of a minor nature and there is no public interest in the prosecution.' So, here there is no obstacle to substantive or procedural criminal law, no lack of evidence and the perpetrator is highly likely to have committed the offence, but yet the proceedings are dismissed. Why? Because the necessity to penalise is so low and if there is no public interest in the prosecution, the case is dismissed.[11] An example is shoplifting. The theft of shop items is widespread and committed on a huge scale. Unless the prosecution office wanted to set an example on general prevention, a single shoplift is a minor offence that will not be prosecuted.

2.2.2.2. Second Example

There are other regulations of non-enforcement, for example, the prosecutor may 'dispense with preferment of public charges and concurrently impose conditions and instructions upon the accused if these are of such a nature as to

---

7 C. Roxin and B. Schünemann, *Strafverfahrensrecht*, 29th edn., C.H. Beck, München 2017, p. 172 et seq.; W. Beulke, *Strafprozessrecht*, 12th edn., C.F. Müller, Heidelberg 2012, p. 307 et seq.

8 C. Roxin and B. Schünemann, *Strafverfahrensrecht*, 29th edn., C.H. Beck, München 2017, pp. 145, 150; W. Beulke, *Strafprozessrecht*, 12th edn., C.F. Müller, Heidelberg 2012, pp. 189 et seq., 197.

9 Federal Statistical Office, *Statistisches Jahrbuch 2017*, p. 315.

10 In the following Code of Criminal Procedure is used for Strafprozessordnung (German Code of Criminal Procedure).

11 H. Diemer in R. Hannich (ed.), *Karlsruher Kommentar zur Strafprozessordnung*, 7th edn., C.H. Beck, München 2013, §153 para. 11 et seq.; S. Peters in H. Schneider (ed.), *Münchener Kommentar zur Strafprozessordnung*, vol. 2, C.H. Beck, München 2016, §153 para. 81 et seq.; T. Pfordte in D. Dölling, G. Duttge, S. König and D. Rössner, *Gesamtes Strafrecht*, 4th edn., Nomos, Baden-Baden 2017, §153 para. 2 et seq.; R. Schnabel in H. Satzer, W. Schluckebier and G. Widmaier (eds.), *Strafprozessordnung*, 3rd edn., Carl Heymanns Verlag, Köln 2018, §153 para. 11 et seq.

eliminate the public interest in criminal prosecution and if the degree of guilt does not present an obstacle' (Sec. 153a I Code of Criminal Procedure). In this case, there is no lack of either suspicion or evidence, but still the proceedings will be terminated.

Why? Because the imposing of conditions and instructions, such as the payment of a sum of money to a non-profit-making institution or to the Treasury, or to participate in a social skills training course etc., compensate the necessity to penalise.[12] Still, severe crimes, such as murder or manslaughter or other felonies can never be compensated in this way.

In these two examples criminal enforcement depends on the nature of the crime (minor offence) and the way of compensation (conditions and instructions). This shows that the enforcement of criminal law and sanctions is the ultima ratio. The ultima ratio rule is based on the principle of proportionality which is derived from the rule of law laid down in Article 20 German Constitution.[13] In criminal law, the ultima ratio principle answers the question whether criminal law should be the adequate reaction to unlawful behaviour.

The legislator initially intended the conviction as the rule and dispensing with the prosecution as the exception. Meanwhile, the rule-exception-relation has reversed and is now the opposite in legal practice. To give an impression of the practical relevance of legal and factual reasons for non-enforcement: of round about 6,330,000 registered criminal cases a year, nearly half of them (3,565,000) can be solved. The other cases remain unsolved because of factual reasons, mainly because the perpetrator cannot be identified.[14] More than a million (1,200,000) of these solved cases need to be subtracted because they are multiple crimes of already recorded suspects. Furthermore, another 70,000 suspects cannot be criminally responsible because of their age. Only 738,000 out the remaining 2,290,000 cases result in a sentence. Sanctions against the others (1.5 million) are not enforced because of factual and legal reasons, mainly because there are not sufficient reasons for suspicion or the guilt is negligible. Another 150,000 cases can be subtracted for acquittal and dispensing with prosecution so that, in the end, 588,000 cases lead to a verdict (including probation, fine and other sanctions) and 34,000 to a conviction of imprisonment without probation.[15]

---

12 H. Diemer in R. Hannich (ed.), *Karlsruher Kommentar zur Strafprozessordnung*, 7th edn., C.H. Beck, München 2013, §153 para. 11 et seq.; S. Peters in H. Schneider (ed.), *Münchener Kommentar zur Strafprozessordnung*, vol. 2, C.H. Beck, München 2016, §153 para. 10 et seq.; R. Schnabel in H. Satzer, W. Schluckebier and G. Widmaier (eds.), *Strafprozessordnung*, 3rd edn., Carl Heymanns Verlag, Köln 2018, §153 para. 12 et seq.

13 B. Grzeszick in R. Herzog, R. Scholz, M. Herdegen and H. Klein (eds.), *Maunz/Dürig Grundgesetz*, 83rd edn., C.H. Beck, München 2018, Art. 20 para. 125.

14 Federal Statistical Office, *Statistisches Jahrbuch 2017*, p 315.

15 Federal Statistical Office, *Statistisches Jahrbuch 2017*, p 315.

2.2.2.3. Third Example

Another very good example for non-enforcement on procedural grounds is the German Code of Crimes against International Law (*Völkerstrafgesetzbuch*). The principle of universal jurisdiction (*Weltrechtsprinzip*) is laid down in its section 1: 'This act shall apply to all criminal offences against international law designated under this Act, to serious criminal offences designated therein, even when the offence was committed abroad and bears no relation to Germany'. Thus, German courts can claim criminal jurisdiction over an accused person regardless of where the alleged crime was committed, and regardless of the accused's nationality, country of residence, or any other relation with the prosecuting entity. Hence, no genuine link to Germany is required.[16]

Why? Because the core crimes laid down in the German Code of Crimes against International Law, such as genocide, crimes against humanity, war crimes and crimes of aggression, are so severe that each State worldwide has the right to bring these criminals to justice.[17] These crimes concern everyone and every nation. But yet, is it is awkward that a German judge holds court in Frankfurt over an Iraqi who commanded a homicide of an ethnic group in Syria and therefore committed a crime against humanity? The German legislator thinks so, or rather that it is not awkward, but ineffective, because how can a German prosecutor receive all the evidence the prosecution needs depending entirely on the cooperation of the Syrian prosecution authorities; how can a German judge not violate national sovereignty by attracting such a case rather than an Iraqi court which has priority jurisdiction over the Iraqi citizen or the Syrian court which has jurisdiction over crimes committed on its territory?

---

16 K. Ambos in W. Joecks and K. Miebach (eds.), *Münchener Kommentar zum Strafgesetzbuch*, 3rd edn., C.H. Beck, München 2017, §1 para. 1 et seq.; C. Safferling, *Internationales Strafrecht*, Springer, Berlin, Heidelberg und New York 2011, pp. 93 et seq.

17 K. Ambos in W. Joecks and K. Miebach (eds.), *Münchener Kommentar zum Strafgesetzbuch*, 3rd edn., C.H. Beck, München 2017, §1 para. 1 et seq.; G. Werle, 'Konturen eines deutschen Völkerstrafrechts' (2001) 18 *JuristenZeitung* 885, 890; G. Werle and F. Jeßberger, 'Das Völkerstrafgesetzbuch' (2002) 15 *JuristenZeitung* 724, 729; A. Zimmermann, 'Bestrafung völkerrechtlicher Verbrechen durch deutsche Gerichte nach In-Kraft-Treten des Völkerstrafgesetzbuchs' (2002) 42 *Neue Juristische Wochenschrift* 3068, 3069; E. Pick in S. Lüder and T. Vormbaum (eds.), *Materialien zum Völkerstrafgesetzbuch. Dokumentation des Gesetzgebungsverfahrens*, LIT Verlag, Berlin, Münster, Wien, Zürich and London 2002; p. 80; F. Jeßberger, 'Universality, Complementarity, and the Duty to Prosecute Crimes Under International Law in Germany' in W. Kaleck, M. Ratner, T. Singelnstein and P. Weiss (eds.), *International Prosecution of Human Rights Crimes*, Springer, Berlin, Heidelberg and New York 2006, pp. 213–23; R. Hannich, 'Justice in the Name of All – Die praktische Anwendung des Völkerstrafgesetzbuchs aus der Sicht des Generalbundesanwalts beim Bundesgerichtshof' (2007) 13 *Zeitschrift für Internationale Srafrechtsdogmatik* 507 510; B. Zypries, 'Strafverfolgung von Völkerrechtsverbrechen: Eine Herausforderung für die deutsche Justiz' in G. Theissen and M. Nagler (eds.), *Der Internationale Strafgerichtshof. Fünf Jahre nach Rom*, Deutsches Institut für Menschenrechte, Berlin 2003, pp. 11–18.

Although section 1 of the International Criminal Code as an implementation of the ICC Statute is still in force and the universal jurisdiction is the central principle of this code, there are ways to avoid the problems mentioned above. In practice, the criminal enforcement of that provision is low and limited to cases where the following criteria are not met. The German Criminal Procedure Code contains a provision (Sec. 153 f Code of Criminal Procedure) which regulates the dispensing with prosecution of criminal offences under the German Code of Crimes against International Law.[18] If criminal offences have been committed outside the territorial scope of the German statute and if the accused is not resident in Germany, the public prosecution office may dispense with prosecuting an offence for which there is criminal liability pursuant to the core crimes of the German Code of Crimes against International Law, 'in particular if

1. no German is suspected of having committed the crime;
2. the offence was not committed against a German;
3. no suspect is, or is expected to be, resident in Germany;
4. the offence is being prosecuted by an international court of justice or by a country on whose territory the offence was committed, a citizen of which is either suspected of the offence, or suffered injury as a result of the offence' (Sec. 153 f II Code of Criminal Procedure).

Here there is a clear reason legal reason for non-enforcement. This shows that a criminal provision which broadens the scope of the referred code is altered and restricted by a criminal procedure provision.[19] With an eye to practicality,

---

18 H. Diemer in R. Hannich (ed.), *Karlsruher Kommentar zur Strafprozessordnung*, 7th edn., C.H. Beck, München 2013, §153f para. 1 et seq; A. Zimmermann, 'Auf dem Weg zu einem deutschen Völkerstrafgesetzbuch – Entstehung, völkerrechtlicher Rahmen und wesentliche Inhalte' (2002) 3 *Zeitschrift für Rechtspolitik* 97, 102; G. Werle, 'Konturen eines deutschen Völkerstrafrechts' (2001) 18 *JuristenZeitung* 885; H. Satzger, 'Das neue Völkerstrafgesetzbuch – eine kritische Würdigung –' (2002) 3 *Neue Zeitschrift für Strafrecht* 125, 132; J. Maclean, 'Gesetzentwurf über die Zusammenarbeit mit dem Internationalen Strafgerichtshof' (2002) 6 *Zeitschrift für Rechtspolitik*, 260, 264; G. Werle and F. Jeßberger, 'Das Völkerstrafgesetzbuch' (2002) 15 *JuristenZeitung* 725 et seq; T. Weigend, 'Das Völkerstrafgesetzbuch – Nationale Kodifikation internationalen Rechts' in O. Triffterer (ed.), *Gedächtnisschrift für Theo Vogler*, C.F. Müller, Heidelberg 2004, pp. 197–212; K. Ambos, 'Völkerrechtliche Kernverbrechen, Weltrechtsprinzip und §153f StPO – Zugleich Anmerkung zu GBA, JZ 2005, 311 und OLG Stuttgart, NStZ 2006, 117 – (2006) 8 *Neue Zeitschrift für Strafrecht* 434, 438.

19 D. Teßner in H. Schneider (ed.), *Münchener Kommentar zur Strafprozessordnung*, vol. 2, C.H. Beck, München 2016, §153f para. 1 et seq; H. Diemer in R. Hannich (ed.), *Karlsruher Kommentar zur Strafprozessordnung*, 7th edn., C.H. Beck, München 2013, §153f para. 1 et seq.; R. Keller, 'Grenzen, Unabhängigkeit und Subsidiarität der Weltrechtspflege' (2006) *Goltdammer's Archiv für Strafrecht* 25, 34; K. Ambos, 'Völkerrechtliche Kernverbrechen, Weltrechtsprinzip und §153f StPO – Zugleich Anmerkung zu GBA, JZ 2005, 311 und OLG Stuttgart, NStZ 2006, 117 –' (2006) 8 *Neue Zeitschrift für Strafrecht* 434, 438;

such a regulation should improve the peace in legal matters in cases where foreign jurisdictions are concerned, as well as promote procedural economy by avoiding expensive and extensive investigations and prosecution when the prospect of success might be low. To get incitation for a German and European Law of Remedies the German Code of Crimes against International Law gives a good example.

3. HOW ARE CRIMINAL SANCTIONS ENFORCED?

Directly linked to the question how substantive criminal law is or is not enforced is the question how criminal sanctions are enforced. The complex nature of criminal regulations offers a variety of reactions to a criminal offence.[20] The two main reactions are imprisonment and fine for culpable persons or measures of rehabilitation and incapacitation for non-culpable persons (Sec. 61 et seq.).

These measures are, for example, mental hospital orders, custodial addiction treatment orders, or supervision orders. But there are also ways to just warn the offender without sentencing him/her or just discharge the sanction. For example, Sec. 60 of the German Criminal Code says that 'the court may order a discharge if the consequences of the offence suffered by the offender are so serious that an imposition of penalties would be clearly inappropriate'. That is when the offender him/herself was seriously injured by the crime he/she committed or suffered thereof a severe financial loss. However, the discharge does not apply if the offender has incurred a sentence of imprisonment of more than one year for the offence. The judge has a margin of discretion to decide if the preconditions for a discharge of the sanction are met. Then the discharge is mandatory. Therefore, the judge can order the enforcement or non-enforcement of a criminal sanction, although all required conditions for a conviction are met.[21] One could even

see in general J. Geneuss, *Völkerrechtsverbrechen und Verfolgungsermessen: §153f StPO im System völkerrechtlicher Strafrechtspflege*, Nomos, Baden-Baden 2013.

20 F. Streng, *Strafrechtliche Sanktionen*, 3rd edn., Kohlhammer, Stuttgart 2012; B. Meier, *Strafrechtliche Sanktionen*, 4th edn., Springer, Berlin, Heidelberg and New York 2014; B. Bannenberg and D. Rössner, *Strafrechtliches Sanktionenrecht*, C.H. Beck, München 2018; G. Kett-Straub and H. Kudlich, *Sanktionenrecht*, C.H. Beck, München 2017; B. Meier and S. Noetzel, *Fallsammlung zum Sanktionenrecht*, Springer, Berlin, Heidelberg and New York 2009.

21 H. Albrecht in U. Kindhäuser, U. Neumann and H. Paeffgen (eds.), *NomosKommentar* Strafgesetzbuch, vol. 1, 5th edn., Nomos, Baden-Baden 2017, §60 para. 3; M. Maiwald, 'Das Absehen von Strafe nach §16 StGB' 681 (1971) 3 Zeitschrift für die gesamte Strafrechtswissenschaft 663, 696; W. Hassemer, 'Das "Absehen von Strafe" als kriminalpolitisches Instrument' in R. Hamm (ed.) *Festschrift für Werner Sarstedt zum 70. Geburtstag*, de Gruyter, Berlin and Boston 1981, pp. 65–80; P. Bringewat, 'Das Absehen von Erziehungsmaßregeln – ein Absehen von Strafe?' (1992) *Neue Zeischrift für Strafrecht* 315, 318; J. Gräfe, *Sinn und System des Absehens von Strafe*, Verlag Dr. Kovac, Hamburg 2012; F. Streng, 'Mittelbare Strafwirkungen und Strafzumessung. Zur Bedeutung

ask to what extent the legislator can choose between civil law, public law and criminal law sanctions. Here again the ultima ratio principle as an expression of the principle of proportionality applies for criminal law. Other instruments as civil law and public law have to be applied before criminal law as the sharpest sword of the State, intervening most strongly in personal rights, can be used to enforce legal peace. Between criminal sanctions or administrative law sanctions (*Ordnungswidrigkeiten*) the legislator has a considerable scope to choose. But the nature and extent of punishment must always be in a reasonable relation to the guilt and to the severity of the offence.[22] Moreover, there are many ways of sentencing that allow reduction of the penalty or measures of rehabilitation and incapacitation and, therefore, influence their enforcement.[23]

4. HOW CAN PRIVATE PERSONS INFLUENCE THE ENFORCEMENT OF CRIMINAL SANCTIONS?

This question especially concerns the relation of private versus public enforcement. The starting point is that criminal law is public enforcement par excellence. Generally, the State enforces criminal sanctions. The State has the monopoly on the use of force.[24] The investigation as well as the prosecution and conviction are executed by the State, represented by the public prosecutor (as part of the executive) and the judge (as part of the judicative power).[25] However, there are exceptions in which private persons can take a role in the enforcement of criminal sanctions. There are remedies which influence the enforcement of a criminal penalty or other sanction. A distinction should be made between the parties to the proceedings: the convicted, the public prosecutor, the victim and witnesses and experts. All of them have special remedies that can influence the enforcement of sanctions. And in all cases private persons oppose the public enforcement.

---

disziplinarrechtlicher Folgen einer Verurteilung für die Bejahung minder schwerer Fälle' (1988) *Neue Zeitschrift für Strafrecht* 485, 467.

22 B. Grzeszick in R. Herzog, R. Scholz, M. Herdegen and H. Klein (eds.), *Maunz/Dürig Grundgesetz*, 83rd edn., C.H. Beck, München 2018, Art. 20 para. 125.

23 S. Maier in W. Joecks and K. Miebach (eds.), *Münchener Kommentar zum Strafgesetzbuch*, 3rd edn., C.H. Beck, München 2016, §67 para. 1 et seq.; G. Schäfer, G. Sander and G. van Gemmeren, *Praxis der Strafzumessung*, 6th edn., C.H. Beck, München 2017; H. Bruns and G. Güntge, *Strafzumessung*, 3rd edn., Carl Heymanns Verlag, Köln 2018; W. Frisch, 'Strafkonzept, Strafzumessungstatsachen und Maßstäbe der Strafzumessung in der Rechtsprechung des BGH' in C. Canaris (ed.), *Festgabe der Wissenschaft zum 50-jährigen Bestehen des Bundesgerichtshofs*, vol. 4, C.H. Beck, München 2000, pp. 269–308.

24 M. Herdegen in R. Herzog, R. Scholz, M. Herdegen and H. Klein (eds.), *Maunz/Dürig Grundgesetz*, 83rd edn., C.H. Beck, München 2018, Art. 79 para. 180.

25 §152 II Code of Criminal Procedure, §170 Code of Criminal Procedure and Art. 92 German Constitution.

4.1. REMEDIES OF THE CONVICTED

The remedies of the convicted are well known as there is the appeal possibility on points of law and facts,[26] appeal on points of law only,[27] complaint,[28] reopening of the proceedings concluded by a final judgment,[29] restoration of the status quo ante[30] and constitutional complaint.[31]

The accused or the convicted, will file all these remedies to obtain a lower sentence or in case of the restoration of the status quo ante or reopening of the proceedings to obtain a better chance for defending him/herself. In any event, the convicted opposes the ruling and, therefore, the public enforcement. If the convicted succeeds, his/her remedy leads at the end to an acquittal. The result is a non-enforcement of the penalty.

4.2. REMEDIES OF THE PUBLIC PROSECUTOR (THE STATE)

Although the prosecutor in his/her role as party to the proceedings represents no private person, he/she can oppose a conviction and demand even an acquittal. With the same remedies as the convicted, the prosecution can

---

26 §312 et seq. Code of Criminal Procedure; see C. Paul in R. Hannich (ed.), *Karlsruher Kommentar zur Strafprozessordnung*, 7th edn., C.H. Beck, München 2013, §312 para. 1 et seq; D. Dölling in R. Wassermann (ed.) *Kommentar zur Strafprozessordnung (Reihe Alternativkommentare)*, vol. 2, subvol. 1, Neuwied 1992, before §312 para 1; S. Beukelmann in H. Radtke and O. Hohmann (eds.), *Strafprozessordnung*, Vahlen, München 2011, §312 para 1.

27 §333 et seq. Code of Criminal Procedure; see J.Gericke in R. Hannich (ed.), *Karlsruher Kommentar zur Strafprozessordnung*, 7th edn., C.H. Beck, München 2013, §333 para. 1; S. Wiedner in J. Graf (ed.) *Beck'scher Online-Kommentar stop mit RiStBV und MiStra*, 30th edn. (01.06.2018), C.H. Beck, München 2018, §333 para. 1 et seq.; BGH 20.12.1955, *NJW* 1956, 478, 480 = *BGHSt* 8, 383, 390; BGH 25. 3.1952, *BGHSt* 25, 242, 246.

28 Sec. 304 et seq. Code of Criminal Procedure; S. Neuheuser in H. Schneider (ed.), *Münchener Kommentar zur Strafprozessordnung*, vol. 2, C.H. Beck, München 2016, §304 para. 1 et seq; A. Zabeck in R. Hannich (ed.), *Karlsruher Kommentar zur Strafprozessordnung*, 7th edn., C.H. Beck, München 2013, §304 para. 1 et seq; OLG Nürnberg 21.5.1948, *HESt* 2, 152, 153; OLG Stuttgart 14.2.2011, *NStZ* 2011, 709, 710 = *Die Justiz* 2011, 184, 185; BGH 01.07.2005, *NJW* 2005, 3078, 3080 = *BGHSt* 50, 180, 188.

29 Sec. 359 et seq. Code of Criminal Procedure; see W Schmidt in R. Hannich (ed.), *Karlsruher Kommentar zur Strafprozessordnung*, 7th edn., C.H. Beck, München 2013, §359 para. 1; T. Singelnstein in J. Graf (ed.) *Beck'scher Online-Kommentar StPO mit RiStBV und MiStra*, 30th edn. (01.06.2018), C.H. Beck, München 2018, §359 para. 1 et seq.

30 Sec. 44 et seq. Code of Criminal Procedure; see B. Valerius in H. Kudlich (ed.), *Münchener Kommentar zur Strafprozessordnung*, vol. 2, C.H. Beck, München 2014, §44 para. 1 et seq; K. Graalmann-Scheerer in V. Erb and C. Stuckenberg, *Löwe-Rosenberg. Die Strafprozessordnung und das Gerichtsverfassungsgesetz*, vol. 1, 26th edn., de Gruyter, Berlin and Boston 2006, §44 para. 1 et seq.; BVerfG 8.8.1990, *NJW* 1991, 351; BVerfG 18.10.2012, *NJW* 2013, 592.

31 Art. 93 I Nr. 4a German Constitution.

influence the outcome of the criminal sentence.[32] They can file a remedy in favour or against the convicted.[33] If they do so in favour of the convicted, they directly oppose the ruling of the judge. The successful appeal then leads to a non-enforcement of the penalty.

4.3. REMEDIES OF OTHERS

4.3.1. Victims

The victims have particular remedies.

4.3.1.1. Private Prosecution (Privatklageverfahren, Sec. 374 Code of Criminal Procedure)

On specific crimes the victim can bring private prosecution against the offender. This remedy in form of particular proceedings is the most important example of private enforcement versus public enforcement. Sec. 374 I Code of Criminal Procedure states that:

> an aggrieved person may bring a private prosecution without need to have recourse to the public prosecution office first; this is possible in respect of the following offences
>
> 1. trespass (section 123 of the Criminal Code);
> 2. defamation (sections 185 to 189 of the Criminal Code) unless it is directed against one of the political bodies specified in section 194 subsection (4) of the Criminal Code;
> 3. violation of the privacy of correspondence (section 202 of the Criminal Code);
> 4. bodily injury (sections 223 and 229 of the Criminal Code);
> 5. stalking (section 238 subsection (1) of the Criminal Code) or threat (section 241 of the Criminal Code);
>
> 5a. taking or offering a bribe in business transactions (section 299 of the Criminal Code);
>
> 6. criminal damage to property (section 303 of the Criminal Code);

32 See above 4.1.

33 §296 II Code of Criminal Procedure; D. Sternberg-Lieben, 'Einstellungsurteil oder Freispruch' (1996) 4 *Zeitschrift für die gesamte Strafrechtswissenschaft* 721, 758; P. Allgayer in H. Schneider (ed.), *Münchener Kommentar zur Strafprozessordnung*, vol. 2, C.H. Beck, München 2016, §269 para. 1; C. Paul in R. Hannich (ed.), *Karlsruher Kommentar zur Strafprozessordnung*, 7th edn., C.H. Beck, München 2013, §296; RG 21.09.1909, *RGSt 42*, 399, 401; OLG Koblenz 19.11.1981, *NJW* 1982, 1770; BGH 25.1.1952, *NJW* 1952, 435, 436 = *BGHSt* 2, 41; OLG Celle 13.09.2000, *NStZ-RR* 2001, 90, 91; see also RiStBV 147 III.

6a. a criminal offence pursuant to section 323a of the Criminal Code, where the offence, having been committed during a state of intoxication, is a misdemeanour referred to in numbers 1 to 6" (Sec. 374 I Code of Criminal Procedure)
7. a criminal offence pursuant to sections 16 to 19 of the Act against Unfair Competition;
8. criminal offences pursuant to section 142 subsection (1) of the Patent Act, section 25 subsection (1) of the Utility Models Act, section 10 subsection (1) of the Semi-Conductor Protection Act, section 39 subsection (1) of the Plant Variety Protection Act, section 143 subsection (1), section 143a subsection (1) and section 144 subsections (1) and (2) of the Trade Mark Act, section 51 subsection (1) and section 65 subsection (1) of the Designs Act, sections 106 to 108 and section 108b subsections (1) and (2) of the Copyright and Related Rights Act and section 33 of the Act on the Copyright of Works of Fine Art and Photography.

All these listed crimes are misdemeanours, meaning unlawful acts punishable by a lesser sentence than one year's imprisonment or by fine (Sec. 12 II Criminal Code) and almost all of them are prosecuted only on request (except Sec. 241 Criminal Code). Why does the law allow private enforcement in these cases? The reason is that these minor offences only affect the legal sphere of (the) offender and victim. As long as there is no public interest (*öffentliches Interesse*), it is up to the victim to bring a private prosecution against the offender.[34] The victim can decide if he/she wants the trespass or defamation to be prosecuted or to let the matter rest. The public prosecutor shall not be obliged to participate in private prosecution proceedings, but the prosecution may be assumed by making an express statement at any stage of the proceedings before the judgment enters into force. The private prosecutor may be assisted by a lawyer. This is a real breakthrough of the principle of public indictment and public prosecution.[35] But to 'tame' the private prosecutor and to prevent troublemakers to occupy the courts, there are some mechanisms. One is that the court may terminate the proceedings if the

---

34 BGH 18.1.1983, *NJW* 1983, 1919, 1921 = *BGHSt* 31, 207; P. Rieß, 'Die Zukunft des Legalitätsprinzips' (1981) *Neue Zeitschrift für Strafrecht* 2, 10; L. Senge in R. Hannich (ed.), *Karlsruher Kommentar zur Strafprozessordnung*, 7th edn., C.H. Beck, München 2013, §374 para. 1 et seq, §376 para. 1 et seq.; B. Valerius in J. Graf (ed.) *Beck'scher Online-Kommentar StPO mit RiStBV und MiStra*, 30th edn. (01.06.2018), C.H. Beck, München 2018, §374 para. 2; see also RiStBV 86 II.

35 B. Valerius in J. Graf (ed.) *Beck'scher Online-Kommentar StPO mit RiStBV und MiStra*, 30th edn. (01.06.2018), C.H. Beck, München 2018, §374 para. 1, who points out that the private prosecution more than ever serves the discharge by the prosecution office as it can refer the victim to private prosecution. In practice the number of successful private prosecution charges is very low; see the empirical data at H. Hilger in H. Hilger and K. Gössel, *Löwe-Rosenberg. Die Strafprozessordnung und das Gerichtsverfassungsgesetz*, vol. 8, 26th edn., de Gruyter, Berlin and Boston 2009, before §374 para. 4.

perpetrator's guilt is negligible. In that case the private prosecutor has to bear the costs. Furthermore, the private prosecutor also has to furnish security for the costs expected to arise for the accused and to pay in advance for fees, so the cost risk for him/her is high and might prevent him/her from filing legal actions. The other way to avoid a legal trial is that the prosecution for most of the mentioned offences may be brought only after conciliation was unsuccessfully attempted by a conciliation board which is to be designated by the Department of Justice.[36] The aim is rather reconciliation than having a trial. Similar to the principle of party disposition in civil law, the private prosecutor can exercise sole control over legal proceedings by withdrawal of charges at any stage of the proceedings. Like a party in a civil lawsuit, the private prosecutor can delimit the subject matter of the dispute. But, as is typical for a criminal trial, the court shall always determine the extent to which evidence shall be taken, so that the taking and hearing of evidence is *ex officio*. Hence, the private prosecution is not purely private enforcement; it has a share of public enforcement. Nevertheless, as long as there is no public interest in the case, only private persons can initiate and enforce the criminal prosecution.

4.3.1.2. Accessory Private Prosecution (Nebenklage, Sec. 395 Code of Criminal Procedure)

Another way for private persons to influence the enforcement of criminal sanctions is the accessory private prosecution. In contrast to minor offences at private enforcement here serious felonies against personal rights are at stake, like for example murder, manslaughter, rape, grievous bodily harm, abandonment and other crimes. To get gratification, to give emphasis to the prosecution and to support and control the prosecutor the private person, in most cases the victim or close relatives of a killed victim, joins as a 'second prosecutor'.[37]

The aim is to enforce the victim's interests by active participation in the trial. By submitting a declaration of joinder, he/she becomes a party to the proceedings with the right for application to take evidence, the right to be present at trial and be represented by a lawyer and the right for appeal and

---

[36] §380 Code of Criminal Procedure; H. Hilger in H. Hilger and K. Gössel, *Löwe-Rosenberg. Die Strafprozessordnung und das Gerichtsverfassungsgesetz*, vol. 8, 26th edn., de Gruyter, Berlin and Boston 2009, §380 para. 23; L. Senge, in R. Hannich (ed.), *Karlsruher Kommentar zur Strafprozessordnung*, 7th edn., C.H. Beck, München 2013, §380 para. 7.

[37] B. Weiner in J. Graf (ed.) *Beck'scher Online-Kommentar StPO mit RiStBV und MiStra*, 30th edn. (01.06.2018), C.H. Beck, München 2018, §395 para. 1; BT-Drs. 10/5305, 13.

other remedies.[38] By exercising their rights, victims may influence the outcome of the judgment and, therefore, the enforcement of criminal sanctions.

4.3.1.3. Compensation (Adhäsionsverfahren, Sec. 403 Code of Criminal Procedure)

Another remedy for the victim in the form of a special proceeding is the compensation of the aggrieved person. The victim or his/her heir 'may, in criminal proceedings, bring a property claim against the accused arising out of the criminal offence if the claim falls under the jurisdiction of the ordinary courts and is not yet pending before another court, in proceedings before the Local Court irrespective of the value of the matter in dispute' (Sec. 403 Code of Criminal Procedure). The main example is compensation for non-economic or economic losses.[39] Although this is private enforcement and only initiated on request of the victim, the public share of the criminal trial is still apparent. The civil claims for damages are titled in the criminal judgment.

4.3.1.4. Proceedings to Compel Public Charges (Klageerzwingungsverfahren, Sec. 172 Code of Criminal Procedure)

If the prosecution office terminated the proceedings because in its view there were not sufficient reasons for preferring public charges, the aggrieved person could contest this decision.[40] The victim is entitled to lodge a complaint against the notification of the termination of proceedings within two weeks after the receipt of such notification. Thus, he/she can compel public charges. If this complaint is dismissed, he/she may apply for a court decision within one month of receipt of notification. The application 'shall be inadmissible where the sole subject of the proceedings is a criminal offence which may be prosecuted by

38 R. Kusch 'Aus der Rechtsprechung des BGH zum Strafverfahrensrecht' (1999) 2 *NStZ Rechtsprechungs-Report Strafrecht* 33, 39; H. Schöch in H. Satzer, W. Schluckebier and G. Widmaier (eds.) *Strafprozessordnung*, 3rd edn., Carl Heymanns Verlag, Köln 2018, §396 para. 1; B. Weiner in J. Graf (ed.) *Beck'scher Online-Kommentar StPO mit RiStBV und MiStra*, 30th edn. (01.06.2018), C.H. Beck, München 2018, §396 para 3.

39 BGH 5.11.2009, *NStZ* 2010, 714, 715; J. Becker, 'Aus der Rechtsprechung des BGH zum Strafverfahrensrecht – 2. Teil' (2004) 3 *NStZ Rechtsprechungs-Report Strafrecht* 65, 68; BGH 21.8.2002, *NJW* 2002, 3560, 3561 = *BGHSt* 47, 378; BGH 14.12.2011–*5 StR 471/11*; BGH 28.11.2002, *NStZ* 2003, 321; BGH 16.12.2008, *NStZ* 2009, 586; A. Zabeck in R. Hannich (ed.), *Karlsruher Kommentar zur Strafprozessordnung*, 7th edn., C.H. Beck, München 2013, §403 para. 1 et seq.

40 BVerfG 27.3.2001 – 2 BvR 2211/97 = NJW 2001, 1563; OLG Nürnberg, NStZ-RR 2000, 212; OLG Nürnberg 11.11.1997 – Ws 1078/97 = NStZ-RR 1998, 143; C. Gorf in J. Graf (ed.) *Beck'scher Online-Kommentar StPO mit RiStBV und MiStra*, 30th edn. (01.06.2018), C.H. Beck, München 2018, §172 para. 2 et seq.

the aggrieved person by way of a private prosecution, or where the public prosecution office has dispensed with preferring public charges in accordance' with Sec. 153 and the following, hence, non-prosecution of minor offences, non-prosecution by imposing conditions and instructions etc. The proceedings to compel public charges ensure the most important principle of legality in criminal law (Sec. 152 II, 170 Code of Criminal Procedure). That principle states the public prosecutor's obligation to accuse and prosecute all cases that provide sufficient reason and grounds for suspicion.[41] It protects citizens from State despotism and arbitrariness and promotes the law enforcement. Therefore, the victim, a private person, can compel the public enforcement of criminal law.

4.3.2. *Witnesses and Experts*

Furthermore, witnesses and experts take part in the proceedings. But they have no remedies that have an impact on the judgment. Even, for example, if a witness is absolutely sure to have seen a severe crime but the court terminates the proceedings, the witness cannot appeal. Although the witness cannot appeal in favour or against the accused, he/she can always bring a remedy in personal matters. For example, the witness can lodge a complaint against a coercive detention or a coercive fine.[42] Similar rules apply with regard to experts, as the provisions concerning witnesses shall apply *mutatis mutandis* to experts except as otherwise provided.[43]

4.3.3. *The Public*

Apart from the mentioned special remedies, everybody has the opportunity to bring a crime of which he/she knows to the knowledge of the police or of the public prosecutor. The public, thus, can initiate prosecution. In this function the public – consisting of private persons – plays a considerable role in criminal law enforcement, and law enforcement depends to a certain extent on the public's willingness to fulfil this function.

---

41 T. Pfordte in D. Dölling, G. Duttge, S. König and D. Rössner, *Gesamtes Strafrecht*, 4th edn., Nomos, Baden-Baden 2017, §152 para. 1; S. Beukelmann in J. Graf (ed.) *Beck'scher Online-Kommentar StPO mit RiStBV und MiStra*, 30th edn. (01.06.2018), C.H. Beck, München 2018, §152 para. 2; BVerfG 21.11.2002, *NJW* 2003, 1030, 1031.

42 BGH 03.05.1989, *BGHSt* 36, 192 = *NJW* 1989, 2702, 2703; LG Berlin 28.09.1994, *NStZ* 1995, 508, 510; OLG Frankfurt 7.4.2000, *NStZ-RR* 2000, 282, 285; KG Berlin 16.12.1999, *NStZ-RR* 2000, 145, 146; G. Sander, 'Zu Einzelheiten der Einstellung eines Ordnungsgeldverfahrens gegen einen Zeugen' (1995) *Neue Zeitschrift für Strafrecht* 509, 510; M. Percic in H. Kudlich (ed.), *Münchener Kommentar zur Strafprozessordnung*, vol.1, C.H. Beck, München 2014, §51 para. 57.

43 §72 Code of Criminal Procedure (Application of Provisions Concerning Witnesses).

5. CONCLUSION

In the first part of this chapter, it was shown that substantive criminal law and criminal sanctions are enforced on a very low scale in Germany. Of more than 6,000.000 registered cases a year only 590,000 lead to a conviction and 34,000 to a sentence of imprisonment without probation.[44] Whereas a huge number of offences remain unsolved, dispensing with prosecution has become the rule, and imprisonment the exception. The dispensing not only relieves the courts and, therefore, promotes economy of the trial, but it realises the concept of criminal law and its sanctions as the ultima ratio.[45] The German Code of Criminal Procedure takes this into account by providing for a range of provisions for non-enforcement. In particular, Sec. 153 f Code of Criminal Procedure, which refers to the code of crimes against international law, showed how unsuccessful proceedings can be avoided and trial economy as well as legal peace be improved.[46] As there is a variety of reactions to a criminal offence the judge has a margin of discretion to enforce or not enforce the criminal sanction even if all required conditions for a conviction are met. But is the legal directive of non-enforcement and its output in legal practice right? The author would agree that it is. The recent tendency of the legislator to create more and more criminal provisions (e.g. the new Sec. 315d, 114, 184 i, 265c Criminal Code) should be rejected strongly. The protection by criminal law shall and must be fragmentary. The opposite would be contrary to the rule of law, as it would even criminalise behaviour that is socially unwanted, but yet not unlawful. The enforcement of criminal law must be the ultima ratio. In contrast to some legal rules of EU internal market law, described as 'open' and 'imperfect' in the sense that they only impose duties without establishing corresponding rights and remedies, the criminal provisions must precisely be defined. They are not 'open' and an act may only be punished if criminal liability had been established by law before the act was committed.[47] The factual requirements and legal consequences of an offence and, therefore, the corresponding rights and remedies are clearly established in criminal law. Thus, criminal provisions allow no regulatory choice for 'private enforcement' and/or 'public enforcement'.

---

44 Federal Statistical Office, *Statistisches Jahrbuch 2017*, p 315.

45 B. Grzeszick in R. Herzog, R. Scholz, M. Herdegen and H. Klein (eds.), *Maunz/Dürig Grundgesetz*, 83rd edn., C.H. Beck, München 2018, Art. 20 para. 125.

46 See in general J. Geneuss, *Völkerrechtsverbrechen und Verfolgungsermessen: §253f stop im System völkerrechtlicher Straferechtspflege*, Nomos, Baden-Baden 2013; R. Keller, 'Grenzen, Unabhängigkeit und Subsidiarität der Weltrechtspflege' (2006) *Goltdammer's Archiv für Strafrecht* 25, 34; K. Ambos, 'Völkerrechtliche Kernverbrechen, Weltrechtsprinzip und §153f StPO – Zugleich Anmerkung zu GBA, JZ 2005, 311 und OLG Stuttgart, NStZ 2006, 117 –' (2006) 8 *Neue Zeitschrift für Strafrecht* 434, 438.

47 Art. 103 II German Constitution and §1 Criminal Code.

The starting point for the second part of this chapter was that criminal enforcement is public enforcement par excellence. The State, represented by its executive and judicial power, has the monopoly of prosecution, accusation and conviction. This is guaranteed by law (see sec. 152 II, 170 Code of Criminal Procedure and Art. 92 German Constitution). Therefore, criminal rules and sanctions are publicly enforced by the State.[48] However, there are exceptions to that principle. The most important one is private prosecution in cases in which the victim initiates and enforces its right for prosecution of the offender. Cases of private prosecution are proceedings without a public prosecutor. In other cases, the parties to the proceedings cannot enforce but rather influence the outcome of a judgment by lodging their remedies. In these cases, the criminal enforcement remains public enforcement but with a big share of private influence. Finally, everybody who knows of a crime can inform the police to have an investigation and eventual proceedings started.

The question is: Should there be more private enforcement in criminal proceedings? In the author's view, it should not. It is a big achievement that independent courts decide on criminal cases and, in a system of checks and balances, an independent prosecution office conducts the criminal investigations. Delivering these powers into the hands of private persons would lead to self-administered justice, to violent mob-justice. The legislator was wise enough to limit the private prosecution to minor offences. However, as long as the administration of justice is exercised by its organs, private persons can and should bring in their rights, review the verdict by a higher appellate court, compel the public enforcement where adequate, support and control the public prosecutor and pursue their civil interests in compensation of losses in a criminal trial. The rights of the accused and of the victims have been strengthened by EU law in the recent years.

Thus, the European Parliament and Council issued a directive in 2012[49] establishing minimum standards on the rights, support and protection of victims of crime. In particular, it improved the procedural rights, the information, compensation and psychosocial help for victims. The directive was implemented in German law in December 2015 (3. OpferrechtsreformG).[50]

---

48 M. Herdegen in R. Herzog, R. Scholz, M. Herdegen and H. Klein (eds.), *Maunz/Dürig Grundgesetz*, 83rd edn., C.H. Beck, München 2018, Art. 79 para. 180; J. Dietlein in V. Epping and C. Hillgruber (eds.) *Beck'scher Online-Kommentar Grundgesetz*, 38th edn. (15.08.2018), C.H. Beck, München 2018, Art. 79 para. 4.

49 Directive 2012/29/EU of the European Parliament and of the Council of 25 October 2012 establishing minimum standards on the rights, support and protection of victims of crime, and replacing Council Framework Decision 2001/220/JHA.

50 Victims' Rights Reform Act of 21.12.2015 (Drittes Gesetz zur Stärkung der Opferrechte im Strafverfahren, Bundesgesetzblatt Teil I Jg. 2015 Nr.55).

Another EU-directive in 2013[51] which enhanced the procedural right of the suspect was implemented in German law in 2017.[52] The EU legislation shows a tendency to increase the influence of private parties in criminal proceedings. This development is positive. Within the current legal system, private parties to criminal proceedings are able to act as a counterbalance to a superior State power. Only a well-balanced trial can at the end lead to justice.

---

51 Directive 2013/48/EU of the European Parliament and of the Council of 22 October 2013 on the right of access to a lawyer in criminal proceedings and in European arrest warrant proceedings, and on the right to have a third party informed upon deprivation of liberty and to communicate with third persons and with consular authorities while deprived of liberty.

52 Accused Persons' Procedural Rights Reform Act of 27.8.2017 (Zweites Gesetz zur Stärkung der Verfahrensrechte von Beschuldigten im Strafverfahren und zur Änderung des Schöffenrechts, Bundesgesetzblatt Jg. 2017 Teil I Nr. 60).

PART III

FUNCTIONS OF REMEDIES

DISGORGEMENT OF PROFITS

Distributive and Deterrant Logics

Benjamin RAUE

1. INTRODUCTION

The law assigns individual property rights in order to achieve an optimal allocation of goods. Exclusive property rights create markets because they force parties to conclude contracts in which they negotiate the price and further conditions for the use of the goods. If this allocation mechanism is undermined by a one-sided appropriation of a good, the legal system must respond by providing remedies for the right holder to restore the market mechanism.[1]

---

1 Cf. M. POLINSKY and S. SHAVELL, 'Punitive Damages: An Economic Analysis' (1998) 111 *Harvard Law Review* 869, 945 f.; G. WAGNER, 'Prävention und Verhaltenssteuerung durch Privatrecht – Anmaßung oder legitime Aufgabe?' (2006) 206 *Archiv für die civilistische Praxis* 352, 376; H.-B. SCHÄFER and C. OTT, *Lehrbuch der ökonomischen Analyse des Zivilrechts*, 5th edn., 2012, pp. 281 f.; J. KÖNDGEN, 'Gewinnabschöpfung als Sanktion unerlaubten

In such a case, the principal remedy is an injunction.[2] An enforceable injunction forces the infringing party back to the negotiation table, thus restoring the contract mechanism.[3]

Nevertheless, there is usually a time gap between the infringement, its discovery by the right holder, and the issuance of an injunction. Damages and disgorgement remedies are aimed to close that time gap by either simulating a state in which the parties would have contracted or by preventing the infringement in the first place. Damages focus on the status of the right holder and aim to restore the status quo ante. Usually, this is a sufficient incentive not to infringe. However, there are cases of *fautes lucratives*, profitable torts, where the gains of the infringer exceed the losses of the infringed party. The disgorgement of those profits is often justified by the simple statement: '*tort does not pay*',[4] or more elaborately: '*right or wrong should not be reduced to a figure in a business calculation*.'[5] Those popular demands serve intuitive justice. Who commits a tort must not profit from their doings. Therefore, he or she should be stripped of all profits, which should be handed over to the victim.

Nevertheless, the reality is not so simple. Let us think of the owner of a car who steals a screw from a neighbour and fixes a minor problem with the car. The owner then sells the car well above market value. Does the owner really have to render the profit to the neighbour as the owner of the screw? Probably not, because the screw made no significant contribution to the ultimate profit.[6] Just like money that is spent for a winning lottery ticket, the screw was a replaceable, random factor in the transaction producing the profits.[7] Therefore, it does not seem fair to deprive the car owner of the profits of the sale.

Tuns: Eine juristisch-ökonomische Skizze' (2000) 64 *The Rabel Journal of Comparative and International Private Law* 661, 679 ff.

2 F. Hofmann, *Der Unterlassungsanspruch als Rechtsbehelf*, Mohr Siebeck, Tübingen 2017, p. 319 with further references.

3 B. Raue, '*Die dreifache Schadensberechnung: Eine Untersuchung zum deutschen und europäischen Immaterialgüter-, Lauterkeits- und Bürgerlichen Recht*' in C. Berger, B. Dauner-Lieb, B. Hess, A. Junker, D. Looschelders, H.-P. Honsel and H.C. Grigoleit (eds.), *Neue Schriften zum Zivilrecht*, vol. 5, Nomos, Baden-Baden 2017, p. 261.

4 Cf. in an exemplary damages case *Rookes v Barnard* [1964] 1 All ER 367, 411 (HL, Lord *Devlin*).

5 German quotation: 'Unrecht darf nicht zum "Rechenexempel" werden', A. Ehrenzweig, 'System des österreichischen allgemeinen Privatrechts' in L. Pfaff (ed.), *Das Recht der Schuldverhältnisse*, vol. II/1, Manz, Wien 1920, p. 732; E. v. Caemmerer, 'Bereicherung und unerlaubte Handlung' in H. Dölle, M. Rheinstein and K. Zweigert (eds.), *Festschrift für Ernst Rabel*, Mohr, Tübingen 1954, pp. 333, 359; D. König, 'Gewinnhaftung' in C. Ficker, D. König K.F. Kreuzer, H.G. Leser, M. v. Bieberstein and E. v. Caemmerer (eds.), *Festschrift für Ernst v Caemmerer zum 70. Geburtstag*, pp. 179, 206.

6 For the significance test, see below 3.1.2.

7 See T. Helms, *Gewinnherausgabe als haftungsrechtliches Problem*, Mohr Siebeck, Tübingen 2007, p. 169.

However, even in cases where the infringed property right has a significant impact on the profitable tort, things are more difficult than it appears at first glance. The content of a novel most certainly contributes to the financial success of a book. Nevertheless, the author of that novel usually agrees in a publishing contract to receive only 5–10% of the sales price of the book.[8] The publisher, who turns the novel into a marketable book, sells those books to bookshops at a discount of around 35% on the net retail price. That attributes 55% of the sales price to the efforts made by the publisher. Accordingly, the market is convinced that 35% of the sales price of the book is attributable to its distribution. The contracting parties therefore assume that the profit made on each level of the book production is attributable to the party who generated it.

Now, the author has lost legal capacity just before signing the contract with the publisher due to a non-recognisable mental illness. There is no good faith acquisition of a copyright licence. Therefore, the publisher did not obtain the necessary rights to publish the book. The publisher and the bookseller infringed the author's copyright. Should the assessment of the individual contribution to the profits change due to the copyright infringement? Should the infringers both be obliged to render all the profits to the author although they did not know and had no reasonable grounds to know that they engaged in an infringing activity?

On the other hand, the case *Blackman v Hustler Magazine*[9] adds to the intuitive justification of the phrase 'tort must not pay'. Larry Flint, the owner and editor of *Hustler Magazine*, was offered the rights to nude photos depicting a woman involved in a scandal with a congressman. Flint did not accept the offered price of $25,000. He preferred to infringe copyright and printed the pictures in his various magazines without the authorisation of the photographer. The revenues of those magazines containing the infringing pictures were $3.9 million.

In all cases in which property rights are infringed, a legal system is obliged to answer three questions: First, whether the owner of an infringed property right is entitled to profits made by the infringer; second, (if so), what proportion the right owner may claim; and third, which costs infringers may deduct from their revenue.

The answers to these questions depend mainly on the function and aim pursued by a disgorging remedy. These complex questions have been addressed in several monographs and papers.[10] In this chapter, the focus will

---

8 Cf. for the example B. RAUE, above n. 3, p. 463.

9 *Blackman v Hustler Magazine* 800 F.2d 1160 (DC Cir. 1986).

10 J. EDELMAN, *Gain-Based Damages: Contract, Tort, Equity and Intellectual Property*, Hart Publishing, London 2002; T. HELMS, above n. 7; B. RAUE, above n. 3, Chapter 4 B; A. JANSSEN, *Präventive Gewinnabschöpfung*, Mohr Siebeck, Tübingen 2017.

be on the fundamental distinction between disgorgement remedies that follow a distributive approach (2.) and will contrast them with remedies that pursue a punishing or deterrent purpose (3.). The chapter aims to provide guidance for courts and legislators tasked with fashioning disgorging remedies, specifically in distinguishing between good faith/negligent behaviour and intentional/grossly negligent behaviour. The chapter does not, however, provide answers regarding the question for which kind of infringements it is advisable to disgorge the profits made by the infringer.[11] The same applies to the question of whether efficient breaches of contract or efficient infringements should be tolerated.[12]

2. DISTRIBUTIVE DISGORGEMENT REMEDIES

Distributive disgorgement remedies aim to ensure the fair distribution of revenue between the infringer and the right holder. There are two basic consequences: First, the right holders should be assigned that part of the revenues that can be attributed to the infringement of their rights; second, infringers are not to be punished by the remedy and should be compensated for their contributions to the revenues.

2.1. ATTRIBUTION OF PROFITS

A distributive remedy must attribute the revenues or profits to one of the involved parties. As the example of the book in the Introduction shows, economic success and resultant profits are never based on a single factor, but on a combination of different factors and contributions.[13] The economic success

---

11 Cf. for proposals for the German law B. Raue, above n. 3, pp. 468 ff., 562 ff., 602 ff.

12 D. Campbell and D. Harris, 'In defence of breach: a critique of restitution and the performance interest' (2002) 22 *Legal Studies* 208, 219 ff.; R.A. Posner, *Economic Analysis of Law*, 8th edn., Aspen Publishers, New York 2011, pp. 117 ff., 120; U. Huber, *Leistungsstörungen: Die allgemeinen Grundlagen – Der Tatbestand des Schuldnerverzugs – Die vom Schuldner zu vertretenden Umstände*, vol. I, Mohr Siebeck, Tübingen 1999, §2 v. 4.

13 This is widely recognised, cf. RG 15.11.1937, *RGZ* 156, 321, 326 – *Braupfanne*; BGH 24.07.2012 – X ZR 51/11 = *BGHZ* 194, 194 para. 18 – *Flaschenträger*; BGH 24.02.1961 – I ZR 83/59 = *BGHZ* 34, 320, 322 f. – *Vitasulfal*; Oberlandesgericht Düsseldorf 15.02.2007 – 2 U 71/05 = *InstGE* 7, 194, 196 – *Schwerlastregal*; E. v. Caemmerer, above n. 5, 333, 356; K. Larenz and C.W. Canaris, *Lehrbuch des Schuldrechts*, 13th edn., vol. II/2, C.H. Beck Verlag, München 1994, §72 I 1 b, III 3 c, pp. 265, 279; D. Reuter and M. Martinek, *Ungerechtfertigte Bereicherung*, Mohr Siebeck, Tübingen 1983, pp. 541 f.; M. Schwab in *Münchner Kommentar*

of a book depends, among other factors, on the copyrighted content, the expertise and organisational structure of the publishers, their pre-financing of the production as well as on the sales and marketing efforts of the bookshop.[14]

As profits cannot be attributed to a single factor, the profits of a business transaction are generally attributed to the person who offered the goods or services on the market and correspondingly bore the risk of loss: *cuius est periculum, eius et commodum esse debet.*[15] That person has to pay for all the resources used in the transaction and is responsible for infringements occurring in the course of business. If those costs exceed the revenue, that person has to bear the losses, not the owners of the resources that were employed. Correspondingly, that person should be entitled to the profits if the revenues exceed the costs.[16]

In intellectual property law, it is often argued that the owner of an intellectual property right is entitled to any profit that is generated with its support.[17] However, intellectual property rights do not guarantee the inventor or creator economic success. Even absolute property rights assign to their owners only the exclusive *chance* to offer the immaterial good on the market.[18]

---

zum Bürgerlichen Gesetzbuch: BGB, vol. 5, 6th edn., 2013, §818 para. 37; T. Helms, above n. 7, pp. 203 ff.; C. Kellmann, *Grundsätze der Gewinnhaftung: rechtsvergleichender Beitrag zum Recht der ungerechtfertigten Bereicherung*, Duncker & Humblot, Berlin 1968, p. 140; H. Haines, *Bereicherungsansprüche bei Warenzeichenverletzungen und unlauterem Wettbewerb*, Carl Heymanns Verlag, Köln 1970, p. 125; H. Büsching, *Der Anwendungsbereich der Eingriffskondiktion im Wettbewerbsrecht*, Nomos, Baden-Baden 1992, pp. 145 f.; B. Ebert, *Bereicherungsausgleich im Wettbewerbs- und Immaterialgüterrecht*, Duncker & Humblot GmbH, Berlin 2001, p. 184.

14 B. Raue, above n. 3, p. 463.

15 Cf. only B. Windscheid and T. Kipp, *Lehrbuch des Pandektenrechts*, vol. II., 8th edn., Rütten & Loening, Frankfurt a. Main 1900, p. 329; S. Lorenz in J. v. Staudinger (ed.), *Kommentar zum Bürgerlichen Gesetzbuch*, vol. 2, 2007, §818 para. 12; K. Larenz and C.W. Canaris, above n. 13, §72 II 3 c, p. 272; W. Wilburg, 'Zusammenspiel der Kräfte im Aufbau des Schuldrechts' (1964) 163 *Archiv für die civilistische Praxis* 346, 350; K.-H. Gursky in J. v. Staudinger (ed.), *Kommentar zum Bürgerlichen Gesetzbuch*, vol. 3, 2013, §987 para. 21; J. Esser and H.L. Weyers, *Schuldrecht. Band II Besonderer Teil: Teilband 2. Gesetzliche Schuldverhältnisse*, 8th edn., C.F. Müller, Heidelberg 2000, §51 I 1 e (general principle); H.-G. Koppensteiner and E.A. Kramer, *Ungerechtfertigte Bereicherung*, 2nd edn., De Gruyter Verlag, Berlin 1988, pp. 122 f. 156, 158.

16 B. Raue, above n. 3, pp. 460 ff.

17 E. Körner, 'Schadensausgleich bei Verletzung gewerblicher Schutzrechte und bei ergänzendem Leistungsschutz' in J. v. Baur, K.J. Hopt and K.P. Mailänder (eds.), *Festschrift für Ernst Steindorff zum 70. Geburtstag am 13. März 1990*, De Guyter Verlag, Berlin 1990, pp. 877, 884 f.; J. Esser and H.L. Weyers, above n. 15, §51 I 1 f; H.H. Jakobs, *Eingriffserwerb und Vermögensverschiebung in der Lehre von der ungerechtfertigten Bereicherung*, Röhrscheid, Bonn 1964, p. 30; dissenting e.g. E. v. Caemmerer, above n. 5, 333, 356.

18 B. Raue, above n. 3, pp. 460 ff.

That opportunity is, however, not a guarantee of economic success. The right holder still needs to invest time, effort, skills, money and luck in order to turn that economic opportunity into actual profit.

If the owners of intellectual property rights have no inclinations to invest in the realisation of the business opportunity (and thus assume risk) or if they lack business acumen, financial reserves, or the time to market their creation, they may license the right to a third party. In this case, however, the licensee will not remit all the profits made by exploiting the licensed property right. The price of the license reflects the value that licensee attributes to the business potential of the licensed intellectual property right. The licence fee must still leave room for the licensees to make their own profits. Otherwise, they would neither be willing to make their own contribution to the market success nor bear the economic risk by offering the goods to the market.

In the book example above, this basic economic principle is reflected in the fact that the author of a novel receives only 10% of the net sale price of a book. The surrender of the remaining profits is the price the author has to pay for not self-publishing. On the other hand, the licensing saves time, costs and effort and the author can concentrate on the art of writing.

There is little justification to change that attribution scheme in the event a property right was infringed in the course of business. This can be demonstrated by the following considerations: let us assume that the owner of the property right was, in fact, entitled to any profit generated by its commercialisation. If the infringing product makes use of one patent, the patent holder would be entitled to the whole profit. The imaginary principle is challenged if the infringing product contains two equally important patents of two different patent holders. According to the above principle, each holder of an absolute right would always be entitled to the full profit generated by the exploitation of the right. This means both owners should be entitled to the full profit. Such an *argumentum ad absurdio* underscores the necessity to share the profits at least amongst the two patent holders. Patents, of course, are just a random example of an absolute property right: the same rule has to apply if the infringer exploited any other absolute right of a third person. This means the profit would have to be apportioned to the different right holders.

In addition, that rule has to include cases in which the infringer made use of its own intellectual property rights. The infringer's property rights had to be included in the profit-sharing scheme – unless one introduces a further rule of law wherein anyone waives any claim to the exploitation of their own rights and efforts by violating other people's rights. However, the latter legal principle does not exist. It would be, in any case, inappropriate, especially when there is no fault on the side of the infringing party. This illustrates the book example from above, where the legal incapacity of the author was not recognisable by the publisher or the owner of the bookstore.

If infringers are entitled to the portion of revenue that can be attributed to their absolute rights, then further questions arise. Why, for example, is the use of the infringer's time, money and other resources not to be accounted for in the attribution of profits? If the inclusion of those elements in the profit-sharing is accepted, this reverts to the original premise – namely, that profit is based on many different factors and should therefore (as it is virtually impossible to attribute exact shares of profit to every single factor),[19] be attributed to the person who bears the economic risk of the undertaking.

Certainly, the owners of the infringed property rights must be compensated for the loss of or the intrusion into their rights. Nevertheless, why should the owners of property rights be entitled to the profits beyond that if they made no arrangements to realise that profit on their own (in which case they would be entitled to damages for financial loss)? The owners of the infringed property rights did not have to bear the economic risk of the infringing undertaking.[20] They are in any case entitled to compensation for the use of their rights, either on grounds of damages or on grounds of unjust enrichment.[21] Their compensation does not depend on the fact that the infringing action was profitable. Consequently, a legal system should not – at least in principle – assign every *profit* generated by a business transaction to the owner of a property or contractual right that was infringed in the course of the business. It should provide remedies that deprive the infringer of the *market price* of unlawfully used resources. That price reflects the value of the inherent *chance* to make profits in conjunction with other necessary factors.

This logic is followed, for example, by the German 'Eingriffskondiktion' (sec. 812 para. 1 s. 1 alternative 2 BGB[22]) which forces the infringer to disgorge the value of the infringing *use* of an intellectual property right and not the profit which was generated by the tort.[23]

---

19 BGH 24.07.2012 – X ZR 51/11 = *BGHZ* 194, 194 para. 20 – *Flaschenträger*.

20 Nevertheless, they have to bear the insolvency risk of the tortfeasor.

21 Cf. B. Raue, above n. 3, pp. 263 f., 319 with further references.

22 Sec. 812 para. 1 BGB (*German Civil Code*) provides: 'Whoever obtains something without legal grounds through the performance of another person or in any other way at his expense is obliged to surrender it.'

23 BGH 24.11.1981 – X ZR 7/80 = *BGHZ* 82, 299, 307 – *Kunststoffhohlprofil II*; BGH 18.12.1986 – I ZR 111/84 = *BGHZ* 99, 244, 248 – *Chanel No. 5*; BGH 27.10.2011 – I ZR 175/10 = *GRUR* 2012, 715 para. 39 – *Bochumer Weihnachtsmarkt*; BGH 29.07.2009 – I ZR 87/07 = *GRUR* 2010, 237 para. 22 – *Zoladex*; C. Zülch and K. Grabinski in G. Benkard (ed.), *Patentgesetz: PatG*, 11th edn., 2015, §139 para. 85; H. Schack, *Urheber- und Urhebervertragsrecht*, 8th edn., Mohr Siebeck, Tübingen 2017, para. 808; M. Rehbinder and A. Peukert, *Urheberrecht*, 17th edn., C.H. Beck, München 2015, para. 1293; S. Lorenz in J. v. Staudinger (ed.), above n. 15, vor §812 para. 60; D. Reuter and M. Martinek, above n. 13, pp. 274 f.

2.2. CONSEQUENCES FOR NON-PUNISHING DISGORGEMENT REMEDIES

A different approach is taken, however, by the common law account of profits. The aim of that remedy is, in the words of Lord Justice Kitchin in *Hollister v Medic Ostonomy*, to

> 'deprive the infringer of the profits he has made from an activity in which he should never have engaged. It therefore ensures the infringer does not benefit from his wrong, but it contains no element of punishment.'[24]

The latter aspect is underlined by Justice Laddie in *BP v Celanese*: 'The account is not a camouflaged method of making the defendant pay punitive compensation.'[25]

A similar non-punitive disgorgement approach was followed by the German *Bundesgerichtshof*[26] before its Gemeinkosten-Ruling[27] in 2000. Here, the holder of an intellectual property right was allowed to claim the infringer's profits as a lump sum approach to calculate damages. The same principles are proposed by a part of the German legal doctrine that argues in favour of a respective interpretation of the 'Eingriffskondiktion': namely, that the court should not disgorge the value of the use of an intellectual property right but the generated profits.[28] A third example of a non-punishing disgorgement of profits is laid down in Art. 13 para. 2 Enforcement Directive 2004/48/EC,[29] which allows the Member States to 'order the recovery of profits' when 'the infringer did

24 *Hollister v Medik* [2012] EWCA Civ 1419 para. 69. For further dogmatic foundations of the remedy cf. L. Bently, 'Accounting for Profits Gained by Infringement of Copyright: When does it end?' (1991) 1 *European Intellectual Property Review* 5 ff.; K. Boosfeld, *Gewinnausgleich: Vergleichende und systematisierende Gegenüberstellung der französischen, niederländischen und englischen Tradition*, Mohr Siebeck, Tübingen 2015, pp. 143 ff.; B. Raue, above n. 3, pp. 181 f. with further references.

25 *Celanese v BP Chemicals* [1999] RPC 203, 231 (Pat). Cf. also *My Kinda Town v Soll* [1982] RPC 15, 55 (Ch); *Imperial Oil v Lubrizol* [1996] 71 CPR (3d) 26, 33 (F.C.A.); *Reading & Bates Construction v Baker Energy Resources* [1995] 1 FC 483 (F.C.A.); *Dart Industries v Decor* [1993] HCA 54 para. 14.

26 Cf. BGH 29.05.1962 – I ZR 132/60 = *GRUR* 1962, 509, 511 – *Dia-Rähmchen II*; Oberlandesgericht Köln 17.03.1995 – 6 U 109/82 = *GRUR* 1983, 752, 753 – *Gewinnherausgabe*. Cf. B. Raue, above n. 3, p. 437.

27 BGH 02.11.2000 – I ZR 246/98 = *GRUR* 2001, 329 – *Gemeinkostenanteil*.

28 J. Esser and H.L. Weyers, above n. 15, §51 I 1 f; H.H. Jakobs, above n. 17, p. 30; E. Fournier, *Bereicherungsausgleich bei Eingriffen in Wettbewerbspositionen im Sinne des §1 UWG: Zugleich ein Beitrag zur Dogmatik des wettbewerbsrechtlichen Leistungsschutzes*, Ed. Iuris, Frankfurt a. Main 1999, pp. 188 ff.; G. Törl, *Die bereicherungsrechtliche Behandlung nichtgegenständlicher Vermögensvorteile*, Köln 1977, p. 146; H. Kaiser, *Die Nutzungsherausgabe im Bereicherungsrecht*, Tübingen 1987, pp. 146 ff.

29 Directive of the European Parliament and of the Council 2004/48/EC of 29 April 2004 on the enforcement of intellectual property rights [2004] OJ L 195/16.

not knowingly, or with reasonable grounds [to] know, engage in infringing activity'.[30] In contrast, the first draft of the directive[31] contained in Art. 17 para. 2 a remedy which allowed recovery of any profits that were not consumed by the payment of damages. That remedy was dropped in the legislative process due to harsh criticism from the Member States.[32]

2.2.1. Deduction of Costs

If the remedy is not aimed to punish the infringers, the latter have to deliver only their net profits.[33] The infringers may deduct any direct costs associated with the infringement, such as materials or labour.[34] Further, they may reduce the amount payable by any additional overhead incurred by the infringement.[35] The same applies to a portion of the general overhead, including the costs of premises and general staff.[36]

The latter, however, is disputed. The Australian High Court, for example, denied the infringer the deduction of overhead costs that would have occurred without the infringement. The court wanted to prevent the infringer from drawing any profit from the infringement.[37] Nevertheless, that argument is not convincing from a distributive point of view, as noted by Justice Laddie in *BP v Celanese*:[38]

> 'The profitability of [the infringing product] is increased by BP not having to have separate services for those plants but sharing them with others in the Acetyls Business Unit. To allow [the patent holder] to take all the benefits of such costs sharing by BP without taking into account the proper proportion of costs borne by the Unit would be unfair to BP and would wrongly increase the notional profits made on [the infringing products].'

---

30 Cf. B. Raue, above n. 3, pp. 94 ff., 129 f.

31 COM (2003) 46: Proposal for a Directive of the European Parliament and of the Council on measures and procedures to ensure the enforcement of intellectual property rights.

32 B. Raue, above n. 3, pp. 91 f.

33 *Hollister v Medik* [2012] EWCA Civ 1419 para. 74; BGH 29.05.1962 – I ZR 132/60 = *GRUR* 1962, 509, 510 f. – *Dia-Rähmchen II*; Oberlandesgericht Köln 17.03.1995 – 6 U 109/82 = *GRUR* 1983, 752, 753 – *Gewinnherausgabe*. In Germany, the deduction is based on sec. 818 para. 3 BGB, D. Reuter and M. Martinek, above n. 13, p. 539; C. Kellmann, above no. 13, p. 140; E. Fournier, above no. 27, p. 200 f.

34 *Hollister v Medik* [2012] EWCA Civ 1419 para. 74.

35 *Hollister v Medik* [2012] EWCA Civ 1419 para. 74.

36 *Hollister v Medik* [2012] EWCA Civ 1419 para. 74, 85 f.; BGH 29.05.1962 – I ZR 132/60 = *GRUR* 1962, 509, 510 f. – *Dia-Rähmchen II*; Oberlandesgericht Köln 17.03.1995 – 6 U 109/82 = *GRUR* 1983, 752, 753 – *Gewinnherausgabe*; Gerechtshof's Gravenhage, 11.5.2006 – *Cordis v. Schneider*, *NJF* 2006, 355 (under 12. und 13.; patent).

37 *Dart v Decor* [1994] FSR 567 = [1993] HCA 54 para. 10. But the HCA allows the infringer to deduct the opportunity costs of alternative, non-infringing products, para. 14. See also the dissenting opinion of *McHugh J.*

38 *Celanese v BP Chemicals* [1999] RPC 203, 236.

It is a general economic truth that no business can be profitable if it fails to recoup any general costs which cannot be directly attributed to a specific product.[39]

The product would not have been manufactured or sold in the absence of general management or a functioning chain of distribution.[40] The division of labour for different products reduces the cost of every unit – but it does not eliminate the costs. Consequently, every product has to contribute to the general costs of a business before it is profitable.[41] As long as the remedy is not aimed at punishing the infringer, even wrongdoers must be entitled to deduct a fair portion of those general costs from the revenues they have received by the infringement.[42]

Still, the deduction of overhead costs must not allow the infringers to 'calculate away' any profit they have made by the infringement. However, courts may prohibit them from attributing a disproportionate amount of costs to the infringing product by relying on the generally accepted accounting practices in the infringer's branch of business, as it is practised in England, the Netherlands and in the USA.[43]

2.2.2. *Apportionment of Profits*

As a further consequence of the non-punishing nature of the remedy, the infringers should not have to surrender *all* the profits gained from the infringement,

---

39 *Schnadig v Gaines*, 620 F.2d 1166, 1172 (6th Cir. 1980): 'The basic truth that no article of manufacture can be profitable in a real sense if it cannot bear its proportionate share of the fixed costs is hardly new.' Further *Tremolo Patent v Hitchcock*, 90 US 518, 528 f. (1874); *Dart v Decor* [1994] FSR 567 = [1993] HCA 54 para. 10 [*McHugh J, dissenting*]; P. Meier-Beck, 'Herausgabe des Verletzergewinns – Strafschadensersatz nach deutschem Recht?' (2005) 8 *Gewerblicher Rechtsschutz und Urheberrecht* 617, 621; B. Raue, above n. 3, pp. 519, 542.

40 *Schnadig v Gaines*, 620 F.2d 1166, 1172 (6th Cir. 1980); Landgericht Düsseldorf 18.12.2007 – 4a O 317/06 = *InstGE* 8, 257, 262 – *Tintentankpatrone*; W. Tilmann, 'Gewinnherausgabe im gewerblichen Rechtsschutz und Urheberrecht' (2003) 8 *Gewerblicher Rechtsschutz und Urheberrecht* 647, 650; U. Dreiss, 'Was sind eigentlich Gemeinkosten?' in R. Einsele and E. Franke (eds.), *Festschrift 50 Jahre VPP*, VPP-Rundbrief, Duisburg 2005, pp. 605 f.

41 *Tremolo Patent v Hitchcock*, 90 US 518, 528 f. (1874); *Schnadig v Gaines*, 620 F.2d 1166, 1172 (6th Cir. 1980); *Dart v Decor* [1994] FSR 567 = [1993] HCA 54 para. 10 [*McHugh J, dissenting*]; C. Meyer, *Betriebswirtschaftliches Rechnungswesen: Einführung in Wesen, Technik und Bedeutung des modernen Management Accounting*, 3rd edn., Schulthess Verlag, Zürich 2012, p. 220; P. Meier-Beck, above n. 36, 617, 621; T. Helms, above n. 7, p. 256.

42 *Celanese v BP Chemicals* [1999] RPC 203, 236 ff. (Pat); Gerechtshof's Gravenhage, 11.5.2006 – *Cordis v Schneider*, *NJF* 2006, 355 (under 12. und 13.; patent); different in trade mark law: Benelux Gerechtshof, 24.10.2005, *IER* 2006, 22 – *Parfums Christian Dior/Delhaize* (under 12. f.); B. Raue, above n. 3, pp. 519, 542 f. with further references; D. Reuter and M. Martinek, above n. 13, p. 539.

43 *Potton v Yorkclose* [1990] FSR 11, 19 (Ch); *Celanese v BP Chemicals* [1999] RPC 203, 232 ff. (Pat); Gerechtshof 's Gravenhage, 11.5.2006 – *Cordis v Schneider*, *NJF* 2006, 355 (under 12. und 13.); *Schnadig v Gaines*, 620 F.2d 1166, 1175 (6th Cir. 1980); *Nike v Wal Mart*,

but only the part they have made as a result of the infringement.[44] The need for that apportionment approach is obvious when one considers the case *BP v Celanese*. BP had infringed a patent that protected a refining procedure at the end of a highly complex and elaborate vinyl acetate synthetisation process.[45] The patent was useful but played only a minor role in the overall process. The case is comparable with the car example from (1.), in which the owner of the screw did not contribute in a significant way to the profits made by the sale of the car. It would be unjustified in both cases if the right holders received profits which could not be attributed to their property rights. Therefore, Justice Laddie apportioned 0.3 respectively 0.6% of the profits to the patent (holder).[46]

The same applies to the copyright owner of a book that was sold without proper consent. As shown above, there were other relevant factors that contributed to the profitable sale of the books – the work of the publisher and that of the bookshop – so it would be unfair to attribute the whole profit of the book sale to the copyright holder.

3. PUNISHING OR DETERRANT DISGORGEMENT REMEDIES

In contrast, a remedy that is aimed to punish an infringer or deter future infringements follows a different logic. The remedy does not aim to distribute gains fairly to the contributing parties, but to deter a potentially infringing party. The punitive or deterrent nature of the remedy should be construed in a way to maximise the deterrent effect. Therefore, the infringer should be deprived of the infringing benefits as comprehensively as possible.

3.1. LIMITING PRINCIPLES

Nevertheless, the deterrent logic needs inherent limiting principles.[47]

---

138 F.3d 1437, 1447 (Fed. Cir. 1998); *Dart v Decor* [1994] FSR 567 = [1993] HCA 54 para. 14 ff. [*McHugh J, dissenting*].

44 *United Horse Shoe and Nail v Stewart* [1888] 5 RPC 260, 266 f. (HL); *Peter Pan* v. *Corsets Silhouette* [1963] 3 All ER 402, 413 (Ch); *Celanese v BP Chemicals* [1999] RPC 203, 219 ff., 230, 251 (Pat); *Baker Energy Resources v Reading & Bates Construction* [1994] 58 CPR (3d) 359, 368 (F.C.A.); BGH 24.07.2012 – X ZR 51/11 = *BGHZ* 194, 194 para. 17 ff. – *Flaschenträger*; BGH 14.05.2009 – I ZR 98/06 = *BGHZ* 181, 98 para. 33, 41 ff. – *Tripp-Trapp-Stuhl*; BGH 07.02.2002 – I ZR 304/99 = *BGHZ* 150, 32, 42 – *Unikatrahmen*.

45 *Celanese v BP Chemicals* [1999] RPC 203 (Pat).

46 *Celanese v BP Chemicals* [1999] RPC 203, 232 ff. (Pat).

47 Cf. B. Raue, above n. 3, pp. 485 ff.

3.1.1. *Intentional or Grossly Negligent Torts*

First, the remedy should be limited to intentional or grossly negligent torts. Every right that a legal system grants to an individual restricts the freedom of the others.[48] It is therefore the goal of every legal system to balance freedom and legal protection. On the one hand, the right holder must be provided with effective remedies. On the other hand, overly effective remedies may be abused by right holders. The House of Lords warned in *Rookes v Barnard* that deterrent remedies, in that case exemplary damages, must be used with caution:

> 'The power to award exemplary damages constitutes a weapon that, while it can be used in defence of liberty [...] can also be used against liberty.'[49]

It is in the public interest that everyone can effectively use the freedoms granted by law. However, laws are seldom black and white. Life is too colourful to be regulated in unambiguous laws. That ambiguity leads necessarily to legal grey areas that must be evaluated by courts. Parties should not be deterred by harsh remedies that discourage the use of freedom. The *US Supreme Court* addressed that problem in *Fogerty v Fantasy* in a copyright case:

> 'Because copyright law ultimately serves the purpose of enriching the general public through access to creative works, it is peculiarly important that the boundaries of copyright law be demarcated as clearly as possible. To that end, defendants who seek to advance a variety of meritorious copyright defenses should be encouraged to litigate them to the same extent that plaintiffs are encouraged to litigate meritorious claims of infringement.'[50]

If bona fide parties are threatened with over-compensatory legal remedies this might promote the existence of phantom rights.[51] Such rights do not exist

---

48 E.-J. MESTMÄCKER, 'Eingriffserwerb und Rechtsverletzung in der ungerechtfertigten Bereicherung' (1958) 13 *JuristenZeitung* 521, 524; H.P. WESTERMANN, 'Sonderprivatrechtliche Sozialmodelle und das allgemeine Privatrecht' (1978) 178 *Archiv für die civilistische Praxis* 150, 169 with further references; A. HAEDICKE 'Die Gewinnhaftung des Patentverletzers' (2005) *Gewerblicher Rechtsschutz und Urheberrecht* 529, 534.

49 *Rookes v Barnard* [1964] 1 All ER 367, 411 (HL, Lord *Devlin*).

50 *Fogerty v Fantasy*, 510 US 517, 527 (1994). To the economic and cultural advantages of imitations B. RAUE, 'Nachahmungsfreiheit nach Ablauf des Immaterialgüterrechtsschutzes' in H. SCHACK (ed.), *Schriften zum deutschen und internationalen Persönlichkeits- und Immaterialgüterrecht*, vol. 024, Vandenhoeck & Ruprecht Verlage, Göttingen, pp. 25 ff.

51 To the concept of phantom rights F. HOFMANN, 'Kontrolle oder nachlaufender Rechtsschutz – wohin bewegt sich das Urheberrecht?: Rechtsdurchsetzung in der EU zwischen Kompensation und Bestrafung' (2018) 1 *Gewerblicher Rechtsschutz und Urheberrecht* 21, 22, 25; F. HOFMANN, 'Disziplinarität, Intradisziplinarität und Interdisziplinarität am Beispiel der Grundsätze "mittelbarer Verantwortlichkeit"' (2018) 15/16 *JuristenZeitung* 746, 751; B. RAUE, above n. 3, p. 473 f.; B. RAUE, 'Die doppelte Lizenzgebühr ist kein Strafschadensersatz – Anmerkung zu

because law assigns them but because third parties respect them due to the harsh sanctions that might be imposed if the trial is lost.[52] Those phantom rights inhibit innovation and, generally, the freedom to act.[53]

Therefore, dissuasive remedies should be limited to cases of obvious infringements of property rights. If it is certain from an ex ante point of view that an act will violate third party rights then – and only then – should the law signal that 'tort does not pay'. This was a lesson Larry Flint had to learn. Instead of paying the offered $25,000 for the pictures he printed without consent of the photographer, he was forced by the DC Court of Appeals to disgorge $2 million of the infringing profits.[54]

3.1.2. *Proportionality Principle*

Second, the disgorgement of profits must observe the proportionality principle.[55]

If the entire profits were to be disgorged even in cases of minor infringements, it would be disproportionate.[56] This is again illustrated by the car example discussed above. It would be disproportionate if the owner of the car were required to surrender all profits to the owner of the screw which itself contributed insignificantly to the generation of profits. The same applies in the *BP v Celanese* case. Therefore, the disgorgement of profits is only justified if the infringement of the right has had a significant effect on the realisation of the profits. For this, the infringed right must have enabled

EuGH ZUM, 349 – Stowarzyszenie "Olawska Telewizja Kablowa"' (2017) 4 *Zeitschrift für Urheber- und Medienrecht* 353, 354.

52 Cf. C. Geiger, J. Raynard and C. Rodà, 'L'application de la directive du 29 avril 2004 relative au respect des droits de propriété intellectuelle dans les États Membres' [2011] Centre d'études internationales de la propriété intellectuelle (CEIPI – Université de Strasbourg) <https://circabc.europa.eu/d/d/workspace/SpacesStore/451321ab-ce2e-4e52-9fa8-f8540f5943ea/ceipi_fr.pdf> accessed 5.8.2019, 12; A. Kur, 'The Enforcement Directive – Rough Start, Happy Landing?' (2004) 35 *International Review of Intellectual Property and Competition Law* 821, 829 f.; J. v. Ungern-Sternberg, 'Schadensersatz in Höhe des sog. Verletzergewinns nach Umsetzung der Durchsetzungsrichtlinien' in R.M. Hilty, J. Drexl and W. Nordemann (eds.), *Schutz von Kreativität und Wettbewerb: Festschrift für Ulrich Loewenheim zum 75. Geburtstag*, C.H. Beck, München 2009, 351, 358; N. Heide, 'Produktpiraterie – Strukturwandel und rechtliche Entwicklungen' (2012) *Betriebs-Berater* 2831, 2834. Cf. also, BGH 15.07.2005 – GSZ 1/04 = *BGHZ* (GSZ) 164, 1, 3 f. – *unberechtigte Schutzrechtsverwarnung*.

53 R.M. Jenny, *Die Eingriffskondiktion bei Immaterialgüterrechtsverletzungen*, Schulthess Juristische Medien, Zürich 2005, para. 562 f.

54 *Blackman v Hustler Magazine* 800 F.2d 1160, 1163 f. (DC Cir. 1986).

55 Cf. Art. 3 para. 2 Enforcement Directive above n. 29; Art. 46, 47 TRIPs (Agreement on Trade-Related Aspects of Intellectual Property Rights); BVerfG 07.12.1994 – 1 BvR 1279/94 = *BVerfGE* 91, 335, 344; BGH 04.06.1992 – IX ZR 149/91 = *BGHZ* 118, 312, 343; A. Kur, *Festschrift für Gert Kolle und Dieter Stauder*, Carl Heymanns, Köln 2005, pp. 365, 370.

56 B. Raue, above n. 3, p. 489.

or at least have had a decisive impact on the realisation of the profits.[57] The remedy should be denied if the infringed right was an exchangeable factor which the infringer could easily have replaced.

3.1.3. *Nature of the Remedy*

Third, the remedy should not be construed as a civil law fine or as punitive damages aimed at maximum sanctioning. Its nature as a disgorging remedy should be respected. Admittedly, the punitive or deterrent effect would be greatest if the infringers had to surrender not only their (net) profits, but all revenues resulting from the infringement. Such a sanction exists, for example, in German criminal law. Sec. 73d StGB forces inter alia drug dealers to hand over their revenues from the drug trade and prevents them from deducting their expenses used to obtain their products.[58] Such a remedy could no longer be qualified as a disgorgement of *profits*. Consequently, the nature of the remedy requires that the infringers be able to deduct all costs that they would have avoided without the infringement. That means that the infringers may deduct all variable costs of the infringing activities, but not the fixed costs. The classification as variable or fixed costs depends on the duration of the infringement. If the infringers of a longer-lasting infringement are able to show that they would have reduced their fixed costs at a certain point without the infringing activity (e.g. by laying off employees), then those costs are deductible.[59]

3.2. RESTRICTED DEDUCTION OF COSTS

Good faith infringers are – as shown above – entitled to deduct a fair portion of their general costs from the revenues because they had contributed to the generation of profit. However, intentional infringers should not be allowed to do so,[60] since they would benefit from the infringement by the contribution to their general costs. Without the infringement, they would have had to cover those costs with other non-infringing activities that would then be

---

57 B. Raue, above n. 3, pp. 490 f. with further examples.

58 Sec. 73d para. 1 StGB (German Criminal Code) provides: 'The expenses of the perpetrator, participant and the other [sic!] are to be deducted when determining the value of the acquired assets. Excluded, however, is what has been spent or used for the commission of the act or for its preparation, except when an obligation to the injured party has been fulfilled'; M. Heger in K. Lackner and K. Kühl, *Strafgesetzbuch: StGB*, 29th edn., C.H. Beck, München 2018, §73d para. 4.

59 E.g. Oberlandesgericht Düsseldorf 08.09.2011 – I-2 U 77/09 – InstGE 13, 199, 203f. – Schräg-Raffstore.

60 BGH 02.11.2000 – I ZR 246/98 = *BGHZ* 145, 366, 374 – *Gemeinkostenanteil*; *Dart Industries v Decor* [1993] HCA 54 para. 10.

less profitable. If the infringers are prevented from keeping this contribution, it gives them a strong incentive to employ their existing resources to new non-infringing activities.

3.3. NO APPORTIONMENT OF PROFITS

A good faith infringer is entitled to keep the portion of profit that can be attributed to the use of their own resources. A bad faith infringer should be encouraged to use their resources for non-infringing activities and, consequently, be deprived of their share of the profits.

Therefore, the infringer's profit should be – after the deduction of flexible costs – transferred in full to the holder of the infringed right, and not be limited to the attributable share of profits.

4. CONCLUSION

Profits belong to the party bearing the economic risk of an activity. If parties infringe property rights of a third party, they should be obliged to pay the market price for the infringing use – but not to render their profit to the right holder.

If, however, a legal system orders bona fide infringers to disgorge the profits of an infringing activity, they should be entitled to recoup their costs, including an appropriate share of their general costs. Furthermore, the holders of infringed rights may only claim that portion of the profits that can be attributed to the use of their right.

Intentional infringers, on the other hand, should be deprived of all benefits that they drew from the infringement. They should be placed in the position they would occupy if they had not infringed. Consequently, they may only deduct direct costs that occurred because of the infringing activity. By stating that 'tort does not pay', the law gives a strong incentive to engage in non-infringing activities.

PREVENTIVE LIABILITY AND SYSTEM OF SANCTIONS IN TORT LAW

Luboš TICHÝ

1. INTRODUCTION

Prevention in a broad sense is a part of existing tort law. As an economic analysis of the law,[1] based on cost and revenue tests, quite persuasively proves, it is advantageous for an economically-thinking individual to respect a certain standard of behaviour (duty of care). It is better to take precautions to prevent damages rather than to be involved in such an incident – whether as an injured party or a perpetrator, and thus as a compensation recipient or, on the contrary, as a compensation payer. Such behaviour should be promoted as well by a general system of protection, including in particular the insurance system.[2]

This chapter addresses prevention in tort law, but in a slightly different way than in which this phenomenon is conventionally addressed.[3] It aims to prove that prevention has specific features and thus can constitute different aim and content than the prevention traditionally understood within tort law. This is, therefore, a case of the so-called prevention in a narrow sense, which concerns situations of emergency or peril to a third person, somebody else's property or general asset, lacking any relation to a potential rescuer.

This kind of prevention has its legal basis in §2901 of the Czech Civil Code/2012. According to this provision, an individual is obliged to intervene in favour of somebody else if he/she 'can, according to his potential and skills, easily avert harm of which he knows or must know that its impending gravity clearly exceeds what must be exerted for the intervention has the same duty.'

---

1 See H. Kötz, H.-B. Schäfer, 'Schadensverhüttung durch ökonomische Anreize', *Archiv für die civilistische Praxis* B 189 (1989), pp. 502–525, D. Dewees, D. Duff, M. Trebilcock, *Exploring the Domain Accident Law*, OUP, Oxford 1998, p. 175 f.

2 C. Ott, H.-B. Schäfer, *Die Präventivwirkung zivil- und strafrechtlicher Sanktionen*, Tübingen 1998, p.142 f.

3 See L. Tichý, *Prävention im Haftungsrecht: Ansatz zu einer Revision*, in P. Apathy et al. (eds.), Festschrift für Helmut Koziol, Wien 2010, p. 905–924; L. Tichý, 'On Prevention Law: Special Focus on Tort Law' in L. Tichý, J. Hrádek (eds.), *Prevention in Law*, Praha 2013, p. 9 f.; L. Tichý, 'Preventive Liability – A New Paradigm in Tort Law?' in H. Koziol, U. Magnus (eds.), *Essays in Honor of Jaap Spier*, Wien 2016, p. 303 f.

The Czech legislator codified – in harmony with the Czechoslovak tradition – a so-called 'tortious preventive liability', which represents a unique phenomenon. A legal (statutory) duty has been imposed on persons referred to as 'Samaritans', who are independent of the person who faces threatening harm. A violation of the duty to intervene can be considered a tort, establish a prerequisite of the preventive liability and, as consequence of it, of a sanction: a secondary duty in the sense of compensation of the damage which could have been avoided.

Hence, the prevention in the broad (traditional) sense is enriched by this specific prevention (prevention in the narrow sense). This preventive liability extends the mechanism (system) of tort law through a new paradigm.

The first task of this chapter is to analyse this preventive liability and to justify it.

The second task of this chapter is to find out the justification of preventive liability. A sanctioned preventive duty means a restriction party autonomy, and hence a strengthening of rectifying function of tort law. According to the Czech model, the breach of this obligation results in compensation of damages (provided other liability preconditions being fulfilled). The question on the adequacy of this concept is therefore appropriate. Like the case of high compensation for damages to personal rights or so-called punitive damages, a question may be placed, whether tort law does not exceed its purpose and whether it does not take over the function of criminal law, as in the case of the mentioned common-law compensations. It can be objected that the very notion of sanction is sort of alien in tort law, and that the sanctioned preventive duty could be regarded as a punishment, asserting that the proposed concept is contrary to constitutional principles regarding this kind of sanction. Therefore, it is highly desirable to address the issue of proportionality of the proposed model.

While substantiating the above-mentioned concept the chapter first elaborates on the traditional notion of prevention in tort law (2.). The third part (3.) deals with the issue of prevention in a broader sense as one of the two main purposes of tort law and explains the difference between this category and prevention in a narrow sense. The fourth part (4.) is description of the roots and the development of prevention in tort law with the focus on prevention in a narrow sense. The fifth part (5.) deals with the need for the preventive duty as a new paradigm of tort law. Here, the chapter analyses the content and the prerequisite of the preventive liability. The sixth part (6.) deals with substantive elements of prevention in tort law, primarily with sanctions. The subject of part seven (7.) is the proportionality of the proposed solution. The eighth part (8.) deals with the policy justification of the concept.

Constraints of space does not allow a discussion of other important aspects of the subject, such as its relationship to negotiorum gestio or negatory action.

2. PREVENTION AS AN OBJECTIVE AND FUNCTION OF TORT LAW

The current position of prevention in the system of tort law is unquestionable. The prevailing opinion[4] in academia recognises its importance and deems it one of tort law's objectives. It is generally recognised that apart from the reparation of damage, tort law also aims at the aversion and prevention of negative consequences stemming from human conduct that take the form of damage. Damage resulting not only from one's own conduct, but also from conduct of third parties may be prevented. As a result, tort law emphasises the importance of carc subsisting in adherence to fundamental rules of conduct.

The legal order affects human conduct in a number of ways and, ultimately, aims to affect this conduct in the sense of the principle of *neminem laedere*, i.e. not to cause damage. This function is referred to as regulation, hence, the regulatory function of law.[5]

The law provides incentive[6] by, on the one hand, reducing insurance payments when one acts in compliance with the law, and on the other by introducing sanctions whose mere possibility of imposition fulfils a general preventive function.[7] The imposition of a sanction and the possibility of its imposition aim to dissuade or deter individuals from conduct that may result in damage. Imposition of sanctions and their threat aims at deterring an individual from wrongful conduct which can lead to a damage. In other words, it encourages them to introduce certain preventive measures.

It is a task of every state to maintain internal peace and security. This is carried out with the help of legislative and judicial power (through the execution of justice). This is articulated in the regulatory function of the state, which can be found in public as well as in private law, including tort law. The regulative

---

4 See, inter alia, H. Koch, 'Die Präventions- und Steuerungswirkung des Schuld- und Wetbewerbsrechts', *Juristenzeitung* 19/1999, p. 922 f.; H. Koziol, 'Prevention under Tort Law from a Traditional Point of View' in L. Tichý, J. Hrádek (eds.), *Prevention in Law*, 2013, p. 33 f.; G. Wagner, 'Prävention und Verhaltenssteuerung durch Privatrecht – Anmaβung oder legitime Aufgabe?', *Archiv für die civilistische Praxis* 206 (2006), p. 352 f.; K. Sailer, *Prävention im Haftungsrecht*, 2005, p. 241 f.; J. Švestka, *Základy teorie prevence v československém socialistickém právu (Theory of prevention in Czechoslovak socialist law)*, Praha 1980, p. 28 f.; L. Tichý, 'Prävention im Haftungsrecht: Ansatz zu einer Revision' in P. Apathy et al. (eds.), *Festschrift für Helmut Koziol zum 70. Geburtstag*, 2010, p. 905 f., H. Kötz, 'Ziele des Haftungsrechts' in J.F. Baum, K.J. Klaus, K.P. Mailänder (eds.), *Festschrift für Ernst Steindorff zum 70. Geburtstag am 13. März 1990*, 1990, p. 644 f.

5 See H. Koch, above n. 4, p. 922, G. Wagner, above n. 4, p. 352 f.

6 See L. Tichý, 'Odpovědnost za škodu a související problematika. Pojištění (Liability for damage and its context. Insurance)' in L. TICHÝ (ed.), *Odpovědnost advokáta za škodu (Lawyer's liability for damage)*, 2012, p. 184 f.

7 See L. Tichý, 'On Prevention in Law: Special Focus of Tort Law' in L. Tichý, J. Hrádek (eds.), above n. 4, p. 9 f.; G. Wagner, above n. 4, p. 352 f.; H. Koziol, *Basic questions of Tort Law from a Germanic Perspective*, 2012, p. 75 f.

function includes both prevention and compensation. The regulative function is thus composed of a compensatory[8] and a preventive function,[9] as well as of deterrence[10] and even punishment.[11] The compensatory function may, with its sanctions, deter and punish in cases when tort law disposes of penal sanctions such as punitive damages.[12]

3. PREVENTION IN THE BROAD SENSE (GENERAL PREVENTION)

Prevention in the broad sense reflects existing tort law, which, inter alia, aims to prevent damage, whether directly or indirectly. As corroborated by the economic analysis of law based on a test of costs and benefits, it is more reasonable for a homo oeconomicus to adhere to a standard of conduct (standard of care) and to take precautions preventing damage rather than participate in it, whether as an injuring or injured party, i.e. as a party receiving compensation or as a party providing it. The whole system of protection, and especially the system of insurance, should motivate an individual to such conduct.

One of the basic factors of the prevention system in a broader sense is duty of care[13] and also the statutory protection (Schutzgesetz).[14] In both cases, the duty of care is a condition of tortious liability. In other words, by violation of a duty of care the first condition of liability is established. The violation of a duty of care is a misconduct which includes elements both of wrongfulness and fault.

The position of a possibly injuring party towards a possibly damaging event is a significant feature of prevention. The general duty of prevention in tort law forms a part of liability for damage as a by-product of its compensatory function. It is a legal duty not to cause damage through one's own conduct, through a source of danger in one's own sphere.

---

8 K. Schlobach, *Das Präventionsprinzip im Recht des Schadenersatzes*, 2004, p. 304 f.

9 H. Kötz, above n. 4, p. 644 f.; H. Koziol, 'Schaden, Verursachung und Verschulden im Entwurf eines neuen österreichischen Schadenersatzrechts. Zugleich ein neuerlicher Versuch der Klarstellung der Idee des beweglichen Systems', *Juristische Blätter (JBl)* 2006, p. 768 f.

10 An excellent example is impact of the so called Präventionsschadenersatz, Cf. G. WAGNER, Präventivschadenersatz im Kontinental - Europäischen Privatrecht, in FS Koziol, 2010, p. 931 f.

11 H. Koziol, V. Wilcox (eds.), *Punitive Damages. Common Law and Civil Law Perspectives*, 2009, passim.

12 Cf. H. Koziol, 'Punitive Damages, Admission into the 7th Legal Heaven or Eternal Damnation?' in H. Koziol, V. Wilcox (eds.), above n. 11, p. 275 f.

13 See C.-W. Canaris, 'Schutzgesetze- Verkehrspflichten- Schutzpflichten' in C.-W. Canaris, U. Diederichsen (eds.), *Festschrift für Karl Larenz zum 80. Geburtstag*, 1983, 27 f.

14 R. Wilhelmi, *Risikoschutz durch Privatrecht*, 2009, p. 64 f.; M. Karollus, *Funktion und Dogmatik der Haftung aus Schutzgesetzverletzung*, 1992, p. 269 f.

Neminem laedere is a principle permeating the legal order as a whole as it is an instrument serving its regulatory function. Nonetheless, it is not distinctive for tort law aiming at compensation for damage resulting from the failure of its regulative function.

The general duty of prevention in a broad sense constitutes a part of the system of tortious liability. Thus, it can be deemed a parallel function accompanying a compensatory function. The emphasis of the preventive function or of prevention as an objective of tort law can be understood as the relocation of the centre of tort law from compensation to prevention. In this sense it is possible to understand authors considering prevention a primary objective of tort law.[15]

This function of tort law, that is based on general prevention, should also include a specific legal notion which is referred to as a preventive liability and is addressed in this chapter.[16]

4. DEVELOPMENT OF PREVENTIVE LIABILITY

The idea of prevention as an orientation of tort law results from recent development. Notably two phenomena which can be seen as its points of origin contributed to the recognition of a preventive function of tort law. First, this was the idea of a totalitarian state directing society and individuals.

A unique regulation of prevention was introduced in the Czechoslovak Civil Code from 1964.[17] It codified a specific duty of prevention, namely the duty of notification and the duty of intervention, including sanction for their violation. §416[18] of the 1964 Civil Code governed the duty of notification in relation to the threatening damage affecting not only the liable person, but also the third parties. The same provision also provided for the duty of intervention.

15 See H. Kötz, above n. 4, p. 644 f.

16 Duty of rescue (preventive duty) is codified in penal codexes of many European legal order including France (No. 223-6 of Penal Code), Germany (§323 c) of the Penal Code) and Czech Republic (§150 of the Penal Code). Prerequisite of a criminal act according to French law is the fault like in Art. 1382 Code Civil. These phenomenons are deemed protected norms (Schutzgesetze) under Czech and German Civil Code (§2010 of the Czech Civil Code and §823 para. 2 of the German BGB). Unlike in French law (Art. 223-6 second sentence) the scope of the liability according German and Czech law is relatively limited.

17 See Act. No. 40/1964 Coll. of April 1, 1964.

18 §416 para. 1 of the Civil Code/1964 read as follows: 'Everybody is obliged to inform competent authorities of a threatening damage. Everybody is obliged to help to avert damage if such help is needed; he is not obliged to do so if he is hindered by relevant circumstance or if he or other person would face a serious danger.'

Another incentive of the notion of preventive liability (and duty of act) and at the same time its justification is not the doctrine of preventive function of tort law based on economic analyses of law, but a codification of 'Samaritan's' duty in §1297[19] of the Austrian proposal and in Art. 4:103 Principles of European Tort Law (PETL),[20] undoubtedly under influence of Austrian scholarship.[21]

Art. 4:103 PETL, published in 2005, sets out the duty to protect others from damage in three cases. While the first two are part of the general duty of prevention, the third case forms the basis for the genuine duty of prevention. It stipulates that the 'duty to act to protect others' may be stipulated provided that the severity of damage on the one side and the simplicity of the averting of such damage on the other call for such a duty.

Similarly to PETL,[22] §1297 of the Austrian proposal[23] sets out three cases with liability for one's violation of the duty to act contained in the third one which requires everyone to prevent damage which can occur to a third party provided that the occurrence of the damage can be easily averted.

This wording was also adopted by the Czech legislator in the second sentence of §2901 of the 2012 Civil Code.[24]

The solutions described here have one common feature. It follows neither from their wording, nor from their context, that the breach of rescuer's duty results in any harm. A person who failed as a Good Samaritan is not threatened by a sanction. Preventive liability can be therefore considered an idle threat. Such a preventive liability has apparently only a declaratory character, and the present deterrence is rather of symbolic nature.

---

19 §1297 of the Austrian proposal: 'Jeder hat den einem anderen erkennbar drohenden Schaden zu verhindern, wenn er zu dem Gefährdeten in einem Naherverhältnis steht, wenn er einen Verkehr zulässt oder eine Gefahrenquelle schafft oder aufrecht erhält oder wenn zwischen dem drohenden Schaden und der mit der Abwendung verbundenen Belastung ein krasses Missverhältnis besteht.'

20 See Art. 4:103: 'A duty to act positively to protect others from damage may exist if law so provides, or if the actor creates or controls a dangerous situation, or when there is a special relationship between parties or when the seriousness of the harm on the one side and the ease of avoiding the damage on the other side point towards such a duty'; L. Tichý, J. Hrádek in *Principles of European Tort Law, Text and Commentary*, 2005, p. 198.

21 H. Koziol, *Österreichisches Haftpflichtrecht*, vol. I, 3rd edn., 1997, 166, 167.

22 See P. Widmer in *European Group on Tort Law, Principles of European Tort Law, Text and Commentary*, 2005, Commentary to §4:103, p. 88.

23 A. Fenyves, Kommentar para. §1297 in I. Griss, G. Kathrein, H. Koziol (eds.), *Entwurf eines neuen österreichischen Schadenersatzrechts*, 2006, p. 51 and P. Widmer, *Der österreichische Entwurf aus der Sicht des Auslandes*, p. 132.

24 'If required by the circumstances of the case or the usages of private life, the person who produced a dangerous situation or who has control over it, or where it is justified by the nature of the relationship between the persons, has the duty to intervene to protect another. The person who can, according to his potential and skills, easily avert harm of which he knows or must know that its impending gravity clearly exceeds what must be exerted for the intervention has the same duty.'

The Czech model, which is outlined immediately below, differs from the above-mentioned attitudes by understanding preventive duty as a legal obligation. Its breach implies the raising of a secondary obligation, thus a sanction in a form of compensation for the damage, which the Good Samaritan would be able to prevent provided he/she fulfilled the preventive duty. Hence, the failing Good Samaritan.

5. PREVENTIVE LIABILITY: A NEW PARADIGM

5.1. BASIS

The basis of liability for damage is the duty not to cause damage at all (*neminem laedere*). This principle is reflected in the duty of care that is governed in mandatory provisions setting out certain procedures or standards. However, many of these rules governing the duty of care do not have the form of a statutory regulation. Despite this, these duties have the character of law and their violation is an element of liability. They constitute wrongfulness or fault.

Nonetheless, the duty of care as traditionally understood pertains solely to the conduct of a liable person, regardless of being a possible injuring party or possible victim. They are required not to cause harm to others or at least mitigate its extent.

In contrast to the conventional duty of care that is a part of general prevention, the performance of the duty of prevention focuses on an activity or a (possible) harmful consequence located outside the sphere of a Samaritan.

It is thus permissible to consider a new paradigm of tort law that would give a new dimension to tort law's preventive function: the duty of prevention whose violation would be sanctioned similarly as a violation of the duty of care, i.e. by compensation of damage.

The duty of prevention exceeds the existing duty of mutual help to avert damage occurring to a third party within the framework of the duty of supervision. These duties namely have a specific legal basis arising from family relationships or from another specific relationship (supervision).

Because the basis of the duty of prevention can be also been seen in the duty of care for an 'unknown' third party, it is, similar to the traditional duty not to cause damage reflected in the liability for one's own conduct, necessary to secure the regulation of this new paradigm on a statutory level and to impose statutory sanctions for the violation of such duty.

Given the novelty of the duty of prevention, its regulation on a statutory level must be explicit as the duty of prevention is a legal duty whose violation is sanctioned, even though its basis can be traced to the principle of trust (see 8.) that is similar to the duty of care. While the duty of care involves in classical criminal law the activity as such, the duty of prevention relates to activity in the sphere of a third party.

The principle of *neminem laedere* is relevant here. However, this principle must be understood as an integral part of everyone's conduct in a society whose functioning is based on the concept of interaction.[25] Life in such society is founded on mutual trust that forms a basis for reliance on a certain standard of conduct while adhering to certain rules of conduct. A certain level of security and certainty and thus also of mutual expectations exists in such a society. This understanding reflects the perception of solidarity based on reciprocity.

The moral subtext plays an important role in such a context. Its level may exceed and does exceed the level of moral rules,[26] yet not under all circumstances and in all societies or legal orders. One does not approach the adherence to Kant's imperatives everywhere.[27]

General stimulation in the form of broader responsibility, even by means of deterrence, is necessary to achieve the revival of certain moral principles. It is more adequate to introduce the duty of prevention in civil law rather than in penal law through punishment according to penal law. Introduction of the Samaritan duty – specific preventive liability – may also be seen as a stimulus for society to move away from its selfish individualism[28] its apathy towards other citizens and to strengthen solidarity.[29] The introduction of the Samaritan duty should also result in cost savings for the benefit of general welfare.

A reasonable person[30] communicates with others based on reciprocity, mutual influence and never gives up their own activity solely for the sake of the security of the others. Reasonable man exercises reasonable care in the interest of others. Such a person should be a standard for the rescuer (Samaritan). With such an average reasonable man, the following abilities are required: (a) the knowledge of the dangerous situation in which a third party may suffer serious mental or physical damage, or (b) competence and skill to prevent or end the dangerous situation by providing assistance or soliciting third parties,

---

25 A. Ripstein, *Three Duties to Rescue: Moral, Civil and Criminal, Law and Philosophy*, 2000, p. 751 f., p. 758.

26 See P. Widmer, above n. 22, p. 132.

27 P. Widmer (above n. 22) speaks of an order of responsibility and solidarity.

28 B.S. Markesinis, S. Deakin, A. Johnston, *Tort Law*, 7th edn., 2013, p. 178 concerning a negative attitude of English courts to the duty of rescue: 'The hostility of the common law to the concept of affirmative duties in tort is long-standing, the product, it has been said, of "values of the era in which private selfishness was elevated to the rank of the public virtue". Though the socio-economic environment is changing, there are few things that the courts are currently prepared to abandon their unwillingness to treat omissions like acts.' (*Baumett v Chelsea and Kinsington Hospital* [1969] 1 QB 428).

29 S. Arnold, 'Verhaltenssteuerung als rechtsethische Aufgabe auch des Privatrecht?' in P. Bydlinski (ed.), *Prävention und Strafsanktion im Privatrecht*, Wien 2016, pp. 39, 47, 53.

30 A. Ripstein, above n. 25, p. 761.

and (c) the knowledge and awareness that a potential victim is unconscious of a serious risk or does not have the ability and skill to save him/herself and that he/she is subsequently unable to ask third parties to provide assistance.

5.2. CONDUCT REQUIRED BY THE DUTY OF PREVENTION AND ITS FORMS

5.2.1. Conduct's Objective

The duty of prevention presupposes conduct aimed at the prevention of harmful conduct or at the prevention of possible damage as well as conduct aimed at the mitigation of damage. It is not a problem of theory but rather a qualification of the facts of a case. In some cases it may be adequate to prevent conduct as such while in others it may be the prevention of a possible situation. Stopping the hand of a violent criminal is the prevention of harmful conduct while the prevention of the collapse of a building is the direct prevention of damage.

Conduct should thus consist of measures preventing the occurrence of damage or at least at its mitigation. Its forms include notification, intervention and even intentional inactivity.

The form of conduct chosen by a Samaritan should correspond with the circumstances of the case, with the Samaritan's possibilities, with the principle of effectiveness, etc. Paradoxically, there may be cases in which intentional inactivity constitutes the most effective solution, such as when preventing the spread of mass psychosis, while in some cases it will be more efficient to notify a person to whom damage may occur or other agencies such as police or firemen of impending danger.

5.2.2. Duty of Notification

Notification of (possible) damage should be primarily directed at the injured party and should be made as soon as a Samaritan learns about the relevant circumstances. The Samaritan should use adequate means, such as a mere exclamation, phone call, the employment of a vehicle, etc.

5.2.3. Duty of Intervention

This duty can be fulfilled directly, i.e. by physical force. Sometimes it may be the most efficient prevention, for instance, when preventing a child from falling into a river. However, intervention may be also indirect, for instance, in form of filing an *actio negatoria* or a motion for an emergency ruling with a court.

5.2.4. *Intentional Inactivity*

Intentional inactivity does not exist in omission, but in intentional passivity that may effectively prevent, for instance, the occurrence of or the spread of mass hysteria.[31]

5.3. SCOPE OF DUTY (PROTECTED INTERESTS AND OTHER FACTORS)

It is a fundamental feature of the duty of prevention that possible or already occurred damage is located outside the personal sphere of a liable person. Thus, the relationship of a liable person to the affected goods/values becomes relevant. The higher the level of their protection, the greater is the responsibility of a Samaritan. Life and health undoubtedly have a higher value than property.

External circumstances are also relevant, notably the difficulty with which the duty of prevention had to be complied with. The final important factor is the Samaritan's personal ability. Effective intervention can be required from a young man rather than from an elderly woman. All these factors must be considered when assessing the violation of the preventive duty.

5.4. PREVENTIVE FUNTION OF TORT LAW AND DUTY OF PREVENTION

As already mentioned above, the Samaritan duty or rescue activity is deemed to be prevention in a narrow sense. It is also submitted that it was not a voluntary conduct, i.e. a mere compliance with one's moral duty. To address the duty of prevention it is necessary to impose a duty of a certain conduct (prevention) and sanction its violation. In other words, it is necessary to provide for a comparatively independent type of tort law liability.

5.4.1. *Unlawfulness and Fault*

The scale of fault is another important preventive liability-reducing instrument, as its key element is the knowledge of a liable person about the existence of their duty. Only when they are able to notice a possible danger (damage, conduct, an event), may they comply with their duty to act. With respect to the specifics of this duty, this legal institution must be seen from the perspective

[31] See §1297 of the Austrian Proposal, above n. 19.

of the injuring party and not of the injured party and thus the fault of the injuring party must be assessed subjectively.

Concerning the level of care, one has to distinguish between professional and non-professional help.[32] In other words, professional rescuers do not fall into the personal scope of this Czech model of preventive liability. Regardless of the legal basis of the position of this group which includes professional rescuer teams, police and to some extent the army, it provides for a higher level of care than the standard of care within this model. Also groups of private guards whose liability is based on contractual basis do not belong to the Czech model.[33]

5.4.2. Damage

The nature of damage undoubtedly plays a significant role with respect to values protected by tort law. Human life and health are on the top of the pyramid, closely followed by other values contained especially in fundamental rights.[34]

5.4.3. Causation and Attribution

To meet one of the elements of attribution there has to be a causal link between the damage emerged and the failure to act by a Samaritan. Omission does not constitute a natural but a legal cause. Omission is causal in relation to damage only if the required conduct could have prevented damage. Causality is connected with the issue of duty of care. Omission is a cause of damage if the damage could have been prevented by one's conduct. Omission must be deemed equal to active conduct as one already has the duty to prevent damage.

A so-called psychical causality will undoubtedly play an important role as many cases will involve exceptional circumstances that affect the human psyche. However, its principle corresponds with the solution of the comparatively complex issue of inactivity and damage. As mentioned above, this will commonly entail omission as the duty of prevention is, in most cases, related to conduct. Occasionally, the duty not to act may be considered (for instance, the duty to give way when driving a car which would constitute a less complicated issue of a relationship between unlawful conduct and occurrence of damage in relation to causality).

---

32 C. Van Dam, *European Tort Law*, 2nd edn., p. 527.

33 A. Ripstein, above n. 25, p. 761. The position of the professional rescuers is essentially different; police, ambulances and firemen are obliged to help by the definition.

34 Regarding damage and damages in greater detail see under 7.

5.4.4. *Limitation of Attribution*

The outer limits of causality's adequacy must be interpreted in accordance with the intensity of unlawfulness and with the intensity of fault in a differentiated manner. Further circumstances are relevant: to what extent did a liable person undertake a certain activity that turned out to be insufficient with regard to the occurrence of damage or to its extent. In other words, a case when a liable person acted yet failed to prevent or could not prevent the damage must be dealt with, as well as a case when a Samaritan tried to notify an injured party but did not succeed.

For exemption from liability, not only the degree of fault is relevant, but notably a relationship between any possible damage and circumstances preventing a Samaritan from compliance with its duties. It involves the relation between the value a Samaritan sacrificed and the damage to be compensated. The first group, i.e. values sacrificed by a Samaritan, includes a threat to life or health of a saviour, or eventually of persons that could be affected. A Samaritan's relationship to all these possible victims of his/her actions also plays a certain role.

6. STRENGHTENING THE PREVENTIVE ASPECT OF TORT LIABILITY AND PRIVATE LAW SANCTIONS

Preventive liability means an extension of the tort law paradigm to the preventive duty, which, in consequences of its breach, represents an expansion of sanction mechanism of a particular tort law, consisting of compensation for damages, which in this case, however, also fulfils the main function of tort law – the remedy function in a situation which could be prevented by respecting the preventive duty.

Incorporating preventive liability into the system of tort law means strengthening its preventive function. It is therefore desirable to ascertain to what extent this institution complies with, or defies, its legal system. This is done this in two ways. The importance of preventive liability is compared to the meaning of other categories, which quite often are also considered part of tort law, although the major opinion asserts they are not actually included. This concerns the issue of punitive damages. The extent of compliance within the system of tort law, on the basis of the proportionality criterion (7.) is ascertained. Before, however, it is necessary to deal with some of the categories that are used to assess some of the phenomena in this area, as parameters of tort law. This mainly concerns the concepts of sanction, punishment, compensation for damages, deterrence and prevention.

6.1. THE CONCEPT OF SANCTION,[35] ITS TYPES AND FUNCTIONING

Sanctions serve various purposes.[36] If the sanction is implemented against the person who violated the norm to restore the impression of justice of the aggrieved party, it is about a repression (eye for eye, tooth for tooth). If the purpose is the restoration of the status that would have existed in compliance with the standard, it represents a restitution. The third purpose consists of deterrence. It is aimed against the violator of the standard or even against society and should deter them from violating the law.

Civil sanctions could be defined as a legal means of prevention of unlawful conduct, or a breach of legal obligations, or its punishment.[37] Their functions can lie in prevention of breach of law, damages, redress in favour of the person injured, punishment of the wrongdoer, removal of the unlawful enrichment of the wrongdoer and enforcement of private law. Vanlerberghe draws a distinction between the penal, reparation and preventive sanctions by emphasising, that the distinguishing need not be always obvious.[38]

Similarly as for the traditional tort liability, which includes a generic duty *neminem laedere* and a secondary duty to compensate for damages if the generic duty is breached, the preventive liability consists of a primary duty to help a person in peril (duty to rescue), which if breached results in a failed rescuer's secondary duty to compensate for damages. Thus, the compensation for

---

35 The term of 'sanction' is not defined in either primary or secondary law (M. Ebers, *Rechte, Rechtsbehelfe und Sanktionen im Unionsprivatrecht*, Mohr Siebeck, Tübingen 2016, p. 261). According to the broad definition, it includes all the legal consequences that serve to ensure the normative or factual force of the law (K.F. Röhl, H.C. Röhl, *Allgemeine Rechtslehre*, 3rd edn., 2008, 218). Such a conception is adopted in the majority of decisions of The Court of Justice of the European Union. What is irrelevant is the fact that in many language versions a term 'sanction' originating from English can be founded and that it is partially understood as a punishment or a penalty. Partly, in secondary law, there is more limited concept of sanction, according to which it is understood the measure which is used against the infringement and which causes some detriment to the liable person (M. Ebers, in this n., p. 262). The Member States' sanctions for the enforcement of European Union law must, in accordance with constant case law, give rise to deterrent consequences (M. Ebers, in this n., p. 282). This is the situation when the sanction is capable of averting the public from unlawful acts (general prevention) and of deterring addressees of norm from other offenses (negative special prevention) (Opinion of Advocate General Kokott, C-387, 391/02, Berlusconi). In addition, sanctions must be able to contribute to reinforcing public confidence in European Union law (positive general prevention, M. Ebers, in this n., p. 282).

36 B. Rüthers, C. Fischer, A. Birk, *Rechtstheorie: mit Juristischen Methodenlehre*, 7th edn., 2013, p. 62.

37 C. van Nispen, p. 1, K. Vanlerberghe, pp. 2–3, quoted by R. C. Meurkens, *Punitive Damages: The civil remedy in American Law, Lessons and Caveats for Continental Europe*, Deventer 2014, p. 287.

38 K. Vanlerberghe, above n. 37, p. 5.

damages as an outcome of a tort law rule constitutes a displeasing consequence, which is described as a sanction. The purpose of tort law is therefore a compensation for damages, which is a sanction.

6.2. DAMAGES AND PUNISHMENT

The difference between both sanctions results from different purposes of criminal law, on the one hand and tort law as part of private law on the other. The criminal law concept of punishment primarily affects the perpetrator. In contrast, the compensation for damages concerns both the perpetrator (as a liable person) and the victim (as an entitled person). During assessment, or ruling on punishment respectively, it is necessary to reflect both the perpetrator and his/her conduct, as well as the outcome (consequence). Only a consequence of an unlawful conduct or unlawful situation, hence the damage itself, is relevant for decision on compensation for damages. Another difference lies in the relation of both sanctions to constitutional law, or constitutional order respectively, mainly including fundamental rights. Rules for punishment are enshrined directly in the Constitution, while fundamental rights effect compensation for damages, its amount and its form only in a very indirect manner. While the punishment follows mainly protection of society and individuals, and is primarily intended to act preventively with its deterrence effect, the sanction of compensation for damages pursues the primary role of tort law, which is a remedy (compensation) for disrupted legal relationship. Preventive or deterrence function works here as a sort of accompaniment.

Damages means in principle compensation for damage.[39] However, there are damages which do not lie in the compensation. These are so called restitutionary damages meaning revocation of unjust enrichment, punitive damages serving as punishment, nominal damages, which basically mean declaratory acknowledgement of delict.[40]

In the European comparison, punishment is not the object or mission of tort law. Thus, the functions of the punitive damages seem to be rather preventive than penal, according to the opinions of Wagner who advocates the punitive damages to a certain extent.[41]

---

39 R.C. Meurkens, above n. 37, p. 287.

40 The function of punishment of tort law is excluded even in the case of painful, because the criminal elements are not in the private law of the place, see J. Hager, Einleitung §823, para. 11 in *Staudinger*, 13th edn.; C. von Bar, *Gemeineuropäisches Deliktsrecht*, para. 605–613; E. Bötticher, *Zur Ausrichtung der Sanktion nach dem Schutzzweck der verletzten Privatrechtsnorm*, p. 385 f.; H.-L. Weyers, *Unfallschäden*, p. 582 f.; D. Kleindiek, *Deliktshaftung und juristische Person*, 199; J. Schmidt, *Schadensersatz und Strafe*, p. 41 f.

41 G. Wagner, above n. 4, pp. 473–474.

Meurkens comes to the conclusion, that while the Anglo-Saxon systems explicitly recognise the mission of the punitive damages, in the German, French and Dutch law some non-compensatory elements are being accepted, even though often only implicitly. Thus, the object of the damages can be deterrent, and even punitive, even though only in some situations.[42] It relates in particular to personal rights and their infringement. In such cases, the compensation of immaterial injuries can exceed the extent of full compensation.

Every measure, that causes certain injury, has always a certain preventive function.[43] The person, to whom this measure is oriented, can experience it as a punishment. That is naturally a completely welcome side-effect of the rules of the private law and, in particular, the rules of the tort law, because it aims at compliance with them. However, it does not mean that these rules are subordinated to the criminal or penal principle.

6.3. PREVENTIVE LIABILITY AND REGULATIVE FUNCTION OF TORT LAW

For a long time, private law has been losing its distinctiveness because of its own regulative instruments, and thus is becoming an imitation of public law. Not only does it allow progress of autonomy of will (party autonomy), but it also regulates it in a certain way as well. It sets the limits and, in that sense, plays a significant regulative function. What is essential is to find a compromise between the protection of confidence and the protection of legal relations. In tort law this optimally means an existence of a sanction in terms of a remedy (compensation) for harm, but also in the meaning of threat of the sanction for the sake of prevention.[44] Preventive compensation of damage is not therefore an expression of archaic concepts, as the literature often mentions,[45] but an instrument of sanction that is frequently used by modern legal orders.

Tort law is located in between of two maxims, namely *casum sentit dominus* on the one hand and *alterum non laedere* on the other. The first means that a breach of a legally protected object results in damage to the proprietor. Therefore, the maxim serves as a basis for tort liability. At the same time, however, the second maxim is a prerequisite for the liability itself, as it prohibits harmful acts. Implementing this principle through law actually leads to emergence of preventive liability and thus to the prevention of harm, and

---

42 R.C. Meurkens, above n. 37, p. 347.

43 F. Bohn, *Der Sanktionsgedanke im Bürgerlichen Recht*, Berlin 2005, p. 229.

44 See also G. Wagner, above n. 4, p. 469.

45 See G. Wagner, *Präventivschadenersatz im Kontinental- Europäischen Privatrecht*; P. Apathy et al. (eds.), *Festchrift für Helmut Koziol*, Wien 2010, pp. 925, 926.

eventually to compensation. The principle of prevention thus takes precedence over the principle of recovery.[46]

The concept of preventive liability introduces a dual obligation. Its peculiarity lies primarily in the 'new' duty to act in a different way than the traditional idea of fulfilling the *neminem laedere* maxim. It is not aimed straight at a direct conflict of an acting person, since it does not concern his/her immediate interest, but the 'conflict' (interest) of a third person. It is undoubtedly an expression of solidarity (see also the distinction between primary and secondary tortuous duties) and claims by Shieman.[47] From a different point of view, based on differentiation of legal norms according to time aspect, it is possible to distinguish between obligations under the law of tort on the one hand, and ex ante obligations (ex post dimension) on the other.[48]

Human behaviour is guided by the ethical and legal norms, both endowed with the instruments corresponding their specific nature. In the latter case, the legal norms accompanied by appropriate instruments have an undoubtedly ethical drive. Legal rules may express ethical rules without imposing sanctions on their breach. These are the so-called imperfect, respectively declaratory legal norms. Such an ethical command can hardly be considered a form of deterrence, which more or less characterises the impact of the so-called 'perfect legal norm' disposing of a sanction. Every sanction is a feature of prevention, and therefore every legal norm has a preventive character.

7. PROPORTIONALITY OF THE PROPOSED SOLUTION

7.1. PROPORTIONALITY IN GENERAL

Proportionality serves as a model of measurement. Measurement in this sense means that, for example, a judge who stands between different alternatives, for example, in a conflict between several legal principles, must decide on the basis of rational criteria for one of these alternatives. While doing so, he/she gathers arguments, evaluates and compares them.[49] The measurement has many similarities with other procedures, such as, for example, a flexible system (bewegliches System) in the meaning of Wilburg. The measurement procedure consists of selecting the elements to be measured and evaluating these elements. This is done on the basis of a benchmark. What is decisive

46 Ibid., p. 934.

47 H. Shieman, *Tort Law and Corrective Justice*, *Law and Philosophy*, 22, 2003, p. 21.

48 See, for example, S. Arnold, 'Verhaltensstörung als Rechtsethische Aufgabe auf des Privatrechts?' in P. Bydlinski (ed.), *Prävention und Strafsanktion in Privatrecht*, 2016, pp. 44, 45.

49 T. Riehm, *Abwägungsentscheidunge in der praktischen Rechtsanwendung. Argumentation – Beweis – Wertung*, München 2006, 4, p. 57.

in this process is the measurement rate, which determines whether a simple prevalence on one side is sufficient, or whether significant disparity is required. What is also important is the finding that each principle, every interest and every legal asset is determined to an optimisation by its nature. Therefore, any restriction must be exceptional in its nature, or rather must include exceptions. It is, as a consequence, a decision on the measurement between different legal positions, or rather interests.[50]

The severity of the sanction can affect the extent of compliance with the rule of law, and so its enforcement. On the one hand, the incentive for the addressee of the norm for compliance with the legal norm is increased by intensity, or more precisely by the scope of an imminent sanction. On the other hand, the intensity of the impending sanction also increases the rate of incentive or stimulus of the entitled to make his/her claim.[51] This again increases the probability of enforcing the legal standard indirectly. This again means increasing the incentive to comply with the standard of conduct.

7.2. 'CRIMINALISATION' OF PRIVATE LAW

According to many opinions, private law includes a number of punishment adaptations, respectively sanctions with a nature of punishment.[52] The concepts of civil and criminal punishment are arguably not as distant as judged.[53] Savigny attributed to tort law even a criminal character. Punishment is a sanction supposing fault which serves the purpose of general and special prevention.[54] It is alleged that criminal law has failed in many areas. Therefore, the need for private law sanctions is increasing.[55] This means development of the right for compensation from a positively static to an actively dynamic notion.

7.3. PUNITIVE DAMAGES AS APROPRIATENESS TEST-ANALYSIS

Criminal (punitive, penal) are such damages that do not correspond to the actual damage of the injured party and cannot be justified by the principle of tort law, hence the principle of compensation. The aim of tort law lies in restoring

50 M. Stürner, *Der Grundsatz der Verhältnismäßigkeit im Schuldvertragsrecht*, 2010, p. 356.

51 D. Poelzig, *Normdurchsetzung durch Privatrecht*, Tübingen 2012, p. 375.

52 Comp. eg. I. Ebert, *Pönale Elemente im deutschen Privatrecht*, 2004, passim. But see the arguments above under 5.2.

53 C. Schäfer, 'Strafe und Prävention im Bürgerlichen Recht', *Archiv für die civilistische Praxis* 202 (2002), pp. 398–434.

54 C. Schäfer, above n. 53, p. 405.

55 R. Möller, *Das Präventionsprinzip des Schadensrechts*, Berlin 2006, p. 370.

the balance between the parties and is therefore different from the idea of punishment for a crime.[56]

Compensation should be regarded as a criminal, if it cannot be regarded as compensation for violation of victim's rights in the sense of reparation of personal injury.[57] Civil and criminal law use their own special categories. Therefore, the civil court must not take into account the sanction imposed on the perpetrator by the criminal court.

Even the judgment in the Caroline von Monaco case[58] reflects 'typical profit' caused by violation of personal rights and does not go beyond the compensatory purpose of tort law, which is to recreate equality between the parties. Although the compensation exceeds the actual loss (damage), it is not assessed on the principle of punishment.

The focus of punitive damages only on deterrence was rejected by case law in favour of their penal function.[59] If American judgments are so orientated on revenge, they cannot be recognised, as these aspects are distant from the continental system of the right to compensation. The distinction between public (criminal) and private compensations is considered to be a cultural achievement which cannot be waived by the re-penalisation of private law. A fine dominates in primitive law systems. Developed legal culture does not know a fine, only a compensation. In principle, the rectifying effect of deterrence is not denied, yet their scope is questioned. In addition to the dominant balancing function, prevention is, at the best, considered a 'desirable by-product'.

7.4. HOW TO UNDERSTAND SANCTION IN TORT LAW

Every sanction faces a question of proportionality. This is a basic and general viewpoint. It is imposed on every sanction, and therefore even in the case of a sanction in the form of compensation. In other words, it is necessary to move from a formal approach to a functional concept, and to assess the admissibility of a sanction by a measure of proportionality. This criterion, with all its vagueness whose 'second face' hides in the advantage of its flexibility, is undoubtedly more appropriate than the perspective of penalisation or punishment. The use of the latter means a double problem because it represents

---

56 See also N. Jansen, L. Rademacher, 'Punitive Damages in Germany' in H. Koziol, V. Wilcox (eds.), *Punitive Damages. Common Law and Civil Law Perspectives*, 2009, p. 77.

57 See BGH 16.12.1975 – VI ZR 175/74 = *Neue Juristische Wochenschrift*, 1976, p. 1147.

58 M. Stathopoulos et al. (eds.), *Festschrift für Apostolos Georgiades zum 70. Geburtstag*, 2006, p. 1121 f.

59 G. Wagner, *Neue Perspektiven im Schadenersatzrecht – Kommerzialisierung, Strafschadensersatz, Kollektivschaden, gut Achten zum 66. Deutschen Juristentages*, Band I (2006), A, p. 81.

a 'two-step' qualification. First of all, as it arises both from doctrine and practice, in the first step the sanction is assessed in terms of its nature, in particular severity, that is, in other words, whether it concerns a punishment in the sense of a civil sanction. If this qualification is admitted,[60] see again the judgement in the Caroline case, the test of proportionality applies. It examines whether this private-law sanction is still within the admissibility limit. Therefore, the second step represents a (judicial) control of civil punishment.

A functional approach of tort law represents the key to clarifying the relationship between compensation for damage and penalty.[61] The prohibition of disproportionateness determines the limit of the extent of the preventive compensation for damage. This is the reason why the continent is basically not confronted with the sums of money seen in US punitive damages. It follows from this principle, namely the principle of proportionality, that the legislator may not use criminal law as the *ultima ratio* of the legal order, if other means are available to achieve the desired purpose. Thus, the relationship between compensation for damage and penalty is determined by the principle of proportionality. In the case that a preventive compensation for damage is adequate, not excessive, and suitable for assuming the function of legal protection, the legislator must avoid the application of criminal law.

The view of the doctrine rejects the identification of the purpose of prevention with the purpose of punishment and concludes that preventive sanctions, especially in economic law, cannot be classified as such into the system of criminal law. A private law standard can follow a preventive purpose without being considered as a norm of criminal law nature. Prevention is a legitimate and recognised function of private law. Only if it is associated with the imposition of certain detriment which does not represent any compensation, does it acquire criminal law nature.[62] Irrespective of this, the criminal law nature is attributable to a private law standard if it has either a preventive character or the purpose of retribution in addition to the compensating function. According to Bohn[63] it is necessary to assess separately the supposition and the effect of the rule of law. Thus, the legal consequences can be classified as a pure compensation, a pure penalty or a mixture of both.

On the other hand, the Czech concept of preventive liability offers a one-step evaluation process which proposes a double assessment: a test of directness

60 See the ruling of BGH 15.11.1994 – VI ZR 56/94 = *Gewerblicher Rechtsschutz und Urheberrecht* 1995, p. 224.and E.J. Weinrib, 'The Case for a Duty to Rescue', *The Yale Law Journal*, 90 (1980) p. 247 f.; G. Wagner, 'Reform des Schadenersatzrechts', *Juristische Blätter*, 2008, 11; P. Sourlas, 'Wirkungsjurisprudence Deliktsrecht' in M. Stathopoulos et al. (eds.), *Festschrift für Apostolos Georgiades zum 70. Geburtstag*, 2006, p. 1121 f.

61 R. Möller, above n. 55.

62 R. Heizmann, *Strafe im schweizerischen Privatrecht*, Bern 2015, p. 51.

63 F. Bohn, above n. 43, p. 37.

(immediateness) and a test of necessity. The first test means that the recipient of the compensation is the directly injured party, i.e. the person to whom the damage was incurred, i.e. the claimholder of compensation for damages caused to his/her property. This claim passes on (e.g. can be inherited) and can also be transferred (sold, donated, etc.). The second test relates to the amount of compensation in the sense of remedying the damage in integrum. For material damage, the admissibility criterion should not cause any problems. For non-material damage, the limits are defined by the standard usual at the place and time.

This concept should be valid in the case of sanctions for breach of preventive obligation as well.

7.5. PROPORTIONALITY OF PREVENTIVE LIABILITY

The rectifying function of tort law can be accomplished by use of its disposition, by use of sanction and its standards, and finally by modification of the scope and importance of the protective laws. The dispositions are not embedded in the factual basis of the preventive liability (5.). Their significance and standards can be very different. This concerns both the intensity rate of fault and the formulation of unlawfulness, as well as the understanding of causal link and attribution. A sanction in the form of compensation for damages can also be drafted in a relatively broad framework, which must not, however, exceed the limits of proportionality, such as understanding the purpose of compensation for damage as a remedy, and not as a means of punishment. A protective law can be provided not only in the form of a criminal law regulation, but also in a variety of specific administrative regulations, especially concerning safety/security.

When ruling on a sanction, and thus assessing compensation for damages, it is necessary to take into account the extent of a particular breach and the reasons for it, similarly as in the case of investigations concerning a breach of the preventive duty. In this respect, the judge exercises a considerably broad discretion.

Its violation must therefore be sanctioned. Hence, it will be up to a court, after consideration of circumstances stipulated for the activation of the duty of prevention, to rule on the liability to participate in damage compensation as a result of one's failure to fully comply with one's duty of prevention. The sanction should thus exist in damage compensation. The liable party in breach of their duty of prevention, in a situation when they could effectively prevent occurrence of damage, should be sentenced to a contribution to financial damage compensation, provided that the damage cannot be compensated otherwise. Elements of liability for prevention should be reflected in the form and extent of compensation.

In principle, however, it is settled that compensation concerns the violation of absolute rights. Only in the case of intentional failure to provide assistance, and therefore a serious breach of the preventive duty, the consequences of violation of other (than absolute) rights may also be compensated.

The issue of compensation for consequences of violation of other (than absolute) rights is, as already mentioned, linked to the issue of the protective law. Although it is likely to come into account very rarely, it is possible to compensate also for consequences of violation of these rights, considering criminal law that affects the failure to provide assistance.

7.6. PREVENTIVE LIABILITY AND RESTRICTION TO THE PARTY AUTONOMY

The preventive liability as a manifestation of preventive function of tort law, or the prevention in the narrow sense respectively, results in an extension of the duty of care by considering a third person, or his/her ownership respectively. Thus, it undoubtedly means a restriction of the freedom of an individual in the position of a potential rescuer, by imposing a preventive duty following the principle of solidarity.

The preventive liability in the author's approach is thus broader than, for example, the concepts mentioned in §1297 of the Austrian ABGB Proposal or in §2901 of the Czech Civil Code from 2012 because it has a general character. In other words, it is not limited to special cases of a particular relationship between the rescuer and the peril, or his/her relation to the victim (potentially injured party). It is the rescuer who, if he/she does not fulfil his/her duties, can justify him/herself by pointing to the general obstacles that prevented him/her from acting. Based on a duty of active conduct in relation to one's own activity or property, it overlaps the *neminem laedere* principle (duty).

The most relevant objection against the introduction of prevention liability stems from adherence to the *casum sentit dominus* maxim whose conservative interpretation refuses, in principle, any compensation coming from the injuring party. In a situation, when every modern legal order deems tort liability an integral part of a social state governed by the rule of law, it follows that the general autonomy of will is restricted to benefit prevention liability. Even so it is necessary to uphold the ideas of K. Wolff[64] and to welcome the reaction of P. Widmer[65] and the introduction of this duty in the reforming draft of Austrian tort law. A general Samaritan's duty has been constructed very narrowly under compliance with comparatively strict conditions. The burden constitutes a minimal restriction to the freedom of an individual and it is

---

64 K. Wolff in H. Klang, *ABGB Kommentar*, 2nd edn., 1951, p.18.

65 P. Widmer, above n. 22.

balanced with indisputable benefits (see 8.2.). In this respect, the imperative of duty of prevention does not differ from the prohibition of a certain conduct that is classed as a more adequate manner of regulation of human conduct.

It may therefore be concluded that preventive liability in comparison to punitive damages cannot be regarded as a criminal law instrument and that, based on the proportionality trial, it complies with the internal system of tort law.

8. POLICY JUSTIFICATION

This author acknowledges that the introduction of a duty of prevention amounts to a change in the paradigm of tort law. Tort law is enriched with a new type of legal liability.

8.1. FLOODGATES: NEW BURDEN FOR THE COURTS?

The argument against liability for prevention may be the imposition of a new burden on judicial systems. These arguments raised under different circumstances, for instance, in relation to the liability for mere damage on property, are not based on certifiable data. There is no comparable experience (with the sole exception of a study conducted in Canada[66] concerning car accidents several decades ago), i.e. no empirically based conclusions on the impact of a change in the system of liability on costs of a dispute are available.[67]

With such a formulation of liability, it is possible to expect a decrease in damage and thus also a decrease in the number of actions filed with the courts for damage compensation, while the number of actions for the violation of the duty of prevention is expected to increase. However, given the benefits of the new paradigm and its deterring effect, this criticism cannot be seen as reasonable.

8.2. REASONS FOR THE INTRODUCTION OF LIABILITY FOR PREVENTION

In modern society human relationships rely on a functioning state governed by the rule of law that is based on mutual trust, not only in relation to state power but also in relation to other individuals, i.e. other citizens. Trust also includes

66 D. Dewees, D. Duff, M. Trebilcock, above n. 1, p. 195 f.

67 J. Spier (ed.), *The Limits of Liability: Keeping the Floodgates Shut*, 1996, passim. This book, however, does not mention any empirical data as regards a possible food of claims.

a certain level of solidarity.[68] Human conduct is based not only on the reliance on the respect of law but also features certain moral values and the imperative of good morals.

The statutory regulation of the duty of prevention corresponds with moral values in many European countries.[69] This is also illustrated in the overview of responses to question 10 in Koziol's questionnaire.[70] In five out of eight jurisdictions there is a legal duty requiring a bystander to prevent a blind person from falling into a ditch.

8.3. CRIMINAL LAW'S PARADIGM: GUARANTOR vs. SAMARITAN

A number of legal orders provide sanctions in their penal codes for negligence or omission to provide help.[71] They frequently contain both generally framed qualified facts of a crime and negligence of help in a cross-border car accident. This solution is based on deterrence by punishment with imprisonment included.

A number of authors[72] in their negative or cautious attitude towards preventive liability refer to the existence of this regulation in criminal law. However, criminal law with its deterrence also limits freedom of conduct party (autonomy), while imposing sanctions upon its breach.

Tort law is not to punish; punitive damages essentially oppose the fundamental principles of a state governed by a rule of law. Tort law aims to amend damage. Preventive liability then sanctions its violations with the duty to contribute to the compensation of damage.

8.4. IN-BETWEEN FREEDOM AND PROTECTION

Even tort law must consider values of freedom and protection (safety). The origin of strict (objective) liability and the development of its relation to subjective liability (fault-based liability) illustrate the understanding of balance

---

68 R. Saladin, 'Menschenrechte und Menschenpflichten' in E.-W. Böckenförde, R. Spaemann (eds.), *Menschenrechte und Menschenwürde*, 1987, p. 269.

69 A woman, who was raped in a car sued a bystander who observed whole event without helping her. The court ruled that the defendant violated his duty according the §323 c) of German Penal Code (above n. 16) ordered to pay 8000 Euro damages. (Oberlandesgericht Düsseldorf 27.7.2004 – I-14 U 24/04 = *Neue Juristische Wochenschrift* 2004, p. 3640).

70 H. Koziol (ed.), *Unification of Tort Law. Wrongulness*, 1998, p. 112.

71 See above n. 16.

72 E.J. Weinrib, 'The Case for a Duty to Rescue', *The Yale Law Journal*, 90 (1980) p. 247 f.; G. Wagner, 'Reform des Schadenersatzrechts', *Juristische Blätter*, 2008, p. 11; P. Sourlas, 'Wirkungsjurisprudence Deliktsrecht' in M. Stathopoulos et al. (eds.), *Festschrift für Apostolos Georgiades zum 70. Geburtstag*, 2006, p. 1121 f.

between these two fundamental values. The concept demonstrates itself through tightening or mitigation of tort liability, or in the tort law system as a whole.

Strengthening the liability of rescuers, a liability under Good Samaritan laws, and the evolution of this branch of tort liability, reflect developments of contemporary western society. At the same time, it takes into account the meaning of values protected by law. The scope of the liability concentrates practically and exclusively only on absolute rights and, among them, namely on the protection of life and health of human. Considering a relatively highly moderate approach to liability preconditions and a significantly restraint conception of sanction, it is possible, even in compliance with flexibly understood conditions of its application, to consider this 'new' liability as a tool which is deeply in accordance with the equilibrium between freedom and protection (safety).

9. CONCLUSION

In conclusion, the following assertions can be made:

1. The hypothesis, that the conception of a preventive liability under the Good Samaritan provision enshrined in the Civil Code (§2901, 2nd sentence) is an integral part of tort law liability, has been proved.
2. The duty to intervene, including notification liability (and thus not only an obligation to intervene, but to notify or not to act as well), which is characterised by a strong aspect of solidarity, and which, when breached, creates a basic precondition for preventive tort liability with consequences in damages, has undisputable privilege in the Czech legal order, side by criminal law liability concerning duty to rescue.
3. The addressee of the duty is a non-participating third reasonable person, who is required through objective standard of due, which can be modified by subjective aspects, and which, with regard to an individual situation, proposes relevant possibilities of exoneration.
4. The Czech concept of a new tort law paradigm succeeds in a proportionality test considering the restriction of individual freedom in comparison with punitive damages. The enactment of the specific preventive obligation in a narrow sense is admissible, as, inter alia, it is balanced with welfare associated with positive consequences of liability under the Good Samaritan provision.
5. The enshrining of preventive liability in the Civil Code succeeds even next to similar preventive obligation regulated by the Criminal Code. It seems more adequate to sanction the breach of the Good Samaritan (preventive) obligation through damages than to punish through a criminal law mechanism. It is mainly in comparison with the latter punishment, a private law sanction seems to be more than adequate.
6. The objection of overloaded courts can be dismissed as unjustified.

PART IV

UNDERLYING PRINCIPLES

COMMON PRINCIPLES OF DAMAGES IN EU PRIVATE LAW?

Christian HEINZE

1. INTRODUCTION

The action for damages has always been an important, if not the most important remedy in private law. Based on the concept of reparation, and, more fundamentally, on the pursuit of justice, one can go back as far as ancient Greek philosophy to find 'a discussion of reparation, extending beyond the criminal law, for all damage inflicted'.[1] It is therefore not surprising that the action for damages is an important remedy also in EU private law. However, as EU private law has not been designed as a complete codification of the law, but rather developed as a fragmentary compilation of regulations, directives, and case law in different substantive fields, it may be asked whether it is possible to identify common principles of damages in EU private law. Is there something like an EU law of damages, or are there several EU laws of damages, possibly as diverse and numerous as there are areas of substantive EU law? In order to approach this question, this chapter will briefly describe the status quo on EU rules on damages and introduce three selected developments in this field (2.). On this basis, it will approach the core issue whether there is and/or should be common principles of damages in EU private law (3.), before outlining, using the example of the definition of damage, how specific such common principles can be (4.). In conclusion, some consequences of the analysis of damages for a possible law of remedies at the EU level shall be described (5.).

2. DAMAGES AS A REMEDY IN EU PRIVATE LAW

2.1. STATUS QUO

First, looking at the status quo: Where can rules on damages in EU law be found, and how do they relate to each other?

2.1.1. Sources

As a starting point to answer the first question, three potential sources of damages claims in EU law can be identified.[2] First, the existence of an action for damages can be an (unwritten) requirement that results from the *principle of effectiveness*.[3] In this situation, one is faced with a substantive right

---

1 For references, see Opinion of AG Trstenjak Case C-300/10, *Almeida*, ECLI:EU:C:2012:414, para. 1.

2 For this categorisation, see C. Heinze, *Schadensersatz im Unionsprivatrecht*, Mohr Siebeck, Tübingen 2017, pp. 106–113. For other examples of damages claims in EU private law, ibid., pp.120–124; B. Raue, *Die dreifache Schadensberechnung*, Nomos, Baden-Baden 2017, pp. 57–79.

3 See D. Poelzig, *Normdurchsetzung durch Privatrecht*, Mohr Siebeck, Tübingen 2012, pp. 306–314; M. Ebers, *Rechte, Rechtsbehelfe und Sanktionen im Unionsprivatrecht*, Mohr Siebeck, Tübingen 2016, pp. 566–628 (Competition Law), pp. 709–725 (Anti-discrimination Law), pp. 843–849 (Consumer Law); J.-U. Franck, *Marktordnung durch Haftung*, Mohr Siebeck, Tübingen 2016, pp. 193–208; C. Heinze, above n. 2, pp. 497–539. For examples of damages claims based on the requirement of effectiveness, see CJEU 20.09.2001, C-453/99, *Courage*, ECLI:EU:C:2001:465, para. 26, 29; CJEU 17.09.2002, C-253/00, *Muñoz*, ECLI:EU:C:2002:497, para. 28, 30 and further references in nn. 6 and 7 below.

established by (either primary or secondary) EU law, but Union law does not provide any (or no complete set of) remedies or sanctions if this right is infringed. National law, subject to the requirements of effectiveness and equivalence, thus governs the remedies, including a possible right to damages. Examples can be found in consumer law,[4] and – before the respective case law was codified in directives[5] – in anti-discrimination law[6] and competition law.[7] A second source of a right to damages can be an *EU directive*. In this case, the directive requires the existence of a right to damages, but it has to be implemented by the Member States. Examples are found in the Product Liability Directive,[8] the Travel Package Directive[9] or the Intellectual Property Enforcement Directive.[10] Finally, EU law itself may establish a *directly applicable right* to damages in an *EU regulation*. The number of such directly applicable provisions is growing, as EU law witnesses a certain trend from directives to regulations,[11] with the consequence that damages rules that were formerly found in directives have now been included in regulations and thus become directly applicable (Article 288(2) Treaty on the Functioning of the European Union (TFEU)). Examples of

4 The 'appropriate measures' under CJEU 25.10.2005, Case C-350/03, *Schulte*, ECLI:EU:C:2005:637, para. 100 can (best) be implemented by a right to damages.

5 See Article 18 of Directive of the European Parliament and of the Council 2006/54/EC of 5 July 2006 on the implementation of the principle of equal opportunities and equal treatment of men and women in matters of employment and occupation [2006] OJ L204/23 and Article 3 of Directive of the European Parliament and of the Council 2014/104/EU of 26 November 2014 on certain rules governing actions for damages under national law for infringements of the competition law provisions of the Member States and of the European Union [2014] OJ L349/1. Even after codification in the directives, it can be argued that the action for damages in these fields is an emanation of EU primary law, namely a requirement of effectiveness of the competition rules of Articles 101, 102 TFEU (see recital 14 3rd sentence Directive 2014/104/EU) or the gender equality rule of Article 157 TFEU (see recital 33 Directive 2006/54/EC).

6 CJEU 10.04.1984, Case 14/83, *von Colson und Kamann*, ECLI:EU:C:1984:153, para. 18, 23; CJEU 02.08.1993, C-271/91, *Marshall II*, ECLI:EU:C:1993:335, para. 25; CJEU 17.12.2015, C-407/14, *Camacho*, ECLI:EU:C:2015:831 = *Europäische Zeitschrift für Wirtschaftsrecht* (EuZW) 2016, 183 para. 28.

7 CJEU 20.09.2001, C-453/99, *Courage*, ECLI:EU:C:2001:465 = *Gewerblicher Rechtsschutz und Urheberrecht (GRUR)* 2002, 367 para. 26; CJEU 13.07.2006, C-295/04 – C-298/04, *Manfredi*, ECLI:EU:C:2006:461 = *EuZW* 2006, 529 para. 61; CJEU 14.06.2011, C-360/09, *Pfleiderer*, ECLI:EU:C:2011:389 = *EuZW* 2011, 598 para. 28.

8 Article 1, 9 of Council Directive 85/374/EEC of 25 July 1985 on the approximation of the laws, regulations and administrative provisions of the Member States concerning liability for defective products [1985] OJ L 210/29.

9 Article 14(2) of Directive of the European Parliament and of the Council (EU) 2015/2302 of 25 November 2015 on package travel and linked travel arrangements, amending Regulation (EC) No 2006/2004 and Directive 2011/83/EU of the European Parliament and of the Council and repealing Council Directive 90/314/EEC [2015] OJ L 326/1.

10 See Article 13(1) of Directive of the European Parliament and of the Council 2004/48/EC of 29 April 2004 on the enforcement of intellectual property rights [2004] OJ L 157/45.

11 For example, see C. Heinze, above n. 2, pp. 112, 517; J. Basedow, '60 Jahre Rechtsharmonisierung oder: vom unaufhaltsamen Drang zur Verordnung' (2018) *EuZW*, 1.

damages provisions in regulations are found in the General Data Protection Regulation (formerly a directive),[12] in the Prospectus Regulation (formerly a directive),[13] and in the different passenger rights' regulations.[14] A directly applicable right to damages is also established by Article 340(2) TFEU. While the case law on this provision is a rich source of inspiration, it deals with state liability, a field where specific interests and concerns (such as the protection of the discretion of public authorities) come into play.[15] The same holds true for the *Francovich*-liability of Member States for wrong implementation of EU law[16] that can be understood as a specific category of state liability.

2.1.2. Relationship between the Different Layers of Regulation

While it is easy to identify several rules in EU private law which deal with damages, it is much more difficult to answer the second question, namely how the different rules relate to each other. As a first observation, it can be said that there is – different from Member State's national laws, e.g. Germany's §823 BGB or Article 1240 (ex Article 1382) of the French Code Civil – no general provision on liability for civil wrongs. Consequently, both the case law of the Court of Justice of the European Union (CJEU) and of the national courts as well as the academic discussion tend to be sector-specific. One mostly finds a discussion of damages in competition law, intellectual property law, consumer law, etc. Relatively few studies try to connect the different fields and discuss the existence and possible content of an overarching law of damages. Moreover, where such studies exist, they tend to focus on matters that are close to the traditional matters of the civil code (such as consumer law or product liability). Other fields such as intellectual property or competition law are neglected, which is unfortunate as it excludes the rich case law in these areas from the analysis.

---

12 See Article 82(1) of Regulation of the European Parliament and of the Council (EU) 2016/679 of 27 April 2016 on the protection of natural persons with regard to the processing of personal data and on the free movement of such data, and repealing Directive 95/46/EC (General Data Protection Regulation) [2016] OJ L 119/1.

13 See Article 11(1) of Regulation (EU) 2017/1129 of the European Parliament and of the Council of 14 June 2017 on the prospectus to be published when securities are offered to the public or admitted to trading on a regulated market, and repealing Directive 2003/71/EC [2017] OJ L 168/12. Article 11(1) is understood to establish only general requirements for the structure of national liability provisions which have to be implemented in the Member States' law.

14 As an example, see Article 7 of Regulation of the European Parliament and of the Council (EC) No 261/2004 of 11 February 2004 establishing common rules on compensation and assistance to passengers in the event of denied boarding and of cancellation or long delay of flights, and repealing Regulation (EEC) No 295/91 [2004] OJ L 46/1.

15 For more details, see C. Heinze, above n. 2, pp. 144–146.

16 CJEU 19.11.1991, C-6/90 and C-9/90, *Francovich*, ECLI:EU:C:1991:428, para. 33.

2.2. DEVELOPMENTS

Looking beyond the status quo, three general trends may be observed.

2.2.1. Horizontal Fragmentation

First, it can be said that the number of sector-specific rules on damages is growing. In the last years, the EU legislator has adopted several new damages rules that add up to the existing number of provisions. Consequently, one witnesses a growing horizontal fragmentation on the level of EU law,[17] i.e. different – sometimes even diverging – damages provisions for related issues.[18] For example, in anti-discrimination law a single issue – damage liability (or remedies in general) for discriminatory practices – is split up into no fewer than five different directives, depending on the ground of discrimination and the status of the victim (employee, self-employed, general citizen).[19] This fragmentation creates a risk of incoherent answers to similar or even identical questions. For example, compensation for immaterial damage is guaranteed by Article 13(1) of the Intellectual Property Enforcement Directive 2004/48, excluded by Article 9 2nd sentence of the Product Liability Directive 85/374 and not addressed in the old Travel Package Directive

---

17 Fragmentation in this context describes primarily fragmentation of legal sources and layers of regulation. This may lead to fragmentation also on the level of substantive policies pursued in different legal instruments and by different lawmakers, or fragmentation by deviation in terminology between the different sources, for different types of fragmentation see J. Smits/ P. Letto-Vanamo in J. Smits/P. Letto-Vanamo (eds.), *Coherence and Fragmentation in European Private Law*, Sellier European Law Publishers, Munich 2009, pp. 1, 4–6.

18 H. Koziol/ R. Schulze, 'Conclusio' in H. Koziol/R. Schulze (eds.), *Tort Law of the European Community*, Springer Wien/New York, 2008, para. 23/6; F. Wilman, *Private Enforcement of EU law before national courts*, Edgar Elgar Publishing Ltd, 2015, para. 10.39. On this trend (and on the definition of coherence and fragmentation), see also J. Smits/ P. Letto-Vanamo, above n. 17, pp. 1, 5 pointing to Europeanisation, Internationalisation and private law making as elements which foster fragmentation; on the concept of coherence see also T. Wilhelmsson, 'The Contract Law Acquis: Towards More Coherence Through Generalisation?' in *Sammelband 4. Europäischer Juristentag*, MANZ, Wien 2008, pp. 111, 130.

19 A right to damages is found in Article 8(2) of Council Directive 2004/113/EC of 13 December 2004 implementing the principle of equal treatment between men and women in the access to and supply of goods and services [2004] OJ L 373/37, Article 18 of Directive 2006/54/EC (above n. 5) and Article 10 of Directive 2010/41/EU of the European Parliament and of the Council of 7 July 2010 on the application of the principle of equal treatment between men and women engaged in an activity in a self-employed capacity and repealing Council Directive 86/613/EEC [2010] OJ L 180/1. Only a general guarantee of effective sanctions is found in Articles 7, 15 of Council Directive 2000/43/EC of 29 June 2000 implementing the principle of equal treatment between persons irrespective of racial or ethnic origin [2000] OJ L 180/22 and Articles 9, 17 of Council Directive 2000/78/EC of 27 November 2000 establishing a general framework for equal treatment in employment and occupation [2000] OJ L 303/16.

(Article 5(2) Travel Directive 90/314;[20] compensation for immaterial damage was awarded by the Court of Justice[21] and is now included in Article 14(2) of the new Package Travel Directive 2015/2302).

2.2.2. *Vertical Fragmentation*

Complicating matters even more is the vertical fragmentation of the EU rules on damages. EU law does not and cannot address all issues that may arise in the context of a damages claim. This is due to different reasons: first, EU legislation focuses mostly on substantive rights and leaves remedies – which are more intertwined with general civil law and thus more difficult to harmonise – to national law.[22] In EU secondary law (directives and regulations), often only a very general obligation of 'effective, proportionate and dissuasive' remedies is found (e.g. Article 24(1) Consumer Rights Directive 2011/83[23]). In this scenario, Union law, in particular the principles of effectiveness and equivalence,[24] defines only the minimum standard for remedies, which remain to be governed by national law. National damages provisions thus apply to the consequences of a violation of Union rights and must provide 'effective' remedies, a standard that is not easy to determine.

In other instances, EU law establishes a right to damages, but its rules on damages are incomplete. This is, in essence, not different from national law where damages provisions in special fields normally do not address all conceivable issues of damages. Different from national legal systems, however, EU law lacks a general tort and civil law that serves as a fall back and 'gap filler'. Consequently, it remains unclear how gaps in EU damages provisions are filled. Article 82 of the General Data Protection Regulation 2016/679 (GDPR) illustrates this 'incompleteness'. The first paragraph of this provision states that 'any person who has suffered material or non-material damage as

---

20 Council Directive 90/314/EEC of 13 June 1990 on package travel, package holidays and package tours [1990] OJ L 158/59.

21 CJEU 12.03.2002, C-168/00, *Leitner*, ECLI:EU:C:2002:163 = *Neue Juristische Wochenschrift (NJW)* 2002, 1255 para. 24.

22 See F. Wilman, above n. 18, para. 2.02, 10.15; F. Hofmann, *Der Unterlassungsanspruch als Rechtsbehelf*, Mohr Siebeck, Tübingen 2017, pp. 100–105.

23 Directive 2011/83/EU of the European Parliament and of the Council of 25 October 2011 on consumer rights, amending Council Directive 93/13/EEC and Directive 1999/44/EC of the European Parliament and of the Council and repealing Council Directive 85/577/EEC and Directive 97/7/EC of the European Parliament and of the Council [2011] OJ L 304/64.

24 Established by CJEU 16.12.1976, Case 33/76, *Rewe*, ECLI:EU:C:1976:188 = *NJW* 1977, 495 para. 5. There is a parallel line of jurisprudence concerning sanctions for infringement of rights or obligations established by directives established by CJEU 21.09.1989, Case 68/88 *Commission/Greece* [1989] ECR 2965 para. 23–24. For further references and a discussion of the relationship between these lines of jurisprudence and related doctrines of EU law C. Heinze, above n. 2, pp. 20–47.

a result of an infringement of this Regulation shall have the right to receive compensation from the controller or processor for the damage suffered'. The following paragraphs of the provision deal with which infringements may lead to liability of data controller or processor, the possibility to exonerate from 'responsibility', joint liability of several controllers/processors, a claim of indemnity/recourse of one of several liable persons, and with the competent courts. At first sight, the provision seems to be rather extensive and 'complete'. However, it is easy to come up with questions that are not (at least not explicitly) answered by the text of Article 82 GDPR. First, it can be asked what is to be understood as compensable damage, and how it is to be calculated. It is true that Article 82(1) GDPR states that damage can be 'material or non-material', and recital 146 3rd sentence adds that '[t]he concept of damage should be broadly interpreted in the light of the case-law of the Court of Justice in a manner which fully reflects the objectives of this Regulation'. However, this still does not answer whether there is damage if, for example, a breach of GDPR obligations concerns personal data which is publicly available from other sources, or how high compensation is to be set for mere 'immaterial' damage. Other issues which are not answered by Article 82 GDPR are whether 'responsibility' in the sense of Article 82(3) GDPR is the same as fault, whether contributory negligence of the data subject can be invoked as defence, or how long the period of limitation is and how it is calculated.

Because of this 'incompleteness', there are open questions of interpretation or even gaps to be filled. In principle, this is possible in two ways: First, it is conceivable to answer open questions by an *autonomous interpretation of EU law*. Under this approach, national courts must interpret Article 82 GDPR and the Regulation as a whole in order to determine an EU autonomous meaning of 'damage'. If uncertainties remain, national courts can or even (as a court of last instance) must refer the question to the Court of Justice to receive an authoritative interpretation. In this process of interpretation, it is possible that, but not fully clear whether national courts and the Court of Justice may, should or even must consider also the meaning of 'damage' in other rules of EU private law. The reference in recital 146 3rd sentence GDPR that '[t]he concept of damage should be broadly interpreted in the light of the case-law of the Court of Justice' suggests that they should look to other fields, as the 'case-law of the Court of Justice' mentioned in this recital is likely to mean case law on other damages provisions, because there was none on Article 82 GDPR or the earlier damages provision in the data protection directive when recital 146 was drafted. As an alternative, open questions of interpretation and gaps can be dealt with by a *subsidiary application of national law* as defined by private international law. While the GDPR is silent on this point, other EU instruments such as the railroad passenger rights regulation refer explicitly to national law. For example, Article 7(2) of Regulation 181/2011[25] states that '[t]he amount of compensation shall be calculated in accordance with applicable national law'.

Which method of interpretation or gap-filling should be applied will depend on the question which has to be answered.[26] Where the courts are faced with the interpretation of a term that is found in the EU instrument (regulation or directive) itself, there is a general presumption of autonomous interpretation of this term.[27] This, however, does not mean that all details will be decided by the Court of Justice. Rather, the Court will define the general contours and basic concepts of a term such as 'damage' (such as whether certain categories of loss are to be compensated, or what general rules of calculation apply). National courts will then apply these principles to individual cases. If, on the other hand, the EU instrument does not address the matter because it falls outside its substantive scope, for example limitation issues in data protection law, the courts will apply the national law as defined by conflict of law rules, but within the limits of the principles of equivalence and effectiveness. Thus, limitation for damages actions for breach of GDPR obligations may not be subject to less favourable rules than those governing similar domestic actions (principle of equivalence), and national rules must not make it in practice impossible or excessively difficult to exercise the rights conferred by EU law (principle of effectiveness).[28]

2.2.3. *Uncertain Impact of the Principle of Effectiveness*

While the principle of effectiveness has steadily become more relevant as EU law has expanded over the last decades, the contours and (minimum) requirements of effectiveness of national remedies in general (and national

---

25 Regulation (EU) No 181/2011 of the European Parliament and of the Council of 16 February 2011 concerning the rights of passengers in bus and coach transport and amending Regulation (EC) No 2006/2004 [2011] OJ L 55/1.

26 While the difference between autonomous interpretation and subsidiary application of national law within the limits of equivalence and effectiveness is important (and the European harmonisation effect stronger in case of autonomous interpretation), both standards can converge if the legislator later decides to codify formerly unwritten requirements of effectiveness. For examples, above n. 5.

27 CJEU 18.10.2011, C-34/10, *Brüstle*, ECLI:EU:C:2011:669 = *EuZW* 2011, 908 para. 25.

28 For the definition of effectiveness and equivalence which are established in permanent jurisprudence, CJEU 17.05.2018, C-147/16, *Karel de Grote*, ECLI:EU:C:2018:320 = *EuZW* 2018, 545 para. 33. For its application to limitation periods in competition law, CJEU 28.03.2019, C-637/17, *Cogeco Communcations*, ECLI:EU:C:2019:263, para. 43, 53: 'In that context, it must be held that a limitation period of three years, such as that at issue in the main proceedings, which, first, starts to run from the date on which the injured party was aware of its right to compensation, even if the infringer is not known and, secondly, may not be suspended or interrupted in the course of proceedings before the national competition authority, renders the exercise of the right to full compensation practically impossible or excessively difficult.' Same view C. Heinze, above n. 2, p. 626 text at footnote 487 and 488.

damages actions to enforce EU law in particular) are far from settled in the CJEU's case law. This uncertainty concerns specific issues such as how long a limitation period must be at the minimum for the damages action to remain effective,[29] or how strict or lenient the effectiveness test is to be applied,[30] and whether this depends on the field of law or nature of EU right concerned. It also concerns more doctrinal questions such as the relationship between the 'general' principle of effectiveness (based on primary law, in particular Article 4(3) TFEU) and requirements established by (later) secondary law. For example, it can be asked whether it is possible for the EU legislator to pass directives or regulations that amend or even fall below requirements established on the basis of the general principle of effectiveness.[31] Vice versa, it is also unclear whether requirements established under the general principle of effectiveness can be applied to later codified rules, possibly even if the later rules concern a different field of law.

To sum up the three trends observed in the EU law of damages, there is a growing number of rules, and, to a lesser extent, unwritten requirements based on the principle of effectiveness. Still, this proliferation does not lead to more, but rather to less certainty and predictability as it remains uncertain whether earlier findings apply to new rules, or whether findings in one field also apply to other areas of the law.

3. COMMON PRINCIPLES OF DAMAGES IN EU PRIVATE LAW?

The vertical and horizontal fragmentation of the law and the uncertain impact of the principle of effectiveness lead to the core question whether it is possible to develop a general concept[32] of damages in EU private law[33]

---

29 Above n. 28.

30 For details on the criteria of effectiveness M. Ebers, above n. 3, pp. 271–290; C. Heinze, above n. 2, pp. 54–75.

31 For details C. Heinze, above n. 2, p. 62; W. Wurmnest/C. Heinze, 'General Principles of Tort Law in the Jurisprudence of the European Court of Justice' in R. Schulze (ed.), *Compensation of Private Losses*, Sellier. European Law Publishers, Munich 2011, pp. 39, 45: 'As a result, the European legislator may, possibly subject to an undeniable core of effectiveness of substantive rights based on primary law, deviate from ECJ case law by legislative action as much as the legislator could abolish the substantive law itself'; J.-U. Franck 'Umbrella pricing and cartel damages under EU competition law', 11 ECJ 135, 138 (2015).

32 On general principles in EU Private Law and the acquis communautaire see A. Metzger, *Extra legem, intra ius: Allgemeine Rechtsgrundsätze im Europäischen Privatrecht*, Mohr Siebeck, Tübingen 2009, pp. 323–413; J.D. Lüttringhaus, *Vertragsfreiheit und ihre Materialisierung im Europäischen Binnenmarkt*, Mohr Siebeck, Tübingen 2018, pp. 150–167.

33 W. Wurmnest, *Grundzüge eines europäischen Haftungsrechts*, Mohr Siebeck, Tübingen 2003, pp. 87–108: 'Anspruchsübergreifende Kohärenz der Haftungssysteme'; N. Reich,

(or at least certain elements as common traits of EU rules on damages). As an alternative, it has been argued that coherence in EU private law aims only at 'the consistent interaction of (…) EU rules', while national private law bears the primary responsibility that the instruments employed by EU legislation are coherent.[34] According to this view, fragmentary legislation by the EU is to be avoided only where it leads to 'inconsistencies in the relevant policy area (…) or in coordination with other measures'.[35] This view seems to prefer a separate analysis of general concepts such as the concept of damages for each sector of substantive law (e.g. consumer law, intellectual property, data protection, anti-discrimination, etc.), unless it leads to 'inconsistencies in the relevant policy area (…) or in coordination with other measures'. In support of such a sector-specific approach, it can be pointed to the sectoral nature of European legislation.[36] It may also appear attractive for reasons of judicial self-restraint, for leaving leeway to decide future cases, and also because it may be perceived as being less intrusive for national law.[37]

While both positions start from different premises, they seem to agree on important points.[38] First, it seems to be accepted by both positions that

---

General Principles of EU Civil Law, Intersentia, Cambridge 2014, pp. 6–7 (general discussion); C. Heinze, above n. 2, pp. 93–106, for examples pp. 497–634; W. Wurmnest, 'Damages' in J. Basedow/K.J. Hopt/R. Zimmermann (eds.), *Max Planck Encyclopedia of European Private Law*, Oxford University Press 2012, Volume I, pp. 444, 447: 'the outlines of a European law of damages are slowly starting to develop'; for contract law J.D. Lüttringhaus, above n. 32, 21. Sceptical S. Weatherhill, 'The "principles of civil law" as a basis for understanding the legislative acquis' (2010) *European review of Contract Law* (6) 1, 74, 80: 'A more coherent system at EU level may lead to a less coherent system at national level. Such a starkly destructive outcome is not inevitable, but this is where the Court's use of general principles may lead, and it is one reason why it is troubling.'

34 T. Ackermann, 'Sektorielles EU-Recht und allgemeine Privatrechtssystematik' (2018) ZEuP 741, 762–763: 'Jedoch ist zu fragen, ob die Kohärenzanforderungen des Unionsrechts nicht eher in eine andere Richtung, nämlich auf das widerspruchsfreie Zusammenwirken der (privat- und/oder öffentlich-rechtlichen) Regelungen für ihre teils sektorübergreifenden, teils sektorspezifischen Politiken, zielen, während das nach wie vor dichtere Gewebe des nationalen Privatrechts die primäre Verantwortung dafür trägt, die von der Union eingesetzten privatrechtlichen Instrumente in einen schlüssigen Zusammenhang zu bringen.'

35 Ibid., p. 767: 'Eine Überwindung fragmentarischer Privatrechtssetzung durch die EU kann im Einzelfall sinnvoll und rechtspolitisch geboten sein, wenn sie von dem Anliegen gedeckt ist, Maßnahmen zu verhindern, die zu Unstimmigkeiten in dem jeweiligen Politikfeld (hier im Bereich des digitalen Binnenmarktes) oder in der Abstimmung mit anderen Maßnahmen (hier etwa mit der Verbrauchsgüterkaufrichtlinie) führen.'

36 Ibid., p. 741: 'However, the concept of a private law system is unsuitable for a democratic polity whose supranational level is formed by the EU. Instead, the systematic quest for unity and consistency should aim at positioning private law rules in the entirety of our legal order. This leads to a better understanding of European legislation and case-law in the field of private law.'

37 On this point, see text immediately before 4.

38 This is not true for those who generally reject the development of common concepts on the EU level, even within a relevant policy area. However, it is not only damaging for the EU legal system to insist on different concepts for each single instrument. Moreover, the idea of coherent interpretation appears to be settled case law at least where a

coherence and consistency of a private law system is desirable *within a relevant policy area*. Therefore, also the proponents of a more cautious approach would seem to agree that there should not be a different concept of damages for each individual EU anti-discrimination directive, but rather a general concept for the entire field of anti-discrimination law. However, it is not always easy to decide where the 'relevant policy area' ends. For example, are the rules in the EU transport regulations and in the EU package travel directive to be regarded as belonging to the same 'relevant policy area'? Are consumer law and the law of unfair commercial practices part of the same policy area? How about consumer and data protection law, or consumer and intellectual property law (e.g. where a consumer acquires copyrighted material)? It is not easy to separate different policy areas in EU legislation, also because most EU legislation relevant in private law is founded on the same competence ground (Article 114 TFEU), i.e. justified by harmonisation necessary for the internal market. Moreover, both views seem to agree on a second point, namely that inconsistency is to be avoided also '*in coordination with other (related) measures*'.[39] An example is coherence and consistency between data protection law and general contract law (and property law) concerning contracts over the use of data or (exclusive) rights in such data.[40]

Thus, in its results the more cautious approach does not appear to be too far from an approach which aims at finding general principles for the entire field of Union law, while admitting at the same time that both the nature of a specific substantive law area as well as the different degrees of EU harmonisation may require exceptions and deviations from the general concept.[41] In the author's view, the more general approach is desirable, mainly for three reasons. First, it is difficult to delineate 'relevant policy areas' or 'related measures'. 'Consistency with other (related) measures' can be – as the example (consumer contract law and data protection law) demonstrates[42] – quite broad. Matters such as the requirements for the fitness for purpose of digital content and product liability

directive 'is based on principles and rules already laid down' in directives in the respective field of law, CJEU 04.10.2011, C-403/08 and C-429/08, *Murphy*, ECLI:EU:C:2011:631, para. 187–188; CJEU 05.07.2012, C-49/11, *Content Services*, ECLI:EU:C:2012:419 = *NJW* 2012, 2637 para. 44.

39 T. Ackermann, above n. 34, p. 767.

40 T. Ackermann, above n. 34, p. 768: 'Nur in wechselseitiger Ergänzung und Abstimmung können diese Teilgebiete des öffentlichen und des Privatrechts dafür sorgen, dass die Autonomie des einzelnen in einer Welt digitaler Transaktionen gewahrt wird.'

41 See C. Heinze, above n. 2, p. 104: 'Es versteht sich von selbst, dass nicht nur aus sachlichen Gründen der betreffenden Rechtsmaterie, sondern bereits infolge der unterschiedlich intensiven Harmonisierungszugriffe des Unionsrechts (…) Unterschiede (…) bestehen können', pp. 538–539 'Derogation durch Sekundärrecht'.

42 The relevant legislation was based on different grounds of competence: The General Data Protection Regulation on Article 16(2) TFEU (see recital 12 of the General Data Protection Regulation 679/2016), the new Directive on certain aspects concerning contracts for the supply of digital goods on Article 114 TFEU.

for physical damage which seemed entirely unrelated when the Product Liability Directive was adopted in 1985 are now considered as related and discussed together. Second, restricting the analysis to material from a certain policy area limits the available information (legislation, case law, legislative materials, etc.) which could be helpful to develop an autonomous (European) answer for a specific question. If national courts and commentators cannot look to models or solutions from other fields of EU law (where the same question might already have been answered), it seems more likely that Member States' courts will resort to solutions which have been accepted in national doctrine, which would in turn compromise the uniform application of EU law. Moreover, a sectoral approach (even if the sector is defined broadly) increases uncertainty as it is necessary to wait for each EU instrument, or at least for each sector of regulation, for decisions of the Court of Justice. Such decisions are rare, and they are likely to answer only specific questions, so that further references to Luxembourg will be necessary if one cannot resort to decisions from other sectors. In addition, a sector-specific analysis may fail to notice (pioneering) developments in one sector which can later become relevant in other sectors. And thirdly, it seems counterintuitive not to look at the field of damages at large, but rather at each substantive law field in separation. In national law, courts and commentators normally do not hesitate to apply decisions from one substantive field of the law to others, and it is difficult to see why this should be fundamentally different on the level of EU law.

For these reasons, it seems preferable to take a presumption of a *general* EU concept of damages as a starting point which allows resorting to decisions or legislation from other sectors of EU private law. This presumption of a general concept of damages can be rebutted depending on the subject matter and legal instrument in question. If, for example, the relevant piece of legislation expressly or implicitly deviates from the understanding of damages in other sectors, the general concept no longer applies. Likewise, it is possible that the level of harmonisation and detail concerning the right to damages is different in different areas of substantive law, or the EU instrument in question may expressly refer certain issues to national law, which also excludes applying a general EU concept. Moreover, the general concept of damages in EU law is necessarily less detailed and specific than in national legal systems. It does not answer each question which may come up in individual cases, but rather aims at general guidelines to safeguard a uniform application of EU law by national courts for the most fundamental issues. The application of the general concepts and guidelines to a given case, including the calculation of the precise damages, will be for the national courts to decide based on the general EU concepts. Such a general concept of damages in EU private law is helpful not only to mitigate the effects of the horizontal fragmentation of EU law. It can also serve as an antidote against the uncertainties caused by vertical fragmentation of EU private law. While the precise requirements of the principle of effectiveness can often be unclear, the concept of damages accepted in other fields of EU law can be a helpful indication of which form of compensation is likely to be acceptable under the requirement of effectiveness. This does not mean that the same form of compensation is required by the principle of effectiveness, but it may indicate what damages rules would be acceptable to comply with the requirement of effectiveness. Thus, the general concept of damages can be 'imported' into the principle of effectiveness to illustrate what form of damages regimes are accepted by Union law, without excluding other national solutions. Finally, such a general concept of damages in EU private law does not question national sovereignty or the autonomy of the Member States. It comes into play where the issue in the law of damages already is a matter of Union law, because a directive or a regulation establishes a right to damages, or because Union law provides for a substantive right for which a minimum level of effective enforcement must be available. In these scenarios, in particular in case of a directive or regulation right to damages, the realm of national law has ended, and the attention focuses not on *whether* the issue is to be answered by Union law, but rather *in which way*. The general concept of damages is one way to develop an answer within EU law, while the adherence to sector-specific damages rules is another. Both solutions are solutions developed on the level of EU law, so it cannot be said that one favours national sovereignty more than the other.

4. THE CONCEPT OF DAMAGE AS AN EXAMPLE OF A COMMON PRINCIPLE

It has been pointed out above that general concepts for damages actions in EU private law can be beneficial to mitigate the horizontal and vertical fragmentation of the law, while at the same time fostering legal certainty and autonomy of Union law. However, it has also been stressed that such general concepts on the level of EU law are less specific than national concepts are. This raises the question how specific common principles for damages in EU private law can be, in particular whether they can be sufficiently specific to provide any helpful guidance to national courts in deciding individual cases. This question shall be answered by presenting the concept of damage as an example. While the level of detail prescribed in a given case by Union law will of course depend on the level of harmonisation in that case,[43] some overarching observations may be made.

[43] Depending on whether only the general principle of effectiveness applies or whether a specific directive or even regulation exists, a European or national concept of damage applies; see C. HEINZE, above n. 2, pp. 579–583.

4.1. NO HIERARCHY BETWEEN RESTITUTION IN KIND AND MONETARY COMPENSATION

In German law, the distinction between 'Naturalrestitution' (restitution in kind, §§249, 250 BGB) and 'Schadenskompensation' (monetary compensation, §251 BGB), i.e. whether the debtor has to reinstate the victim into the position before the damage occurred (restitution in kind), or whether the debtor owes 'only' monetary compensation, is fundamental as 'Naturalrestitution' takes precedence over 'Schadenskompensation'. Moreover, the limits placed on compensation of non-economic harm for monetary compensation (§253 BGB) do not apply to restitution in kind. Such a hierarchical relationship between restitution in kind and monetary compensation for damages cannot be observed in Union law.[44] Only for damages in a contractual relationship, Union law seems to have a certain preference for claims to (subsequent) performance before turning to monetary compensation,[45] probably also due to the proximity of the other party to provide the desired performance. The absence of a hierarchical relationship between restitution in kind and monetary compensation does not mean that Union law excludes restitution in kind. Rather, Union law permits national law to impose on the aggrieved party 'any form of reparation that accords with the general principles of non-contractual liability common to the laws of the Member States, including, if it accords with those principles, compensation in kind'.[46]

---

44 See CJEU 19.12.2013, C-174/12, *Hirmann*, ECLI:EU:C:2013:856 = *EuZW* 2014, 223 para. 69 (Member States' choice), see also CJEU 25.10.2005, C-350/03, *Schulte*, ECLI:EU:C:2005:637 = *NJW* 2005, 3551 para. 80; Article 8:402(1) Acquis Principles 2009: 'Damages are a money payment of the amount necessary to put the creditor into the position in which it would have been if the obligation had been duly performed'; K. Oliphant 'The Nature and Assessment of Damages' in H. Koziol/R. Schulze (eds.), *Tort Law of the European Community*, Springer Wien/New York, 2008, para. 11/29: 'no general obligation (…) to make restoration in kind'; C. Schubert, *Die Wiedergutmachung immaterieller Schäden im Privatrecht*, Mohr Siebeck, Tübingen 2013, p. 433 (on immaterial damage).

45 See the hierarchy between Article 13(2), (3) and Article 14(2) Package Travel Package Directive 2015/2302; see also Article 8(1)(b), (c) and Article 9 Air Passenger Rights Regulation 261/2004 and Article 13(2) and (4) and recital 50 of Directive (EU) 2019/771 of the European Parliament and of the Council of 20 May 2019 on certain aspects concering contracts for the sale of goods, amending Regulation (EU) 2017/2394 and Directive 2009/22/EC, and repealing Directive 1999/44/EC [2019] OJ L 136/28; on the primacy of subsequent performance see K. Riesenhuber, *Europäisches Vertragsrecht*, De Gruyter, Berlin/Boston 2nd edn., 2006, para. 793.

46 CoFI 08.11.2011, T-88/09, *Idromacchine*, ECLI:EU:T:2011:641, para. 81; W. Wurmnest, above n. 33, pp. 235–236.

4.2. DEFINITION OF DAMAGE

The fundamental principle under Union law is that compensation 'must enable the loss and damage actually sustained (...) to be made good in full'.[47] This principle can be found in several areas of EU law, from competition law,[48] consumer contract law[49] and product liability law[50] to travel law[51] and air passenger compensation.[52] It can also be observed in state liability law,[53] anti-discrimination law,[54] intellectual property law,[55] data protection law,[56] compensation under the fund of liability insurers for motor vehicle accidents[57] and probably also in cases of payment default[58] and capital market law.[59]

Full compensation means that, in principle, all detriment capable of being compensated from the point of view of Union law must be compensated (i.e. also immaterial damage,[60] loss of profit,[61] loss of value of a compensation

---

47 CJEU 17.12.2015, C-407/14, *Camacho*, ECLI:EU:C:2015:831 = *EuZW* 2016, 183 para. 33.

48 Article 3(1) Cartel Damages Directive 2014/104: 'full compensation for that harm'; the leading decision in CJEU 13.07.2006, C-295/04 – C-298/04, *Manfredi*, ECLI:EU:C:2006:461 = *EuZW* 2006, 529 para. 97 cites CJEU 02.08.1993, C-271/91, *Marshall II*, ECLI:EU:C:1993:335, *infra* note 57.

49 CJEU 25.10.2005, C-350/03, *Schulte*, ECLI:EU:C:2005:637 = NJW 2005, 3551 para. 100 which can be understood as requiring removing all risks of loss from the consumer to the bank, for details C. Heinze, above n. 2, pp. 303–306.

50 CJEU 10.05.2001, C-203/99, *Veedfald*, ECLI:EU:C:2001:258 = *NJW* 2001, 2781 para. 27; CJEU 05.03.2015, C-503/13 and C-504/13, *Boston Scientific*, ECLI:EU:C:2015:148, para. 49.

51 Opinion of AG Tizzano Case C-168/00, *Leitner*, ECLI:EU:C:2001:476, para. 29; now recital 34 7th sentence of Travel Package Directive 2015/2302.

52 CJEU 13.10.2011, C-83/10, *Sousa Rodriguez*, ECLI:EU:C:2011:652 = NJW 2011, 3776 para. 38.

53 CJEU 04.10.1979, C-238/78, *Ireks-Arkady*, ECLI:EU:C:1979:226, para. 20; CJEU 03.02.1994, C-308/87, *Grifoni*, ECLI:EU:C:1994:38, para. 40; see also for civil services claims CJEU 21.02.2008, C-348/06 P, *Girardot*, ECLI:EU:C:2008:107, para. 76.

54 CJEU 02.08.1993, C-271/91, *Marshall II*, ECLI:EU:C:1993:335, para. 26, 31; CJEU 11.10.2007, C-460/06, *Paquay*, ECLI:EU:C:2007:601, para. 46; CJEU 17.12.2015, C-407/14, *Camacho*, ECLI:EU:C:2015:831 = *EuZW* 2016, 183 para. 33, 37; today Article 10 Directive 2010/41, Article 18 Directive 2006/54.

55 Article 13(1) 1st sentence and recital 26 1st sentence Intellectual Property Enforcement Directive 2004/48; CJEU 17.03.2016, C-99/15, *Liffers*, ECLI:EU:C:2016:173 = *GRUR* 2016, 485 para. 25.

56 Recital 146 6th sentence General Data Protection Regulation 2016/679.

57 CJEU 04.12.2003, C-63/01, *Evans*, ECLI:EU:C:2003:650 = EuZW 2004, 146 para. 64, 67.

58 Article 6(3) 1st sentence of Directive (EU) 2011/7 of the European Parliament and of the Council of 16 February 2011 on combating late payment in commercial transactions [2011] OJ L 48/1.

59 CJEU 19.12.2013, C-174/12, *Hirmann*, ECLI:EU:C:2013:856 = *EuZW* 2014, 223 para. 43.

60 CJEU 22.04.1997, C-180/95, *Draehmpaehl*, ECLI:EU:C:1997:208 = *NJW* 1997, 1839 para. 34 (anti-discrimination law); CJEU 12.03.2002, C-168/00, *Leitner*, ECLI:EU:C:2002:163 = *NJW* 2002, 1255 para. 22 (travel law); CJEU 06.05.2010, C-63/09, *Walz*, ECLI:EU:C:2010:251 = NJW 2010, 2113 para. 29 (passenger rights in air transport);

payment as a result of the passage of time,[62] or the costs of enforcing the law[63]), that symbolic compensation is not sufficient,[64] and that maximum limits for damages are inadmissible[65] unless Union law excludes certain damage positions from compensation or provides for its own limits of liability (as in Articles 9, 16 Product Liability Directive 85/374). A gradation of compensation based on the degree of fault (intent or (slight) negligence) – which may exclude full compensation in cases of light negligence – is rare in EU law.[66]

Furthermore, it is becoming apparent that the concrete losses which constitute recoverable damage are to be determined by a comparison of assets of the injured person with and (hypothetically) without the damaging event according to the 'Differenzmethode'.[67] Within this comparison, a 'normative control'[68] applies, for example to determine whether or not a benefit received after the damaging event can relieve the tortfeasor from the burden to pay compensation, and the objectives of the infringed Union law norm (and the

---

Article 13(1) lit. a Intellectual Property Enforcement Directive 2004/48; CoFI 08.11.2011, T-88/09, *Idromacchine*, ECLI:EU:T:2011:641, para. 61 (state liability).

61 CJEU 13.07.2006, C-295/04 – C-298/04, *Manfredi*, ECLI:EU:C:2006:461 = *EuZW* 2006, 529 para. 95 (competition law); CJEU 05.03.1996, C-46/93 and C-48/93, *Brasserie du Pêcheur*, ECLI:EU:C:1996:79 = *NJW* 1996, 1267 para. 87, 90 (state liability); Opinion of AG van Gerven Case C-271/91, *Marshall*, ECLI:EU:C:1993:30, para. 18 (anti-discrimination law); Article 13(1) lit. a Intellectual Property Enforcement Directive 2004/48; CJEU 26.03.2009, C-348/07, *Semen*, ECLI:EU:C:2009:195 = *EuZW* 2009, 304 para. 19 (commercial agency).

62 Normally, but not necessarily by means of interest, for details C. Heinze, above n. 2, pp. 631–634.

63 Recital 26 3rd sentence Intellectual Property Enforcement Directive 2004/48 and Article 8:402(3) Acquis Principles 2009. Where special provisions on recuperation for (legal) costs exists, these may be conclusive, see also Article 14 Intellectual Property Enforcement Directive 2004/48.

64 CJEU 10.04.1984, Case 14/83, *von Colson und Kamann*, ECLI:EU:C:1984:153, para. 24; CJEU 25.04.2013, C-81/12, *Accept*, ECLI:EU:C:2013:275 = *EuZW* 2013, 469 para. 64. For a different view in civil servants' law W. Wurmnest, above n. 33, pp. 237–238.

65 CJEU 02.08.1993, C-271/91, *Marshall II*, ECLI:EU:C:1993:335, para. 30; see also on commercial agent's compensation CJEU 26.03.2009, C-348/07, *Semen*, ECLI:EU:C:2009:195 = *EuZW* 2009, 304 para.25; CJEU 03.12.2015, C-338/14, *Quenon*, ECLI:EU:C:2015:795 = *EuZW* 2016, 221 para. 30.

66 For a rare example Article 94(2) Council Regulation (EC) No 2100/94 of 27 July 1994 on Community plant variety rights, OJ L 227/1. See also recital 17 Intellectual Property Enforcement Directive 2004/48.

67 CJEU 04.10.1979, Case 238/78, *Ireks-Arkady*, ECLI:EU:C:1979:226, para. 13; CJEU 26.06.1990, C-152/88, *Sofrimport*, ECLI:EU:C:1990:259, para. 30; U. Magnus in Research Group on the Existing EC Contract Law (ed.), *Principles of the Existing EC Contract Law (Acquis Principles)*, Sellier. European Law Publishers, 2007, Article 8:402 para. 1; S.J. Geibel, 'Die Richtlinie über die Haftung für Kartellrechtsverstöße: Förderung der Privatinitiative zur Durchsetzung des Rechts und Eckstein für ein Europäisches Schadensrecht?' in C. Stumpf/ F. Kainer/C. Baldus (eds.), *Privatrecht, Wirtschaftsrecht, Verfassungsrecht – Privatinitiative und Gemeinwohlhorizonte in der europäischen Integration – Festschrift für Peter-Christian Müller-Graff*, Nomos, Baden-Baden 2015, pp. 558, 564. See also Art. 8:402 para. 1 Acquis Principles 2009.

68 BGH 26.09.1997, V ZR 29/96 = *NJW* 1998, 302, 304 – *Normative Kontrolle*.

legal system in general) must be taken into account. This leads to differences between contractual and non-contractual liability, because the reference point of the difference method (i.e. the point of comparison for the hypothetical situation without the damaging event) for contractual damages is the proper performance of the contract, whereas in non-contractual damages the aggrieved party must be placed in the same position as he/she would be without the damaging intervention.[69]

4.2.1. *Material Damage*

There are three categories of compensation for material damage, namely compensation for bodily injury and personal injury, for damage to property and for pecuniary loss.[70]

4.2.1.1. Bodily Injury

Compensation for bodily injury[71] plays a rather subordinate role in current Union law, because only few of its liability rules are relevant for bodily injury. However, where it is relevant, as in product liability law, travel law and air traffic law, compensation of bodily injury is fully guaranteed.[72]

4.2.1.2. Damage to Property

Compensation for damage to property is also generally guaranteed by Union private law. However, limitations of liability are more permissible than in the case of bodily injury.[73] Nevertheless, these exceptions do not question the general principle of full compensation for damage to property.[74] Compensation for property damage also includes compensation for consequential damage caused by the property damage.

---

69 K. Oliphant, above n. 44, para. 11/3.

70 Following W. Wurmnest, above n. 33, p. 275. See also the categorisation in Opinion of AG Capotorti Case 238/78, *Ireks-Arkady*, ECLI:EU:C:1979:203.

71 For a definition CJEU 24.10.2013, C-22/12, *Haasová*, ECLI:EU:C:2013:692, para. 47; CJEU 24.10.2013, C-277/12, *Drozdovs*, ECLI:EU:C:2013:685, para. 38; see also A. Vaquer, 'Damage' in H. Koziol/R. Schulze, *Tort Law of the European Community*, Springer, Wien/New York 2008, para. 2/33; K. Oliphant, above n. 44, para. 11/37.

72 See Article 9 lit. a Product Liability Directive 85/374; Article 17(1) in conjunction with Article 14(2), (4) 3rd s Package Travel Directive 2015/2302; Article 21(2) lit. a Montreal Convention; see also Annex No. a Unfair Contract Terms Directive 93/13. For details and further references see C. Heinze, above n. 2, pp. 589–590 at footnotes 346–350.

73 A. Vaquer, above n. 71, para. 2/34; K. Oliphant, above n. 44, para. 11/45; for examples see Article 9(b) Product Liability Directive 85/374; Article 14(4) 3rd sentence Travel Package Directive 2015/2302; in air passenger law see Article 22(2), (5) Montreal Convention.

74 CJEU 12.03.2002, C-168/00, *Leitner*, ECLI:EU:C:2002:163 = *NJW* 2002, 1255 para. 23.

4.2.1.3. Financial Loss

While the body of Union law governing physical injury and damage to property is rather small, compensation for financial loss plays an important role due to the proximity to the market of numerous rules of Union law. In this respect, the Court of Justice has confirmed in competition and state liability law that the principle of effectiveness requires not only compensation for positive damage (damnum emergens) but also compensation for loss of profit (lucrum cessans).[75] Similar principles can be found in intellectual property law[76] and data protection law,[77] and the case law on liability for defective information about consumer withdrawal rights also points to an obligation under Union law to compensate pure financial loss, since the Court of Justice obliges the Member States to pass on the risk from the consumer to the financing bank.[78] There are therefore indications that Union law in principle also imposes an obligation to compensate pure financial losses, including lost profits,[79] insofar as the structure of the liability situation and the protective purpose of the liability provision do not indicate otherwise and the financial loss is causally linked to the infringement.[80]

If compensation for loss of profit and pure pecuniary loss is thus in principle part of the compensation (unless, as in the Product Liability Directive, for example, an explicit exception is made in legislation[81]), the question arises as to how this compensation is to be determined. In contrast to property damage or bodily injury, where the material damage can be calculated with some degree of certainty on the basis of the costs of treatment or repair and the loss of service (at least for employees), the calculation of pure financial loss, in particular of lost profits raises the question of how (successfully) the aggrieved party would have acted on the market without the infringement (intellectual property law) or what prices he/she would have had to pay on competitive terms (competition law). Since this normally cannot be established with mathematic precision,

---

75 CJEU 05.03.1996, C-46/93 and C-48/93, *Brasserie du Pêcheur*, ECLI:EU:C:1996:79 = *NJW* 1996, 1267 para. 87; CJEU 13.07.2006, C-295/04 – C-298/04, *Manfredi*, ECLI:EU:C:2006:461 = *EuZW* 2006, 529 para. 95; see A. Vaquer, above n. 71, para. 2/22 et seq. on the categories of damnum emergens and lucrum cessans.

76 Article 13(1) lit. a Intellectual Property Enforcement Directive 2004/48; for example A. Metzger, 'Schadensersatz wegen Verletzung des geistigen Eigentums gemäß Art. 13 Durchsetzungs-RL 2004/48' in O. Remien (ed.), *Schadensersatz im europäischen Privat- und Wirtschaftsrecht*, Mohr Siebeck, Tübingen 2012, pp. 209, 216–217.

77 T. Kosmides, *Zivilrechtliche Haftung für Datenschutzverstöße*, Herbert Utz Verlag, München 2010, p. 112 (on Article 23 of the old data protection directive 95/46).

78 CJEU 25.10.2005, C-350/03, *Schulte*, ECLI:EU:C:2005:637 = *NJW* 2005, 3551 para. 100–101.

79 See Article 8:402 (2) Acquis Principles 2009; U. Magnus, above n. 67, Article 8:402 para. 5, 9.

80 CJEU 14.03.2013, C-420/11, *Leth*, ECLI:EU:C:2013:166, para. 35.

81 See Article 9 lit. a and b Product Liability Directive 85/374; Article 17 Montreal Convention.

Union law uses different approximation methods. These can, in principle, be traced back to four models, namely market simulation, the setting of lump sum compensation, the calculation of damages based on the infringer's profit, and liability for presumed causal processes. These are possible, but not the only ways to determine financial loss; the list is not exhaustive.

The most obvious method for determining the loss of profit is *market simulation*[82] which is found in competition law when calculating damages using the comparative market concept (by finding comparable markets without the unlawful restriction of competition and comparing the development of prices). However, practice in competition law shows also the limits of this concept. It seems to be reasonably practicable as far as compensation for the overcharge in price due to a cartel is concerned. However, damage caused by the loss of demand, which can in principle also be compensated in competition law, has so far rarely (if at all) been claimed in practice. This finding corresponds to the experience with the calculation of damages on the basis of lost profits in intellectual property law, which was hardly relevant in Germany for a long time until the Federal Supreme Court simplified the requirements.[83] Because of these difficulties, it may be necessary to resort to approaches other than the simulation of market developments.

Such an approach is *lump sum compensation* for damages, which can be found in particular in intellectual property law, where Article 13(1) lit. b Intellectual Property Enforcement Directive 2004/48 permits setting the damages 'as a lump sum on the basis of elements such as at least the amount of royalties or fees which would have been due if the infringer had requested authorisation to use the intellectual property right in question'.[84] In addition, it can also be found in the compensation of intangible losses, in particular in the compensation claims under Article 7 of the Passenger Rights Regulation 261/2004, and in the lump sum compensation of recovery costs under Article 6(1) of the Payment Default Directive 2011/7. For competition or consumer contract law, the model

---

[82] For capital market law see D. Poelzig,'Private Enforcement im deutschen und europäischen Kapitalmarktrecht – Eine Untersuchung anhand des Marktmanipulationsverbots unter Berücksichtigung des Entwicklungen im europäischen Kartellrecht' (2015) *Zeitschrift für Unternehmens- und Gesellschaftsrecht* 801, 833.

[83] See T. Dreier, *Kompensation und Prävention*, Mohr Siebeck, Tübingen 2002, pp. 254–255: 'geringe Zahl konkreter Schadensberechnungen in Deutschland'; BGH 02.11.2000 I ZR 246/98 = *GRUR* 2001, 329 – *Gemeinkostenanteil* has relaxed the requirements for claiming infringer's profits.

[84] On the Plant Variety Regulation 2100/94 CJEU 05.07.2012, C-509/10, *Geistbeck*, ECLI:EU:C:2012:416, para. 43. For an application see Opinion of AG Cruz Villalón Case C-103/11 P, *Systran*, ECLI:EU:C:2012:714, para. 187. More generally D. Poelzig, above n. 3, p. 492: 'zeichnen sich die marktregulierenden Schadensersatzregelungen oft dadurch aus, dass sie die Voraussetzungen an die Schadensfeststellung und -berechnung absenken und pauschalisieren.'

of lump sum damages is normally not appropriate because it is hardly possible to determine a typical, lump sum amount of damage.[85]

The calculation of damages on the basis of the *infringer's profit* is also found in intellectual property law.[86] This method, too, although it can also be found in the determination of fines in public enforcement of capital market law,[87] is only suitable to limited cases outside intellectual property law, because competition offences and other infringements of market conduct law are not concerned with the infringement of exclusive rights. As a consequence, it is difficult to justify attributing the infringer's profits to the victim of the infringement as damages, because the profits could be caused by other reasons and may exceed the actual loss of the victim.

A final approximation for the purposes of compensation of pure financial losses is liability for *presumed causal processes*. Even if compensation for lost chances is not generally required by the principle of effectiveness,[88] the protective purpose of the infringed Union law provision may in specific cases require the presumption of a certain causal course which leads to a concrete damage scenario. A prominent example here is the liability for defects in the consumer's instruction about his rights to withdrawal. In this context, the principle of effectiveness requires that the consumer should be presumed to have revoked the contract in good time if the instruction was correct,[89] so that the consumer should be placed in the same position as he/she would have been if he/she had withdrawn from the transaction by revoking the contract in time. In practice, this is related to liability for lost chances for presumed causal processes. However, the presumption of a causal process is stricter than liability for lost chances, insofar as the aggrieved party is liable for the full loss (and not only a percentage corresponding to the chance), unless he/she can rebut the presumption of conduct of the consumer (which will be impossible to prove in many cases).

---

85 For the discussion on a presumed minimum overcharge in cartel cases of 10% C. Brömmelmeyer, 'Die Ermittlung des Kartellschadens nach der Richtlinie' 2014/104/EU (2016) 2 NZKart pp. 7–9.

86 Cf. Article 13(1)(a) Intellectual Property Enforcement Directive 2004/48: judicial authorities shall take into account all appropriate aspects, 'including (...) any unfair profits made by the infringer'. For the understanding of the infringer's profit as an alleviation of proof (or a rebuttable presumption) in proving damage of the right holder see K. Boosfeld, *Gewinnausgleich*, Mohr Siebeck, Tübingen 2015, 200 et seq.; B. Raue, above n. 2, pp. 107–113.

87 On the infringer's profits in administrative sanctions see CJEU 23.12.2009, C-45/08, *Spector Photo Group*, ECLI:EU:C:2009:806 = *EuZW* 2010, 227 para. 73.

88 For details C. Heinze, above n. 2, 220; less sceptical M. Weitenberg, *Der Begriff der Kausalität in der haftungsrechtlichen Rechtsprechung der Unionsgerichte*, Nomos, Baden-Baden 2014, p. 799: damages for lost chances an accepted category, but a general concept still in development.

89 For details C. Heinze, above n. 2, pp. 310–315.

4.2.2. Immaterial Damage

Due to the structure of the EU liability rules and a general tendency towards a higher weighting of intangible interests, Union law in principle[90] requires compensation for losses[91] 'which do not relate to a person's assets, wealth or income and, as such, cannot be quantified in an objective manner by reference to a market price or value' (non-material or immaterial damage).[92] This is most clearly confirmed in travel and air traffic law: while the Leitner ruling considered the loss of holiday enjoyment as a loss to be compensated under Article 5(2) of Directive 90/314[93] (now expressly recital 34 sentence 6 of Directive 2015/2302), the Court of Justice in Walz extended compensation for loss of luggage to the immaterial damage caused by the loss.[94] Particularly important is the compensation for immaterial damage in the Air Passenger Rights Regulation 261/2004: the compensation claim in Article 7 of Regulation 261/2004 is aimed at a lump sum compensation for inconvenience, in particular the loss of time due to flight delay, flight cancellation or denied boarding.[95] However, even in competition law[96] compensation for immaterial damages is guaranteed, even if it is of only minor practical significance due to the pecuniary nature of these offences. An obligation to compensate for immaterial damages exists also in motor vehicle liability insurance law,[97] anti-discrimination law,[98] intellectual property law,[99] data protection law,[100]

---

90 Unless this is expressly excluded as in Article 9 Product Liability Directive 85/374.

91 Opinion of AG Wahl Case C-371/12, *Petillo*, ECLI:EU:C:2013:652, para. 39; A. Vaquer, above n. 71, para. 2/36 et seq.; W. Wurmnest/C. Heinze, above n. 31, 39, 59–60; C. Schubert, above n. 44, 464, 562. But see CJEU 22.06.2016, C-280/15, *Nikolajeva*, ECLI:EU:C:2016:467 para. 57: reasonable compensation under Article 11(2) of the Trade Mark Regulation 2017/1001 does not include compensation for moral prejudice.

92 Definition from Opinion of AG Wahl Case C-371/12, *Petillo*, ECLI:EU:C:2013:652, para. 38 with reference to H. Rogers, *Damages for Non-Pecuniary Loss in a Comparative Perspective*, Springer, Vienna/New York 2001, p. 246.

93 CJEU 12.03.2002, C-168/00, *Leitner*, ECLI:EU:C:2002:163 = *Neue Juristische Wochenschrift (NJW)* 2002, 1255 para. 23.

94 CJEU 06.05.2010, C-63/09, *Walz*, ECLI:EU:C:2010:251 = NJW 2010, 2113 para. 29.

95 CJEU 19.11.2009, C-402/07 and C-432/07, *Sturgeon*, ECLI:EU:C:2009:716, para. 52; CJEU 23.10.2012, C-581/10 and C-629/10, *Nelson*, ECLI:EU:C:2012:657, para. 52, 54.

96 Proposal for a Directive of the European Parliament and of the Council on certain rules governing actions for damages under national law for infringements of the competition law provisions of the Member States and of the European Union, COM (2013) 404, p. 13: 'The notion of actual loss referred to in this provision is taken from the case-law of the Court of Justice, and does not exclude any type of damage (material or immaterial) that might have been caused by an infringement of the competition rules.'

97 CJEU 24.10.2013, C-22/12, *Haasová*, ECLI:EU:C:2013:692, para. 47, 50; CJEU 24.10.2013, C-277/12, *Drozdovs*, ECLI:EU:C:2013:685, para. 44.

98 CJEU 22.04.1998, C-180/95, *Draehmpahl*, ECLI:EU:C:1997:208, para. 34 (today Article 18 2nd sentence Directive 2006/54); C. Schubert, above n. 44, 457, 465.

99 Article 13(1) lit. a) Intellectual Property Enforcement Directive 2004/48: 'elements other than economic factors, such as the moral prejudice caused to the right holder by the infringement'.

state liability law,[101] and probably also in case of payment default.[102] Immaterial damages are thus generally eligible for compensation under Union private law.[103]

At the same time, however, Union law does make a distinction between immaterial damage that can and cannot be compensated.[104] The most recognised private law[105] category of compensation for immaterial damage is compensation for pain and suffering.[106] It is recognised, for example, in the liability of the Union under Article 340(2) TFEU[107] and in travel law.[108]

An (additional) compensation for immaterial damage is available even if the right holder asks to set the damages as a lump sum on the basis of the amount of royalties, Article 13(1) lit. b), CJEU 17.03.2016, C-99/15, *Liffers*, ECLI:EU:C:2016:173 = *GRUR* 2016, 485 para. 25–26. For a further example see Opinion of AG Cruz Villalón Case C-103/11 P, *Systran*, ECLI:EU:C:2012:714, para. 198. It is still uncertain which forms of damage can be considered as immaterial damage in case of an infringement of intellectual property rights, for diverging views in the Member States C. Heinze, 'Die Durchsetzung geistigen Eigentums in Europa' (2009) *Zeitschrift für Europäisches Privatrecht*, 282, 308; A. Metzger, above n. 76, 209, 222–223.

100 Article 82(1) General Data Protection Regulation 2016/679; for examples of possible harm recital 85 1st sentence.

101 CJEU 03.02.1994, C-308/87, *Grifoni*, ECLI:EU:C:1994:38, para. 37; CoFI 09.07.1999, T-231/97, *New Europe Consulting*, ECLI:EU:T:1999:146, para. 53–54; CJEU 28.05.2013, C-239/12 P, *Abdulrahim*, ECLI:EU:C:2013:331, para. 72, 76; CoFI 08.11.2011, T-88/09, *Idromacchine*, ECLI:EU:T:2011:641, para. 61 (damage to reputation); CoFI 29.05.2015, T-217/11, *Staelen*, ECLI:EU:T:2015:238, para. 290; for actions by EU civil servants CJEU 22.12.2008, C-198/07 P, *Gordon*, ECLI:EU:C:2008:570, para. 19, 60.

102 The lump sum reimbursement of recovery costs under Article 6(1) of Directive 2011/7/EU of the European Parliament and of the Council of 16 February 2011 on combating late payment in commercial transactions, [2011] OJ L 48/1, amounting to 40 Euro also applies if the recovery was carried out using one's own labour, which was previously regarded in Germany as a mere loss of leisure time and thus as pecuniary loss not eligible for compensation, T. Dornis, 'Die Entschädigungspauschale für Beitreibungsaufwand – Neujustierung von Kompensation und Prävention im europäischen und deutschen Vertragsrecht?' (2014) *Zeitschrift für Wirtschafts- und Bankrecht*, 677, 680. But see the restrictive interpretation in CJEU 11.04.2019, C-131/18, *Gambietz*, ECLI:EU:C:2019:306, para. 27.

103 W. Wurmnest, above n. 33, 289; W. Wurmnest/C. Heinze, above n. 31, 39, 59–60; see also Article 8:402(4) Acquis Principles 2009: 'Damages cover non-pecuniary losses only to the extent that the purpose of the obligation includes the protection or satisfaction of non-pecuniary interests.'

104 For the possibility to restrict compensation for immaterial losses in case of light injuries CJEU 23.01.2014, C-371/12, *Petillo*, ECLI:EU:C:2014:26, para. 43 et seq. (in the context of Directive 2009/103/EC of the European Parliament and the Council relating to insurance against civil liability in respect of the use of motor vehicles, and the enforcement of the obligation to insure against such liability [2009] OJ L 263/11).

105 A. Vaquer, above n. 71, para. 2/40. In public law, other forms of compensation for immaterial damages are possible, see Opinion of AG Wahl Case C-371/12, *Petillo*, ECLI:EU:C:2013:652, para. 40, 44.

106 Opinion of AG Wahl Case C-371/12, *Petillo*, ECLI:EU:C:2013:652, para. 42: Compensation of immaterial damages in particular where damage is connected with physical or psychological suffering.

107 CJEU 03.02.1994, C-308/87, *Grifoni*, ECLI:EU:C:1994:38, para. 37; CJEU 07.10.1982, Case 131/81, *Berti*, ECLI:EU:C:1982:341, para. 14–15; CJEU 08.10.1986, Case 169/83, *Leussink*, ECLI:EU:C:1986:371, para. 18 et seq.; C. Schubert, above n. 44, p. 466.

More difficult is compensation for psychological suffering without connection to a body injury. While the Court was sometimes restrictive in older cases concerning liability of the Union,[109] more recent decisions tended to be more generous. Thus, in motor vehicle liability insurance law, the immaterial damage suffered by persons close to the victim of a road accident must be included in the scope of compulsory motor vehicle liability insurance if the applicable national liability law provides for such compensation.[110] Losses in connection with violations of personal rights in a broader sense, in particular data protection offences or unlawful discrimination, are also recognised as (immaterial) damage to be compensated. The same holds true for reputation damage.[111] In intellectual property law, the compensation of immaterial damages serves primarily to protect the author's personality rights, but at the same time, it covers incalculable market confusion and damage to the reputation of the right holder, which, however, could also be regarded as part of the material damage (damnum emergens).[112] A loss sometimes discussed in connection with immaterial damage is compensation for lost chances. This should, however, better be regarded as a form of material damage; it does not appear to be generally required by EU law.[113]

Other forms of immaterial damages are strongly influenced by the specific nature of the liability rule in question and unlikely to be generalised.[114] This applies to the compensation for lost holiday enjoyment in travel law,[115] for the loss of time and inconvenience in the Air Passenger Rights Regulation[116] or

108 In travel law, compensation for pain and suffering seems to have been accepted even before the Leitner decision, see CJEU 12.03.2002, C-168/00, *Leitner*, ECLI:EU:C:2002:163 = *Neue Juristische Wochenschrift (NJW)* 2002, 1255 para. 10; Opinion of AG Tizzano Case C-168/00, *Leitner*, [2002] ECR I-2631 para. 30 (pain and suffering falling under the damages claim in Article 5(2) of the old Package Travel Directive 90/314).

109 CJEU 08.10.1986, Case 169/83, *Leussink*, ECLI:EU:C:1986:371, para. 22.

110 CJEU 24.10.2013, C-22/12, *Haasová*, ECLI:EU:C:2013:692, para. 47, 50, 55; CJEU 24.10.2013, C-277/12, *Drozdovs*, ECLI:EU:C:2013:685, para. 46–47.

111 On liability of the Union Case CoFI 08.11.2011, T-88/09, *Idromacchine*, ECLI:EU:T:2011:641, para. 61; A. Vaquer, above n. 71, para. 2/41.

112 For uncertainties of what may be 'immaterial damage' in intellectual property law above n. 99.

113 For references above n. 88.

114 With a similar approach C. Schubert, above n. 44, p. 466: 'Grundsätze für ersatzfähige immaterielle Schäden haben sich vor allem im Rahmen der Haftung nach Art. 340 Abs. 2 AEUV entwickelt, so dass vor allem Gefühlsschäden als Nichtvermögensschäden anzusehen sind. Daneben ist anhand des Gegenstands der Richtlinien zu ermitteln, welche ideellen Einbußen typischerweise mit der Verletzung der Richtlinienvorgaben einhergehen, so dass ihre Entschädigung vom Normzweck der Richtlinie getragen ist.'

115 CJEU 12.03.2002, C-168/00, *Leitner*, ECLI:EU:C:2002:163 = *Neue Juristische Wochenschrift (NJW)* 2002, 1255 para. 23.

116 CJEU 23.10.2012, C-581/10 and C-629/10, *Nelson*, ECLI:EU:C:2012:657, para. 46, 48, 51.

the compensation of immaterial damage in the event of loss of luggage[117] and probably also to the compensation of collection costs in the event of default in payment in business transactions.[118] However, there are indications that the compensation for one's own efforts could well lead to a more general rethinking of this issue in national law.[119]

In summary, compensation of immaterial losses can be regarded as a general principle of EU law. This generally includes compensation for pain and suffering. It also includes compensation for infringements of personal rights and interests in the broader sense, such as damage to reputation, unlawful discrimination or data protection offences. In addition, the influence of the (protective) purposes of the respective liability norm is particularly evident in the scope of the compensable immaterial damages, which leads to a differentiation of the compensable immaterial losses. This ranges from economic intangible loss such as market confusion, the compensation of which is relevant in the case of market-related offences such as infringements of intellectual property rights, to compensation for loss of holiday enjoyment or inconvenience caused by delays in travel and passenger transport law and compensation for own efforts to recover debts in the event of default in payment in business transactions. The differentiation proves that Union law has no reservations about extending the categories of losses eligible for compensation if this appears appropriate for the regulatory objectives of the specific provisions concerned.

In order to quantify immaterial damage, it is possible to resort to lump sum payments (for standardised losses) and comparable previous cases.[120] This is particularly prominent in the case of lump sum compensation claims under the Air Passenger Rights Regulation, but the calculation of lost holiday enjoyment on the basis of travel price, duration of impairment and intensity of impairment also points to lump sum compensation. On the other hand, a merely symbolic compensation seems to be unsuitable for compensation of immaterial damages due to a lack of sufficient deterrent effects.[121]

---

[117] CJEU 06.05.2010, C-63/09, *Walz*, ECLI:EU:C:2010:251 = NJW 2010, 2113 para. 29.

[118] Article 6 Directive (EU) 2011/7 of the European Parliament and of the Council of 16 February 2011 on combating late payment in commercial transactions [2011] OJ L 48/1.

[119] See T. Dornis, above n. 102, *Zeitschrift für Wirtschafts- und Bankrecht* 2014, 677, 681 on German law.

[120] See W. Wurmnest, above n. 33; for a comparative perspective J. Ady, *Ersatzansprüche wegen immaterieller Einbußen*, Mohr Siebeck, Tübingen 2004, p. 126 et seq., and C. Schubert, above n. 44, p. 287.

[121] CJEU 10.04.1984, Case 14/83, *von Colson und Kamann*, ECLI:EU:C:1984:153, para. 24. But see also the Opinion of AG Cruz Villalón Case C-103/11 P, *Systran*, ECLI:EU:C:2012:714, para. 198 (1.000 Euro as symbolic damages for a copyright infringement by the Commission); for a more favourable view in EU civil servants regulations W. Wurmnest, above n. 33, pp. 237–238.

4.2.3. *Non-Compensatory Damages*

Finally, it can be said that Union law does not oblige the Member States to introduce non-compensatory damages.[122] Recent legal developments rather suggest that, on the contrary, Union law is sceptical towards an obligation to pay over-compensatory or multiple damages.[123] Still, the regulatory objectives, in particular the concern for prevention, impact the interpretation of the requirements to find liability under EU law. This may lead to an extension of the categories of compensable losses (e.g. to the mere loss of time or the inconvenience of flight cancellation[124]) or limit liability-restricting instruments such as the consideration of benefits the aggrieved party obtained due to the damaging event ('Vorteilsausgleichung') or the interruption of the causal process. The idea of prevention thus impacts on the interpretation of the different elements of the liability norm (requirements for liability, categories of compensable losses, restrictions of liability), but does not require the introduction of non-compensatory damages.

5. CONCLUSION

To conclude, it can be said that damages – and remedies in general – in EU private law face an increasing vertical and horizontal fragmentation. The traditional sector-specific approach to damages, as to remedies in general, reduces certainty and foreseeability. It is therefore desirable to develop a general concept of remedies to give guidance to national courts. Such a general concept should be informed by an overarching analysis of the most relevant sectors of EU private law which includes different layers of regulation (primary law, in particular the principle of effectiveness, directives, regulations). The EU law of remedies is thus more complex (due to different layers) and less specific (details left to national courts), but equally needed as in national law.

---

122 CJEU 17.12.2015, C-407/14, *Camacho*, ECLI:EU:C:2015:831 = *EuZW* 2016, 183 para. 34, 37, 40; U. Magnus, above n. 67, Article 8:401 para. 10, Article 8:402 para. 7.

123 See Article 3(3) Cartel Damages Directive 2014/104; see also (on the Commercial Agents Directive 86/653) CJEU 03.12.2015, C-338/14, *Quenon*, ECLI:EU:C:2015:795, para. 34, 39–40. This is remarkable because damages under Article 17(2) of the Commercial Agents Directive are otherwise not regulated by Union law.

124 U. Magnus, above n. 67, Article 8:402 para. 8: 'Even the penalty available under the Denied Boarding Regulation aims mainly at the compensation of the discomfort and possible costs of passengers whose flights were cancelled or overbooked.'

A MANIFESTO ON PROPORTIONALITY AND COPYRIGHT LAW

'Taking Remedies Seriously'

Orit FISCHMAN AFORI

1. INTRODUCTION

In the last decades intellectual property law has been facing a severe crisis. Intellectual property law is accused of not promoting a fair and balanced regime. It is also blamed for not being efficient, in utilitarian terms, since it mainly serves right-holders' interests while neglecting the vast public interest.[1]

In theoretical terms, this crisis could be described as a debate about the initial allocative or distributive justice assumptions of intellectual property law. In other words, the debate is whether the initial allocation of entitlements, through the exclusive intellectual property rights, is just, fair and efficient.[2]

---

1 See, for example: J. LITMAN, 'The Politics of Intellectual Property' (2009) *Cardozo Arts & Entertainment Law Journal* 27, 313; W. PATRY, *Moral Panics and the Copyright Wars*, OUP, Oxford 2009, pp. 1–41.

2 For the general theme of allocative justice, fairness and efficiency see: J. RAWLS, *A Theory of Justice*, Harvard University Press, Cambridge 1971, pp. 76–77.

Accordingly, contemporary scholarly writings propose various ways to ease the crisis, through an allocative justice discourse, which therefore is focused on the redefinition of intellectual property rights. Since the focus is on the redefinition of rights, there is an excessive discourse on the exceptions and limitations to the rights, as a vehicle for promoting fairness.[3] Thus far, therefore, intellectual property discourse has been focused almost entirely on the scope of the rights.

Yet, rights and exceptions are subject to the strict regime of international intellectual property law.[4] Therefore, this discourse has reached, to a significant extent, a dead end.[5] This chapter constitutes a manifesto that stresses another powerful path for easing the crisis – and that is through remedies.

Remedies are left to national courts' discretion and are crafted on a case-by-case basis. Therefore, they may play a major role in realising a de facto fair, balanced and more efficient intellectual property law.[6] The main argument is that remedies are a powerful and pragmatic tool, which may promote the end-result that allocative justice has failed to achieve.

2. THEORETICAL BACKGROUND OF THE ROLE OF REMEDIES

The theoretical background of the role of remedies is essential for a better understanding of their importance in designing substantive law. The line of the argument relating to the potential function of remedies in promoting fairness and efficiency is the following: Fairness and/or efficiency are the goals underlying any law.[7] These goals are crafted through allocative justice entitlements, namely rights and duties. Corrective justice, in contrast to allocative justice, aims at promoting fairness and efficiency within two concrete parties, by transferring resources from one party to another, in order to

---

3 See, for example: P.B. HUGENHOLTZ and M.R.F. SENFTLEBEN, *Fair Use in Europe. In Search of Flexibilities*, Amsterdam 2011, pp. 6–9, <https://ssrn.com/abstract=1959554> accessed 09.01.2019.

4 The restrictions on exceptions to copyright are imposed by the Berne Convention for the Protection of Literary and Artistic Works, July 24, 1971; Art. 9 (2) and 13 Agreement on Trade-Related Aspects of Intellectual Property Rights (TRIPS).

5 R.M. HILTY, 'Copyright Law and the Information Society – Neglected Adjustments and Their Consequences' (2007), *International Review of Intellectual Property and Competition Law* 38, 135.

6 This idea was explored in a previous article by this author: O. FISCHMAN AFORI, 'Flexible Remedies as a Means to Counteract Failures in Copyright Law' (2011) *Cardozo Arts & Entertainment Law Journal* 29, 1.

7 J. RAWLS and E. KELLY (eds.), *Justice as Fairness. A Restatement*, Belknap Press, Cambridge 2001.

maintain the initial allocation of entitlements that were set by allocative justice considerations.[8] Therefore, the actual vehicle for executing corrective justice are the remedies granted. In that sense, remedies are the legal mechanism enabling execution of justice within two concrete parties, yet within the vast framework of the initial allocative assumptions imbedded in law.

The importance of remedies in promoting both fairness and efficiency should be further stressed: rights and remedies are closely interrelated in the sense that remedies affect the scope of the rights.[9] For example, the question whether a right holder is entitled to monetary relief or injunctive relief as well may assist in classifying the right as a 'property rule' or a 'liability rule', according to Calabresi and Melamed's seminal proposition.[10]

Moreover, there is a growing understanding that remedies are a complimentary means for implementing policy considerations. Dworkin, in his seminal book *Taking Rights Seriously*,[11] stressed the importance of structuring the theoretical underpinning of the rights' discourse. Time is ripe for taking remedies seriously as well.

Currently, the law of remedies (assuming that there is such a discipline), to a significant extent, is not structured and is underdeveloped, at least in the common-law jurisprudence. Remedies, unfortunately, are sometimes perceived as the ancillary part of the judicial process, or as the technical part at the end of the trial or legal procedure. However, in fact, the remedial part has at least an equal importance as the liability or rights' discourse. For example, in criminal procedures, many defendants are more anxious about the exact punishment that would be imposed than about the question of whether they would be found guilty; and in civil procedures, both parties are highly interested in the accurate calculation of the remedies that would be granted. Yet, most scholarly writings are devoted to analysing rights and duties and the structuring of remedies is less appealing.[12]

3. OPEN STANDARDS IN THE LAW OF REMEDIES: AN ADVANTAGE AND NOT AN OBSTACLE

Since the law of remedies is underdeveloped, it is followed by many uncertainties, with all the accompanying side effects. Nevertheless, the flip side of the coin

---

8 E.J. Weinrib, *The Idea of Private Law*, OUP, Oxford 2012.

9 G. Calabresi and A. D. Melamed, 'Property Rules, Liability Rules and Inalienability: One View of the Cathedral' (1972) *Harvard Law Review* 85, 1089.

10 Ibid.

11 R. Dworkin, *Taking Rights Seriously*, Harvard University Press, Cambridge 1977, pp. 15–16.

12 For further reading see O. Fischman Afori, supra note 5; see also P. Gewirtz, 'Remedies and Resistance' (1983) *Yale Law Journal* 92, 585–587.

of uncertainty is flexibility. Usually, in legal jurisprudence one should decide whether to opt for certainty or flexibility. For example, when legal systems choose between rules and standards, the choice is between very certain rules with no judicial flexibility or opting for uncertain and flexible norms to be further elaborated by courts.[13]

In that respect, the law of remedies, even though it reflects the concrete and pragmatic part of the legal process, is crafted as a set of legal standards. Namely, there is no certainty, yet much flexibility is given to the court. The proposition presented here is that the flexibilities in the craft of remedies should be used by courts in a wise manner to facilitate solving some of the many problems created by the rights' discourse. In other words, the open standards and flexibilities implemented in the law of remedies are an advantage and not necessarily an obstacle. More specifically, as will further elaborated below, the flexibilities in granting remedies could be used by courts for easing some of the basic failures in private copyright law.

4. THE ROLE OF 'PROPORTIONALITY' IN EASING FAILURES IN COPYRIGHT LAW

Copyright law must strike a balance between competing interests: on the one hand the interests of authors – usually identified as 'property rights' – and on the other hand the public's interest in using protected materials – usually located within the freedom of expression realm. Therefore, the discourse taken inside copyright law has always been around the constitutional sphere. However only in the last decade it has been acknowledged upfront as being a core constitutional or a human rights' discourse.[14]

As is the case with any two competing human rights, there is need for a legal mechanism or formula that enables reconciliation of the constitutional conflict. One such tool, that within a gradual process is overtaking the copyright discourse, is the notion of proportionality.

It should be stressed that the use of internal copyright law standards, such as exceptions and limitations, for reconciling the constitutional conflicts of copyright law have reached, to a large extent, a dead end. Therefore, copyright law discourse would be expected to move gradually into using constitutional standards, aimed at balancing conflicting interests.

---

13 See for example L. Kaplow, 'Rules Versus Standards: An Economic Analysis' (1992) *Duke Law Journal* 42, 557; K.M. Sullivan, 'The Justices of Rules and Standards' (1992) *Harvard Law Review* 106, 22.

14 C. Geiger, 'Constitutionalizing Intellectual Property Law? The Influence of Fundamental Rights on Intellectual Property in Europe' (2006) *International Review of Intellectual Property and Competition Law* 37, 371.

Here comes the link between the two themes – the role of flexible remedies in easing copyright failures and the perception that basic copyright conflicts reflect constitutional tensions – and this is because the framework for applying the constitutional measure of proportionality is the remedies granted for copyright infringement. Namely, courts should address questions of freedom of speech, the free flows of ideas and other constitutional issues when civil remedies are granted. This is particularly the case regarding one of the most important remedies in the online environment – site-blocking orders, which is a kind of injunction that raises questions of balancing competing human rights.

5. THE MEANING OF THE NOTION OF PROPORTIONALITY

Proportionality is an accepted mechanism for balancing competing fundamental rights. It is a significant open standard which assists in organising the various fundamental rights.[15]

The legal notion of proportionality was developed in German public law, beginning in the nineteenth century. It reflected a move to a 'counter-formalistic' approach to the legal system.[16] The modern notion of 'proportionality' is rooted in constitutional law, and it denotes the understanding that constitutional rights are relative and not absolute and should therefore be balanced against each other on a case-by-case basis.

Yet, the general notion of proportionality in European constitutional law has developed into a concrete multi-factor test, consisting of (1) proper purpose, (2) necessary means and (3) a cost/benefit analysis.[17] It seems, therefore, that 'proportionality' reflects the 'logicality', 'rationality' or 'reasonability', embedded in courts' inherent judicial capacity. The notion of proportionality reflects some general values and therefore has spread on a global scale.

6. INTRODUCTION OF 'PROPORTIONALITY' INTO EUROPEAN INTELLECTUAL PROPERTY DIRECTIVES

The first move that introduced the notion of proportionality into European copyright law was through the framework of remedies. Two key directives have emphasised the link between remedies and the requirement of proportionality.

---

15 For the various functions of the notion of proportionality in EU law see: E. Ellis (ed.), *The Principle of Proportionality on the Laws of Europe*, Hart Publishing, Oxford 1999; particularly see therein D. Feldman, 'Proportionality and the Human Rights Act 1998'.

16 A. Barak, *Proportionality: Constitutional Rights and their limitations*, Cambridge University Press, Cambridge 2012, p. 177.

17 T. Tridimas, *The General Principles of EU Law*, OUP, Oxford 2000, pp. 90–93.

The directive on harmonisation of certain aspects of copyright and related rights in the information society[18] states that the 'measures, sanctions and remedies against infringements of intellectual property rights should not only be effective but also proportionate'.

Furthermore, the directive on the enforcement of intellectual property rights[19] states that 'those measures, procedures and remedies shall also be effective, proportionate and dissuasive and shall be applied in such a manner as to avoid the creation of barriers to legitimate trade and to provide for safeguards against their abuse'.

7. PROPORTIONALITY: AN APPEALING PATH TO COPYRIGHT LAW

The global use of the notion of proportionality as a criterion for limiting constitutional rights is highly appealing to civil copyright law for various reasons.

Current copyright law discourse focuses on the necessity to limit the scope of copyright to enable its coexistence with other significant interests. Thus, the need for measures, whether internal or external, for such end is clear. Moreover, copyright law is basically structured as 'rights and limitations', which is very akin to the 'balancing' discourse. Therefore, the introduction of the 'external' measure of proportionality for limiting the scope of copyright is a natural and consistence move.

Furthermore, current copyright law is in a global crisis, in light of the digital environment. It is increasingly difficult to reconcile fundamental rights, such as freedom of expression, privacy and data protection, with copyright enforcement. Therefore, to enable copyright law to survive in online contexts, copyright law enforcement needs to be reasonable and balanced. The notion of proportionality serves as a prime mechanism for ensuring that various human rights' interests are taken into consideration properly.[20]

And, most importantly, the measure of proportionality is a remedial tool. Whereas courts have very limited discretion in crafting the scope of copyright, international copyright law leaves remedies discretionary, in the sense that there are no strict rules and remedies are left to be determined by domestic principles.

---

18 Directive of the European Parliament and of the Council 2001/29/EC of 22 May 2001 on the harmonisation of certain aspects of copyright and related rights in the information society [2001] OJ L 167/10.

19 Directive of the European Parliament and of the Council 2004/48/EC of 29 April 2004 on the enforcement of intellectual property rights [2004] OJ L 195/16.

20 J. Griffiths, 'Constitutionalising or Harmonising? – the Court of Justice, the Right to Property and European Copyright Law' (2013) *European Law Review* 38, pp. 65–78.

Therefore, remedies have a great potential for serving as a means of promoting policy goals through adjudication.

The acute need for a remedial balancing mechanism in copyright law promotes the understating that the introduction of the external proportionality measure into internal civil copyright law may be a 'game changer' in the development of copyright law.

8. THE CJEU MOVE

The European Court of Justice (CJEU) had made the first move in realising the proportionality measure, as a remedial vehicle designed by the directives.

To begin with, in 2006 the CJEU handed down its first comprehensive decision in the case of Promusicae,[21] stressing the role of 'proportionality' within the intellectual property arena. The guidance given to national courts was clear: 'When the Directives are applied on national level, it is important to ensure that the interpretation adopted does not conflict with other general principles of EU law, headed by the principle of proportionality'.[22] Following the Promusicae case, the focal point of any copyright/remedies discourse would now be on the standard of proportionality.

In 2011, the CJEU handed down two decisions discussing the legality of a Belgian decision ordering an Internet service provider (ISP) to block access to certain infringing internet websites (the 'SABAM' cases)[23] – namely site-blocking orders.

In reliance on the Promusicae holding, the EUCJ further developed the rule, by refining the proportionality measurement as an internal constitutional benchmark. The Court held that:

> '... national authorities and courts must strike a fair balance between the protection of copyright and the protection of the fundamental rights of individuals who are affected by such measures. Accordingly, in circumstances such as those in the main proceedings, national authorities and courts must, in particular, strike a fair balance between the protection of the intellectual property right enjoyed by copyright holders and that of the freedom to conduct a business enjoyed by operators such as ISPs ...'[24]

---

21 CJEU 29.01.2008, C-275/06, *Productores de Música de España (Promusicae)/Telefónica de España SAU*, ECLI:EU:C:2008:54 = WRP 2008, 334.

22 Ibid., para. 70.

23 CJEU 24.11.2011, C-70/10, *Scarlet Extended SA/Société Belge des Auteurs, Compositeurs et éditeurs SCRL (SABAM)*, ECLI:EU:C:2011:771 = GRUR 2012, 265; CJEU 16.02.2012, C-360/10, *Belgische Vereniging van Auteurs, Componisten en Uitgevers (SABAM/ Netlog NV*, ECLI:EU:C:2012:85 = GRUR 2012, 382.

24 CJEU 24.11.2011, C-70/10, *Scarlet Extended SA/Société Belge des Auteurs, Compositeurs et éditeurs SCRL (SABAM)*, ECLI:EU:C:2011:771 = GRUR 2012, 265, par. 45–46.

The final conclusion was that the Belgian order did not strike a proportionate balance and therefore the blocking order was rejected.

In March 2014, the CJEU laid down another brick in elaborating the notion of proportionality in copyright law, this time discussing an Austrian site-blocking order (the 'Telekabel' case).[25] The Court stressed the conflict between copyright and the freedom to conduct a business, which was concretised as a right of 'any business to be able to freely use, within the limits of its liability for its own acts, the economic, technical and financial resources available to it'.[26] Yet, this time the blocking order was approved, since the ISP was given a leeway with respect to the way it should be applied, namely in a manner that would minimise the harm and costs of the ISP.

This last CJEU ruling reinforces the need to concretise the balancing metaphor. A more down to earth, pragmatic analysis, to be conducted by national courts is no doubt required.

9. ENGLISH COURT DECISIONS

In England, it was Justice Arnold who opened the door to the new standard of proportionality in copyright cases. In a long series of decisions, commencing 2011, he has gradually implemented and developed the proportionality test. Not surprisingly, these cases involved ISPs function as a gatekeeper, and mainly discussed the 'hot' issue of site-blocking orders. In all these cases remedies served only as the gateway to introduce the proportionality test. However, it was further elaborated as a means to strike a balance between the competing human rights involved: copyright and freedom of speech, or copyright and privacy. Therefore, the impact of the proportionality test was not limited to the remedies, but rather affected the substantive questions of the limits to the copyright. The clear line in all these decisions is that the granting of the remedies should be inspected very carefully and should be tailored to each case according to the potential harm to the various constitutional rights.

In July 2011, the decision of *Twentieth Century Fox Film Corporation and others v British Telecommunications plc* ('Fox', 'BT') was handed down.[27] Fox pleaded for a site-blocking order, claiming damages for infringement of its property rights by illegal downloading. BT claimed that the grant of a site-blocking order would injure their subscribers' right to receive information, which is part of the freedom of speech. Justice Arnold opened his decision

---

25 CJEU 27.03.2014, C-314/12, *UPC Telekabel Wien GmbH/Constantin Film Verleih*, ECLI:EU:C:2014:192 = GRUR 2014, 468.

26 Ibid., para. 49.

27 *Twentieth Century Fox Film Corporation and others v British Telecommunications plc* [2011] EWHC 1981 (Ch) = [2012] 1 All ER 806.

by stressing the need to strike a balance between two competing human rights: property right and freedom of information, both protected under the EU Charter. Thereafter, Justice Arnold analysed the constitutional conflict reflected within the copyright law case, and eventually determined that the granting of the order under the circumstances was proportionate.

A following decision was handed down in 2012, in the case of Golden Eye.[28] This case concerned the need to balance copyright against the right to privacy, since the ISP was asked to disclose details of customers who had allegedly infringed copyright. Justice Arnold looked closely at the specific terms of the order that was granted and discussed every condition through the prism of the proportionality or balancing test. The Golden Eye ruling elaborated the proportionality test by using the benchmarks of 'necessity' and 'efficiency', as are often used in constitutional law discourse.

The next decision concerning site-blocking orders was handed in 2013, in the EMI Records case.[29] Once again, the conflict was between copyright and freedom of expression. Justice Arnold held that every order should be inspected by courts, *ab intio*, since 'the proportionality of a blocking order is bound to be a context-sensitive question'[30] and should be therefore considered only on a case-by-case basis. This last decision is a reminder that the proportionality measure is a remedial tool, aimed at promoting pragmatic results in each case, and therefore should be always open to courts for reconsiderations.

This line of decisions is extending, and in each decision more elaborations are introduced as to the function of proportionality as a balancing measure for copyright remedies. For example, the last decision handed down in 2017 in the Premier League case[31] elaborated the idea that a blocking order could be granted for a very limited time, as part of the concrete balance of interests at stake, which involved live broadcasting.

10. CONCEPTUALISING THE USE OF THE PROPORTIONALITY TEST IN COPYRIGHT LAW

Synthesising the above insights brings up several core questions that may assist in analysing the function of the proportionality test in a coherent way.

First, it should be asked what the accurate location of the proportionality test is? Is it a substantive test for balancing copyright against other fundamental rights or is it a test for calibrating remedies – especially site-blocking orders?

28 *Golden Eye (International) Ltd and others v Telefonica UK Ltd* [2012] EWHC 723 (Ch).
29 *EMI Records Ltd and others v British Sky Broadcasting Ltd and others* [2013] EWHC 379 (Ch).
30 Ibid., para. 95–99.
31 *Football Association Premier League v British Telecommunications* [2017] EWHC 480 Ch.

Apparently, in recent case law, courts are using the proportionality test for both purposes.

The next question is whether there is a necessary link between the two possible functions of the proportionality test, namely the rights-oriented discourse and the calibration of a remedies discourse? The answer is that all these cases raise the constitutional challenge of balancing copyright against other fundamental rights. The reconciliation of such conflict was made on a pragmatic level, by matching the appropriate remedies to the type or intensity of the constitutional conflict.

In that sense, the use of the proportionality test in recent copyright case law could be conceptualised as a measure for conducting a constitutional remedy analysis, within the civil copyright law realm. Therefore, proportionality is not simply a rhetorical tool. It is not a way for replacing one open standard with another. Rather, proportionality serves as the legal path for introducing the constitutional balancing mechanism into various areas of private law, through the 'back door' of remedies. Yet, remedies, in fact, are the 'front door' of laws, since the scope of the rights is affected by the remedies granted. Therefore, remedies should be indeed taken seriously.

ASKING INNOCENT THIRD PARTIES FOR A REMEDY

Origins and Trends

Martin Husovec

1. INTRODUCTION

This chapter,[1] focuses on a specific type of remedy, the emergence of which has been witnessed in the European intellectual property law in the last couple of years. As the following stories will demonstrate, its historical pedigree is a mixture of European and national influences and its field of application is highly technological space. The overall story is relevant for a broader audience for several reasons. First, it shows that remedies are a very important instrument when trying to adjust the policy layers to particular industries and their social problems. Second, it gives a glimpse into the process of Europeanisation

1 This chapter is based on the author's previous research, referenced throughout the chapter. The author has made several extensions of his existing work, however, the core remains published in previous works: M. Husovec, *Injunctions Against Intermediaries in the European Union: Accountable, but not Liable?*, Cambridge University Press, Cambridge 2017; M. Husovec, 'Injunctions against innocent third parties: case of website blocking' (2013) 4(2) *Journal of Intellectual Property, Information Technology and E-Commerce Law (JIPITEC)* 216; M. Husovec, *Accountable, Not Liable: Injunctions Against Intermediaries*, TILEC Discussion Paper No. 2016-012, Tilburg 2016.

of remedies, and how such a process can embrace, but also confuse national traditions. Third, the issue of injunctions against intermediaries provides an exciting account of merge and clash of common law and civil law traditions and their conceptions of remedies. And fourth, not less importantly, it shows that remedies can be a subject that can excite young people.

Intellectual property rights are surely familiar concept to most people. Many people know, perhaps from their own experience or that of their children, that enforcement of intellectual property rights in the online environment is not the easiest thing to do. For starters, the environment is anonymous, and thus creates a low-risk space for infringements where personal accountability is hard to achieve. Moreover, the same space is encouraging all sorts of modern user creativity, which is not always in line with old-school copyright laws. For these and many other reasons, infringements are not easy to stop. For music and other industries, they represent a persistent problem which they try to tackle and resolve.

In the past, the first generation enforcement approach was to target users, the source. The attempts were made to align user behaviour with the old copyright laws. Those who were fans of tape recorders might remember this well. Already back then, there was a surge of litigation, both in Germany and the United Kingdom. The House of Lords in 1987, heard a high-profile case concerning reel-to-reel tape recorders and how they should be made illegal. The reason was that home copying of tapes significantly cut into margins of music industry since it was taking place free of charge and substituting sales of official tapes. Lord Templeman, who delivered the judgment for the court in *Amstrad* case closed his opinion with the following words:

> [t]hese proceedings will have served a useful purpose if they remind Parliament of the grievances of the recording companies and other owners of copyright and if at the same time they draw the attention of Parliament to the fact that home copying cannot be prevented, is widely practised and brings the law into disrepute.[2]

In the case, the House of Lords faced a tough question. Are producers of tape recorders contributing to infringing behaviour of their customers by wrongful means? In other words, are they accessories? Saying yes, meant making tape recorders illegal. Saying no, meant allowing them. However, next to these two options, the court was also asked to construe a novel equitable duty of care, which could serve as the basis for an injunction that was requested. This, according to the plaintiffs, should restrain the producers of tape recorders from supplying their machines without taking some steps to reasonably ensure

2 *CBS Songs Ltd v Amstrad Consumer Electronics Plc* [1988] AC 1013.

that copyright would not be infringed by their use. They were essentially asking for redesign.

Lord Justice Slade, sitting at the Court of Appeal, squarely rejected any duty in equity, arguing that:

> If the alleged duty in equity existed in the present case, it seems to me that a similar duty would have existed in each of the line of cases beginning with *Townsend v Haworth*. This, it would appear, was never even suggested by any of the members of this court responsible for those decisions. The suggestion, with due respect to the argument, is, in my opinion, ill founded.[3]

Before the House of Lords, Lord Templeman argued that:

> The court has no power to make such orders and judges are not qualified to decide whether a restraint should be placed on the manufacture of electronic equipment or on the contents of advertising. No one is to blame for the present situation. Copyright law could not envisage and now cannot cope with massproduction techniques and inventions which create a vast market for the works of a copyright owner but also provide opportunities for his rights to be infringed. Parliament could place limitations on the manufacture or sale of certain types of tape recorder and could prescribe notices and warnings to be included in advertisements.[4]

But where did the UK litigators even get an inspiration for these advertising notices? In 1955, the German Federal Supreme Court heard a similar case concerning reel-to-reel tape recorders.[5] The issue at stake was whether the sellers of such recorders should be obliged to use so called GEMA-notices, GEMA, being the biggest collective society for music in Germany. In what became to be known as the *Grundig Reporter* decision,[6] the Court opined that, even if a producer does not him/herself engage in the copying of copyrighted works and thus copyright infringements, he/she can nevertheless face injunctions which were meant to help the plaintiff to collect licensing fees from citizens. The Court accepted the proposed measure of so called 'GEMA notices' which were meant to inform users of the devices in advertising that they needed to pay GEMA for home-copying. This litigation lasted over a decade,[7] and its climax

---

3 *Amstrad Consumer Electronics Plc v British Phonographic Industry Ltd* [1986] FSR 159 Court of Appeal.

4 *CBS Songs Ltd v Amstrad Consumer Electronics Plc* [1988] AC 1013; [1988] WL 624207 House of Lords at 1060.

5 BGH 18.05.1955, I ZR 8/54 = *GRUR* 1955, 492.

6 BGH 18.05.1955, I ZR 8/54 = *GRUR* 1955, 492.

7 BGH 18.05.1955, I ZR 8/54 = *GRUR* 1955, 492; BGH 22.01.1960, I ZR 41/58 = *GRUR* 1960, 340; BGH 12.06.1963, Ib ZR 23/62 = *GRUR* 1964, 91; BGH 26.06.1963, Ib ZR 127/62 = *GRUR* 1964, 94; BGH 29.05.1964, Ib ZR 4/63 = *GRUR* 1965, 104 – *Personalausweise*.

was when GEMA requested that sellers should ask their customers to show ID and sign the commitment to pay licenses before they purchase devices. Unlike GEMA-notices, this was seen as going too far, and was rejected by the Court. The conflict ended by a notoriously known private-levy system.

Now what the English and German mini-stories show is that injunctions against intermediaries are not a novel phenomenon. They were around for quite some time. They also show that technological shifts often demand some intervention by the judiciary, and often that response is hard to fit into yes and no answers of the tort or copyright law. Non-infringing intermediaries in the copyright law have an important role to play, but as the music industry in the UK (without injunctions) and Germany (with them) both survived for many years, their impact should not be overestimated.

To clarify the concept of injunctions against innocent third parties: what is meant is a separate private cause of action by which an individual is required to perform, or is restrained from performing, a particular act, issued against a person who neither committed a tort, nor acted against the scope of the right. This means that such person is neither primary, nor secondary infringer. As the English would say, he/she is a by-stander who got mixed up with third-party wrongdoing.[8]

Before returning to the English and German stories as they unfolded until today, the modern time of 2000s should be considered. This is when the European enforcement framework for intellectual property rights was drafted. As will be shown later, this has a lot to say about how the national traditions later evolved.

2. EUROPEAN ORIGINS

The most important European story of injunctions against innocent third parties started with the InfoSoc Directive (2001) and Enforcement Directive (2004). They both contained provisions allowing two types of orders. First, the orders against third parties that possess some information that can be relevant to IP enforcement. These third parties can include entities such as banks or internet access providers. And second, the orders against intermediaries. In particular, the latter injunctions were phrased in a very vague way.

The wording of the provisions is as follows: '[m]ember States shall ensure that right holders are in a position to apply for an injunction against intermediaries whose services are used by a third party to infringe a copyright or related right' (Art 8(3) InfoSocDirective). The Enforcement Directive, then substituted 'copyright or related right' with 'an intellectual property right' (Art 11 EnfD).

---

8 *Norwich Pharmacal Co v Customs & Excise Commissioners* [1974] AC 133.

A few scholars at the time foresaw that the provision constituted a dramatic shift. The provision turned out to be broadly misunderstood and to some extent downplayed or misconstrued by national legislators. In fact, its goal was a new policy intervention, namely, to seek accountability for help where no (tortious) liability exists.[9] Because accessory liability was not harmonised on the European level, and there was a lack of political will to do so, it was a smart move how to create an additional tool for right holders. It was only until very recently that the full potency of this provision was revealed after the Court of Justice of the European Union decided its first cases concerning intermediaries.

Looking at the wording, it has few conditions for its addressees: (1) an intermediary, (2) whose services are used, (3) by a third party, (4) to infringe, (5) an intellectual property right. If the conditions are met, the plaintiff can ask for an injunction, however, subject to general limitations of Article 3 Enforcement Directive,[10] and of the national implementation. The following discussion will focus more on the cause of action, its nature and history, than limitations or actual cases.

For a while, many scholars argued that the term 'intermediary' in fact means that such an intermediary has to be an infringer, be it primary, or as an accessory. This was refuted by the Court most openly in the *Tommy Hilfiger* case,[11] where the Court summarising its own cases stated that:

> [the provision] obliges Member States to ensure that an intermediary whose services are used by a third party in order to infringe an intellectual property right may, *regardless of any liability of its own in relation to the facts at issue*, be ordered to take measures aimed at bringing those infringements to an end and measures seeking to prevent further infringements (emphasis added).[12]

The goal of these measures was also disputed. Some argued that only corrective measures are possible, others that prohibitory orders are equally possible. The CJEU eventually decided that *preventive role* is one of the main goals of the measures. In addition, in the common law parlance, one would say that these injunctions take form of mostly mandatory, as opposed to prohibitory injunctions. The CJEU expressed both of these preferences when it held that: '[n]or can the intermediary be required to exercise general and permanent oversight over its customers. By contrast, the intermediary may be forced to take measures which contribute to avoiding new infringements of the same

9 M. Husovec, *Injunctions Against Intermediaries in the European Union: Accountable, but not Liable?*, Cambridge University Press, Cambridge 2017, preface.

10 Enforcement Directive (Directive of the European Parliament and of the Council 2004/48/EC of 29 April 2004 on the enforcement of intellectual property rights [2004] OJ L 195/16).

11 CJEU 7.7.2016, C-494/15, *Tommy Hilfiger*, ECLI:EU:C:2016:528 = *GRUR* 2016, 1062.

12 CJEU 7.7.2016, C-494/15, *Tommy Hilfiger*, ECLI:EU:C:2016:528 = *GRUR* 2016, 1062 para. 22.

nature by the same market-trader from taking place.'[13] To this day, one of the unsolved issues is how far such preventive measures can really stretch and what should be the cost allocation under these measures. The national approaches differ, as will be shown below.

It is worth noting that these newly created measures do not form part of an international standard of protection. For the time being, save for some limited exceptions, they are uniquely European. None of the international treaties in the area of intellectual property law mandates them.[14]

3. ENGLISH ORIGINS

The origin of English injunctions against innocent third parties is equity. Equity was a system that developed as a reaction to the harshness or inflexibility of common law. It systematically grew from a system of petitions to the king for his mercy to a fully-fledged judiciary. Naturally, a rivalry between the court of common law and the court of equity soon developed. Although equity eventually prevailed, when Sir Francis Bacon became Lord Chancellor, he immediately made a number of gestures to the common law judges.[15] Soon the principle would be established that equitable remedies, such as injunctions, would be applied only if the remedies of common law were inadequate.[16]

Since early common law was only providing compensation, until 1854 the Court of Chancery was the only court with power to grant injunctions.[17] In the late 19th century, the courts of common law and the courts of equity in the UK were fused into a single jurisdiction by the Supreme Judicature Act 1875. The Act, however, did not fuse the sources of law, equity and common law, but only vested their administration in the hands of the same judges.[18] Section 25(8) of the Supreme Judicature Act 1875 provided that 'an injunction may be granted (…) in all cases in which it shall appear to the court to be just or convenient that such order shall be made'. The provision, however, did not amend or change those powers, but only declared them. As explained by Lord Goff: 'That power is unfettered by statute; and it is impossible for us

13 CJEU 7.7.2016, C-494/15, *Tommy Hilfiger*, ECLI:EU:C:2016:528 = *GRUR* 2016, 1062 para.34; CJEU 12.7.2011, C-324/09, *L'Oréal v eBay*, ECLI:EU:C:2011:474 = *GRUR* 2011, 1025.

14 M. Husovec, *Injunctions Against Intermediaries in the European Union: Accountable, but not Liable?*, Cambridge University Press, Cambridge 2017, p. 215.

15 D. Wright, *Remedies*, Federation Press, 2010, p. 4.

16 Ibid.

17 *Cartier International AG & Ors v British Sky Broadcasting Ltd & Ors* [2014] EWHC 3354 (Ch) [94].

18 I. Spry, *Equitable Remedies*, 4th edn., Sweet & Maxwell, 1990, p. 323.

now to foresee every circumstance in which it may be thought right to make the remedy available.'[19] This does not mean that the judges are absolutely free of any restrains. The injunctions are granted only if they accord with the principles of equity, since equity is their ultimate source.

Prior to 1973, with two notable exceptions,[20] injunctions, including information disclosures, had to be sought against whom an independent cause of action could be reasonably maintained. In 1973, the House of Lords handed a seminal patent judgement where it allowed that even an innocent third party could be requested to disclose information about infringers. In this case, a patent holder tried to discover the identity of the importers of infringing goods, but without success. He therefore decided to request their identity from the Customs. This is because every importer is legally obliged to report this information.

The main holdings of the *Norwich Pharmacal* case is embodied in the following passage written by Lord Reid:[21]

> They [previous cases] seem to me to point to a very reasonable principle that if through no fault of his own a person gets mixed up in the tortious acts of others so as to facilitate their wrong-doing he may incur no personal liability but he comes under a duty to assist the person who has been wronged by giving him full information and disclosing the identity of the wrongdoers. I do not think that it matters whether he became so mixed up by voluntary action on his part or because it was his duty to do what he did. It may be that if this causes him expense the person seeking the information ought to reimburse him. But justice requires that he should co-operate in righting the wrong if he unwittingly facilitated its perpetration.

Over the years, considerable case law has developed and *Norwich Pharmacal* has become an often-cited authority in support of various orders against innocent third parties, not only in the UK, but the entire common law world. The Norwich jurisdiction is, however, limited to assistance by information disclosures. It was a matter of time before the equitable duties of innocent third parties would be pushed further. That case soon arrived in a form of a lawsuit for asking for a website blocking injunction to be issued against an innocent access provider. The court has previously granted many of these injunctions, however, on the basis of statutory copyright law, which was transposing the European Union law. The *Cartier* case concerned trade marks which had no comparable statutory basis for website blocking.[22] As a consequence,

19 Lord Goff in House of Lords decision *South Carolina Insurance Co v Assurantie Maatshappij De Zeven Provincien NV* [1987] AC 24 at p. 25, pp. 44–45.

20 *Upmann v Elkan* [1871] 7 Ch App 130; *Orr v Diaper* [1876] 4 Ch. D. 92.

21 *Norwich Pharmacal Co v Customs & Excise Commissioners* [1974] AC 133, Lord Reid [12].

22 *Cartier International AG & Ors v British Sky Broadcasting Ltd & Ors* [2014] EWHC 3354 (Ch).

English courts had to consider whether equitable jurisdiction could support such cause of action. Justice Arnold at the High Court of England and Wales issued a decision recognising that such injunctions are possible, subject to further conditions. This decision was confirmed by the Court of Appeals.[23] Although the court eventually reached the UK Supreme Court,[24] only the issue of costs was considered there.

In the end result, the *Cartier* case essentially generalises equitable duties of innocent third parties beyond mere provision of information. It constitutes an important development for the equitable jurisdiction, and is likely to have an impact in other areas of law too. In particular, the question arises whether these new measures cannot at least partly address the self-restraint of English judges in the area of accessory tortious liability. Although of relevance only for repeated interactions where harm could be prevented in the future, the practical consequences should not be underestimated. If *Amstrad* was to be decided today, it could have therefore ended up very differently.[25]

4. GERMAN ORIGINS

Unlike English tradition, the German story of these measures revolves around one of the most foundational provisions of its civil code, namely §1004 BGB. This provision was the first legislative fusion of rei vindicatio and actio negatoria. Pandectists accepted that both claims were in fact of the same quality and origin, but differ only in the type of interference they aim to protect from. The unity of both claims in the BGB is apparent from the text of §1004,[26] where actio negatoria is defined as a course of action protecting against any other interference than withdrawal of possession, which means any different interference than the one protected under rei vindicatio.

This negative formulation, however, also had another consequence. Namely, because the interference in the case of actio negatoria was very abstract and only negatively formulated, it was impossible to reach exactly the same clarity

23 *Cartier International AG & Ors v British Sky Broadcasting Ltd & Ors* [2016] EWCA Civ 658.

24 *Cartier International AG and others v British Telecommunications Plc and another* [2018] UKSC 28.

25 M. Husovec, *Injunctions Against Intermediaries in the European Union: Accountable, but not Liable?*, Cambridge University Press, Cambridge 2017, p. 208 ff.

26 §1004 BGB *(German Civil Code)*:'If the ownership is interfered with by means other than the removal or retention of possession, the owner may require the disturber to remove the interference. If further interferences are to be feared, the owner may seek a prohibitory injunction. (2) The claim is excluded if the owner is obliged to tolerate the interference.' Translation provided by the Langenscheidt Translation Service, http://www.gesetze-im-internet.de/englisch bgb/englisch bgb.html.

as under rei vindicatio, which protects against one certain type of interference (withdrawal of possession[27]). It was therefore possible to positively describe the addressee for rei vindicatio, but not for actio negatoria. In addition, pandectists also changed the thinking from actio, a procedural remedy, to a material claim exercisable also outside of the courts. The outcome was a very broad and uncertain scope of addresses under action negatoria of §1004. Reinhold Johow, who authored the proposal of the BGB for the property law chapter, explained this by saying that '[w]hereas delictual claims should require at least an act, for injunctive claims merely an objective interference with the property should suffice'.[28] He emphasised that 'which grounds need to be seen as sufficient, is determined merely from consideration of *usefulness*, while the justification of claims arising from the wrongful behaviour is deduced from the principle of the atoning justice'.[29]

Interpretation of §1004 BGB, even after more than hundred years, is far from settled. The deeper meaning of virtually each word is disputed. The controversy is so intensive that Canaris and Larenz, the two academic superstars of German private law, did not hesitate to name it 'the darkest and most disputed chapter of private law'.[30] The most significant controversies concern (1) the relationship between claims under §1004 BGB and tort law (§823 BGB[31]) and (2) the demarcation of a person accountable under §1004 BGB.

For intellectual property law, German courts have tried to identify an appropriate 'attribution principle' under §1004 BGB that would best delineate a person who must comply with injunctions. Although the courts to date cite a formula originating from the BGB's explanatory note (*Motive*), they do not really apply it.[32] The courts, in their attempts to define such a person,

---

[27] §985 BGB *(German Civil Code)*:'The owner may require the possessor to return the thing.' Translation provided by the Langenscheidt Translation Service, http://www.gesetze-im-internet.de/englisch bgb/englisch bgb.html.

[28] R. Johow, *Die Vorlagen der Rektoren für die erste Kommission zur Ausarbeitung des Entwurfs eines Bürgerlichen Gesetzbuches – Sachenrecht, Teil 1, Allgemeine Bestimmungen, Besitz und Eigentum* (first published 1880, De Gruyter 1991) 984 ('zur Beseitigung des das Eigenthum beeinträchtigenden Zustandes') 991.

[29] Ibid., p. 992.

[30] K. Larenz and C.-W. Canaris, *Lehrbuch des Schuldrechts II*, 13th edn., C.H.Beck, Munich 1994, p. 675.

[31] §823 BGB *(German Civil Code)*: '(1) A person who, intentionally or negligently, unlawfully injures the life, body health, freedom, property or another right of another person is liable to make compensation to the other party for the damage arising from this. (2) The same duty is held by a person who commits a breach of a statute that is intended to protect another person. If, according to the contents of the statute, it may also be breached without fault, then liability to compensation only exists in the case of fault.' Translation provided by the Langenscheidt Translation Service, http://www.gesetze-im-internet.de/englisch bgb/englisch bgb.html.

[32] See M. Husovec, *Injunctions Against Intermediaries in the European Union: Accountable, but not Liable?*, Cambridge University Press, Cambridge 2017, p. 154.

often refer to the principles of tort law, such as causality or later also duty of care.[33] The resulting case law is, in the author's view, legitimately criticised by Picker as 'a type of subsidiary tortious claim' (*Art sekundärem Deliktsanspruch*) abridged of the culpability requirement.[34] The years of case law and countless scholarship have shown that the newly created 'disturbance liability' (*Störerhaftung*) doctrine could be easily transplanted to tortious setting, and experience only few set-backs.[35]

All this is to say that German situation is complicated. Unlike the English story, it is very messy and interconnected with tortious liability. Especially so, if one adds to the mix German underdeveloped negligence-based tortious accessory liability in most of IP law. Today's 'disturber's liability' in German law, serves both situations that could be resolved under healthy tortious doctrine, and cases that need stepping out of the tort law. What can be said, however, is that its roots are in property law, although its subsequent development was heavily influenced by the tort law that it is meant to supplement. One of the driving reasons for this, however, can have more to do with the fact that damages and injunctions are conceptualised as a form of claim (*Anspruch*) and married with costly consequences of (pre-trial) incompliance. After all, had injunctions been only viewed as a possibility to apply to the court, there would have had been no need to elaborate any *pre-trial* 'duties to review' (*Prüfungspflichten*) of their addressees. Potential innocent third parties would simply await the case, and then argue before the court about the scope of the proposed assistance measures. Judges would have simply relied on the proportionality or reasonableness principles when handing down the judgments in order to contain it. But since obligations of private parties to respect content of such obligations arise *before* any judicial intervention, and pre-trial non-compliance leads to legal consequences, most notably costs, the need arose to delimit pre-trial obligations by some other means. Duties to review (= special duties of care) are simply a response to this problem.

5. FROM YESTERDAY'S TO TOMORROW'S IP ENFORCEMENT

Today, the cause of action against innocent third parties is being used in the intellectual property law in order to reach out to intermediaries, such as

33 See for instance: H. Köhler, '"Täter" und "Störer" im Wettbewerbs- und Markenrecht – Zur BGH-Entscheidung "Jugendgefährdende Medien bei eBay"' [2008] GRUR 1.

34 E. Picker, *Der negatorische Beseitigungsanspruch*, Mohr 1972, p. 31.

35 BGH Geschäftsführerhaftung (2014) I ZR 242/12, para. 15 (relaxing the duties of care for the executive director over her company's actions); see for more extensive debate: M. Husovec, *Injunctions Against Intermediaries in the European Union: Accountable, but not Liable?*, Cambridge University Press, Cambridge 2017, p. 179.

access provider, banks, social networks and similar services. The emerging body of case law concerning website-blocking, filtering, and password-locking is simply manifestation of the use of this remedy in practice. To some extent, these measures show how they can complement tort law, by removing pressure from it in cases where exposing to tortious liability could endanger the infrastructure and its stability. In particular, they decompress doctrines of accessory liability. For instance, exposing internet access providers to tortious liability for user-infringements could raise its costs for consumers, lower stability of infrastructure due to high legal risks, and not necessarily improve much the prevention of harm. From this perspective, injunctions against innocent third parties add a new tool to the toolkit of the legislator who instead of awaiting negotiations between stakeholders, takes a position in allocating the entitlement to the right holders.[36] It empowers the courts to make tough decisions about how effective and efficient enforcement measures should look like.

The two presented jurisdictions show how these injunctions developed in two major European jurisdictions. They paint a picture of enthusiastic English judicial intervention, and self-centric (but also complicated) German debate. While English judges embraced the cause of action and its European origin, the German judges often side-stepped the European context, unless it was hard to ignore, and even then, any references usually made little if any difference to the outcome. This has changed only recently when EU law was instrumental in overcoming strict consequences of a legislative intervention employed by the German legislator.[37] The case studies also show that while the English context clearly distinguishes between tortious claims and innocent third parties, the German context would not use these terms, and the application space of the remedies is often more mixed, doing the (policy) job also for the underdeveloped negligence-based accessory liability. Apart from the above, the most essential differences between two systems seems to be: (1) how they conceptualise the duty, and (2) allocate the costs of (in)compliance. Therefore, the following section examines these issues.

6. WHAT DUTY?

One of the most important divergences between the two systems concerns how they conceptualise the remedy itself. This follows from the doctrines employed for injunctions in the private law as such. While the English approach views

---

36 See for in-depth debate: M. Husovec, *Accountable, Not Liable: Injunctions Against Intermediaries*, TILEC Discussion Paper No. 2016-012, Tilburg 2016.

37 BGH 26.7.2018, I ZR 64/17 = *GRUR* 2018, 1044 – *Dead Island*.

them as a possibility to request the court to intervene, the German approach views them as entitlements, subjective claims, preceding any application to the court.[38] The history behind this is very interesting, and some of the chapters in this book already discuss this.

To contrast two approaches in this context, consider what Lord Sumption says in *Cartier*:

> the duty to assist identified by Lord Reid was not a legal duty in the ordinary sense of the term. As Lord Reid himself put it in Norwich Pharmacal, the intermediary came under the duty without incurring personal liability. *This is really only another way of saying that the court had an equitable jurisdiction to intervene* (emphasis added).[39]

The German view would attribute legal effects to injunctions against innocent third parties even prior to an application before the court.[40] This is because the debt (obligation) of an injunction-addressee corresponding to the claim to injunction of a right holder is automatically formed *ipso facto* when the required (substantive) conditions are met. This happens *before* the courts get involved. Such obligation is formed at the point when the 'committal danger' (*Begehungsgefahr*), the risk of occurrence of an undesired act, is established.[41] For some providers, this differs depending on whether they act for profit or not.[42] While this aspect of the remedy does not pose problems to more negligence-tasting situations of secondary liability, where it feels justified to trigger them, it definitely stands out in cases of remote third parties, such as internet access providers.

It is therefore no wonder that controversy around the scope of preventive duties imposed on WiFi operators triggered a legislative response in *Bundestag*. The societal problem was that the German owners of WiFi connections

---

38 See for in-depth treatment of the issue: F. Hofmann, *Der Unterlassungsanspruch als Rechtsbehelf* (Mohr Siebeck 2017), pp. 13–83; F. Hofmann, 'Markenrechtliche Sperranordnungen gegen nicht verantwortliche Intermediäre' (2015) 2 *Gewerblicher Rechtsschutz und Urheberrecht* 123.

39 *Cartier International AG and others v British Telecommunications Plc and another* [2018] UKSC 28, para. 11.

40 For instance, an obligation to pay cost of incompliance. See M. Husovec, 'Holey cap! CJEU drills (yet) another hole in the e-Commerce Directive's safe harbours' (2017) 12 (2), *Journal of Intellectual Property Law & Practice*, pp. 115–125.

41 BGH 26.7.2018, I ZR 64/17 = *GRUR* 2018, 1044 – *Dead Island*; BGH 17.8.2011, I ZR 57/09 = *GRUR* 2011, 1038 para. 38–47. – *Stiftparfüm*; O. Teplitzky, *Wettbewerbsrechtliche Ansprüche und Verfahren*, Carl Heymanns Verlag, 2011, p. 32 ff, p. 119 ff; K. Bacher, *Die Beeinträchtigungsgefahr als Voraussetzung für Unterlassungsklagen im Wettbewerbsrecht und in anderen Gebieten des Zivilrechts*, Centaurus-Verlagsgesellschaft Pfaffenweiler, 1996; J. v. Staudinger (ed.), *Bürgerliches Gesetzbuch*, 13th edn., Sellier-de Gruyter, 1993, §1004; F. Hofmann, *Der Unterlassungsanspruch als Rechtsbehelf*, Mohr Siebeck, 2017, §10.

42 BGH 26.7.2018, I ZR 64/17 = *GRUR* 2018, 1044 – *Dead Island*.

were required to password protect them in order to prevent third-party infringements. If they did not, they could receive cease and desist letters, which they would have to reimburse. To avoid this, the German parliament amended the act which implements the E-Commerce Directive, limiting the preventive duties and compliance cost that can be imposed on WiFi operators, but also creating a new statutory basis for special injunctions against them.[43]

In the first case applying this new legal landscape – *Dead Island*, BGH shifted its position, and instead of referring to disturbance liability as a legal basis, it expanded the reach of this statutory injunctive powers to generally cover providers who qualify under the so-called mere conduit safe harbour.[44] This created a split, as other providers, including those covered by other safe harbours like hosting, continue to be covered by the general doctrine of 'disturbance liability'. Website-blocking requests, which are always aimed at mere conduits, such as WiFi operators or access providers, thus obtained a new statutory basis that the Court distinguished from general disturbance liability, although its content seems to incorporate some of the principles of the older case law.

Most importantly for this discussion, BGH emphasised that these blocking orders are about *positive acts*, and not necessarily about merely prohibitory orders.[45] However, at the same time, it emphasised that this conceptualisation is not dissimilar from the old doctrine, which required 'usually'[46] the same, although covered in different language because the plaintiffs did not have to specify the acts in their lawsuits.[47] These latest developments bring about partial convergence of two systems in the area of mere conduit covered services. For other types of services, conceptualisation of the remedy under disturbance liability in Germany, and equitable relief in the UK, remains rather distinct. Although European law unites the discussion about two instruments, it is also unlikely to entirely iron out domestic differences.

7. COSTS OF COMPLIANCE

Closely connected with the last point is the issue of costs. Because costs are inextricably linked to the very jurisdiction to grant the measures, they determine the nature of the remedy. The cost allocation creates an impression of the conceptual context of the jurisdiction, and its daily use is influenced

43 See §§7 and 8 of the Telemedia Act (*Telemediengesetz*) G v. 28.9.2017 (BGBl. I S. 3530).

44 BGH 26.7.2018, I ZR 64/17 = *GRUR* 2018, 1044 – *Dead Island* (ratio decidendi).

45 BGH 26.7.2018, I ZR 64/17 = *GRUR* 2018, 1044 para. 57 – *Dead Island*.

46 Ibid.

47 Ibid.

by it. To illustrate this point, consider how English and German concepts practically converge if one allocates the costs in a uniform manner for a pre-trial phase.

In *Cartier*, Lord Sumption argued that, '[a]s a matter of English law, the ordinary principle is that unless there are good reasons for a different order an innocent intermediary is entitled to be indemnified by the rights-holder against the costs of complying with a website-blocking order'.[48] As a consequence, '[t]here is no legal basis for requiring a party to shoulder the burden of remedying an injustice if he has no legal responsibility for the infringement and is not a volunteer but is acting under the compulsion of an order of the court.'[49] In addition to compliance costs, pre-trial costs and trial costs are then normally also paid by right holders.

To contrast this, German practice asks providers to pay the pre-trial costs and trial costs.[50] The reason for this is the fact that the sending of a cease and desist letter shall be reimbursed to its sender.[51] The underlying idea is that such letters help rightfully targeted defendants by giving them an opportunity to save costs of litigation. In consequence, this means that even if the court is never involved in the dispute, the addressee of the letter can be obliged to provide some pre-trial compensation. In addition, as a losing party, it will have to pay the costs of litigation. It is worth noting that countries like Slovakia or the Czech Republic do not trigger the same consequences, at least pre-trial, despite relying on the same conceptual framework. So this policy choice is not inherent in the concept of *Anspruch*. In the German system, these expected costs drive much of compliance, without an actual need to involve the courts in the enforcement. Recently, the German legislator decided to weaken these effects when it decided to free WiFi operators of any pre-trial and out-of-court costs.[52] This statutory change might send a ripple through the system, but it is too early to say if it will influence the German situation beyond legislated cases of WiFi operators.

The regulatory split between WiFi operators and other providers leads to an interesting situation. When the German legislator stripped injunctions against WiFi operators of their pre-trial and out-of-court cost implications, the remedy that was left ended up looking a lot more like its common law counterpart. Although it is not compensated for, it has – at least from a practical point

---

48 *Cartier International AG and others v British Telecommunications Plc and another* [2018] UKSC 28, para. 31.

49 *Cartier International AG and others v British Telecommunications Plc and another* [2018] UKSC 28, para. 33.

50 M. Husovec, 'Holey cap! CJEU drills (yet) another hole in the e-Commerce Directive's safe harbours' (2017) 12 (2), *Journal of Intellectual Property Law & Practice*, pp. 118 ff.

51 Cf. Art. 97a of the German Copyright Act.

52 See Section 7(4) of the Telemedia Act (*Telemediengesetz*) G v. 28.9.2017 (BGBl. I S. 3530).

of view[53] – no legal effects prior to the judicial decision. Awaiting judicial coercion is thus a perfectly rational choice for defendants. Notice how this also changes the worries about overextending the injunctive obligations. Since the courts will always determine the scope, BGH could easily relax any considerations of duties to review, and resort only to proportionality analysis. In fact, the first decision on the matter – *Dead Island* – seems to do exactly that.

BGH moreover decided to emphasise that the content of such remedy is an entitlement to positive action; in a common law parlance, also known as mandatory injunctions. Interestingly enough, BGH even considered this aspect to be implicit in the earlier case law. Thus, perhaps preparing the ground for broader convergence of this statutory injunction against mere conduits, and injunctions based on the doctrine of disturber's liability originally based on §1004 BGB.

To summarise this briefly, once pre-trial costs are removed from equation, the duty to assist imposed by means of injunctions against innocent third parties looks very much the same in both systems.[54]

As regards compliance costs, German doctrine does not offer any compensation. However, such compensation is known in the area of assisting by providing information.[55] As explained elsewhere, the nineteenth century authors of the BGB openly discussed a possibility that costs of compliance born by non-wrongdoers can be an issue. In the official explanatory note, one finds a cautionary note from the members of the committee saying that: '[a]gainst the reasonableness of the obligation to pay the costs (...) the doubt can be raised and it considered to be justified only towards those who, by erecting a facility, also committed a tort.'[56]

The intuition underlying this historical debate was that if non-wrongdoers are asked to help in assuring compliance, perhaps one should think twice before imposing too high costs on them. After all, had they been blameworthy, this would have been stated in the tortious context first. If it was not, then perhaps they should be treated differently. This debate was resolved in favour of a simply

---

53 F. Hofmann, Modifizierte Haftung von Internetzugangsprovidern, (2018) 9 *juris Praxis Report Wettbewerbs- und Immaterialgüterrecht (jurisPR-WettbR)* Anm. 1.

54 See on also debate in M. Husovec, 'Holey cap! CJEU drills (yet) another hole in the e-Commerce Directive's safe harbours' (2017) 12 (2), *Journal of Intellectual Property Law & Practice*, pp. 124 ff.

55 In the area of information disclosures, even German law requires that non-infringers are compensated. All intellectual property statues require 'necessary effort' (erforderlichen Aufwendungen) to be reimbursed – see M. Husovec, *Injunctions Against Intermediaries in the European Union: Accountable, but not Liable?*, Cambridge University Press, Cambridge 2017, p. 177 ff. (debating the origin and application practice); Cf. Art. 101 UrhG *(Act on Copyright and Related Rights)*.

56 See B. Mugdan (ed.), *Die gesamten Materialien zum Bürgerlichen Gesetzbuch für das Deutsche Reich: Band III*, Deker's Verlag, 1899–1900, p. 237.

administrable solution, namely, the defendants should bear the costs. This debate should serve as a reminder that if the compliance efforts of innocent third parties become very costly, perhaps one might want to consider exceptions to this rule.

8. CONCLUSION

To conclude, an injunction against innocent third parties is a novel tool of enforcement of intellectual property rights. It allows right holders to demand assistance in enforcement also from the persons who engage in no wrongdoing of their own. The measures thus surpass classical categories of primary and secondary infringers (accessories) and relieve the pressure from solving every intervention through tortious means. The legal history of these measures in the civil and common law world is very different, but not too far apart. Perhaps the European legal basis can continue to provide inspiration to unite two streams of traditions, and deliver a more coherent and effective policy response to evolving problems of the digital IP enforcement. While doing so, it might provide further lessons on how English and German concept of remedies can coexist and influence each other.

PART V

REMEDIES IN CONTRACT LAW AND INTELLECTUAL PROPERTY

REMEDIES IN EUROPEAN CONTRACT LAW

Themes and Controversies

Christian TWIGG-FLESNER

1. INTRODUCTION

In this chapter, the evolution of remedies in European contract law, particularly consumer contract law, will be discussed. This discussion will reveal how the European Union (EU) has gradually developed its approach towards remedies in this sphere, starting with the Consumer Sales Directive (1999/44/EC),[1] followed by the revised Package Travel Directive (2015/2302/EU)[2] and the recently

1 Directive of the European Parliament and of the Council of 25 May 1999 on certain aspects of the sale of consumer goods and associated guarantees [1999] OJ L 171/12. This Directive will be repealed from 1 January 2022.

2 Directive of the European Parliament and of the Council of 25 November 2015 on package travel and linked travel arrangements, amending Regulation (EC) No 2006/2004 and Directive 2011/83/EU of the European Parliament and of the Council and repealing Council Directive 90/314/EEC [2015] OJ L 326/1.

adopted directive on digital content and digital services (2019/770/EU)[3] and the revised consumer sales directive (2019/771/EU).[4] Several themes can be identified. First, despite the increasingly detailed approach to remedies in the aforementioned directives, it is striking that many aspects of EU consumer contract law are characterised by an incomplete approach. Many rights granted to consumers are provided without specifying a corresponding remedy. Key examples here are the widespread use of information duties (most recently under the Consumer Rights Directive (2011/83/EU)[5]),[6] and the fact that the consequences of a consumer having suffered loss because a trader relied on a contract term which has subsequently been found to be unfair under the Unfair Contract Terms Directive (93/13/EEC)[7] are not addressed at the European level. This leads to the second theme: the fact that European contract law measures depend on supplementation of the European rules by national law, i.e. to the extent that remedial schemes in the directives are incomplete or missing altogether, national law is required to fill those voids. This has resulted in quite a complex interaction between EU legislation (or rather, the national provisions implementing those directives) and national laws in the affected areas. The third theme is the European Commission's policy to shift from the minimum harmonisation approach which characterised most of the first-generation consumer contract directives (and is still applicable in the case of consumer sales (for now) and unfair contract terms) to a maximum harmonisation approach.[8] This has resulted in more detailed provisions on all aspects of the second-generation directives (such as the second Package Travel Directive) and reduced the scope of the Member States to adapt EU provisions to align them more effectively with the related areas of national law.

---

3 Directive (EU) 2019/770 of the European Parliament and of the Council of 20 May 2019 on certain aspects concerning contracts for the supply of digital content and digital services [2019] OJ L 136/1.

4 Directive (EU) 2019/771 of the European Parliament and of the Council of 20 May 2019 on certain aspects concerning contracts for the sale of goods, amending Regulation (EU) 2017/2394 and Directive 2009/22/EC, and repealing Directive 1999/44/EC [2019] OJ L 136/28.

5 Directive of the European Parliament and of the Council of 25 October 2011 on consumer rights, amending Council Directive 93/13/EEC and Directive 1999/44/EC of the European Parliament and of the Council and repealing Council Directive 85/577/EEC and Directive 97/7/EC of the European Parliament and of the Council [2011] OJ L 304/64.

6 See H. Schulte-Nölke, C. Twigg-Flesner and M. Ebers (eds.), *EC Consumer Law Compendium*, Sellier, Munich 2008, p. 480.

7 Council Directive of 5 April 1993 on unfair terms in consumer contracts [1993] OJ L 95/29.

8 G. Howells, C. Twigg-Flesner and T. Wilhelmsson, *Rethinking EU Consumer Law*, Routledge, Abingdon 2017, ch. 1, pp. 19–22.

2. THE EVOLUTION OF REMEDIES

As already noted, a recurring theme in the development of European contract law, especially European consumer contract law, is the rather piecemeal development of any provisions dealing with remedies. The two areas where there are long-standing and detailed provisions dealing with remedies are the directives on consumer sales and package travel (especially in its revised version), and these will be analysed in depth below. It is worth noting that the European Commission's attempt to introduce a complete set of remedies via its proposal for a Common European Sales Law (CESL),[9] which was the legislative proposal resulting from a decade of work on the idea of a European contract law,[10] did not gain sufficient support and was ultimately withdrawn. Following the adoption of the directive on digital content (2019/770/EU) and the revised directive on the sale of consumer goods (2019/771/EU), a further stage in the evolution of the EU's approach to consumer contract remedies has been reached.

2.1. REMEDIES IN THE FIRST CONSUMER SALES DIRECTIVE

The first time a fairly detailed set of provisions dealing with remedies was introduced into EU consumer contract law was in Article 3 of the first Consumer Sales Directive (99/44/EC). These remedies are available for a consumer against the seller of goods in circumstances where the goods are not in conformity with the contract (under Article 2). It is important to stress that, despite discussions about holding the producer of non-conforming goods liable alongside the seller, this was not introduced in the Consumer Sales Directive, and so the consumer's only claim is against the contractual seller of the goods in question.[11]

2.1.1. Preconditions to Claiming a Remedy

The minimum requirement under the Directive is that the seller is liable for any lack of conformity which becomes apparent within two years from the date of delivery of the goods.[12] As the Consumer Sales Directive is of a minimum harmonisation standard, it is open to individual Member States to extend this period. The Directive also permits a reduction of this period in

---

9 Proposal for a regulation of the European Parliament and of the Council on a Common European Sales Law COM(2011) 635 final.

10 This is charted in C. Twigg-Flesner, *The Europeanisation of Contract Law*, 2nd edn., Routledge, Abingdon 2013.

11 Art. 3(1) Consumer Sales Directive.

12 Art. 5(1) Consumer Sales Directive.

respect of second-hand goods, for which consumer and seller may agree on a shorter period of no less than one year during which a lack of conformity must materialise.[13] The burden of establishing a lack of conformity, and therefore the entitlement to one of the remedies under Article 3, is generally on the consumer. However, the Directive reverses this burden for any lack of conformity which arises within six months from delivery. In that situation, the Directive creates a rebuttable presumption that the goods were not in conformity with the contract when they were delivered.[14] The seller can then rebut this presumption by adducing evidence that the lack of conformity was caused by something which happened after the goods had been delivered to the consumer. The Directive itself envisages that this would be so where the presumption would be incompatible with either the nature of the goods or the nature of the lack of conformity.

As a final restriction on the consumer's ability to seek a remedy, a Member State may provide that a consumer has to notify the seller of the lack of conformity within two months of discovering the lack of conformity.[15]

2.1.2. The Remedies

The Consumer Sales Directive makes available four remedies to a consumer: repair, replacement, price reduction or rescission of the contract. A notable absence is any right to compensation (damages), an issue to be returned to later. It does once more flag up the complex interaction between European rules and national laws, because the remedies required by the Directive are not complete and leave some matters to national law.

One point to note at the outset is that the consumer does not have a free choice as to which remedy he/she prefers. Whilst it is always open for a seller to offer a consumer any of these remedies,[16] the Directive has separated the remedies into a two-stage hierarchy. The first level provides only a choice between repair or replacement of the non-conforming goods. Prioritising these two remedies reveals the particular approach underpinning the remedial regime of the Directive, and also offers a pointer to the preferred approach to remedies which has started to evolve in European contract law: in focusing on repairing or replacing non-conforming goods, the seller is effectively held to the contract, and the consumer is entitled to require the seller to do what is necessary to ensure the performance of the seller's contractual obligation to deliver goods which are in conformity with the contract. This focus on performance is common to many

---

13 Art. 7(1) Consumer Sales Directive.
14 Art. 5(3) Consumer Sales Directive.
15 Art. 5(2) Consumer Sales Directive.
16 Cf. Recital 12 Consumer Sales Directive.

European jurisdictions, but is in stark contrast to the general position in the common law, where remedies for breach of contract tend to be limited to a claim for damages and, in some instances, the right to terminate the contract.

The assumption is that the consumer has a choice between repair or replacement. There is no definition of 'replacement', but repair is defined as 'in the event of lack of conformity, bringing consumer goods into conformity with the contract of sale'.[17] Either remedy must be provided free of charge,[18] i.e. without imposing any costs on the consumer, although this does not generally require the seller to advance the cost of returning the goods to the consumer, unless the cost would be a such a burden on the consumer that he/she would not seek a remedy at all.[19] This means that national law may not, for example, permit the seller to ask for compensation to reflect the fact that the consumer may have had a period of time where the goods could be used without difficulty. This was confirmed by the CJEU held in *Quelle*,[20] where a consumer had been able to use a cooker for about 18 months before it was replaced due to a lack of conformity. A provision which was then part of German law permitted a request by the seller for some compensation, but the CJEU held that this was not compatible with Article 3 of the Directive.[21]

There are limitations to the consumer's ability to select these remedies, however. Repair or replacement cannot be requested if the chosen remedy is impossible to provide, or where the remedy would be disproportionate.[22] Whenever a consumer has chosen one of repair or replacement, the seller could therefore claim that it is impossible to provide that remedy, or that doing so would be disproportionate. One would expect that the threshold for either limitation would be set at quite a high level. For example, it should not be enough for a seller to argue that he/she does not have facilities or trained staff to undertake repairs to succeed in arguing that repair would be impossible. On the other hand, the lack of any spare parts (especially where these are not supplied by the producer of the goods) might suffice.[23] Moreover, one would generally expect that it would be possible to replace mass-produced goods when

17 Art. 1(2)(f) Consumer Sales Directive.

18 'Free of charge' refers to 'the necessary costs incurred to bring the goods into conformity, particularly the cost of postage, labour and materials' (Art. 3(4)).

19 CJEU 23.05.2019, C-52/18 *Christian Fülla v Toolport GmbH*, ECLI:EU:C:2019:447.

20 CJEU 17.04.2008, C-404/06, *Quelle AG v Bundesverband der Verbraucherzentralen und Verbraucherverbände*, ECLI:EU:C:2008:231.

21 P. Rott, 'The *Quelle* Case and the Potential of and Limitations to Interpretation in the Light of the Relevant Directive' (2008) 12 *European Review of Private Law* 1119–1130.

22 See Art. 3(3), first sentence.

23 An interesting issue which will likely emerge is whether the ability to use 3D scanning and printing technology to create at least some spare parts would change this assumption in the future, although there would undoubtedly be complex intellectual property issues at play.

these were bought as new goods.[24] One instance where replacement might be impossible is where the goods were required for a particular purpose,[25] but it transpires that the goods would never be suitable for that purpose.

A more difficult restriction on the consumer's ability to request either repair or replacement might be the seller's claim that providing the chosen remedy would be disproportionate. According to the Directive, this will be the case where the chosen remedy 'imposes costs on the seller which, in comparison with the alternative remedy, are unreasonable'.[26] A preliminary question is what might be meant by 'the alternative remedy'. It might seem obvious that the alternative remedy to repair would be replacement, and vice versa, rather than price reduction or rescission. This was confirmed by the CJEU in *Weber* and *Putz*.[27] One of the questions the CJEU had to deal with in that case was whether the proportionality criterion in Article 3 was 'relative' or 'absolute', i.e. whether repair could only be disproportionate when compared to replacement (and vice versa), or whether repair/replacement could be disproportionate because of the inherent cost of providing that remedy, without the need to show that those costs would be significantly higher than those of proving the alternative remedy. The Court said that:

> Article 3(3) defines the term 'disproportionate' exclusively in relation to the other remedy, thus limiting it to cases of relative lack of proportionality. Furthermore, it is clear from the wording and purpose of Article 3(3) of the Directive that it refers to two remedies provided for in the first place, namely the repair or replacement of the goods not in conformity.[28]

This means that a seller can only argue that the remedy chosen by the consumer is disproportionate when compared to the other remedy, and that this only relates to a comparison between repair and replacement.

To be regarded as unreasonable, it seems that more is required than simply pointing out that the other remedy is less costly to provide; the threshold is that the difference in costs has to be *significant*.[29] A number of factors have to be taken into account when determining whether the costs of providing the chosen remedy are unreasonable. They are:

1. the value the goods would have had if they had been in conformity with the contract,

---

24 Recital 16 assumes that the replacement of second-hand goods would generally be impossible, although that might be debatable.

25 Cf. Art. 2(2)(b) Consumer Sales Directive.

26 Art. 3(3) Consumer Sales Directive.

27 Joined cases C-65/09, *Weber v Wittmer*, and C-87/09, *Putz v Medianess Electronics*, ECLI:EU:C:2011:396.

28 Joined cases C-65/09, *Weber v Wittmer*, and C-87/09, *Putz v Medianess Electronics*, above n. 27, para. 68.

29 Cf. Recital 11 Consumer Sales Directive.

2. the significance of the lack of conformity, and
3. whether the alternative remedy could be completed without significant inconvenience to the consumer.

Taking account of the value of conforming goods suggests that, in the case of low-value mass-produced goods which are easily replaced, repair might more readily be regarded as disproportionate compared to replacement. On the other hand, where goods are of high value, even complex repairs might still be below the threshold for disproportionality.

Similarly, where there is only a small difference in value between the goods as delivered and their market value, replacement might be regarded as disproportionate, especially if repair could be effected easily and at low cost.

The second aspect, the significance of the lack of conformity, might be relevant, for example, where the goods are of a high-value and the lack of conformity means that the goods cannot be used at all. In such a situation, an expensive repair might still be regarded as proportionate; however, if the goods are of low value, repair would be disproportionate when compared to replacement.

The third factor focuses on the impact of providing the opposite remedy to the one chosen by the consumer on that consumer. If the alternative remedy were to cause significant inconvenience to the consumer, then this might swing the balance of the overall assessment of disproportionality back in favour of the remedy requested by the consumer.

Once it has been determined which of repair or replacement a consumer will receive, the seller is required to provide that remedy within a reasonable time and without any significant inconvenience to the consumer.[30] Relevant considerations for determining what would be a reasonable time and not a significant inconvenience are the nature of the goods and the purposes for which the consumer required them.

These factors also determine whether a consumer has to return non-conforming goods to the seller's business premises, or whether the seller can be required to collect the goods or repair them at the consumer's premises. In *Fülla*,[31] the CJEU ruled that there is no single rule regarding the place where the consumer has to make goods available to the seller; instead, this has to be determined on a case-by-case basis on the basis of the requirements that any remedy has to be provided free of charge, within a reasonable time and without significant inconvenience. This issue will be particularly relevant in the context of distance selling or in the case of bulky goods. Thus, sometimes, it may be quicker for the consumer to take or send the item back to the seller, whereas in other instances, the seller can be expected to go to the consumer's premises.

---

30 Art. 3(3) Consumer Sales Directive.

31 CJEU 23.05.2019, C-52/18 *Christian Fülla v Toolport GmbH*, ECLI:EU:C:2019:447.

These factors are also relevant for moving from the first to the second stage of the remedial hierarchy in the Directive. Thus, if the seller does not manage to provide a repair or replacement within a reasonable time and without any significant inconvenience, then the consumer can request a reduction of the price, or ultimately rescission of the contract.[32] A further instance when the second stage remedies become available is when repair or replacement are not available or have not managed to rectify the lack of conformity.

Once more, limitations are placed on the availability of these remedies. In particular, rescission will not be available if the lack of conformity is only minor. In addition, even where the consumer is able to rescind the contract, his/her right to a full refund of the purchase price may be off-set by an allowance in favour of the seller to reflect the use the consumer may have had of the goods.[33]

2.1.3. No Provision on Damages

This overview of the remedies under the Consumer Sales Directive reveals quite a complex scheme, ostensibly designed in such a way as to balance the interests of consumer and seller. However, despite all this, one important issue has not been addressed: the availability of damages. Damages may be important for several reasons. First, damages could be awarded to reflect the fact that a consumer has not received the goods he/she expected, and that he/she should be compensated for this. Secondly, damages are available to compensate a consumer for any consequential losses suffered as a result of the non-conformity. There are numerous instances of consequential losses, such as loss of clothing or food from a faulty kitchen appliance, the need to hire a car whilst the non-conforming vehicle is undergoing repairs, or the need to engage a professional to remove the non-conforming goods and install conforming ones. This matter is something that would have to be dealt with under whichever national law applies to the contract of sale between the seller and the consumer.

The consequences of not having a provision in the Directive on the availability of damages is illustrated by the somewhat strange decision in two combined cases, *Weber* and *Putz*.[34] In *Putz*, the consumer had bought a dishwasher online and had this installed by a third party unconnected with the seller. The dishwasher had a lack of conformity, and the consumer successfully asked for a replacement. In *Weber*, the consumer had tiles and laid the floor himself, but then noticed a flaw in the glaze which meant that the tiles were not in conformity and would need to be replaced.

---

32 Art. 3(5) Consumer Sales Directive.

33 This is not a substantive rule, but it is stated in Recital 15.

34 Joined cases C-65/09, *Weber v Wittmer*, and C-87/09, *Putz v Medianess Electronics*, above n. 27.

It was noted above that repair or replacement have to be provided free of charge, but in both cases, there was the need to remove the non-conforming goods, and to reinstall conforming goods. The CJEU therefore had to consider whether the cost of doing this would have to be borne by the seller, despite the fact that installation had not been part of the seller's contractual obligations. The CJEU's reasoning is somewhat convoluted. It starts by noting, correctly, that if the consumer could not recover the cost of uninstalling the non-conforming goods and installing the replacement goods, this would result in an additional financial burden that would not have occurred if the goods had been conforming ones when delivered. This, the Court argued, would mean that replacement had not been provided 'free of charge'. In both cases, the actual cost of replacement was high. In *Weber*, the purchase price of the tiles was €1,380, and the cost of replacing them ran to €5,830. The CJEU stressed that a seller could not refuse to replace goods simply because the cost of doing so was disproportionate based on the value of the goods had they been in conformity and the significance of non-conformity. However, as this reasoning could expose a seller in circumstances similar to those in *Weber* and *Putz* to potentially very high expenses, the CJEU continued by limiting the consumer's right to reimbursement of the costs of removing and reinstalling the goods to a 'proportionate amount'. There is nothing in the Directive itself that would provide any basis for this interpretation, but the Court justified its conclusions on the basis that the Directive:

> aims to establish a fair balance between the interests of the consumer and the seller, by guaranteeing the consumer, as the weak party to the contract, complete and effective protection from faulty performance by the seller of his contractual obligations, while enabling account to be taken of economic considerations advanced by the seller.[35]

Limiting the seller's obligation to reimburse the consumer to a 'proportionate amount' creates further room for arguments between seller and consumer, although the CJEU also emphasised that this should not 'result in the consumer's right to reimbursement of those costs being effectively rendered devoid of substance'.[36] This has added an incredibly complex gloss to the availability of replacement in many common situations.

It was suggested above that this decision could have been avoided, had there been clarity in the Directive about the relationship of the performance-focused remedies with any entitlement to damages. The Court's reasoning was restricted by the need to give an answer to the questions which had been referred to it, but the effect of this is that there is some confusion between the consumer's right to have goods replaced free-of-charge, and the consumer's right to damages

35 Ibid., para. 75.
36 Ibid., para. 76.

in respect of consequential losses. Perhaps the CJEU should have treated this issue differently: the cost of having to remove and replace non-conforming goods could have been treated as an irrelevant consideration in applying the proportionality test, and the extent to which the consumer would be entitled to be compensated could have been characterised simply as being recoverable through a claim for damages at national law,[37] perhaps with the proviso that a claim for such consequential losses should be permissible in principle so as not to violate the principle of effectiveness (*effet utile*).[38]

2.2. REMEDIES UNDER THE PACKAGE TRAVEL DIRECTIVE

The revisions made in the second Package Travel Directive (2015/2302/EU) are interesting because they suggest that a clear preferred approach for remedies for breach of contract has emerged in European contract law. The second Package Travel Directive has been extended to cover a wide range of aspects of package travel contracts. In line with the first Directive, a package is defined as a combination of at least two different travel services (which include accommodation, carriage of passengers, vehicle hire and other tourist services).[39,40] Article 13 places the responsibility for the performance of the package on the organiser (defined as a trader who combines and sells/offers for sale packages either directly or through another trader),[41] which means that a traveller[42] can seek redress from the organiser if the holiday does not proceed as agreed.

As a first step, a traveller is under a duty to notify the organiser of the package without undue delay of 'any lack of conformity which he perceives during the performance of a travel service'.[43] One thing which immediately stands out is the term 'lack of conformity', which is familiar from the Consumer

37 Cf. B. Kresse, 'Anmerkung zu EuGH C-65/09 *Weber v Wittmer* u. C-87/09 v. 16.6.2011' (2012) 20 *European Review of Private Law* 255–262.

38 See also A. Johnston and H. Unberath, 'Joined cases C-65/09 *Weber v Wittmer* and C-87/09 *Putz v Medianess Electronics*' (2012) 49 *Common Market Law Review* 793–808. For an example of how the application of national rules on damages would work, see the Scottish case of *Peebles v Rembrand Builders Merchants Ltd* [2017] G.W.D. 15–236, Sh.Ct. (involving faulty roof tiles).

39 Art. 3(1) Package Travel Directive.

40 Art. 3(2) Package Travel Directive.

41 Art. 3(8) Package Travel Directive.

42 The definition of 'traveller' is broader than the definition of consumer found in other directives. It covers 'any person who is seeking to conclude a contract, or is entitled to travel on the basis of a contract concluded, within the scope of this Directive' (Art. 3(6) Package Travel Directive). It includes persons covered by a contract but who may not be a party to that contract.

43 Art. 13(2) Package Travel Directive.

Sales Directive. It sounds somewhat artificial when applied to package travel contracts. The term has been defined as 'a failure to perform or improper performance of the travel services included in a package',[44] and it might have been more straightforward to have used 'improper performance' instead. However, using the language of 'conformity' evokes an image of coherence in the way a breach of contract is labelled under European contract law.

Once a lack of conformity has been notified by the traveller, Article 13(3) requires the organiser to 'remedy the lack of conformity', unless this (a) is impossible; or (b) would entail disproportionate cost, taking into account (i) the extent of the lack of conformity and (ii) the value of the travel services affected. For either instance, Article 14(1) makes available the right to an 'appropriate price reduction' for the period of travel during which there was a lack of conformity (except where the lack of conformity was somehow attributable to the traveller).

Although the language of the Package Travel Directive is more generic in talking of remedying the lack of conformity, the purpose is, of course, to correct an improper performance. The corresponding remedy in the Consumer Sales Directive would be 'repair'.

Moreover, there are also instances where the lack of conformity is such that the organiser of the package would effectively have to provide a 'substitute performance' – akin to the right to a 'replacement' under the Consumer Sales Directive. Thus, Article 13(5) of the Package Travel Directive requires an organiser to offer suitable alternative arrangements of equivalent or higher quality to ensure the continuation of the package where a significant proportion of the travel services cannot be provided as agreed. If the alternative arrangements are of lower quality, then the organiser has to reduce the price by an appropriate amount. The traveller will generally be bound to accept the alternative arrangements made by the organiser, except where they are not comparable to what had originally been agreed, or if the price reduction by the organiser is inadequate.[45]

Whilst there are obvious parallels between the remedial schemes in the Consumer Sales Directive and the second Package Travel Directive, there are also provisions in the latter on issues which have not been covered in the former. One such provision is Article 13(4) of the Package Travel Directive, which applies when the organiser does not remedy the lack of conformity within 'a reasonable period set by the traveller'. In this situation, the traveller can do what is needed to rectify the lack of conformity him/herself, and then request reimbursement of any necessary expenses from the organiser. The traveller will not have to give the organiser the opportunity to rectify things by

44 Art. 3(13) Package Travel Directive.
45 Art. 13(5) Package Travel Directive.

setting a time limit if the organiser refuses to provide a remedy or an immediate remedy is required.[46] In that case, the traveller can take the necessary steps at once.

The significance of this provision is that it addresses the situation where the organiser does not act and gives the green light to the traveller to do what is necessary and then seek reimbursement from the organiser.

The remedial approach of the Package Travel Directive is heavily balanced in favour of ensuring performance of the contract. On the one hand, this is understandable in view of the particular nature of a package travel contract: the traveller will be on holiday, for a limited period of time, and will wish to enjoy as much of his/her time away as possible. On the other hand, it does tie the traveller into the performance the package in circumstances where the trip may already have been spoilt by the non-conformity.

The possibility for a traveller to terminate the contract are limited to circumstances where the lack of conformity 'substantially' affects performance of the package.[47] Before the traveller can terminate, he/she has to set a reasonable period of time for organiser to remedy the lack of conformity. If this substantial lack of conformity is not remedied within that period, then the traveller can terminate the contract and request a price reduction or compensation, as appropriate.[48] If package included the carriage of the traveller, then following termination by the traveller, the organiser has to repatriate the traveller using equivalent transport, and do so without undue delay and at no extra cost to traveller.[49]

However, unlike the Consumer Sales Directive, the Package Travel Directive also includes a provision dealing with compensation. This had, of course, already been part of the first Package Travel Directive.[50] Under the first Directive, a retailer or organiser of a package holiday was liable if there is had been an improper performance of the contract. This liability included, in particular, an entitlement to compensation for damage (including non-material damage such as loss of enjoyment)[51] due to a failure fully to perform the contract, except where neither retailer nor organiser were at fault.[52] In the new Package Travel Directive, this right to compensation is enshrined in Article 14(2),

---

46 Art. 13(4) Package Travel Directive.

47 This can also be compared to the Consumer Sales Directive, which makes a right to rescission available only in respect of a lack of conformity which is not 'minor'.

48 Art. 13(6) Package Travel Directive.

49 Art. 13(6), 3rd para. Package Travel Directive.

50 Council Directive 90/314/EEC of 13 June 1990 on package travel, package holidays and package tours [1990] OJ L 158/59.

51 The CJEU ruled that this included non-material damage: C-168/00, *Simone Leitner v. TUI Deutschland GmbH & Co. KG*, ECLI:EU:C:2002:163.

52 Arts. 5(1) and (2) (first) Package Travel Directive (90/314/EEC).

according to which a traveller is entitled to 'appropriate compensation ... for any damage which the traveller sustains as a result of any lack of conformity'. Such compensation also extends to 'non-material damage, such as compensation for loss of enjoyment'.[53] Whilst this provision goes further than other Directives, Article 14(2) is anything but a comprehensive provision on damages. There are several limitations on the entitlement to damages in Article 14(3). The organiser will not be liable to pay compensation where the lack of conformity is attributable to the traveller, or attributable to a 'third party unconnected with the provision of the travel services included in the package travel contract and is unforeseeable or unavoidable', or where the lack of conformity is due to unavoidable and extraordinary circumstances.

However, there is no indication whether the entitlement to damages resulting from the lack of conformity is restricted by a criterion of remoteness such as foreseeability. Furthermore, it is not made clear whether the liability to pay damages is strict or whether there has to be some inquiry into the possible fault of the organiser. The limitations to the right to compensation mentioned above suggest that, at best, this is a hybrid form of liability which does not depend on showing fault on the part of the organiser, but which allows the organiser to evade liability to pay compensation where either the traveller or an unconnected third party are shown to be responsible for the lack of conformity.

Nevertheless, this provision is important because it finds a place for damages/compensation in a remedial regime which is primarily performance-oriented. It is therefore a further step in the evolution of the remedial schemes in European contract law. Overall, the Package Travel Directive provides a more complete system of remedies than the Consumer Sales Directive.

Taken together, these two directives offer a strong indication about the preferred approach to remedies in European contract law. The latter's main objective is to ensure performance of the contract, and so the remedies which are prioritised are those dealing with correcting performance (repair) and substitute performance (replacement), with other remedies such as price reduction and termination given restricted availability. The difficult issue of how to relate a performance-oriented remedial scheme with an entitlement to compensation for damages has been tackled to some extent in Article 14 Package Travel Directive, but there are unresolved aspects which, at present, rely on guidance from the CJEU.

A clear direction of travel in the development of remedies has emerged, however. As a next step, their further development in recently adopted legislation merits discussion.

---

53 Recital 34 Package Travel Directive. This reflects the ruling in C-168/00 *Simone Leitner*, above n. 49.

3. THE NEW DIRECTIVES ON DIGITAL CONTENT AND DIGITAL SERVICES, AND ON CONSUMER SALES

As noted in the Introduction, the European Commission had attempted to introduce broader legislation on remedies for certain types of sales contracts via the Common European Sales Law,[54] drawing on the work of the research group which produced the so-called Draft Common Frame of Reference (CESL).[55] Although the scope of CESL had been limited to sales contracts, its provisions were often expressed in more general contract law language, and had CESL been adopted, one might have expected its provisions to be extended to other types of contracts eventually. Some of the ideas from CESL have re-emerged, in much reduced and limited form, in the new directives on digital content and digital services (2019/770/EU) and on consumer sales (2019/771/EU).[56] Both directives were adopted in April 2019 and national implementing legislation must take effect from 1 January 2022.

3.1. THE DIGITAL CONTENT AND DIGITAL SERVICES DIRECTIVE

Following the withdrawal of the proposal for CESL, the European Commission put forward more limited proposals for new legislation in the context of its Digital Single Market agenda. The first of these was a proposal for a directive on certain aspects concerning contracts for the supply of digital content, now adopted with an extension to digital services (hereafter 'Digital Content and Digital Services Directive' or 'DCSD').[57]

The basic structure of the DCSD aligns with the EU's legal regime on consumer sales, in the sense that a trader supplying digital content/services would be required to supply that content 'in conformity with the contract' and would consequently be liable for a failure to supply the digital content/services, as well as any lack of conformity which exists at the time of supply or, where

---

[54] See C. Twigg-Flesner, 'Remedies for Faulty Goods – The Impossibility of Balancing the Interests of Consumers, Traders and Coherence of the Law' in E. Buttigieg (ed.), *Rights and Remedies for the Consumer in the European Union*, University of Malta, 2001.

[55] Study Group on a European Civil Code/Research Group on the Existing EC Private Law (Acquis Group) (eds.) *Principles, Definitions and Model Rules on European Private Law – Draft Common Frame of Reference*, Sellier, Munich 2009.

[56] See G. Howells, 'Reflections on Remedies for Lack of Conformity in Light of the Proposals of the EU Commission on Supply of Digital Content and Online and Other Distances Sales of Goods' in A. De Franceschi (ed.), *European Contract Law and the Digital Single Market*, Intersentia, Cambridge 2016.

[57] Proposal for a directive of the European Parliament and of the Council on certain aspects concerning contracts for the supply of digital content COM (2015) 634 final ('pDCD').

the supply is over a period of time, during that period.[58] A failure to supply would entitle a consumer to terminate the contract of supply after the trader has been reminded to perform.[59] One important novelty of the DCSD needs to be noted here: the DCSD applies to contracts for the supply of digital content where the consumer has either paid a price for the digital content, or where the consumer has agreed to provide personal data to the trader (except for personal data necessary to supply the digital content/service).[60] It therefore extends to most 'free' digital content/services, such as apps for smartphones.

The main remedy[61] provided for in the DCSD is the right to have the digital content/services brought into conformity with the contract free of charge.[62] This right would be subject to familiar limitations, i.e. the remedy must not be impossible or disproportionate.[63] As far as the disproportionality restriction is concerned, the criteria would be akin to those in the first Consumer Sales Directive.

The parallels with the Consumer Sales Directive would continue into the trader's obligation to provide a remedy within a reasonable time and without causing significant inconvenience to the consumer. Relevant considerations here would be the nature of the digital content/services and the purpose for which the consumer required the content/service.[64]

There are a number of instances when alternative remedies to bringing the digital content/service into conformity with the contract would become available. Once more, one condition is that the initially-chosen remedy is impossible or disproportionate.[65] New conditions added in the DCSD are that the trader has not brought the digital content/services into conformity,[66] the lack of conformity appears despite the trader's attempts at cure,[67] the lack of conformity is so serious to justify price reduction/termination,[68] or the trader has either declared that he/she will not provide a remedy to bring the digital content/services into conformity within a reasonable period of time and without

58 Art. 11 DCSD.

59 Art. 13 DCSD. Immediate termination is possible where the trader has refused to perform, or where the digital content/digital service is required by a specific date.

60 Art. 3(1) DCSD.

61 For a discussion of the remedies in the pDCD see M. Behar Touchais, 'Remedies in the Proposed Digital Content Directive: An Overview' in R. Schulze, D. Staudenmeyer and S. Lohse (eds.), *Contracts for the Supply of Digital Content: Regulatory Challenges and Gaps*, Nomos, Baden-Baden 2017.

62 Art. 14(3) DCSD.

63 Art. 14(2), first paragraph, DCSD.

64 Art. 14(3), DCSD.

65 Art. 14(4)(a) DCSD.

66 Art. 14(4)(b) DCSD.

67 Art. 14(4)(c) DCSD.

68 Art.14(4)(d) DCSD.

significant inconvenience, or where this is clear from the circumstances.[69] This final condition has a prospective element to it, i.e. significant inconvenience would not need to have been caused already, nor would the consumer have to wait for a period of time before it is clear that the trader will not provide the remedy.

The alternative remedies would be either price reduction (only where a price was paid for the digital content/service), or termination of the contract.[70] The DCSD would make it clear that the price reduction is to be calculated on the basis of a proportionate reduction, i.e. in proportion to the reduced value of the digital content/service as supplied, compared to the value which the digital content/service would have had, had it been in conformity with the contract.[71]

In order to terminate the contract, the consumer would have to give notice to the trader 'by means of a statement ... expressing the decision to terminate'.[72]

The DCSD deals with the consequences of termination in Arts. 16–18 DCSD. These provisions are rather complex, not least because digital content/services is/are not tangible and therefore not easily returned, as well as the fact that a consumer may have provided personal data in return for the digital content/services or used the digital content/services to create or provide both personal and non-personal data.

The most straightforward provision relates to the refund of the purchase price, where the consumer has paid for the digital content/services. In this situation, the trader will have to refund the price without undue delay, and within 14 days at the latest.[73]

Things get more complicated with regard to personal and non-personal data supplied by the consumer through the digital content/service. First of all, in respect of personal data,[74] the trader has to comply with the corresponding provisions of the General Data Protection Regulation (2016/679/EU).[75]

For non-personal data, the trader has to refrain from using any non-personal data and other content provided or created by the consumer.[76] Exceptions to this requirement cover content/data which has no utility beyond the digital content/services, content/data relating to the consumer's activity whilst using the digital content/services, data which has been aggregated by the trader and cannot be disaggregated, and content generated with other consumers jointly

---

69 Art. 14(4)(e) DCSD.
70 Art. 14(4) 1st para., DCSD.
71 Art. 14(5) DCSD.
72 Art. 15 DCSD.
73 Arts. 16(1) and 18 DCSD.
74 Art. 16(2) DCSD.
75 Regulation (EU) 2016/679 of the European Parliament and of the Council of 27 April 2016 on the protection of natural persons with regard to the processing of personal data and on the free movement of such data, and repealing Directive 95/46/EC [2016] OJ L 199/1.
76 Art. 16(3) DCSD.

and the others continue to use that content.[77] The trader will further be obliged to enable the consumer to retrieve all the content generated or provided by that consumer.[78] All of this would have to be possible without charge, without hindrance by the trader, and within a reasonable time and in a commonly-used format.[79] Furthermore, the trader will be entitled take steps to prevent further use of the digital content/services by the consumer, for example, by preventing access to the digital content/services or by disabling the consumer's user account.[80]

As far as the consumer is concerned, the consumer would also be under several obligations. As digital content or digital services cannot simply be returned due to their intangible nature, the consumer will be required to stop using the digital content/services, and he/she must not make them available to third parties.[81] Where the digital content had been provided on a tangible medium, the consumer will, if so requested by the trader, be obliged to return the durable medium to the trader at the latter's expense without undue delay.[82] However, the trader has to request such return within 14 days from being notified of termination.[83] The consumer will not have to pay for using the digital content/services for the period before termination when the digital content/service was not in conformity.[84]

If the contract for the supply of the digital content/services involved payment by the consumer and was intended to run for a period of time (e.g. a subscription to a video streaming service), then any reimbursement by the trader after termination would only be required in respect of the period when the digital content/service was not in conformity with the contract.[85]

The foregoing highlights the complexity of DCSD's remedial regime. However, there is one provision from the proposal for the Digital Content Directive which could have become important: a right to damages. This would have been available in respect of any economic damage to the consumer's digital environment,[86] caused either by the lack of conformity or outright failure to supply the digital content.[87] Such damages would have had the effect of placing the consumer in as close as possible a position as he/she would have been in, had

77 Art. 16(3)(a)-(d) DCSD.
78 Art. 16(4) DCSD.
79 Ibid.
80 Art. 16(5) DCSD.
81 Art. 17(1) DCSD.
82 Art. 17(2) DCSD.
83 Ibid.
84 Art. 17(3) DCSD.
85 Art. 16(1), second paragraph DCSD.
86 Defined as 'hardware, software and any network connection used by the consumer to access or make use of digital content or a digital service' (Art.2 (9) DCD).
87 Art. 14(1) pDCD.

the digital content been supplied and been in conformity with the contract.[88] Furthermore, consistent with the performance-focus of the remedial scheme, such damages would have reflected what a common lawyer would call the 'expectation interest', i.e. the monetary equivalent to the expected performance (which would not have resulted in economic damage to the consumer's digital environment). Whilst the scope of this provision would have been limited to certain consequential losses,[89] and with detailed provisions for claiming such damage, to be determined at Member State level,[90] it would nevertheless have been an important development.

However, this particular Article did not make it into the DCSD as adopted: following discussions in the Council of the EU, it was resolved to delete Article 14 from the proposal, because the Council did not see any need for such a provision and because of the diversity of national rules regarding a right to damages.[91]

3.2. THE NEW CONSUMER SALES DIRECTIVE

In parallel with the proposal for the DCD, the European Commission also proposed a new directive on the online and other distance sale of goods.[92] Following the 'Fitness Check' of the consumer *acquis*,[93] the Commission revised its proposal to extend it to all contracts for the sale of goods to consumers.[94] The new Directive (2019/771/EU) ('new CSD') will replace the existing Consumer Sales Directive and, additionally, be of a full harmonisation standard, removing the ability of individual Member States to adopt rules more favourable to consumers. A further innovation is that the new CSD will cover so-called 'goods with digital elements', i.e., tangible goods incorporating or inter-connecting with digital content/services required for the goods to perform their functions.[95]

---

88 Ibid.

89 Cf. S. Martens, 'Contracts for the Supply of Digital Content – Consequential Loss' in R. Schulze, D. Staudenmeyer and S. Lohse (eds.), *Contracts for the Supply of Digital Content: Regulatory Challenges and Gaps*, Nomos, Baden-Baden 2017.

90 Art. 14(2) DCD. This means that issues such as remoteness or fault would be determined nationally, rather than for the EU as a whole.

91 See paras. 15 and 16 of the 'Basic Principles and Political Guidelines for Future Work' in the Council document minuting the policy debate regarding the proposal (2 June 2016, Council document no. doc.9768/16).

92 Proposal for a directive of the European Parliament and of the Council on certain aspects concerning contracts for the online and other distance sales of goods COM(2015) 635 final.

93 European Commission, *Report of the Fitness Check*, SWD(2017) 209 final. On this, see C. Twigg-Flesner, 'From REFIT to a Rethink: Time for fundamental EU Consumer Law Reform?' (2017) 6 *Journal of European Consumer and Market* 185–189.

94 COM(2017) 637 final, see above n. 4.

95 Art. 2(5) new CSD.

The remedies for non-conformity are now distributed over four separate articles, rather than the single and rather densely worded Article 3 in the first Consumer Sales Directive. Putting the various aspects into separate paragraphs/articles clarifies the application of aspects such as the proportionality test, and also increases the clarity of the remedial scheme.

There are also additional elements to the remedial scheme which provide more detail on the operation of some of the remedies. However, overall, the remedies under the new Directive are the same as before:[96] repair or replacement ('bringing the goods into conformity') as primary remedies, with price reduction and termination (a change of terminology from 'rescission' in the first Consumer Sales Directive) as second tier remedies. Article 13 of the new CSD makes it clear that the consumer has a choice between repair and replacement, except where the chosen remedy would be impossible or disproportionate compared to the opposite remedy.

The triggers for the second tier of remedies would be expanded to include circumstances where (i) the seller has not repaired or replaced the goods as required,[97] or where both would be impossible or impose disproportionate costs on the seller;[98] (ii) the lack of conformity reappears;[99] (iii) the lack of conformity is so serious as to justify moving to the second tier immediately;[100] or (iv) the seller has refused to provide a remedy, or where it is clear from the circumstances that the seller will not do so.[101] Furthermore, a consumer who has not yet paid for the goods in full will be entitled to withhold any remaining payments until the seller has brought the goods back into conformity with the contract.[102] Also, Member States may determine (but are not obliged to do so) whether a consumer's entitlement to a remedy should be affected by the consumer's contribution to the non-conformity.[103] The provision may seem odd because the liability of a seller to provide goods in conformity with the contract would be determined at the time the goods are delivered to the consumer,[104] but perhaps a relevant factor here might be an insufficiently clear explanation of the particular purpose for which the goods are required. Article 11(1) new CSD extends the duration of the presumption of non-conformity from the current six month period to one year from delivery.

96 Art. 13(1) new CSD.
97 Art. 13(4)(a) new CSD.
98 Art. 13(3) new CSD. This provision seems to reflect the 'second proportionality criterion' from the CJEU's ruling in C-65/09, *Weber v Wittmer*, and C-87/09, *Putz v Medianess Electronics*, ECLI:EU:C:2011:396, discussed above.
99 Art. 13(4)(b) new CSD
100 Art. 13(4)(c) new CSD
101 Art. 13(4)(d) new CSD.
102 Art. 13(6) new CSD.
103 Art. 13(7) new CSD.
104 Art. 10(1) new CSD.

It was seen earlier that the first Consumer Sales Directive said very little about replacement of non-conforming goods, and there is still no definition of 'replacement'. However, Article 14 of the new CSD introduces three rules to clarify how the right to repair or replacement operates. The first is that the seller has to take back the non-conforming goods at his/her own expense.[105] Two other rules follow CJEU rulings under the first Consumer Sales Directive. Thus, a consumer will not have to make any payment to the seller to reflect the normal use made of the goods prior to their replacement.[106] Moreover, in a situation where goods were installed 'in a manner consistent with their nature and purpose', the seller will be required to take back the non-conforming goods, which involves either removing the non-conforming goods and installing the repaired goods or their replacement, or bearing the cost of this. This reflects the decision in *Weber* and *Putz*.[107] The proviso from that case that the costs of removal and re-installation have to be 'proportionate' is found in Article 13(3) of the new CSD.[108]

A further clarification has been introduced with regard to the method by which a reduction of the price would be calculated. Although it had been assumed that price reduction under the Consumer Sales Directive (CSD) would follow the proportionate reduction approach already familiar to most EU legal systems from the UN Convention on the International Sale of Goods (CISG), this was not clear from the wording of Article 3 CSD itself and left open the possibility that a national court would apply a difference-in-value calculation instead. Article 15 of the new CSD confirms that the calculation is based on the decrease in the value of the goods as delivered compared to the value of conforming goods.

Finally, the consumer's right to terminate the contract is also more clearly set out in the new CSD. First, a consumer has to give notice to the seller, by means of a statement, to terminate the contract.[109] Secondly, if the contract of sale relates to several goods, but only one or some of them are not in conformity, then the consumer is effectively given a partial right of termination only, restricted to the non-conforming goods and any other goods which had been acquired as accessories for the non-conforming goods.[110] Following termination, the

---

105 Art. 14(2) new CSD.

106 Art. 14(4) new CSD, reflecting the decision in C-404/06, *Quelle AG v Bundesverband der Verbraucherzentralen und Verbraucherverbände*, above n. 19.

107 Joined cases C-65/09 *Weber v Wittmer* and C-87/09 *Putz v Medianess Electronics* [2011] ECR I-5257.

108 See the discussion above.

109 Art. 16(1) new CSD.

110 Art. 16(2) new CSD.

seller has to refund the price paid for the goods covered by the termination on receipt of the goods or of evidence that the consumer has returned the goods.[111] Also, the goods have to be returned by the consumer to the seller at the seller's expense.[112]

One important matter has not be addressed in the new Consumer Sales Directive: the potential entitlement to the consumer for damages. However, Recital 61 of the new CSD stresses that whilst consumers should be entitled to such compensation, the right to damages is already part of all the national laws of the Member States and no provision on this was needed in the new CSD.

The additional provisions which have been introduced by the new CSD are dealing with detailed points regarding the various remedies. This is undoubtedly due to the shift to maximum harmonisation, which tends to result in a higher degree of micro-regulation of matters falling within the scope of a directive. It is, however, important to note that the final version of the new CSD contains far fewer detailed rules than had originally been proposed, leaving some room for the Member States to address related issues through their national laws (acknowledged variously in recitals and articles of the new CSD).

4. A COHERENT APPROACH TO REMEDIES IN EUROPEAN CONTRACT LAW?

The foregoing discussion of selected areas of European contract law reveals a number of findings regarding the overall coherence of the EU's approach to remedies. First, it is clear that the preference is for a system of remedies which prioritises performance of contractual obligations. This is evident in remedies such as repair and replacement in the context of sales, or the obligation to remedy a non-conformity in the Package Travel Directive. Indeed, in the latter Directive, the language has a more generalist contract law flavour, which might suggest that a similar approach could be adopted in other areas of European contract law in the future. Secondly, termination of a contract is a remedy of last resort, and only available if a breach of contract is 'substantial' or 'not minor', and only after attempts to secure full performance of a contract have not succeeded. To that extent, one can clearly identify the contours of a European approach to contract law remedies. However, the Achilles' Heel of EU contract law is its difficult (or non-existent) link with a right to claim damages, particularly with regard to damages for consequential losses. This is an issue where national law continues to face the task of having to integrate EU-based provisions with

111 Art. 16(3)(b) new CSD.
112 Art. 16(3)(a) new CSD.

national rules on damages – despite the fact that, at least from a consumer perspective, dealing with consequential losses may often be of as much, if not greater, concern than the primary remedy to address a non-conformity. Perhaps the main reason for the absence of any provisions on damages are the divergent approaches at national level (e.g. the fact that some jurisdictions permit damages on a strict liability basis, whereas others require fault), something which could arguably speak against any EU rules on damages.[113] However, if one of the objectives of all of these directives is to make it easier for consumers to shop online and abroad, then not dealing with a significant issue such as this remains a serious omission.

Moreover, it is also important to stress that there are still many areas of European contract law where no remedies are stipulated in EU measures for any breach of rights granted by those directives. Some of this may be explained by the difficult balance between ensuring adequate regulation at the European level in the interest of the internal market and the demands of subsidiarity in areas of competence shared between the EU and its Member States.[114] This often results in little more than basic instructions to the Member States to do something – for example, in its recent proposal for a 'New Deal' directive (on which political agreement was reached in Spring 2019, although the final Directive had not yet been formally adopted at the time of finalising this chapter), a provision which will result in the introduction of private remedies in respect of unfair commercial practices, including compensation for damages, does little more than to require the Member States to do something, but is woefully short on specifics.[115]

As for the many areas of EU consumer contract law for which there are no remedies stipulated expressly, it is arguable that national law might nevertheless be required to provide at least for a claim for damages, based on the principle of effectiveness. In *Courage v Crehan*,[116] the CJEU rules that a claim for damages as a result of a breach of Article 101 TFEU. Furthermore, in *Antonio Munoz Cia SA v Frumar Limited*,[117] the CJEU established that regulations could be enforced in civil proceedings, even though the claimant was not a direct beneficiary of that regulation, to deal with an infringement of that regulation by another party. Whilst in both cases, directly applicable provisions were in issue (something

---

113 Cf. P. Machnikowski, 'Regulation of Damages on National or European Level' in R. Schulze, D. Staudenmeyer and S. Lohse (eds.), *Contracts for the Supply of Digital Content: Regulatory Challenges and Gaps*, Nomos, Baden-Baden 2017, and Recital 61 new CSD.

114 Art. 5(3) Treaty on European Union.

115 See e.g. M. Loos, 'The Modernisation of European Consumer Law: A Pig in a Poke' (2019) 27 *European Review of Private Law* 113; C. Twigg-Flesner, 'Bad Hand? The "New Deal" for EU Consumers' (2018) 15 *Gemeinschaftsprivatrecht* 166.

116 Case C-453/99, *Courage Ltd v. Bernard Crehan*, ECLI:EU:C:2001:465.

117 Case C-253/00, *Muñoz and Superior Fruiticola*, ECLI:EU:C:2002:497.

stressed by the CJEU) there remains scope for extending the *Munoz* principle beyond these areas to rights introduced by directives into national law.[118]

5. CONCLUSION

Having been one of the more neglected aspects of European contract law initially, the shape of a coherent system of remedies has started to crystallise, although it is still limited to few types of specific contracts and some way away from a generalised approach. The emerging system is performance-focused, although it has thus far not properly addressed the place of damages in the overall remedial scheme, leaving this to the national laws of the Member States. However, even though it would be appropriate to say that there are foundations of a system of remedies in European contract law, it would be wrong to say that there is a clear basis for a *European* law of remedies in evidence: ultimately, the EU's approach is quite traditional and resembles an approach found in the majority of the Member States, and, indeed, the UN Convention on the International Sale of Goods. It lacks features which would reflect the particular demands of developing the internal market, such as a system of remedies which would move beyond the obligation to provide a remedy imposed on the immediate contractual supplier and extend this obligation to other parties, such as a producer, the operator of an online platform, or members of a specific distribution network.[119] Unless the EU's approach to remedies becomes more courageous, the development of remedies in European contract law will replicate much of what is already common to the Member States and achieve little more than establishing a common approach with no obvious benefits.

---

118 Cf. the discussion of this by T. Wilhelmsson and C. Twigg-Flesner, 'Pre-contractual information duties in the *acquis communautaire*' (2006) 2 *European Review of Contract Law* 441, 467.

119 Cf. R. Bradgate and C. Twigg-Flesner, 'Expanding the Boundaries of Liability for Quality Defects' (2002) 25 *Journal of Consumer Policy* 342.

THE INTERSECTION BETWEEN ECONOMIC JUSTIFICATIONS FOR IP RIGHTS AND COST OF ENFORCEMENT IN THE ENGLISH COURTS

Jonathan Moss

1. INTRODUCTION

This chapter is a written report of a presentation given by the author in October 2018 at the University of Erlangen conference on 'Themes and Controversies in EU IP Remedies'.[1] The chapter takes a different approach to the many other excellent papers that were presented at the conference. This difference in approach reflects the author's background as a barrister practising in IP (intellectual property) litigation in the UK. What follows here arises from what the author has observed in over 10 years of litigation experience in intellectual property – not only in the UK, but also in the US and other EU jurisdictions. Whilst this chapter is addressed primarily from the viewpoint of someone

---

1 The author would very much like to thank Professor Franz Hofmann for inviting him to speak at this conference. He would also like to thank all the other speakers who so gamely engaged with the more practical approach that this presentation entailed.

practising in England, it must be made it clear that this is essentially an anecdotal view, although, it reflects the views of many practitioners the author has spoken to in every major jurisdiction where IP rights are litigated. It is therefore certainly not an English only problem. It is to be hoped that this discussion will encourage further research into this area.

In summary, the author's view is that the actual mechanism of enforcing intellectual property rights through litigation in the English courts can sometimes, be economically inefficient when viewed in isolation – i.e. the cost of litigating a right can outweigh the value of the right in that one off case. As many IP rights exist because of an economic justification for their existence, their very raison d'etre is challenged if the ultimate mechanism for their enforcement by way of litigation is economically inefficient. Put simply, is the very existence of IP rights being challenged if the court systems cannot make enforcing them economically efficient? This issue, and issues arising in relation to this, are addressed in this chapter.

This discussion identifies a problem in certain cases. Different IP rights are afflicted by this potential problem to differing degrees. This chapter serves to raise the issue and start a debate, and therefore any generalisations made will, invariably, not be true of all cases or all IP rights.

This chapter comprises four sections. Section 1 contains a brief overview of the principles relating to the calculation of financial remedies and injunctive relief for IP rights under English Law. Section 2 addresses the core problem of how the economic justification for IP rights can be undermined by the enforcement of those rights in the courts.

Section 3 addresses the potential problem of observation bias that arises by looking at reported cases, as the vast majority of IP litigation is settled before it ever gets to court. Section 4 suggests some potential solutions that could be help alleviate the problems of economically inefficient litigation.

2. CALCULATION OF FINANCIAL REMEDIES AND INJUNCTIVE RELIEF UNDER ENGLISH LAW

Under English law, intellectual property infringement actions are a species of tort law and so damages are calculated on the basis that they are to be compensatory.[2] This differs from the measure of damages in contract law where damages are

[2] The term 'damages' will be used in this chapter to cover both damages and an account of profits. Under English law, the remedy of an account of profits is general available as an alternative to the award of damages. An account of profits awards the claimant the profits made by the infringer which are directly attributable to the infringing action. Account of

calculated to award the claimant the expectation value of their bargain. It is, however, important to bear in mind that in some cases intellectual property damages will be calculated as expectation damages if the underlying cause of action lies in contract rather than in tort. The two most common examples of this are suing on a licence and suing upon a settlement agreement.

Damages under English law are not there to punish the defendant, nor are they to provide a windfall to the claimant. This is best summed up by Lord Nicholl, *AG v Blake*, at 279–280, where he states:

> The general rule is that, in the oft quoted words of Lord Blackburn, the measure of damages is to be, as far as possible, that amount of money which will put the injured party in the same position he would have been in had he not sustained the wrong … Damages are measured by the plaintiff's loss, not the defendant's gain.

Under English law a claimant can claim damages in the three following categories:[3]

1. Directly lost sales (i.e. one infringing sale replaces one genuine sale).
2. If not competing directly, then a reasonable royalty.
3. If no direct or indirect competition, then court must award the claimant something.

The most common measure of damages that is dealt with in practice is the second category of 'reasonable royalty'. Damages that fall under this category would arise in, for example, a patent case where the patent owner does not manufacture a product and is therefore due a royalty on all the infringing items sold by a defendant. There is an entire line of case law which deals with how such a royalty is calculated.

The first category of damages of directly lost sales requires the claimant to show that they have actually lost sales to the competitor defendant. It is perfectly possible for a claimant to break their damages claim amongst these different categories, for example, they could show that 30% of the sales of the defendant led to directly lost sales, whereas the remaining 70% should be calculated on a reasonable royalty basis.[4]

---

profits is generally viewed as leading to a lower monetary remedy. For the purposes of this chapter, the awarding of damages or an account of profits makes little difference in terms of expense of litigating.

3 See for example the discussion in *Blayney v Clogau St David's Gold Mines* [2002] EWCA Civ 1007.

4 This could happen if, for example, the defendant traded in two geographic areas, only one of which overlapped with where the claimant sold their own products.

3. ECONOMIC JUSTIFICATION FOR IP RIGHTS UNDERMINED BY ENFORCEMENT IN THE COURTS

There is significant literature in the academic realm of intellectual property law on the justification for why IP rights exist. This literature looks at rights individually and, in many cases, the justifications for why certain IP rights exists have elements of both economic and moral justification. This is not the place to examine all those various theories, but nevertheless the justifications exist and for some rights, the extent of the right has been determined due to economic considerations.[5]

Many academic papers which look at the justification for intellectual property rights start from a position that monopolies are not desirable. The oft-quoted remark of Justice Millar in the US Supreme Court case of *Butchers' Union Slaughterhouse v Crescent City*, 1884, sums up this view:

> I hold it to be an incontrovertible proposition of both English and American public law, that all mere monopolies are odious, and against common right.

Different jurisdictions take different views on why various IP rights exist. The justification for copyright protection in, for example, France, appears (to this author at least) to be based more on the Lockian ideal of the author being entitled to the fruits of the labour than the approach taken in many common law jurisdictions.

However, even in common law jurisdictions, there is certainly a view that copyright contains more of a moral element to justifying its existence than, for example, patents. Even within patent law, there is great debate about whether time limited monopolies of, normally, 20 years are necessary. The argument goes that such a term for the patent monopoly is needed to allow research and innovation. Few could argue that this is necessary for many drug patents – it is unlikely that without such a monopoly that pharmaceutical companies would spend billions on research when a generic could then just take that work and make the drug at a very low cost.

This chapter does not seek to engage with the various models and justifications posed for all the IP rights. The premise for this discussion is that the scope of protection for the vast majority of IP rights are justified on the basis that they are economically justified. By this, it is meant that the legislatures of those countries have decided that statutory monopolies should be granted to IP right holders because the existence of such monopolies is economically beneficial to society as a whole. This chapter therefore seeks to address one issue head on

---

5 The most obvious example of this is the term of a patent – 50 years would stifle competition, 5 years would be far too short to get a proper return.

which the author has observed regularly in practice. This is the problem that the cost of enforcing IP rights through the courts can be economically inefficient in itself because it is often more expensive to litigate a right than the right is worth. It is true that the economic inefficiencies of many IP rights have been considered as a whole. Two obvious examples are the literature on patent thickets and on patent trolls. However, it is probable that there has not been enough consideration of how IP rights interact with the individual court system in which they are litigated. Part of the reason why this has happened is obvious even in the EU where many IP rights are totally harmonised, that harmonisation does not extend to procedural law. For example, there is no harmonisation that a case must require a letter before action, or allow a defendant chance to respond with a reasonable amount of time to do so.

One key area where IP rights differ is how those various IP rights come into existence in the first place. For example:

- Substantive applications, including examination, are required for patents and trade marks to be granted. These examinations include open registers and an open period of opposition where interested parties can seek to stop the registration of those rights.
- Formality based registration exists for registered designs. Whilst registered designs are placed onto an open register, searching these registers can be hard – due to it being hard to search pictures if you do not know who may have registered a design.
- Copyright and unregistered design right comes into existence immediately so long as some basic conditions are met.

One general trend from the above is that the more 'economic' of the IP rights (patents and trade marks) are subject to greater registration thresholds, which in turn increase the cost of acquiring them. This is reflected in the fact that an entire portion of the legal market, patent and trade mark attorneys, are involved in the registration of these two rights. It is therefore clear that for the more 'economic rights' the granting of those rights is considered to require a certain degree of control in order to ensure that their granting is economically efficient.

However, the enforcement for all IP rights in the UK is the same. There is no real difference enforcing a patent in litigation than there is enforcing a copyright or trade mark. Whilst there are some procedural differences laid down in the Civil Procedure Rules (CPR) which say how pleadings should be drafted, etc. for different rights, the same solicitors, barristers and courts are used to litigate all IP rights.

Under English law, litigants face a system where:

- There is a right to an adversarial trial.

- The burden of proof is on the claimant (and the burden of proof is the 'balance of probabilities').
- The successful litigant will have their costs paid for by the losing party (sometimes referred to as the 'English rule' in American legal literature).

The burden of proof is not lowered for different IP rights, and due to the adversarial nature of English court proceedings, a defendant can put a claimant to proof on their entire claim. In copyright cases, for example, this can be highly costly. This is because a claimant may need to seek ex-employees to give evidence that they created a certain copyrighted work. For copyright, there is a statutory presumption that where a company's name is on a document that it is owned by that company. However, it is not too hard in contest litigation to find a way to cast some doubt on that – which means that in practice the presumption only goes so far in reducing costs should a defendant decide to put ownership and subsistence in issue.

The effect of the 'loser pays' model of a court system is that the enforcement of intellectual property rights can, in some cases, become economically inefficient. This can arise in two ways and is certainly not a problem that afflicts only claimants.

One common problem facing a claimant is that they want to enforce their rights, but the costs of doing so are too great for the ultimate value of the right. This costs comes not only in terms of court fees and lawyer fees, but also the large amount of management time required to run a case and, should the matter proceed to trial, time required of witnesses to be available for cross-examination. A claimant may therefore have a strong case to enforce their rights, but decide not to because looked at in isolation it is not cost-effective. For example, if a defendant is sued to patent infringement, and the matter proceeds all the way to trial (with the likely need for expert evidence), then the cost of that trial will be the same in terms of lawyer's fees regardless of whether the defendant has sold £300,000 or £800,000 of infringing product. One can immediately see where problems may arise when the value of the case is lower.

In such cases one answer may be that the claimant gets an injunction which stops further infringement, but the defendant may have already decided to stop selling, in which case the value of that injunction is greatly reduced – as such injunctions are only binding on the parties to the litigation.

From a defendant's point of view, the cost of invalidating a right may be greater than the costs of simply rebranding or coming up with a new product that designs around the existing right to avoid infringement. This could be the case even when they are advised that they have a very strong case. Furthermore, even if the defendant comes out of such a case having invalidated the right, and assuming they recover a large portion of their costs, they have merely helped their competitors in clearing the field – and there is rarely any economic incentive in doing that.

The above, in the author's view, shows a system that has not fully come to grips with the economic nature of the very rights that are being litigated. Society has decided that these rights should exist for economic reasons, but yet their enforcement can often be economically inefficiently when looked at in isolation.

For example, if the damages that would be awarded are worth £100,000, but the cost of litigating the case is £90,000 was that case really worth fighting? On one view, it is, because the claimant had a net gain of £10,000 and will almost certainly have obtained an injunction stopping the defendant from undertaking that infringing activity again. The claimant will also have an ancillary benefit of other players in the market knowing, should the judgment be publicised, that the claimant is someone willing to fight cases all the way to trial.

This example of course ignores the fact that the £90,000 costs spent by the claimant in this case may be recoverable from the defendant. Two problems, however, arise with cost recovery. First, it is almost unheard of for a claimant to recover all their costs from a defendant. The usual figure is something which more likely floats around the 70–80% mark of the claimant's total costs depending on how the case was fought. Secondly, the defendant may not have any money left after the defendant has paid their own lawyers and the damages.

When it comes to very high value litigation, which in the author's experience arises most often in patents cases, the damages could run into the tens of millions, with lawyer fees in the region of £2–5million. The concern about the litigation system being economically inefficient is much less at that extreme end of the bell curve. The real concern from this author's point of view are the cases that are in the middle of the bell curve of value – where there really is a genuine concern on behalf of litigants that the costs of fighting the case may not be worth the overall gain (even when non-direct financial benefits are factored in). These cases often involve small and medium enterprises (SMEs) and start-ups (which can often be worth a lot on paper but do not have the cash in hand to necessarily litigate as easily as they may like).

At this point it should be emphasised that there is no suggestion that the right to an adversarial trial or the burden of proof should be altered in IP cases – those are cornerstones of the entire common law legal system. Where changes could be made is perhaps in individual mechanisms for certain rights.

One such mechanism that is available in the English courts under the CPR which does reflect the economic value of litigating a patent. This is called a 'Certificate of Contested Validity' and it can be granted if a patent's validity is challenged and the patent is held to be valid. Should a future litigant seek to attack the validity of that patent, they are free to do so, but they are at a risk of getting costs awarded against them on an indemnity basis.[6]

---

6 Which effectively means that all the patentees costs would be payable by the party seeking revocation if the attack on the patent fails.

It should also be pointed out that in England at least, there are effectively three tiers of courts where IP claims can be brought. The small claims track applies to cases where the value of the claim is worth up to £10,000. Few IP cases fall into this court save for instances of single copyright infringement (for photos for example).

A significant volume of cases is dealt with in the Intellectual Property Enterprise Court (IPEC) which is a sub-division of the High Court. This is for cases with a value up to £500,000[7] and it has special rules on how proceedings can be streamlined – i.e. trial length is capped at two days and there is strong case management control that leads to limited disclosure. The IPEC also has limits on costs exposure, meaning that a losing party cannot be ordered to pay more than £50,000 in costs to the winning side save in exceptional circumstances.

The 'normal' High Court then deals with all other IP claims.[8] It has generally broader disclosure and trials also tend to be longer. Whilst the High Court does have strong case management, it is not as tightly controlled as the IPEC.

Litigants in the IPEC face a situation which is more akin to how cases without cost shifting are dealt with in the US. Whilst a losing party knows that it may have to pay £50,000 to the winning side, they can control their own costs to a certain degree and therefore know their maximum exposure regardless of how much the other side decides to spend.

In the author's view, the IPEC has led to more cases being fought because of this greater certainty about costs exposure – put simply, litigants are not as concerned about being on the end of a huge costs bill from the other side should they lose. They are, therefore, often more willing to fight.

However, this increased certainty comes with a cost. This cost is that if the case is going to cost a lot to litigate (for example, there is going to have to be a large volume of documentation and witness evidence produced) then claimants may not bring the case because they know that even if they have a very strong case, the defendants can keep them fighting the case and only be on the hook for £50,000 in costs. The rules of procedure in relation to pleadings, etc. are slightly altered in the IPEC, but the requirement to prove a claimant's case on the burden of proof and the necessity of cross-examination do not change.

The IPEC has, undoubtedly been a good thing for IP litigation in England, but it certainly does not solve all the problems of the potential for inefficient enforcement of economic rights.

7 Though the parties can agree that this value cap is waived.

8 It should be pointed out that the Intellectual Property Office can hear certain types of litigious actions in relation to patents, but it is not extensively used.

4. POTENTIAL OBSERVATION BIAS ARISING FROM LOOKING AT REPORTED CASES

The author has had numerous discussions with practitioners and clients from all over the world about what has happened in various reported cases from the English courts. One common comment is that there are very few reported decisions on the value of any damages awards for certain types of cases. The problem with looking at the outcome of reported decisions is that they represent a tiny proportion of the infringement cases which are started in the English courts. Those cases which are started are, in turn, reflective of only a small proportion of potential cases which are settled before any claim form is formally issued.

The problem with looking at reported cases is twofold. First, it shows generally only those cases that were worth fighting. Cases where the merits strongly point in one direction are much more likely to settle than cases which are finely balanced. Litigation is virtually always binary with a winner and a loser. Therefore looking at these (often) finely balanced cases is not illustrative of commercial reality because the court has naturally come down on one side or another. The results of cases that settle before judgment is handed down generally do not see the light of day.

Secondly, the lack of reported decisions on how damages are calculated for a given type of IP right means that it can be hard to advise with certainty on the value of any infringement. In practice, it is not uncommon to give a range of damages which may cover an order of magnitude in difference.

It is therefore suggested that any research in this area is going to require some form of qualitative angle – i.e. asking practitioners and clients how they have reacted, rather than trying merely to do some form of quantitative analysis.

5. POTENTIAL SOLUTIONS TO HELP ALLEVIATE PROBLEMS OF ECONOMICALLY INEFFICIENT LITIGATION

The study and consideration of how economic rights can be economically enforced is one that should be considered in greater depths by scholars and practitioners alike. Any consideration of this area will, as mentioned above, necessarily require the close interaction between the academic side of the law and those who are involved in enforcing it on a daily basis. There are a number of possible responses to the problems outlined in this chapter.

Before setting out those responses, the question of whether there really is a problem as outlined must be addressed, or whether the 'costs' of litigating are merely there because every system will, invariably, have its in-built inefficiencies?

After all, the overall IP system is, generally, and certainly in the author's view, highly effective in our modern economy. Thus why the need for change? The short answer to this is that there is always room for improvement, and one should never assume that everything will remain as it is.

The main reason for wanting to improve the economic efficiency of IP enforcement is that no one knows what the future landscape will look like for IP rights. The internet has changed the game. AI may change the game further. It is surely best to try and make things right before they may break – as at that point, it may be too hard to right the course.

The first response is to continue with the status quo and accept there is a threshold where IP enforcement is just not economically efficient. This would have a greater impact on SMEs and particularly start-ups. Imagine a scenario where Uber or Facebook ran into IP issues early on and could just not finance the litigation. Is that the sort of IP system one wishes to present to the world? One problem with working out whether or not the current system is stifling innovation is that if economically inefficient enforcement has led to a future billionaire dollar company failing at the first hurdle, this will never be known.

Another possible response is to create different types of litigation for sub-classes of rights. For example, the threshold for proving unregistered design-right ownership (an often costly part of that sort of litigation) could be reduced, or the burden changed. For example, the courts could decide that, when ownership of copyright is put in issue, if there is a prima facie case that the claimant is the owner, but the defendant challenges this, there are costs consequences to doing so.

The court could also decide that the strict requirement of expert evidence is not necessary for certain matters – a better solution could be that removing the need for independent expert evidence would be to allow in-house expertise to be put forward. For low value cases, that would certainly be more desirable than having to pay external experts. Consider, for example, the difference between needing expert evidence in UK patent proceedings compared to the lack of such evidence in European Patent Office Opposition Proceedings. Although in EPO proceedings those hearing the case are technically qualified, but then so are most UK IP judges.

Finally, the Certificate of Contested Validity approach in patents could, in certain circumstances be adapted for other rights – such as for anyone challenging a trade mark on absolute grounds when such a challenge has already been made in previous litigation and failed. Such a certificate could have a double effect. First, it may encourage a trade mark proprietor to litigate a case which on its own is not economically efficient, as it allows the proprietor to gain future 'value' from that litigation should they succeed.

Secondly, it would reduce the incentive for defendants to fight unnecessary cases in courts with limited costs recovery, such as the IPEC. The existence of a certificate of contested validity for trade marks could, for example, lead to the costs cap in the IPEC being lifted or otherwise modified (it could be doubled or increased to a certain extent).

6. CONCLUSION

It must re-emphasised that in the author's opinion the system is not broken in England or elsewhere. The issues raised in this discussion are based on anecdotal experience, but, nevertheless, are reflective of genuine concerns in the market amongst some participants. Only further research into whether this really is an issue or not, will answer that question. This chapter has aimed to stimulate ideas and it is to be hoped that this issue will be investigated further in the future, hopefully with the assistance of those on the academic side of the profession who are often better placed to analyse such problems from an outside perspective – albeit one with a deep understanding of how the underlying legal system works.

INDEX

ABOUT THE EDITORS

Franz Hofmann is Professor of Law at the Friedrich-Alexander-University Erlangen-Nürnberg, where he holds the Chair of Private Law, Intellectual Property and Technology Law. Before his appointment in 2016, he was a Lecturer in Law at the Ludwig-Maximilians-University München and the University of Bayreuth. In 2009, he obtained an LLM degree at the University of Cambridge. His recent research focusses on legal implications of digitalisation (e.g. copyright in the digital single market and liability for new technologies) and questions of enforcement, particularly remedies in the fields of private law and intellectual property law.

Franziska Kurz is a Research Assistant at the Chair of Private Law, Intellectual Property and Technology Law at the Friedrich-Alexander-University Erlangen-Nürnberg. She holds an MJur from the University of Oxford, where she also spent a research visit. At the Friedrich-Alexander-University Erlangen-Nürnberg, she teaches private law and works on her doctorate. Her research interest focusses on questions concerning remedies, comparative contract law and intellectual property law.

Ingram Content Group UK Ltd.
Milton Keynes UK
UKHW051628140623
423436UK00007B/62

9 781780 687858